9-11

WITHDRAWN

THE
MAN WHO
NEVER DIED

THE
MAN WHO
NEVER DIED

---

*The Life, Times, and Legacy of Joe Hill,
American Labor Icon*

WILLIAM M. ADLER

BLOOMSBURY

NEW YORK BERLIN LONDON SYDNEY

Published by Bloomsbury USA, New York

All papers used by Bloomsbury USA are natural, recyclable products made from wood grown in well-managed forests. The manufacturing processes conform to the environmental regulations of the country of origin.

LIBRARY OF CONGRESS CATALOGING-IN-PUBLICATION

Adler, William M.
The man who never died : the life, times, and legacy of Joe Hill,
American labor icon / William M. Adler.—1st ed.
p. cm.
Includes bibliographical references and index.
ISBN-13: 978-1-59691-696-8 (hc)
ISBN-10: 1-59691-696-6 (hc)
1. Hill, Joe, 1879–1915.   2. Working class—United States—Songs and music.
3. Folk singers—United States—Biography.   I. Title.
HD8072.A35 2011
331.88'6092—dc22
[B]
2011009821

First U.S. Edition 2011

1 3 5 7 9 10 8 6 4 2

Designed by Adam Bohannon
Typeset by Westchester Book Group
Printed in the U.S.A. by Quad/Graphics, Fairfield, Pennsylvania

For Robin and Zeke
and
For Peter R. Decker

JOE HILL
MEMORIAL EDITION
OF THE
I.W.W.
SONG BOOK

PRICE
10c
EACH
50 FOR $2.50
100 " $5.00
1000 " $35.00
CARRIAGE
PREPAID

PRICE 10 CENTS

ADDRESS
I. W. W. PUBLISHING BUREAU
1001 W. MADISON ST., CHICAGO, ILL.
U. S. A.

You don't remember the Wobblies. You were too young. Or else not even born yet. There has never been anything like them, before or since . . . They were workstiffs and bindlebums like you and me, but they were welded together by a vision we don't possess. It was their vision that made them great. And it was their belief in it that made them powerful. And sing! You never heard anybody sing the way those guys sang!

—JAMES JONES, *FROM HERE TO ETERNITY*, 1951

These people do not belong to any country, no flag, no laws, no Supreme Being. I do not know what to do. I cannot punish them. Listen to them singing. They are singing all the time, and yelling and hollering, and telling the jailers to quit work and join the union. They are worse than animals.

—SAN DIEGO CHIEF OF POLICE KENO WILSON, 1912

I dreamed I saw Joe Hill last night
Alive as you and me.
Says I, "But Joe, you're ten years dead."
"I never died," says he.
"I never died," says he.

—ALFRED HAYES AND EARL ROBINSON,
"JOE HILL," 1936

CONTENTS

INTRODUCTION

"Don't Waste Any Time Mourning"

It was a funeral the likes of which Chicago had never seen. As early as dawn they began gathering, a great singing swarm of humanity, tens of thousands of the city's dispossessed and disinherited. "The ghetto, the slums, the lodging house quarters and the manufacturing districts are buzzing with preparations," the *Chicago Daily Tribune* reported that morning, adding that "hand-bills in a dozen different languages" had urged attendance at the rites. By ten o'clock, when the service began, five thousand celebrants, not just the poor but also intellectual "parlor radicals" and leftists of many stripes, including anarchists, unionists, Socialists, nihilists, and ordinary, nondenominational "wage slaves"—"'bums' and hoboes generally, of whom less than 10 per cent were American," the *New York Times* sniffed—were packed into every seat and wedged into every cranny along the back and side walls of the West Side Auditorium. It was Thursday, November 25, 1915, an unseasonably warm Thanksgiving morning; already the temperature had climbed into the fifties, and the windows of the great second-floor hall were opened wide, and verse after verse, song after song, cascaded outside the block-long building.

> *Workers of the world, Awaken,*
> *Break your chains, Demand your rights.*
> *All the wealth you make is taken*
> *By exploiting parasites.*
> *Shall you kneel in deep submission*
> *From your cradles to your graves?*

1

Is the height of your ambition
To be good and willing slaves?

Outside the West Side Auditorium, at the intersection of Taylor and South Racine, a milling and singing throng—one writer called it a "mob" of thirty thousand people and reported the streets jammed "from curb to curb for over a mile" and all traffic at a halt—echoed the verses resounding from the upstairs hall. As the song built to its final verse, the mighty street chorale swelled to a crescendo.

Workers of the world, awaken!
Rise in all your splendid might;
Take the wealth that you are making,
It belongs to you by right.
No one will for bread be crying,
We'll have freedom, love and health.
When the grand red flag is flying
In the Workers' Commonwealth.

The grand red flag belonged to their union, the Industrial Workers of the World (IWW). A union, yes, but it might better be described (in its own vernacular) as a loose confederation of workstiffs and bindlebums: hard-rock miners and muckers, timberbeasts, lint-heads, shovel stiffs and straw cats, fruit tramps, dock wallopers, pond monkeys, sewer hogs, and stump ranchers. They called themselves Wobblies, though no one is sure why.*

The IWW's heyday lasted for only a brief, electrifying moment at the dawn of the twentieth century: when industrial capitalism was new and raw and brutal, and when the union's vision of a new worker-controlled order—an "industrial democracy"—seemed, if not on the verge of becoming reality, not preposterous either.

The idea of industrial democracy was as subversive as it was simple: "plain folk running society for their own benefit," as one historian distilled it; "socialism with its working clothes on," as William "Big Bill" D. Haywood, a founder of the IWW, liked to say. More explicitly, the program called for all workers to form industrial unions under the scarlet-and-black standard of the IWW, the "One Big Union." Eventually the IWW

---

* The most oft-cited theory credits a Chinese cook in a railroad camp in the Pacific Northwest who mispronounced "I-W-W" as "Eye-Wobble-U, Wobble-U."

would call a general strike. Capitalism would screech to a halt like traffic on the West Side of Chicago on that Thanksgiving morning. Industrial unions would take over the machinery of production in the United States, not for profit but for the public good. From there, the workers' commonwealth would ripple across the oceans.

Where you stood on the concept of industrial democracy depended on whether you sat in a passenger coach or a boxcar. To its legion of critics who rode the rails in comfort, the IWW was a toxic brew of feckless ideology and reckless imagination. "America's most damnable enemy" and "America's cancer sore" were representative sentiments. And yet the Wobblies struck a deep, responsive chord among hundreds of thousands of disenfranchised and unskilled laborers, particularly in the raw, extractive industries of the West, where the economy was unstable, the jobs were transitory, and workers saw themselves regarded by employers as beasts of burden devoid of humanity.

THE FUNERAL SERVICE on that warm Thanksgiving day in Chicago was testimony to the power of song, a power the IWW had recognized right from its start. "We have been naught," the delegates to the 1905 founding convention sang. "We shall be all." Wobblies sang in jails, on picket lines, in fields, factories, and mines, in train yards and city streets and hobo jungles. The very act of mass singing seemed to embolden and inspire people of varied backgrounds—emigrants from different parts of the world, who spoke different languages, whose skins were of different color—to unite under the IWW flag for the common goal of social and economic justice. "They had never heard the song before," the novelist B. Traven wrote of a group of strikers, "but with the instinct of the burdened they felt that this was their song, and that it was closely allied to their strike, the first strike of their experience, as a hymn is allied to religion. They didn't know what the IWW was, what a labor organization meant, what class distinctions were. But the singing went straight to their hearts."

A Swedish émigré named Joe Hill wrote their songs. Not all of them, of course, but it was he, says the historian Joyce L. Kornbluh, who "more than any other one writer, had made the IWW a singing movement." The songs were scathing critiques of capitalism—blunt, defiant, satirical, wry, cocky—and distinctly Hill. But Joe Hill, the IWW's beloved troubadour of dissent, had written his last. Six days earlier, at the age of thirty-six, he had been silenced—executed by a Utah firing squad.

The stage on which Hill's coffin rested was blanketed in scarlet and black and shrouded with floral offerings from IWW branches through-out the country and across the world. Accompanying the flowers were inscriptions in a variety of languages: Swedish, Hill's native tongue; Russian; Hungarian; Polish; Italian; German; Yiddish; Lithuanian; and English. Hanging above the coffin was a huge red banner:

IN MEMORIAM, JOE HILL
WE NEVER FORGET
MURDERED BY THE AUTHORITIES OF THE STATE OF UTAH,
NOV. 19, 1915

Joe Hill had been shot for the murder of a Salt Lake City grocer twenty-two months earlier, in January of 1914, a crime of which he had been convicted on the wispiest of evidence. The victim was John G. Morrison, a forty-seven-year-old former police officer and the father of six. (A son, Arling, seventeen, was killed alongside him. Hill was tried for the elder Morrison's murder; an alleged accomplice was wanted for the boy's killing.)

At trial the state of Utah introduced no motive, no murder weapon, no positive identification of Hill. Its case leaned entirely on circumstantial evidence, and primarily on the fact that Hill had received a gunshot wound on the night the Morrisons had been killed. The state tried to show that the younger Morrison, in the moment before he'd died, had fired the shot that had torn through Hill's chest. But the prosecutor could not show conclusively that Morrison's gun had been fired, let alone that Hill had been at the store.

Nor did he need to. For one thing, the trial judge could not have been more partial to the prosecution. For another, Hill did not help himself when he started a ruckus by firing his court-appointed lawyers in open court, and, most egregiously in the eyes of the local press and the appellate court, when he refused to testify. Whether out of naïveté or hubris, it was as if he could not fathom a conviction. As he later acknowledged, "I never thought I was going to be convicted on such ridiculous evidence." But that was before the state checkmated him. As to proof of the defendant's guilt beyond a reasonable doubt, the prosecutor pointed to what was found in Hill's pocket: his IWW red card.

FOR A DOZEN YEARS before America entered World War I, the Industrial Workers of the World was the nation's most revered and reviled labor organization. It was a union unlike any other: homegrown rebels and immigrant agitators divided by tongue, ethnicity, race, sex, and nationality and yet united in their militant, take-no-prisoners response to what they considered the assault on workers' rights perpetrated by American industry and capital. The IWW was something more, too: a powerful movement that transcended unionism. A "fighting faith," Wallace Stegner wrote, "the shock troops of labor."

Stegner was correct; the IWW was a kind of faith. "The true and one religion!" IWW orators shouted at potential converts. From atop soapboxes or rickety wooden stepladders on the street corners of skid road America, Wobbly "jawsmiths," or "soapboxers," preached the fiery gospel of social revolution. "The working class and the employing class have nothing in common," they would say, quoting the first line of the preamble to the IWW constitution. Then they might explain union doctrine in folksy terms anyone could understand: "Your interest is to have short hours and big pay and slow work and a small wheelbarrow and a small shovel. And the boss's interest is just the opposite. The boss's interest is to have long hours, small pay, and big shovels and big wheelbarrows and hurry up."

From Karl Marx, of course, the IWW borrowed its bedrock teachings: the history of society was the history of class struggle; reform of capitalism was impracticable; self-organization required class consciousness, and only through organization at the point of production could workers generate the power to build a new and just society; religion was a form of oppression by the ruling class. And yet, as the Western weekly IWW paper, the *Industrial Worker*, pointed out, for all its adherence to Marxian economics, the union's "tactics and methods" were indigenous, "born from the every-day experience" of men like "the obscure Bill Jones on the firing line, with stink in his clothes, rebellion in his brain, hope in his heart, determination in his eye and direct action in his gnarled fist." Or as Big Bill Haywood, a Utah native and onetime miner, punned, "I've never read Marx's *Capital*, but I have the marks of capital all over me."

In fact, the marks of capital, most of it Eastern capital, were all over the American West. At the turn of the twentieth century, when only 15 percent of Americans lived west of the Mississippi River, the region was a virtual colony: dependent on the exportation of inherently unstable natural resources—primarily minerals and timber—and on its principal colonizers: Wall Street and New England financiers and industrialists. The prevailing attitude of these extractive enterprises, as the Western historian Patricia Nelson Limerick has written of mining in particular, was "Get in, get rich, get out." It was an ethos as raw as the materials. Not only did it imply the plunder of natural resources, but it also suggested that those resources—and the profits from them—would be mined regardless of the environmental or human toll.

Perhaps, then, Marx would not have been surprised to learn that the West was the industrial battleground on which American class warfare was most fully realized. Major combat predated the founding of the IWW. Fighting broke out in the early 1890s and lasted through 1917, when the federal government heeded demands from Western states that it legislate and prosecute the IWW out of business on the pretext of "treasonable conspiracy" to interfere with the war-production effort.

The skirmishes began when mine operators and state militias allied to fight striking members of the newly formed Western Federation of Miners, a radical forebear of the IWW. The early strikes ostensibly concerned demands for the eight-hour day or higher wages, but as Melvyn Dubofsky notes in *We Shall Be All*, his indispensable history of the IWW, the overarching issue was the resolution of "a raw struggle between employers and employees for economic power." Those strikes were followed in 1903 and 1904 by a string of violent clashes over the basic right to organize in the mining districts of Colorado. The battling miners might not have read Marx, but by virtue of their "every-day experience" they could grasp his fundamental tenet: the interests of labor and capital were irreconcilable. And from the crucible of those brutal and bloody wars was their idea formed for a revolutionary labor organization, something as radical and militant as the Western Federation of Miners, but bigger and inclusive of all: "the amalgamation of the entire working class into one general organization," as Bill Haywood envisioned it.

When Haywood gaveled to order the founding convention of the IWW in June of 1905—the "Continental Congress of the Working Class," he called it—the country stood at an unmapped economic crossroads: somewhere beyond Jeffersonian agrarianism, but not yet inexorably on the path to modern industrial capitalism. There was another philosophical route, socialism, which a large cross section of the populace saw not as some alien, un-American plot but as a legitimate detour around the inequities of capitalism. "People spoke of the cooperative commonwealth and the coming nation with hope, expectation, and meaning," the historian John Graham writes. Socialism thrived; in 1911, voters in no fewer than eighteen American cities elected the Socialist Party candidate as mayor, and every week the Kansas-based Socialist newspaper *Appeal to Reason* circulated more than five hundred thousand copies nationally. In 1912, the party's presidential nominee, Eugene V. Debs, won nine hundred thousand votes, outpolling the Republican incumbent, William Howard Taft, in seven states.

Woodrow Wilson won that election. A Democrat, he had the support of the Progressives, the reform movement that campaigned for an end to corporate monopolies, for government oversight of industry and labor, and for moral regeneration. Progressives had restricted child labor, regulated food and drugs, passed occupational-safety laws (thirty-five thousand people perished annually in industrial accidents) and legal protections for women workers, and had pushed for education and prison reform and for prohibition. To their detractors in business, Progressives were meddlesome scolds intent on diminishing company profits; to the radical wing of labor, the reforms—*all reforms* within the moving parts of capitalism—were inadequate: "mere tinkering with the machinery."

In 1904, a pioneering social worker named Robert Hunter published a landmark book, *Poverty*, that supported radical labor's critique of Progressivism as useless for lifting the working poor out of the quicksand of capitalism. (Hunter was an interesting case: a Socialist *and* a millionaire—his wife was an heiress to a Wall Street fortune.) Extrapolating from data collected by various state and federal agencies, Hunter estimated that of the ninety million people the U.S. Bureau of the Census had counted in 1900, ten million lived in poverty. Another researcher looked at wage scales in 1904 and 1905 and determined that "at least" two-thirds of male workers earned less than six hundred dollars annually—the "absolute yearly minimum" one could live on.

As low as wages were in the first decade of the century, they would sink lower still, relative to purchasing power, over the second decade. In 1914, one economist found real wages "rapidly falling," even as new technology and the economies of mass production lowered manufacturing costs. Income inequality rose as fast as Henry Ford's unrelenting assembly lines rolled out Model Ts. A very few families were accumulating so much capital so fast that one contemporary historian thought wealth in America to be "almost as unevenly distributed as that of Europe and its slums nearly as desperate."

The numbers are telling: A federal study in 1915 found one-third to one-half of the population living at a "near-starvation level" while 2 percent of Americans owned 60 percent of the nation's wealth. And though there was a rising middle class of professionals and skilled craftsmen who benefited from the new industrial order—those whose jobs automation could not replace, or who were needed to install or operate or repair complex machinery—many workers were shoved into the abyss of grinding poverty, condemned to its degradations and attendant ills: chronic hunger, infectious disease, illiteracy, homelessness, and hopelessness. As Hunter found,

> A very large proportion of the working classes are propertyless; a very large mass of people, not only in our largest cities, but in all industrial communities as well, live in most insanitary conditions; there is a high death-rate from tuberculosis in most of our states; a large proportion of the unskilled workers receive, even when employed, wages insufficient to obtain the necessaries for maintaining physical efficiency; . . . the number injured and killed in dangerous trades is enormous; and lastly, there is uncertainty of employment for all classes of workers.

Even as the IWW preached revolution, it practiced an old-fashioned "pork-chop unionism" aimed at redressing just those sorts of societal ills. It fought for better pay, safer working and living conditions, shorter hours. "We can talk of Utopia afterwards," Bill Haywood said. "The greatest need is employment." And those who were among the neediest and who were most receptive to industrial unionism—a unified system of labor organization that mirrored the ways of modern industrial innovation and combination—were the unskilled and discounted migratory workers of the West.

Those workers, whom the famous private detective Allan Pinkerton once dismissed as "worthless things to be dreaded, shunned, driven and despised," were the IWW's core constituency. Haywood had promised delegates to the founding convention, "We are going down in the gutter to get at the mass of workers and bring them up to a decent plane of living." To haul those workers out of the gutter required militancy, and militancy guaranteed reprisal—and usually bloodshed. Town after town denied IWW members the right of free speech and assembly, of use of the mails, of fair trials; the union's halls and offices were raided, its papers unlawfully seized, publications suppressed.

Despite, or perhaps because of, the reprisals, the IWW taught and practiced nonviolent resistance. "Direct action gets the goods!" Wob-

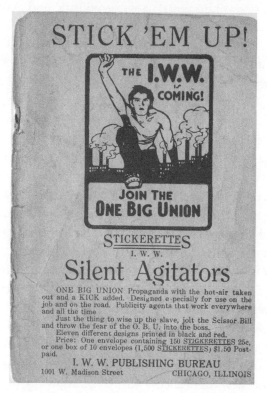

The novel stickerettes represented a low-cost, high-visibility advertising campaign for the union. This ad ran on the inside cover of the Joe Hill Memorial Edition of *The Little Red Songbook*.

blies evangelized in song, from soapboxes, and on gummed "stickerettes" that members plastered everywhere: on boxcars, in skid road hangouts, at job sites.*

The saying meant that neither bullets nor ballots could deliver economic justice to exploited, unorganized, and unskilled workers; that it took organized agitation—agitation in defiance of state-sanctioned authority and law, either in the workplace (via strikes or slowdowns or methods of what Wobblies vaguely termed "sabotage"†) or on the street (employing mass civil disobedience to assert the right to free speech or

---

* "Now all the bosses and their stools will think they're out of luck / To see the spots of black and red where Stickerettes are stuck; And after they have scratched them off and shook their fists and swore / They'll turn around and find again about a dozen more." —from "Stick 'Em Up," by the IWW writer "Shorty." The tune was borrowed from Joe Hill's song "Stung Right," whose tune Hill had appropriated from the 1897 hymn "Sunlight, Sunlight."

† Haywood's definition: "To push back, pull out, or break off the fangs of capitalism."

other constitutional liberties)—to wrest political and economic power from capitalists.

The slogan also clearly reflected the IWW's profound philosophical differences with the American Federation of Labor—or "American Separation of Labor," as Wobblies knocked the country's dominant labor organization. Under the leadership of the imperious Samuel Gompers, the AF of L had no quarrel with capitalism; rather, it saw itself as a full collaborative partner with industry and government. (Its motto, "A fair day's wage for a fair day's work," could hardly have been more at odds with the IWW's own call for "Abolition of the wage system.") As self-styled "aristocrats of labor," the AF of L welcomed only skilled workers, who were organized—or separated—by craft. It shunned migratory workers, those unskilled gutter-dwellers of whom Haywood spoke, as well as women, most minorities, and certain immigrant groups.

To the IWW, craft (or "graft") unionism was a rusted relic of labor organization: a weapon as futile against the onslaught of twentieth-century industrial capitalism as a Civil War musket against a battery of machine guns. The only way to combat industrial capitalism, the IWW believed, was through industrial unionism. For apart from new technology in factories and on farms that had begun displacing many skilled workers, there were also new, unbridled forms of business organization to contend with: large, absentee corporations that had replaced local owners and were themselves subordinate to monopolistic business trusts.

Consider United States Steel, the epitome of oligopoly and the first corporation in American history to be capitalized at over a billion dollars. J. P. Morgan formed the steel trust in 1901 by combining Andrew Carnegie's vast steel holdings with his own. The result was a sprawling empire of vertical integration, as if one steel-company town had annexed all other steel-company towns. The trust owned the mines that produced the iron ore. It owned the rail lines that shipped the ore from mine to waterway, the steamships that hauled the ore, the blast furnaces that smelted the ore, and the mills that finished the steel rails. A U.S. Steel employee "sees on every side evidence of an irresistible power, baffling and intangible," a researcher observed in 1911. "It fixes the conditions of his employment; it tells him what wages he may be expected to receive and where and when he must work."

To organize the steel trust by craft, as the AF of L had done— smeltermen in one union, railroad workers (themselves subdivided by trade: engineers, brakemen, conductors, and so on) in others, dockers, miners, and millworkers in others, each with their own respective locals, each with their own officers, and all with distinct contracts and contract-expiration dates—was to play one union off against another, and into the grateful hands of the trust. If, for example, miners walked off the job to protest dangerous working conditions, leaders of an allied local, the dockworkers, say, could force the miners' union back to work by denying strike benefits to dockers who wanted to walk out in sympathy. Whether out of loyalty to the trust, venality, or both, competing local union leaders forged for U.S. Steel an invaluable product: a fire wall against a general strike.

The IWW's idea was to organize *all* steelworkers into *one* union, so that when, for instance, railroad engineers struck, not only would brakemen and conductors honor the strike, but so would smeltermen and sailors. As Joe Hill wrote in "Workers of the World, Awaken," the first song sung at his funeral,

> *If the workers take a notion,*
> *They can stop all speeding trains.*
> *Every ship upon the ocean*
> *They can tie with mighty chains.*
> *Every wheel in the creation,*
> *Every mine and every mill,*
> *Fleets and armies of the nation,*
> *Will at their command stand still.*

Hill's song reiterated the IWW refrain that one source alone, working-class solidarity, could generate the power to stop all speeding trains, and that it was nothing short of that power—control of all industry, every ship, every mine, every mill—to which labor must aspire. "Power, in the last analysis, determines everything," George Speed, an itinerant IWW philosophizer and lumberjack, once said. Speed was speaking of economic power, for "political power is a reflex of economic power," he explained, adding, in more familiar terms, "The fellow who owns the property makes the law."

THE WOBBLIES were prolific writers, churning out dozens of periodicals and propaganda pamphlets. But it was their songs—songs of hope and unity and humor spun out of anger and frustration at life's injustices—that resonated with the masses. As Joe Hill explained in a letter from jail,

A pamphlet, no matter how good, is never read more than once, but a song is learned by heart and repeated over and over; and I maintain that if a person can put a few cold, common sense facts into a song, and dress them . . . up in a cloak of humor to take the dryness off them, he will succeed in reaching a great number of workers who are too unintelligent or too indifferent to read a pamphlet or an editorial in economic science.

Many IWW songs parodied gospel tunes favored by the Salvation Army—or "Starvation Army," as Hill disparaged the organization's "long-haired preachers," who "come out every night" to advise starving workers of their eternal reward:

> *You will eat, bye and bye*
> *In that glorious land above the sky;*
> *Work and pray, live on hay,*
> *You'll get pie in the sky when you die.*

The lyric is from "The Preacher and the Slave," Hill's best-known song (the biting, final line of the chorus endures in the American vernacular). It parodies the hymn "Sweet Bye and Bye," and it became the signature song of the IWW. He probably wrote it in San Pedro, California, in the spring of 1911, shortly before serving as a soldier in the Mexican Revolution. San Pedro was the location of the new Los Angeles Harbor, where from time to time he worked longshore, and where he could frequently be found at a Christian rescue mission. He was not there to save his soul, but because the kindly director—a minister, no less—allowed Hill to work out his songs on the mission piano. "The Preacher" was first printed in 1911 on small four-song cards and later reprinted in august compilations such as Upton Sinclair's anthology of social protest, *The Cry for Justice*, and Carl Sandburg's definitive history of American folk music, *The American Songbag*. It and some two dozen of Hill's other songs were also published in the IWW's weekly publications, the *Industrial Worker* and *Solidarity*, and in *The Little Red Songbook*, a widely circulated, pocket-size, more or less annually updated collection of IWW tunes.

AFTER "WORKERS OF THE WORLD, AWAKEN," mourners sang a few more of Joe Hill's compositions, including "The Rebel Girl," his tune for

Elizabeth Gurley Flynn, one of the IWW's leading soapboxers. In the last months of Hill's life, Flynn had championed his cause like few others; she and a well-connected friend had even talked their way into the White House, where they had pleaded his case before a sympathetic Woodrow Wilson.

Following two tenor solos, one in Swedish, the other in Italian, Big Bill Haywood took the stage. He *was* a big man for his day, though maybe not quite a "great towering hulk of a man," as a social worker in Chicago once described him. At forty-six, Haywood stood a shade under six feet tall and weighed about 230 pounds. His face was "like a scarred mountain," his friend John Reed once wrote, and with his megaphone voice and unmatched gift for oratory—"his speech was like a sledge-hammer blow, simple and direct," Flynn remembered—Haywood was labor's leading jawsmith. "He had tremendous magnetism," recalled a reporter who frequently covered his speeches. "Huge frame, one blazing eye, voice filling the hall. When he shouted, 'Eight hours of work, eight hours of play, eight hours of sleep—and *eight dollars a day!*' that last line came [like] a clap of thunder."

At Joe Hill's funeral, however, Big Bill was not his stentorian self. As he stood alongside the casket, his voice was "strangely husky," observed his friend Ralph Chaplin, himself a songwriter ("Solidarity Forever") and at the time an editor of *Solidarity*. Haywood spoke only briefly, recounting his final correspondence with Hill. He told of the farewell wire he had received on November 18, the last night of Hill's life. "Good bye Bill," Hill had written. "I will die like a true blue rebel. Don't waste any time in mourning. Organize."

"Good bye, Joe," Haywood said he had replied, "you will live long in the hearts of the working class. Your songs will be sung wherever the workers toil, urging them to organize!"

Then, uncharacteristically, Haywood grew quiet. He introduced the principal orator, Orrin N. Hilton, a renowned criminal and labor lawyer from Denver who had represented Hill on appeal and to whom Hill had grown close in his final months. Then Haywood sat down, turned his head from the stage, and stared blankly out the window.

Hilton was as effusive as Haywood had been reticent. The attorney spoke for more than two hours, some minutes of which were devoted to eulogizing his client: "this dreamer of dreams, this singer of songs, this player of music, who sought to lighten the dreary gray and unrelieved blackness of the lives of his fellow workmen."

But Hilton devoted the bulk of his address to attacking the indignities and inequities of the Utah justice system, and to arguing the impolitic case he was unable to make while Hill was alive: that the Church of Jesus Christ of Latter-day Saints—the Mormon church—was complicit in the "willful, cold-blooded murder" of his client by the capitalist class of Utah. He called the church a "hideous, slimy monster" and a "mighty empire . . . dominated by greed, selfishness and a plentitude of power . . . that will visit with vengeance upon any questioning of that power."

Hilton reserved special condemnation for the governor of Utah, William Spry, "a Mormon of the Mormons" and a man of "crass brutality." (The governor had not warmly received two pleas for mercy from President Wilson. Spry had advised the president, "Mind your own business, you are interfering with justice" in Utah, in Hilton's accurate paraphrase.) "It makes the heart sick to contemplate the fiendishness of men like Spry," Hilton said. "He defies and insults the federal government, because it is one of the foundation stones of Mormon belief that the . . . federal government is an oppressor secretly to be defied and regarded as an intruder; that the line must always be drawn between the self-styled saints on the one side and the gentiles [non-Mormons] on the other."

Hilton's conclusion struck a poetic, prescient note. "We delight today to drop a tear upon this coffin and a flower into this grave," he said. "I think there is one thought that comes to us all on an occasion of this kind, and that is that our beloved dead do not ever wholly die; that the twilight lingers after the setting of the sun . . . So it will be, men and women, with Joe Hill."

The lengthy oration over, the five thousand mourners trooped downstairs and outside while an orchestra (conducted by Rudolf von Liebich, a leading anti-capital-punishment activist) played Chopin's Funeral March. The crush on the street was so great that the dozen pallbearers were initially unable to reach the waiting hearse. It was not until the forty-piece band of the Rockford, Illinois, IWW local elbowed its way outside and encouraged the crowd to join its impromptu parade twice around the block, all the while singing Joe Hill's songs, that the crowds parted sufficiently for the pallbearers to lay the coffin atop the hearse.

The Rockford band then led the procession a mile or so northeast toward the elevated train station at Harrison and Halsted streets. The band held aloft an enormous red silk flag, emblazoned with the IWW emblem on either side and replete with a wooden shoe above the pole. (The shoe symbolized sabotage, a tactic derived from the actions of workers during the Industrial Revolution in France, who, legend had it, threw their wooden shoes—or *sabots*—into the machine cogs.) Thousands

The throng outside West Side Auditorium parts for the pallbearers after the funeral service. The IWW later sold this and the picture below, of the procession, as souvenir postcards. (Top: Walter P. Reuther Library, Wayne State University; bottom: Labadie Collection, University of Michigan)

of marchers wore on their sleeves red ribbons or IWW pennants inscribed with DON'T MOURN—ORGANIZE or WE NEVER FORGET or HE DIED A MARTYR. "The whole street seemed to move and sing as the throng inched through the West Side streets," Ralph Chaplin recalled in his memoir. "As soon as a song died down in one place, it was taken up by other voices along the line." West Siders flung open their windows as the procession approached, or filed out onto porches and roofs; the more adventurous scaled signposts and telephone and arc-light poles. When the flower bearers marched in unison, Chaplin noted, "their brightly colored floral pieces, tied with crimson ribbons, formed a walking garden almost a block in length."

At the El stop, funeral organizers and dignitaries—pallbearers, flower bearers, members of the singing and speaking committees—boarded an advance train of five reserved cars bound for Graceland Cemetery, to "highball" it there in time to meet the hearse and prepare for the coming multitude. Once the reserved train had departed (not without difficulty: so many sought to board it that committeemen had to lock arms to bar those without credentials), the regular trains to Graceland were filled to capacity for more than an hour with singing mourners. The crowds so overwhelmed the cemetery chapel that the proceedings were moved to a grassy, tree-lined hill, where the warm, humid air and leaden sky lent an appropriate mist, Chaplin remembered.

James "Big Jim" Larkin, an Irish industrial unionist, spoke the final words over Joe Hill's grave. He began on a grace note, tendering his condolences to the widow Morrison, but hardly exhaled before declaring that Hill was executed in retribution for being a Wobbly. Then Larkin praised the IWW for ever hewing "true to the line of working-class emancipation"* and for having produced "a great soul like Joe Hill, whose heart was attuned to the spirit of the coming time and who voiced in rebellious phrases his belief in the working class." As evidence of Hill's heroic character and commitment to the One Big Union, Larkin quoted from a letter Hill had written "on the verge of eternity" to his friend and champion Elizabeth Gurley Flynn, who had rallied national and international support for his cause—the right to a fair trial—and

---

* Set up in contrast was the unnamed AF of L, which Larkin, at variance with standard graveside comportment, chided as "a breed of sycophants masquerading as labor leaders, whose sole purpose in life seems to be apologizing for and defending the capitalist system of exploitation."

demands for Utah to spare his life. Hill, while appreciative, had urged Flynn to stop spending time and money on his case. Larkin said that Hill had written her that it was senseless "to drain the resources of the whole organization and weaken its fighting strength just on account of one individual."

Finally, said Larkin, let the death of Joe Hill be not in vain. "Let his blood cement the many divided sections of our movement, and our slogan for the future be: Joe Hill's body lies mouldering in the grave, but the cause goes marching on."

LIKE JOHN BROWN, the mouldering abolitionist whose own cause went marching on long after he was hanged, in death Joe Hill entered the pantheon of martyred American folk heroes. Both were the subjects of anthemic songs—"John Brown's Body" and "Joe Hill" (also known as "I Dreamed I Saw Joe Hill Last Night")—and both (owing partly to those songs) seem to float with Paul Bunyan and John Henry and Johnny Appleseed in a celestial realm somewhere between fiction and legend. But Hill, like Brown, was no cartoon character or comic book staple. As Hill's friend and fellow Wobbly Alexander MacKay said, "He earned his mythology the hard way."

One aim of this book is to examine how Hill earned his mythology; how he came to decide that if a cause was important enough to live for, it was worth dying for. Yet even a cause worth dying for does not mean one *has* to die. Joe Hill had a choice. He could have testified as to the circumstance of his shooting. He could have produced at least one supporting witness. He could have lived. Why did he choose to die? What did he hope to achieve through martyrdom? What was the calculus of self-sacrifice?

To attempt to solve that complex equation, one must consider Hill's beliefs and character, and thus his beginnings: how did his impoverished and often sickly boyhood in a Swedish port city shape his ideology and activism, his music, his humor, and his fateful decision to emigrate? Like many immigrants, he took a new name upon arriving in the United States. Who was he before he became the emblematic Joe Hill, labor martyr, before symbolism and myth attached to his name like barnacles to a ship?

And why did he join the IWW? What was it that attracted and inspired him and hundreds of thousands of other "wage slaves" to join at one time or another, often at considerable peril? Partly it was because these were people with nothing to lose: unskilled transients who slung their bindles on their backs and beat their way through hobo jungles and rail yards to cities for the promise of work; who squandered their last dollars on employment agents who cheated them out of jobs, wages, and their dignity; who lived in wretched tent camps or in vermin-infested bunkhouses, sometimes with as many as five hundred men packed and stacked like cordwood. These were men who labored twelve hours or more daily, seven days a week, in workplaces as unsafe and unhealthy as their sleeping quarters, and who, when they dared protest those conditions, were, the fortunate ones, merely fired and blacklisted.

They also joined the IWW because with the peril of membership came a sense of belonging: to a brotherhood bonded by their red cards and their songbooks and the belief that the IWW was the best and only tool for building a new and better world. As Ralph Chaplin wrote, "At all times—on the soapbox, on the picket line, and even in prison—we were aware of being part of something more important than our own unimportant selves."

UNTIL RECENTLY, what I knew of Hill I'd gleaned from the famous eponymous folk song. I'd heard recordings of Paul Robeson, the thundering, incomparable baritone, performing "Joe Hill" at Carnegie Hall in the 1940s, of Joan Baez at Woodstock in 1969, of Pete Seeger on his sloop *Clearwater*, and I'd heard it warbled in union halls and on picket lines. I didn't know the song by heart, or who had written it.* But I knew the basic story: in retaliation for organizing miners in Salt Lake City, a union man was framed and executed for murder:

> "The Copper Bosses killed you Joe,
> They shot you Joe," says I.
> "Takes more than guns to kill a man,"
> Says Joe "I didn't die."

And I knew that to union folk and other activists his fighting spirit lived on:

---

* The lyrics, written by Alfred Hayes and published in *New Masses* in 1934, were set to music in 1936 by Earl Robinson when the two met at a leftist summer camp in New York State.

And standing there as big as life,
And smiling with his eyes,
Joe says, "What they could never kill
Went on to organize."

"Joe Hill ain't dead," he says to me.
"Joe Hill ain't never died."
Where workingmen are out on strike,
Joe Hill is at their side.

As a student of labor history and folk music, I knew, too, that Hill's life and music had inspired Woody Guthrie. Indeed, in the 1940s, Guthrie wrote a long first-person prose poem, "Joe Hillstrom," that revisited the trial and execution. (Hillstrom was the unabridged surname Joe adopted after he immigrated to the United States.) Guthrie's narrative stuck close to the facts and raised the question on which the entire legal case had hinged: whether the gunshot wound Hill had received on the night of the murders had been inflicted at the crime scene, as the state had contended, or whether, as Hill had confided that night to his treating physician, he'd been shot by an unnamed friend in a row over the affections of an unnamed woman. Guthrie wrote, "Just because I've got a fresh bullet hole / You claim that I killed the Morrisons in their store." But as Guthrie's Joe explains,

I was courting a woman and had a fight with a man
He fired a pistol that lodged in me
Old Prosecutor Leatherwood can beat out his brains
But I'm not going to tell you this lady's name.

Hill and Guthrie are "links on a chain of political music," the folklorist Lori Elaine Taylor notes in her introduction to a 1990 compilation of Hill's songs on the Smithsonian/Folkways label. Taylor, citing Pete Seeger, goes on to connect Hill and Guthrie to Bob Dylan, Phil Ochs, and other writers and singers of socially conscious folk music.* Dylan wrote "Song for Woody"; Ochs wrote "Bound for Glory" (about Woody) and another song titled "Joe Hill," set to the tune Woody had borrowed

---

* To name a baker's handful of exemplars: Steve Earle, Ani DiFranco, Anne Feeney, Si Kahn, David Rovics, and Utah Phillips, himself a latter-day Wobbly troubadour until his death in 2008.

for "The Ballad of Tom Joad." A generation later, Billy Bragg recorded Phil Ochs's "Joe Hill" and wrote one of his own called "I Dreamed I Saw Phil Ochs Last Night." And in 1995, Bruce Springsteen wrote "The Ghost of Tom Joad," a song that not only evoked Guthrie (and John Steinbeck) but also resounded with a clear echo of Earl Robinson and Alfred Hayes's original "Joe Hill" ballad.

Springsteen (1995):

> *Wherever there's somebody fightin' for a place to stand*
> *Or decent job or a helpin' hand*
> *Wherever somebody's strugglin' to be free*
> *Look in their eyes Mom you'll see me.*

Robinson and Hayes (1936):

> *From San Diego up to Maine,*
> *In every mine and mill,*
> *Where workers strike and organize*
> *It's there you'll find Joe Hill.*

IT WAS BOB DYLAN'S three-page paean to Hill in his memoir, *Chronicles: Volume One*, that piqued my interest. Dylan recounted that during his early days in New York he'd been hearing the "Joe Hill" song around, that he knew Hill was "real and important," but that he didn't know who Hill was. He asked an acquaintance, the proprietor of the Folklore Center, in Greenwich Village, who dug up a few pamphlets about Hill.

"What I read could have come out of a mystery novel," Dylan wrote. "Joe Hill was a Swedish immigrant who fought in the Mexican War. He had led a bare and meager life, was a union organizer out West in about 1910, a Messianic figure who wanted to abolish the wage system of capitalism—a mechanic, musician and poet. They called him the workingman's Robert Burns."

"Joe wrote the song 'Pie in the Sky,'" Dylan continued, "and was the forerunner of Woody Guthrie.* That's all I needed to know."

I needed to know more. What animated Hill's progression from

---

* "The Preacher and the Slave" is often referred to as either "Pie in the Sky" or "Long Haired Preachers."

bindlestiff to songwriter to martyr? How did Hill come to write his songs, and what, in his music, can be heard of the culture *and* counterculture and passions of a little-known but transformative era in American history: when the urban-industrial future was supplanting the agrarian past, and when class war between labor and capital raged as never before or since?

And why, I wondered, do the legend and legacy of Joe Hill endure? Why do people still sing songs by and about him? Is it because of his influence on latter-day troubadours of dissent?* Is it because in death, as the *New York Times* fretted the day after his execution, he was thought to be "much more dangerous to social stability than he was when alive"? Is it because his story exposes the roots of so many hardy perennials: the struggles over a new economic order; rising inequality and the myth of a classless society; the limits of dissent and free speech; the causes and consequences of radical thought; the danger to democracy of a compliant and sensational press; the right to due process of law; separation of church and state; states' rights; the meaning of patriotism; the use of economic power to leverage political power; the right to freely organize unions; the morality of capital punishment; and the politics of nativism and immigration reform?

Finally, what of the murder for which Hill was convicted and executed? Who was the victim, why was he killed, and who wanted him dead? If Hill did not shoot John Morrison, as he maintained to his death, who did? A century on, could the whodunit be solved? And the most intriguing question of all: if Hill was innocent, what informed his choice to die a martyr rather than clear his name and live?

That Hill was tried in a hothouse of fear and hatred of the IWW is doubtless; none of his earlier biographers has suggested that he received, or could have received, a fair trial. Some mid-twentieth-century writers, notably Wallace Stegner (who portrayed Hill in both fiction and nonfiction), decided that Hill was "probably guilty." Stegner seems to have based his verdict largely on the prosecution-friendly trial coverage in the Salt Lake City press, as well as on lurid and demonstrably false reports about Hill's alleged criminal background—"as violent an IWW as ever lived," Stegner calls him.

The playwright Barrie Stavis, also writing at midcentury, devoted five years to a nonfiction study of Hill. He used the notes for a 1951 play,

---

* In 1986, the musicologist Wayne Hampton called Hill the most influential writer of twentieth-century protest music. He also cited Hill, Guthrie, and Dylan, along with John Lennon, as the century's four leading "guerrilla minstrels."

the title of which I borrowed (with Stavis's blessing) for this book. Both Stavis and the prolific labor historian Philip S. Foner, who published a book about the case in 1965, argue Hill's innocence; Foner declares the case "one of the worst travesties of justice in American labor history."

Was Hill a murderer? There's no telling, according to the biographer Gibbs M. Smith, whose *Joe Hill* is often referred to as the standard English-language life of Hill. (Two Swedish writers have also published biographies.) Writing in 1969, Smith concluded, "The question of Joe Hill's guilt or innocence is no more certain today than it was in 1915."

As of this writing, though, the answer *is* more certain. During five years of investigation, I have uncovered evidence, here revealed for the first time, that both persuasively suggests Hill's innocence and points to the guilt of another man. As to the former: I obtained a letter that describes in detail the circumstances surrounding the gunshot wound Hill received on the night John Morrison and his son were killed at their grocery, and that corroborates Hill's story that a friend shot him during an argument over a mutual love interest. (The state's case rested on the premise that Hill's wound was inflicted during a shoot-out at the grocery.) Hill refused to testify at trial—the burden of proof was the state's, he repeatedly asserted—and he went to his death without telling who shot him or the name of the woman with whom he and his romantic rival were entangled.

Now, for the first time, the woman herself takes a figurative step forward. Her name is Hilda Erickson, and though she is long since dead, her testimony as to the fateful events of the night of January 10, 1914, has been recovered and preserved via a letter she wrote in 1949. In the hand-written letter, which only recently was found in an attic in Michigan, Erickson unequivocally recollects who shot Hill, why, and what Hill told her the next day about the confrontation.

Erickson's revelation begs several questions: Why didn't she or Hill's shooter, a fellow Swede by the name of Otto Appelquist, speak up while they had a chance to save Hill's life? Why did Hill himself decline to testify; why, as Woody Guthrie sang, did Hill tell the prosecutor, "I'm not going to tell you this lady's name"? And if, in fact, Hill and Appelquist were busy fighting over Hilda Erickson at the hour when John Morrison and his son were shot dead, then who was the actual murderer?

A FAR MORE COMPELLING CASE could and should have been made against the initial, obvious suspect: a murderous career criminal (of remarkably similar background and appearance to Hill) whom witnesses reported "acting strangely"—lying on a snowy sidewalk not far from Morrison's grocery and moaning as if he was drunk or wounded—some ninety minutes after the murders. Later that night, police detained him in the immediate vicinity of the crime scene. A search of his person turned up an item that perhaps was not as incriminating as an IWW red card, but nevertheless would seem to have merited further investigation: a bloody handkerchief. Instead, once Hill was in custody and determined to be a notorious Wobbly musician, police released the logical suspect.

The Utah authorities knew him by the name Frank Z. Wilson, but as I learned from piecing together his life story through archival materials— court records, mug shots, rap sheets, and administrative correspondence from a youth reformatory and from jails and prisons all over the United States; federal census and immigration records; news articles; and his own writings—"Wilson" was merely one of no fewer than sixteen aliases he used. I also learned that over the six weeks preceding the night the Morrisons were killed, Wilson had been on a violent crime spree in the area, and that he was wanted for questioning (under different names, of course) in other nearby cities. This and further new information does not prove that Frank Z. Wilson murdered John Morrison. It does suggest that Wilson fit the profile of Morrison's killer, and it proffers evidence for a stronger circumstantial case than was made against Hill.

Why detectives let Wilson go one can only speculate. As Hill's lawyer and eulogist, Orrin Hilton, told an Eastern reporter on the eve of the execution, "People living at a distance from Utah cannot possibly understand the influences which are at work there."

NOR AT THIS REMOVE is it easy to understand the essential question of Hill's life: why he chose to die rather than try to save himself. After years of turning over the existing evidence and turning up new evidence myself, I have come to believe he was innocent of murder, by which I mean to say that he could have spared himself had he wished to by revealing the circumstance of his shooting. But like many Wobblies, Joe Hill was principled to the point of recklessness, and no less stubborn than he was principled. Time and again, the Utah Board of Pardons offered to commute his sentence from death to life if only he would provide a verifiable alibi; time and again, he said no. Despite persistent appeals from his lawyers and friends that he break his silence—"You will be worth more to the organization alive than dead," Bill Haywood pleaded—Hill kept mum. "I am going to get a new trial or die trying" is all he had to say.

His time behind bars had given him a certain degree of control over his destiny. No longer was he subject to the whims and everyday humiliations of employment agents or job foremen or railroad bulls; no longer did he have to hustle for the next meal or boxcar or flophouse. To be locked up was to be free to think and write, and he wrote constantly. "One thing this jail has made out of me is a good correspondent," he remarked.

Jail also made a kind of literary soapboxer out of him. He philosophized in the Wobbly press on any number of issues: the efficacy of sabotage, the need to recruit more women, the ravages of unemployment and hunger. He did so in songs, of course, and in poems, essays, and cartoons. As productive as he was, he seemed to develop an appreciation of sorts for his confinement. As he told a friend, "I can dope out my music and 'poems' in here and slip them out through the bars and the world will never know the difference."

Even before his legal appeals were exhausted, there were signs that Hill's thinking had begun to evolve. The public's reaction to his plight was extraordinary. He was hailed as a hero, a symbol of working-class resistance, and it seems plausible that he felt he needed to act the part. In what ways did his iconic status affect his thinking, shape his identity and destiny? For one thing, contrary to Haywood's entreaty that he was "worth more to the organization alive than dead," Hill apparently came to believe, consciously or unconsciously, that he could better serve the union by dying. And later, once it was clear that he would not be granted a new trial, he perhaps came to see his death as *necessary*, or at the very least as valuable propaganda for advancing the cause of industrial unionism. The cause needed a martyr, someone to incite his fellow workers, to inspire them not to mourn but to organize, and he cast himself in that swaggering role. In a valedictory letter published in the IWW weekly *Solidarity*, he vowed that he would not "'eat my own crow' just because I happen to be up against a firing squad."

Death imbued his life with meaning. What, after all, attests more powerfully to a righteous cause than the willingness to die for it? No longer was he Joe Hillstrom, another anonymous working stiff tramping around the West with a bindle on his shoulder and a red card in his pocket. Now his place in history was secure. "I have lived like an artist and I shall die like an artist," he often said. He was Joe Hill, more a legend than a man.

I

IN THE SWEET BY AND BY

Short is my date, but deathless my renown.
—HOMER, *THE ILIAD*, BOOK 9

1.

Fanning the Flames

Joe Hill arrived in Salt Lake City from Los Angeles around the middle of August 1913. He probably came via boxcar on the San Pedro, Los Angeles, & Salt Lake Railroad, the main line between its namesake cities. The route took him over the San Bernadino Mountains, in Southern California, across the Mojave Desert into Las Vegas, through the high-desert badlands of northern Nevada to Caliente, and up through red-rocked southern Utah to Salt Lake.

He had been living in a tar paper shack on the docks of the Los Angeles Harbor, in the city's San Pedro district. The IWW's much larger union rival, the management-friendly American Federation of Labor, controlled the hiring system on the wharves, and since an ill-fated IWW-led dock strike the previous summer, employment for a Wobbly longshoreman, or dock walloper, had been hard to come by—especially for one of the strike's most visible organizers: Hill had been secretary of the strike committee. In June, he had been arrested for vagrancy and sentenced to thirty days in jail. He was released on July 9. Out of jail and out of work, Hill decided to make a new start.

On the San Pedro waterfront he had befriended two brothers, John and Ed Eselius, who were fellow Swedes from Murray City, Utah, a working-class suburb of Salt Lake. The brothers had also had difficulty finding and keeping work on the wharves. In late spring or early summer of 1913, they returned to Murray and the smelting jobs they had forsaken. The Eseliuses suggested that Hill and another Swede, Otto Appelquist, follow them back home. (Appelquist had shared Hill's waterfront shack, and the brothers had bunked nearby.) They told of work to be had in Utah, either in the smelters or up in the silver mines of Park

City, in the Wasatch Range, east of Salt Lake. And indeed, their house sat across the road from a copper smelter—one of a handful of smelters that had fundamentally changed Murray's landscape over the last two decades. (Smelting is the vastly pollutive and toxic process of extracting metal from ore.*) From the town's agricultural roots had sprouted a heavy-industrial economy fueled by immigrant labor. By 1910, a majority of Murray's population of four thousand—fourfold that of forty years earlier—were recent European immigrants.

They came for jobs at the American Smelting and Refining Company, the world's largest lead smelter. ASARCO was a subsidiary of the Guggenheim syndicate, the sprawling New York–based concern that owned mines and smelters throughout the United States and Mexico. Nearly half of Murray's workforce was employed by ASARCO. Most others worked at another smelter or in related industries: the railroad that hauled the ore to the smelters from the mines of Bingham Canyon and Park City, or the brickyard that produced the firebrick that lined the smelter furnaces and smokestacks.

John and Ed Eselius invited Hill and Appelquist to stay with their family while they lined up jobs. Appelquist took them up on the offer right away. By the time Hill arrived in August, Appelquist was working construction on a "skyscraper" in downtown Ogden, thirty-five miles north of Salt Lake.

IF BY THE MIDDLE of August, Hill's name was not yet widely recognized, his songs were. Across the West that spring and summer of 1913, it seemed workers everywhere—from Northern California to Salt Lake City to Denver—were singing "Mr. Block," a tune he had written at the beginning of the year. Block was a common worker, anonymous and disposable to the employing class, a condition Hill wrote about with authority. But the senseless, bumbling Block was no Wobbly. Rather, his head was "made of lumber, and solid as a rock." He was blind to his class position—the metaphorical block upon which, the IWW taught, capitalism was built. So often was it sung and with such gusto did workers implore the hapless Mr. Block to "tie on a rock to your block and jump in

---

* As the smokestacks rose in Murray, so, correspondingly, did the number and severity of health problems among residents and smelter workers. The incidence of cancer, complications during pregnancy and birth, and lung ailments all increased drastically between 1890 and 1920; lung disease alone accounted for nearly 20 percent of all deaths between 1900 and 1920.

The Eselius family's home in Murray, where Hill was arrested. (Special Collections Department, J. Willard Marriott Library, University of Utah)

the lake, / Kindly do that for Liberty's sake" that one California journalist remarked, "Of all the [IWW's] songs, the greatest favorite now is 'Mr. Block.'"

Soon Hill would be as well known as his songs. Charged with a heinous crime five months after he arrived in Utah, he would become infamous first, a cause célèbre second, and finally a martyr, known the world over.

HILL TRAVELED a long way to Salt Lake, not every mile by boxcar. He was born Joel Hägglund in Sweden in 1879, one of six siblings who survived to adulthood. Both his parents loved music, and the entire family would sing together at home and church. Before he turned eight, his father gave him a violin. He practiced incessantly and also took to writing and performing satirical songs about his family.

His father, a railway conductor, died from injuries suffered in an accident on the job just after Joel turned eight. His oldest sibling was twelve. The family was destitute. Some days there was nothing to eat. Joel stayed in school until his twelfth birthday and then went to work in a rope factory. When he was about seventeen, he contracted tuberculosis. The disease nearly killed him. When he recovered, he went to work at the port in his hometown.

In 1902, when he was twenty-two, his mother died. Joel and his siblings sold the house and went their separate ways. Joel and an older brother used their proceeds for steamship tickets to America. They arrived in October 1902. The record of Joel's next five years is hazy. Like thousands of others, he worked his way west, traveling up and down the Pacific coast from British Columbia, Canada, to Baja California, Mexico. We know that in 1906 he was caught in the San Francisco earthquake; he covered the story for his hometown paper. And we know that he bumped into a boyhood friend there, and that together they hoboed up to Oregon. By 1908, he had joined the IWW in Portland, and later that year he went to Spokane, Washington. There was no work; the region had yet to recover from the Panic of 1907. He and fellow Wobblies hanging around the IWW hall started writing parodies of Salvation Army hymns to be played and sung during street meetings and as a rejoinder to the Army's "long-haired preachers" who struck up their own band to drown out the IWW soapboxers.

When Hill left Spokane, probably in the summer of 1910, he didn't stay put anywhere for long. He returned to Portland, rambled down the California coast to the docks at San Pedro, then headed inland to the San Joaquin Valley, the state's agriculture capital, where he worked construction, and back to San Pedro. In the middle of 1911, he crossed from San Diego into Tijuana, where he fought with rebel troops in the Mexican Revolution. (His antiwar song "Should I Ever Be A Soldier" probably dates from his time in Mexico. "Do your duty for the cause, / For Land and Liberty," he writes, alluding to the rebels' slogan, "Tierra y Libertad.")

It was during 1911 that he began to deeply mine his gifts as a songwriter. Soon after he returned to the States from Mexico, the *Industrial Worker* began promoting the fourth edition of the IWW's *Little Red Songbook*, which included what is probably his best and best-known song, "The Preacher and the Slave." And over the next couple of years, he would write a great majority of the *Songbook*'s tunes. (Of the seven songs in the 1912 edition, four were Hill's, and he wrote ten of the dozen songs in the 1913 edition.)

His songs were so popular because of his singular talent for boiling down complex social and economic issues into darkly funny parodies, and because he set the songs to familiar tunes that were easily memorized, usually hymns or popular songs of the day. (He arranged "Mr. Block," for instance, to a durable 1908 Tin Pan Alley hit, "It Looks to Me Like a Big Night Tonight.") And there was nothing abstract or detached about his songs. They were written in the crucible of the moment, not for performance or posterity but, as *The Little Red Songbook* stated, "To Fan the Flames of Discontent." Whether workers gathered on a Salt Lake City street corner, in a hop field in Northern California, in a union hall in Butte, Montana, or in a logging camp near Spokane, they sang as if Joe Hill's distinctive voice was theirs, and as Hill would have been the first to say, they were right.

HILL HAD IMMIGRATED through New York City in 1902 and within a year had entered the westward migrant stream. The West is where the unskilled jobs were, where wage-workers were needed to dig and saw and pick and blast the natural resources from the recently tamed frontier, to haul and sort and refine the raw materials, and to pack the resultant commodities and ship them to distant markets and industrial centers. The economy was boom-and-bust. A dip in, say, the spot price of copper could trigger swells of unemployment that rippled like harvest wheat. Even in boom times, however, employment agents kept their skid road hiring halls overflowing with surplus workers. And surplus workers— regardless of the going rate for copper futures—ensured surplus misery: low wages, long hours, and appalling living and working conditions. Employers had no incentive to spend money on improvements. Government regulation was nil; Western politicians considered labor regulation— wage and hour laws, for instance, or a prohibition on children's work—a throttle on the engine of economic growth. (To be fair, the antiregulatory stance was widespread throughout the land; Congress passed no comprehensive worker-protection legislation until the Fair Labor Standards Act of 1938.)

The other institution that might have provided Western workers with a measure of relief was the American Federation of Labor. Its members, though, as previously discussed, were mainly higher-paid skilled craftsmen with stable employment. It was unsuited for, and uninterested in, organizing low-wage unskilled workers who drifted, or were driven, from job to job. There was, briefly, one exception within the AF of L: the Western Federation of Miners. But the WFM, which was founded in 1893 and soon thereafter joined the AF of L, was a poor fit—too radical, too militant, too inclusive. Where the AF of L believed that individual trade unions should put their own concerns above those of other trade unions, the WFM believed in solidarity among all kinds and classes of workers. After a brief, unhappy marriage, the two federations parted in 1897.* A year later, the miners' federation tried again to unify the labor movement. That time it stuck closer to home. Out of a meeting in Salt Lake City, a new federation was born, the Western Labor Union. It embraced the slogan of the old Knights of Labor, "An injury to one is the concern of all." (For about two decades prior to the founding of the AF of L in 1886, the Knights of Labor was America's preeminent labor organization.) The Western Labor Union was headquartered in Butte, where the WFM had been founded. In 1902, the WLU moved to Chicago and changed its name to the American Labor Union. In 1905, along with the Western Federation of Miners and other radical unions, it was absorbed by the new Industrial Workers of the World.

BY 1900, SALT LAKE CITY, with a population of 54,000, trailed only Denver (population 134,000) in size among the cities of the intermountain West. The landscape, natural and built, was striking: a blooming desert valley surrounded by two mountain ranges and the Great Salt Lake, with the magnificent six-spired temple of the Church of Jesus Christ of Latter-day Saints—the Mormons—looming over the valley. The city's population had nearly quadrupled since the transcontinental railroad had been joined at nearby Promontory Point, Utah, in 1869. A year later the tracks had been laid to Salt Lake City, and by 1900 a dozen rail lines crisscrossed the city.

With the coming of the railroads, a mining boom emerged. Branch lines were extended into the mine-laden canyons of the nearby Wasatch and Oquirrh ranges. For the first time, mining companies could efficiently transport their precious minerals—gold, copper, silver, and lead—to local mills and smelters and on to far-flung markets. With a hyperbolic push from the region's exuberant promoters, Salt Lake became a commercial and industrial hub. As the Utah historian John S.

---

* They would reconcile a decade later, after the WFM, under new conservative leadership, quit the IWW in 1907 over an ideological breach.

McCormick paraphrases the remark of a visiting journalist, "Utah was one large mining camp and Salt Lake City was its Main Street."

IT WAS NOT SUPPOSED to be that way. Led by their prophet Brigham Young, the Mormons founded Salt Lake City in 1847. It was to be a self-sufficient "Kingdom of God" until the second coming of Christ. A half century later, Christ had yet to appear, but the United States government had, intent on imposing its laws on a territory that preferred its own.

"Brother Brigham" had led the Mormons' well-chronicled exodus from Illinois to the Great Basin because it was a remote and harsh desert—"a place on this earth," he reckoned, "that nobody else wants." The isolation appealed to the Mormons. "We do not intend to have any trade or commerce with the gentile world . . . ," Young said. "I am determined to cut every thread of this kind and live free and independent, untrammeled by any of their detestable customs and practices."

The prophet's vision of cooperative self-sufficiency was as rational as it was radical. For the whole of their existence, practically since the day in 1830 when the twenty-four-year-old church founder, Joseph Smith Jr., had published the Book of Mormon, church members had been persecuted brutally and relentlessly. In every state where they tried to establish a "gathering place," they were treated as "little better than vermin, rats, and razorbacks." Their tumultuous search for a settlement led from New York to Ohio, where Smith was tarred and feathered; to Missouri, where the governor ordered the "extermination" of Mormons and where Smith was jailed for treason and murder (he escaped); and finally to Illinois, where in 1844, near the Mormon settlement of Nauvoo, a vigilante mob murdered Smith.

Why did mainstream America regard the early Mormons as pests to be eradicated? Were they persecuted because people feared the very domination they would later achieve in Utah through their industriousness, organization, and loyalty to the faith to the exclusion of outsiders? Why were the Mormons regarded as the Industrial Workers of the World would be two generations later: as a subversive menace to civil society? Perhaps because the ideas and beliefs the early Mormons espoused were in their own way as deviant and dangerous as the revolutionary ideology the IWW preached. In the age of the rising, pre–Civil War market economy and what Smith disparaged as its presiding society of "bankers, lawyers, and businessmen," the Mormons advocated collective ownership of property. They saw no need to separate the functions of church and state. And most notoriously, they held that plural marriage was fundamental to attaining salvation. (Smith took at least thirty-three wives, and Brigham Young, his successor as prophet, married fifty-five women, including seven or more of Smith's widows.) Only Indians were more intolerable to Jacksonian America. As John McCormick writes of the early Mormons, "They were theocratic in a democratic society. They were polygamous in a monogamous society. And they were utopian socialists in an emerging capitalistic order."

And, like the IWW's legion of soapboxers, Mormon missionaries were devoted and accomplished proselytizers; they were winning Protestant converts. Both the IWW's and the Mormons' potent combination of recruiting success and deviance bred fear and misrepresentation and vilification. But where the IWW spread the gospel of the One Big Union and the coming industrial democracy, the Mormons foresaw a theocracy, a society organized, as Brigham Young envisioned, as "one great family of heaven."

EVENTUALLY MORMONS warmed to capitalism. By the early 1890s, they pretty much had to. The desolate "place on this earth" that was once beyond the grasp of U.S. law was no longer. Through a series of punitive acts of Congress, the United States effectively seized Utah Territory. The federal government disincorporated the church and ordered its significant property confiscated; it criminalized polygamy and disenfranchised its practitioners; it stripped from the church local control of political and judicial offices. The country surrounded Utah, and Utah had no alternative but to surrender: the church officially renounced polygamy and made other concessions. In January of 1896, Utah joined the Union as the forty-fifth state.

Any residual feelings on Utah's part for its utopian-socialist past were sublimated by its desire to embrace statehood. It longed to recast its reputation as a freakish "other"—a separatist theocracy peopled by, in Wallace Stegner's words, "a bunch of fanatics having revelations or talking gibberish." Utah expended a lot of energy trying to convince the rest of the country that, as Governor William Spry felt needed to be said as late as 1915, "American ideals are as great here as anywhere else . . . The people are patriotic, progressive, Godfearing and intelligent."

For decades before statehood, the Mormon church had tolerated unions. (Most union members, of course, would also have belonged to the

The Salt Lake City skyline, 1915. Among the visible buildings are the Salt Lake Temple and the new state capitol building. (Used by permission, Utah State Historical Society, all rights reserved)

church.) With Utah's transition to capitalism, however, the church became "more and more critical of unionism," a Utah labor historian, J. Kenneth Davies, writes. In 1902, Mormon church president Joseph F. Smith Sr., who in his capacity as prophet presided over a conglomerate of church-owned businesses, including an iron mine, proclaimed the despotism of union labor.* On that occasion his gripe concerned the "closed shop"; he called union-only workplaces "a species of tyranny which I am totally opposed to."

A year later, the church injected itself into a mine workers' strike. Mining camps in Utah, like most places, relied on the weak organization and strong backs of cheap immigrant labor. In the fall of 1903, some of those immigrant miners organized. They joined the United Mine Workers and launched a strike in the coalfields of Carbon County that would last for more than a year. When the employer, Utah Fuel Company, put

---

* In a bit of confounding nomenclature, Joseph F. Smith Sr. was a nephew of church founder Joseph Smith Jr.

out the call for strikebreakers, a high church official in Salt Lake announced in the tabernacle that jobs in the coalfields were there for the taking. A United Mine Workers organizer offered his blunt assessment of the church's decision to side with the mining company: "The Mormon church ha[s] commenced a fight to annihilate union labor in Utah." Moreover, the church-owned *Deseret Evening News* engaged in rank nativism; it chided the predominantly Italian strikers for being, well, Italian. "These Italians have refused to amalgamate with Americans or learn the English language and have lived with the intention of getting out of this country all they could and then returning to their native land of olives and dirt."

The Carbon County strike ultimately failed, as did a subsequent walkout by five thousand predominantly Greek copper miners at Bingham Canyon in 1912, yet both heralded a new labor militancy in the state.

The IWW opened its first hall in in Salt Lake City, under the banner of Local 69, in the summer of 1910. By that fall it had attracted three hundred members—and, with its calls for "abolition of the wage system" and its own sort of utopian-socialist society, the attention of the authorities as well. "Even here in sleepy, saintly Salt Lake," an *Industrial Worker* correspondent noted, "the [wage] slaves are waking up. The master, too."

Most of the local's early activity centered on maintaining its right to conduct open-air meetings in the city, rather than focusing on industrial organizing in the hinterland. Along with its sometime ally, the Socialist Party, during the fall of 1910 the IWW drew large, enthusiastic crowds to outdoor meetings at Liberty Park, a sixteen-acre swath of verdant open space southeast of downtown. The city took notice: it tightened its outdoor-assembly policy. But it did so not in the ham-fisted manner that would paralyze other Western cities—Spokane, Fresno, and San Diego, most notoriously—where police roughed up and rounded up hundreds of Wobblies who refused to surrender their First Amendment right to peaceable assembly. (More than one was arrested while reciting the Bill of Rights or the Declaration of Independence.) That tactic only encouraged Wobblies from all over the country to swarm those cities, fill the jails, and demand individual trials. The inevitable result was a gummed-up legal system, far more publicity and recruits for the IWW than it could have generated itself (although the press was wildly sensational), and a widening of the class divide between labor and capital.

Salt Lake City took another tack. So as not to appear quarrelsome with anyone's right to free expression, it exercised prior restraint in the name of public safety. On one occasion that the union billed as a "monster meeting," Salt Lake police arrested all six scheduled speakers *before* the meeting, charging them not with intent to purvey revolutionary propaganda or to insult God and country, but with "obstructing the street in placing a soap box thereon." (The cases were dismissed when the prosecutor failed to prove who the "placer" was.)

By the summer of 1913, as Joe Hill prepared to leave California for Utah, Local 69 was actively, if furtively, organizing. As many as fifteen hundred shovel stiffs were building a six-mile grade on the Denver & Rio Grande Railroad for the state's largest and most powerful contractor, Utah Construction Company. The road was near the central Utah town of Tucker, in coal-mining country. Workers lived in squalid tent camps, where the amenities were nil: they slept on the ground, they relieved themselves wherever they could, they had no access to laundry and only the crudest bathing facilities, and the food was insubstantial on good days, rancid on others. The stiffs were made to toil long, backbreaking hours for low wages; indeed, if someone *were* to break his back or suffer some other serious injury or illness, he was out of luck: there was no accessible hospital—despite the mandatory hospitalization fee workers paid. That was life for the rootless, floating army of bedraggled laborers who roamed the West. If someone quit, there was always another hungry hobo waiting and willing to take his place.

Only this time, nearly everyone quit. Agitators from Local 69 had infiltrated the tent camps and begun holding meetings. On June 10, the stiffs laid down their shovels and drew up their demands: a twenty-five-cent daily raise and one hour less work a day; decent food and bedding; and sanitary bathing and laundry facilities to enable them "to live under conditions something approaching human."

On July 10, the IWW's Western weekly, the *Industrial Worker*, reported the outcome of the strike in Utah: TUCKER CONTRACTORS CONCEDE DEMANDS. The shovel stiffs could not have won without the support of the trainmen of the Denver & Rio Grande Railroad. The trainmen barred anyone from riding the struck line unless they showed an IWW red card or a pass from the strike committee. Ultimately the company conceded the twenty-five-cent raise, it shipped in boxcar-loads of new bedsprings and mattresses, and it dispatched a team of carpenters to install sanitary bathing and toilet facilities in the tent camps. By the end of June, the IWW had justifiably and loudly proclaimed victory. "Direct Action gets the goods!" a Local 69 member reminded his fellow workers in the afterglow of the strike, adding that the hard-wrung concessions at Tucker were but a signpost on the revolutionary road the IWW was grading to-ward "the final abolition of the peonage system."

It was a huge win for the IWW, and an alarming loss for the Utah establishment. "You IWWs caught us with our pants down this time," a Utah Construction Company official candidly acknowledged to a striker. "But I can assure you, that before the end of a year every damn single IWW will be run out of the state of Utah."

Rather than deport Wobblies by, say, herding them into boxcars and stranding them without provisions in the desert in July—as did strike-breakers in southern Arizona—Utah Construction's hired thugs exacted payback closer to home: they attacked IWW members during a peace-able street meeting in downtown Salt Lake City.

Their primary target was a strike ringleader named James F. Morgan, a forty-five-year-old traveling soapboxer whom one newspaper described as a "fanatic IWW screacher" blessed with a "cast-iron voice" that dispensed "fire-eating oratory." Morgan had been jailed during the strike and held for sixty days. On the evening he was sprung, August 12, hundreds of Wobblies turned out in downtown Salt Lake for an open-air celebration of the strike and Morgan's release.

Morgan was to be the main speaker. As usual, the meeting began with a song; on that evening they chose Joe Hill's "Mr. Block." The workers' chorus had just condemned Mr. Block to everlasting punishment in the company of plutocrats. (In the last verse, Hill kills off the wretched Block. Block asks St. Peter for a chance to meet the titans of capitalism: "'the Astorbilts and John D. Rockefell.' Old Pete replied, 'Is that so? / You'll meet them down below.'")

That was when a twenty-man armed posse seemed to come from no-where. (The men had emerged from a bar across the street.) One man drew a heavy revolver and clubbed Morgan on the back of his head. "The sound was sickening," a bystander reported. Morgan slumped to the ground. Someone began kicking his face. Others joined in. Blood spurted from the back of his head, his nose, mouth, eyes. He lost con-sciousness.

A full-fledged riot broke out: fists flew, bullets flew, blood, lots besides Morgan's, spilled. Morgan, who was clubbed silly before he could speak a word from the soapbox, was charged with inciting a riot and assault with intent to commit murder. (The charges were eventually dismissed.)

Salt Lake City chief of police Brigham F. Grant promptly announced that as long as he remained in charge, the IWW would "hold no more street meetings." Sam Scarlett, secretary of Local 69, argued that the free speech clause of the U.S. Constitution trumped local fiat, adding, "and we as citizens propose to uphold the Constitution." To do so, Local 69 put out the call to IWW branches across the West to send reinforcements. "I expect ten thousand of them to come here," J. F. Morgan told a reporter.

"What will they do here?" the reporter asked.

"Any damn thing they want to do," Morgan replied.

Though thousands of free speech fighters never materialized in Salt Lake, enough small clusters of "suspicious" men—"groups of threes and fours and by the half-dozens"—converged on the city to cause "a feeling of uneasiness among the guardians of the city's peace." The sheriff announced that hundreds of vigilantes—he called them "volunteers"—had offered to assist should there be further IWW trouble. "The only trouble we will have," he added, "if trouble does start, will be to restrain those volunteers who would want to take the punishment . . . into their own hands."

Joe Hill answered the call from Local 69. Whether he timed his arrival to participate in the "trouble," or whether the timing was coincidental, we don't know. We do know that he got to Salt Lake within days of the riot, at a high-water mark for hostilities. And we know that Hill and Otto Appelquist bunked with the Eselius family in Murray through the rest of August and into the first week of September. They then took jobs at the Silver King mine in Park City, about thirty-five miles and a jagged mountain range east of Murray. Hill got sick, probably in early December, and was laid up for two weeks in the Miners Hospital in Park City. Appelquist accompanied him back to the Salt Lake area, where Hill recovered in time to make a great hit playing Swedish folk songs on piano and violin at holiday sing-alongs at the Eseliuses' and other Swedish families' homes.

They stayed with the Eseliuses over Christmas and into the new year. It was a tight squeeze, what with three generations of the family crammed into a four-room cabin: two bedrooms, each with two beds, a kitchen, and a parlor with a folding iron cot on which Hill and Appelquist slept. There were John and Ed Eselius, the brothers who had befriended Hill and Appelquist in San Pedro; their brother Victor; their widowed father, Carl; their widowed sister, Betty Eselius Olson; and three of Betty's four children—all but Hilda Erickson, who boarded in Salt Lake.

TWO WEEKS into the new year, there would be a double murder at a family-owned grocery store in Salt Lake. The initial prime suspect would be an ex-convict whom the police knew as Frank Z. Wilson. Wilson was murderous, he was vengeful, and he was seen acting "strangely" within walking distance of the crime scene some ninety minutes after the murders.

On the same night, Joe Hill received a gunshot wound. Hill told the doctor who treated him that a friend had shot him over a woman. But Hill never named either one—not then, not at trial, and not during the appellate case or in subsequent hearings. He argued instead that the burden of proof lay with the state; that he should not have to prove his innocence.

If he was innocent, why the silence? Perhaps because at first he thought he would win the case, if not at trial, then surely on appeal. But as the months in prison wore on—from arrest to execution, the process took twenty-two months—his case drew worldwide publicity, tens of thousands of letters and telegrams of protest, rallies in many major cities, and the intervention of the president of the United States. Eventually, Hill appeared to see himself as his supporters saw him: as a heroic prisoner of the class war. But was he also a prisoner of his celebrity? No more did he think of himself as just a "common pacific coast wharfrat," as he used to say. He was a hero, a living symbol of courage and conviction and rebellion, and once he had glimpsed himself in that heroic light, he went willingly to the darkness.

2.

The Man Who Wouldn't Be Held Up

January 10, 1914, was "an ideal winter's day," the *Deseret Evening News* reported, "dry, clear and cold, with lots of ozone in the atmosphere to brace up one's physiology." Into the chill of the Saturday night that followed, under a moon so ripe and bright that it all but rendered the newfangled street lamps redundant, the big crowd spilled from the Empress, the gleaming new vaudeville palace in Salt Lake City's bustling theater district. For "those never changing Empress prices"—a dime to perch in the crow's roost of the upper balcony, twenty cents for a spot in the lower balcony or on the floor level, and thirty cents for a high-hat seat—an itinerant troupe of performers had treated the audience to ninety minutes of "thrills, chills and shrills": death-defying, high-wiring acrobats, crooners and belters and hoofers, sight gags and slapstick and hokum, an ingenue late of Broadway, "Dare-Devil" motorcyclists, and the featured attraction, "Louis's Christmas," a one-act marital farce.

As always, too, there were the melodious stylings of the Empress house orchestra and Mutual Weekly's silent newsreel footage of events spanning the globe. After seven years of construction, the waterway between the Atlantic and the Pacific, the Panama Canal, was nearly complete. There was no word yet from Europe on the coming war; combat was still seven months off. From London came the astonishing news of a likely cure for cancer: radium treatments. A cancer researcher declared that some patients who entered the cancer ward of his hospital to die were "apparently cured" within a month. And from Dayton, Ohio, Orville Wright announced his latest invention, a "fool-proof" balancing device, or "automatic stabilizer," for use in commercial air travel. Wright said he anticipated the day "when it will be just as safe to board an aeroplane and take a long trip as it is at present to make a journey behind a locomotive."

There was also labor news from Michigan that must have had Utahns buzzing. A long and bitter strike by copper miners in that state was on the verge of spreading nationwide; the Western Federation of Miners was threatening to call a general strike of its entire U.S. membership. The union's chief counsel was none other than Orrin Hilton. "It means a struggle to the bitter end," Hilton said, regarding the mine owners' refusal to bargain in good faith. "They wanted everything and would concede nothing." Later that year, Hilton would take on another client, Joe Hill, for whom he would struggle, literally, until Hill's last breath. Hilton would take Hill's case on appeal. Ironically, though, this time it would be Hilton's client who would not "budge an inch." Hill wanted a new trial, and he, too, would concede nothing, even though it would secure his doom.

The other big labor news of the week came from neighboring Colorado, where the state had just deported the octogenarian union organizer Mary "Mother" Jones from its southern coal-mining precincts during a strike called by the United Mine Workers. (Three months later, on April 20, 1914, the Colorado National Guard fired on, and set fire to, the tent colony in Ludlow, Colorado, where striking miners and their families were living. Of the nineteen people who died, twelve were children.)

THE CURTAIN DROPPED just before nine o'clock, and as the five hundred or so early-show patrons funneled from the Empress and each of the theater's neighboring rivals—the Orpheum, the Pantages, and the Utah—the late-show audiences were cueing up. The sidewalk below the Empress's huge, roof-mounted electrified tiara and the surrounding streets were snow-crusted and all but impenetrable: thousands of men in overcoats and bowlers and women in ankle-length corset dresses and tailored hats milled about, some doubtless discussing which of the many nearby cafés and saloons to visit for a late bite or a nightcap, perhaps the Royal or the White Way, or maybe they'd brave the lines at Keeley Ice Cream, adjoining the Empress. Tourists in for a night on the town, and maybe a visit to Temple Square after Sunday church, had only to stroll a block north to the Kenyon Hotel, or to the Rex or the Lucid, all of which boasted modern rooms at moderate prices. And there were those, of course, whose night was ending and who were jostling their way to the corner of First South and Main for a streetcar homeward.

One middle-aged couple, Frank and Phoebe Seeley, decided that rather than elbow their way onto a trolley, they would walk home under the glowing moon. They lived on First West between Washington and Jefferson streets, not quite a mile and a half south of the theater. It was likely a rare evening out for the Seeleys; they had two teenagers and a five-year-old, and Frank worked nights as a conductor on the Denver & Rio Grande Railroad. As they strolled south along West Temple, the clamor and bustle of Saturday night on Main Street receded. There was the occasional clip-clop of a horse-drawn wagon, the squeal and buzz of a motorized streetcar tethered to its overhead power lines, and even a few wheezy automobiles, but for most of their eight-block walk down the ramrod-straight street, there was but the sight of their own breath in the frosty air and the crunch underfoot of packed snow.

It was about nine-thirty when the Seeleys neared the intersection of West Temple and Eighth South. They noticed a light in the corner grocery, peered into the storefront, and beheld a bucolic scene: a snoozy cat in the window and beyond it the industrious owner and two of his sons. The Seeleys were two blocks from home when they turned west on Eighth South. There they crossed paths with two men walking side by side, one a bit taller than the other, one (it was unclear which) with a scar on the side of his face or neck, both with their hands buried in their coat pockets, and at least one wearing a red bandanna around his neck. The passable portion of the cobblestone sidewalk narrowed, and Phoebe stepped in front of Frank to walk single file. Neither of the approaching men yielded, crowding Phoebe off the sidewalk. "This angered me slightly," Frank would later say. He turned and glared at the taller of the impolite men, but no words were exchanged, and both parties continued on their way.

That fleeting, unpleasant encounter would haunt the Seeleys, probably for the rest of their lives.

ONLY THE DAY BEFORE, readers of Salt Lake City's four dailies had been heartened by the news of a police department report that fewer grave crimes had been committed in 1913 than in the previous year. Chief of Police Brigham Grant acknowledged that arrests were on the rise—there had been more than ten thousand altogether—but pointed out that most of those charged were jobless transients given more to vagrancy and drunkenness than to, say, stealing or blowing safes. The chief was the half brother of Heber J. Grant, a Mormon apostle who four years later would become president of the Church of Jesus Christ of Latter-day Saints. Brigham Grant had a bushy salt-and-pepper mustache, beetled eyebrows, and an evident streak of morality—he had been appointed in 1911 with a mandate to scrub the town of vice in the wake of eight years of non-Mormon city government. (And yet he himself was "an old-time gambler who had lived quite a lusty life," as one scholar notes.) And although Grant's administration would itself soon stand accused of misconduct and corruption, the chief's latest annual report practically crowed that "race horse touting, pay-off games, dollar matching, negresses enticing and robbing men, as well as other bunko games have become practically a thing of the past." The report was greeted with editorial acclaim. That Saturday morning, the *Salt Lake Tribune*, for one, applauded the department's "gratifying efficiency." The paper noted, however, the chief's observation that since the turn of the new year "criminals and other undesirable characters" had been "pouring into the city," and it also printed Grant's prescient warning that "the police will probably have their hands full."

FEW IN TOWN that day could have been more anxious about an influx of criminals than John G. Morrison, the proprietor of the grocery store the Seeleys had just looked in on. As the Seeleys passed by, Morrison and his two boys were preparing to close for the night. Morrison was forty-seven years old and a former police officer. He had worn a badge for only fifteen months, and although it had been a half dozen years since he had turned it in, he had come to profoundly regret his time in uniform and had had more than his share of disquieting confrontations with the city's "undesirable elements." Like many in town, he habitually kept a loaded gun within reach, but he was less reserved than most about using it. His gunplay, particularly after thwarting a holdup the previous September, had accorded him a certain celebrity: by early 1914, he was renowned as the ex-cop who wouldn't be held up. But the reputation burdened him, and lately he'd begun to confess his fears and regrets to his confidants; he spoke forebodingly, as if he knew his life was in imminent danger. Just that afternoon he had told his good friend John Hempel, a former police captain with whom he had served, that he would give up all his hard-earned savings, some eight hundred dollars, if only "I could have my name blotted out of the police department's record."

John Gibson Morrison was five feet ten inches tall, with a thick, dark pompadour and high cheekbones that some said evidenced Indian heritage. His was a large farming family, his father's forebears having emigrated from Scotland to New England to Kentucky to Morgan County in central Missouri, where by 1851 John's father, Thomas Perry Morrison, was settled in a house he had forged out of rock and mortar on some ninety acres of rolling farmland. Between 1846 and 1851, Tom Morrison had six children with his first wife. She died young, and in 1858 he was remarried, to Alverna Smith Hanby. Alverna had two children from her prior marriage, and together Tom and Alverna had six more. The fourth of those, John, was born on July 8, 1866. According to John's grandson John Arling Morrison, Tom Morrison was known as a brawler, "a real roughneck farmer" who liked to mix it up about politics. "He was tough on his kids, and he wanted to make them tough."

By the time John left home in 1892, he was plenty tough. What his father had not pounded into him, the desperate economic conditions had. A weed-borne pestilence killed some family members; persistent drought and recurring dust storms plagued the land. Crop prices fell for a decade, interest rates soared, banks failed. (That winter in St. Louis, 175 miles east of the Morrisons' farm, ten thousand insolvent farmers and hard-bitten city dwellers formed a third political party, the People's Party, to organize for economic reform.)

John was twenty-five or twenty-six years old when he crossed the plains to Salt Lake City, twelve hundred miles from Morgan County. When he first gazed skyward at the spires of the Salt Lake Temple, Utah was not yet a state; it would be four years before the territory gained admission to the Union. And although the city had not become the Mormon utopia that Brigham Young had envisioned, the two-hundred-foot-high temple dominated the political, cultural, economic, and social landscape as much as it did the built environment in its shadow.

To a newcomer to Salt Lake City such as Morrison, the church must have seemed pervasive; its leaders controlled economic development, law enforcement, a major newspaper, education, and most cultural activities. On April 6, 1893, not long after he arrived, more than forty thousand people—virtually everyone in town—crowded onto and around Temple Square for the dedication ceremonies of the Salt Lake Temple. It was forty years to the day since Brigham Young had laid the cornerstone. The prophet had not lived to attend the festivities—he had died in 1877—but John Morrison likely was there with his sweetheart. Following prayer and song, temple president Lorenzo Snow led the multitude in the thrice-shouted "*Hosanna, hosanna, hosanna, to God and the Lamb, amen, amen,*

amen." It is unlikely that Morrison added his voice to the hosannas, and it is certain that he was not allowed inside the holy building: it was closed to "gentiles,"—non-Mormons—and Morrison was no Mormon.

His girlfriend, however, was descended from Mormon pioneer stock. Harriet Maria Nowlin, known as Marie, was a petite, vivacious twenty-year-old whose maternal grandfather, Briant Stringham, had been among those handcart pioneers who had accompanied Brigham Young from Illinois in his fabled advance party of 1847. Marie Nowlin was born in 1872 to a seventeen-year-old mother whose own mother was one of Stringham's four wives. Marie's father was a deadbeat, given, it was said, to "chasing rainbows" and deserting his family for lengthy periods of time. When Marie turned seven, her exasperated mother left her father for good. She took Marie and her three younger siblings back to the house in Salt Lake in which she had been raised. Eventually she was able to remodel and operate it as a boardinghouse.

Marie and John met at a downtown skate park. He had recently opened a cigar stand nearby, on the corner of First South and Main, a few blocks from Marie's house. That she would take up with a gentile was scandalous enough to her family. That she would take up with a gentile who sold cigars for a living when the prophet Joseph Smith had plainly revealed that "tobacco is not for the body," well, that could only have inflamed matters. And not only was Marie dating a tobacco-promoting gentile, but she was *fornicating*—a sin in the Book of Mormon graver than all but murder and denial of the Holy Ghost. And not only was

John Morrison at his cigar stand, circa 1893. (Courtesy Morrison family)

Marie unchaste, but she was pregnant with the tobacco-peddling gentile's child. John and Marie were married on May 17, 1893. Three months and ten days later, their first child died in childbirth.

Shortly after they were married, John sold his cigar stand and opened a store, J. G. Morrison Staple and Fancy Groceries. It was located on the south end of town, the gentile section, near the new City & County Building, a five-story stone-and-masonry structure with a clock tower that soared 250 feet in the air—higher, by design, than the temple's spires up the street.

In Morrison's years as a shopkeeper, he would have to defend himself against robbers on two occasions. Once was in 1903, not long after the family—by then John and Marie had four of their six children who would live to maturity (four others died in childbirth or as infants)—had moved into rooms in the rear of the grocery, at Fourth South and First West streets. The other instance occurred a decade later—four months before he was murdered. He was not one to shirk. And his bravery and readiness to use firearms not only earned him a reputation but also would be relevant to how his murder was seen. He had faced down potential killers, had returned fire. When he was killed, the police seemed certain that the motive had been revenge, not robbery. And further, that the murderer had sought revenge against Morrison for his having foiled a previous holdup.

On February 2, 1903, the family was finishing supper when a trio of masked men burst in. Morrison ran into the store. Told to throw up his hands, he instead dropped behind the counter and sprinted back to the living quarters. "Where's my shotgun?" he cried. "Give me the gun!"

Morrison grabbed the shotgun, reentered the store, leveled the gun at the robbers, and . . . it wouldn't fire. Now the holdups took aim: three errant shots whizzed by Morrison's head, another bullet grazed his left wrist, and another tore through his pant leg. Once again Morrison dashed into the living room. With one of the bandits in hot pursuit, he hid behind a pile of boxes while Marie fetched his Colt .45.

"Where's that son of a bitch that ran in here?" the bandit asked, pointing his gun at a servant girl in the kitchen. "Throw up your hands!"

"O my God! O my God!" the girl screamed.

The bandit retreated to the store. Morrison found his pistol and, "standing behind the counter and showcase in full view of the hold-ups, began pumping lead in their direction." He emptied his six-shooter, shattering one assailant's right hand; the man crumpled to the hardwood. Morrison rushed back to his parlor to reload; the others dragged their comrade to the street. BRAVE GROCER PUT THREE BOLD ROBBERS TO FLIGHT, read the front-page headline in the next morning's *Tribune*.

Morrison's pluck and skill with a revolver caught the attention of the incoming chief of police, George A. Sheets. But Sheets, a gentile, lasted only a month on the job before the Utah Supreme Court tossed him out of office; it ruled that the city council had confirmed him without a quorum. It would take three years, during which an anti-Mormon third party, the American Party, was swept into municipal power, for Sheets to regain his job. In January 1906, he shot back, promptly firing seven loyalist Republican (Mormon) police officers and replacing them with fellow American Party members, among them John Morrison.

During Morrison's brief tenure as a police officer, he was commended for bringing into custody untied horses, or "fiery steeds"; the *Tribune* saluted him as the "Copper Who Cops Animals." And he was cited in the newspapers for helping to rescue a raving, suicidal mother of seven from herself. Unrecorded in police files or the press is whether Morrison worked any cases that would have incited lasting enmity. In the aftermath of his murder, this would be a critical question. Certainly Morrison *believed* that to be so, as he implied to Hempel and others. Perhaps that was why he resigned after only fifteen months, or maybe it was because he had given policing a try and missed the retail business. Both of those reasons likely factored into his decision, but the timing of his resignation suggests it was because the department was neck-deep in scandal. The very day Morrison resigned, April 10, 1907, Chief Sheets himself was jailed on a charge of conspiracy in connection with a robbery.

Once Morrison returned to civilian life, he moved the business about a half mile from the original store into a spacious new brick building at the corner of West Temple and Eighth South streets. Although he shared the building's cost and space with a close friend who was a butcher, his finances were tight enough that he finished the deal by swapping two handwoven Indian blankets in lieu of cash. The store fit nicely into the neighborhood. The Westside, as it was known, was home primarily to working-class residents, many of whom, like Frank Seeley, worked at one of the nearby railroad depots. The Morrisons piled into a two-story, two-bedroom house for which John scraped together 850 dollars. It was around the corner from the store and just up the street from the Seeleys, at First West and Eighth South. John was not home much: he opened the grocery early, at six o'clock in the morning, and closed late, sometimes not until ten P.M.

When he wasn't tending to business or family, Morrison devoted

Marie and John Morrison with three of their sons. Merlin, left, was inside the store when his father and brother Arling, front, were slain. Perry, the eldest son, stands behind Arling. (Courtesy Morrison family)

himself to his Masonic fraternal organization, the Ancient Order of United Workmen. For a time he was the leader, or Master Workman, of Salt Lake Valley Lodge No. 12. The lodge met on Thursday evenings, conducting charitable events, banquets, and excursions. Beyond the benefits of fellowship, the AOUW offered members a benefit not otherwise available to most: life insurance. For a monthly assessment of a dollar and a half, Morrison (or, rather, his beneficiaries) would be eligible for a payment upon death of a thousand dollars.

On two occasions before he was murdered, his family very nearly had to file a claim. On an early evening in September of 1908, Morrison and another fellow were on a grocery-delivery run in Morrison's horse-drawn wagon when the rig halted on a streetcar track. Along came a car, which overturned the wagon and threw Morrison and his passenger to the ground. The accident partially blinded Morrison, whose night vision, especially, was impaired, and the wagon pinned his passenger, who suffered internal injuries so severe that it was thought he might not recover.

Five years later, Morrison almost died. That time it was no accident. On September 20, 1913, he was the target of what the *Deseret Evening News* called a "sensational holdup" attempt. It occurred four months before his murder, and he believed that the culprits, whoever they were, would come at him again.

Morrison had just closed the store on a Saturday night. He'd sent his two sons the two and a half blocks home ahead of him while he tidied up. At ten-forty-five, he stuffed the day's proceeds, 192 dollars, into his pockets and took his usual route. He was a few doors from his house when two thieves stepped from the shadows, aiming twin revolvers at his face. Rather than surrender his day's earnings, Morrison assumed what one reporter called an "unaccommodating disposition": he whipped out his heavy Colt .45. Shots were exchanged over the course of a minute or maybe two. Miraculously, none of the three duelists was wounded seriously during the "merry fusillade," although bullets struck nearby houses and one of Morrison's shots may have hit one of the foiled bandits in the leg; one shrieked and hobbled away to their getaway vehicles: a pair of bicycles. MORRISON SIMPLY WON'T BE HELD UP, the next morning's *Salt Lake Herald-Republican* marveled.

The invincible grocer could not have been entirely surprised by the holdup attempt. Five weeks earlier, the *Tribune* had published the story of a burglar who had been caught in the act at a grocery store two blocks south of Morrison's. When the police booked the dapper twenty-six-year-old—he was dressed in a jacket and tie and a broad-banded fedora—he told the desk sergeant that he and his crime partner (who had escaped) had planned to rob two other groceries as well—*including Morrison's*.

And one month after Morrison's shoot-out, police arrested an eighteen-year-old suspect, Walter Roice, in a string of bicycle thefts. Roice not only confessed to those crimes but also named his co-conspirators: Charles and William Samuelson. The brothers Samuelson, ages eighteen and sixteen, were the sons of a convicted burglar and were themselves on probation for an earlier bicycle theft. They were also wanted by the police in connection with the severe beating and robbery of a man in downtown Pioneer Park. Roice gave up the Samuelsons for that offense and went on to say that the brothers had told him it was they who had attempted to hold up Morrison on September 20. The police invited Morrison to the jail to make their case against the Samuelsons, but he was unable to identify them, due, he said, to his inability to see much of anything at night since the streetcar accident five years earlier.

However poor his night vision, Morrison clearly saw he was a marked man—not for the contents of his cash register, but for vengeance, and by someone he was acquainted with. It is unlikely that Morrison believed the Samuelson boys were his assailants. He told several people, including his wife, that he was "positive" he knew at least one of the culprits. "The fellow who tried to kill me didn't want to rob me," Morrison told an acquaintance. "He ordered me to throw up my hands, and if I had obeyed, he would have killed me . . . He knows me and he knows my habits. He knew just the moment when I was to leave the store . . . and he knew where to get me."

To his neighbor John Holt, Morrison said that "unless he was badly mistaken," he knew one of the men who had attacked him that night "as well as he knew anyone in the neighborhood." He told another neighbor, Herbert Steele, that the suspect "even comes in this store. I'm positive of this, too, although I know I cannot prove it for I only saw him in the dark that night. What's more, this fellow knows I suspect him and he will get me the next time."

BY NINE-FORTY on January 10, 1914, John Holt was winding down for the evening, munching an apple and reading the newspaper in the front room of his home. Holt was an English-born building contractor in his middle fifties. He and his wife lived at 777 West Temple Street, directly across the street from the J. G. Morrison Grocery, where Morrison and two of his sons, Merlin, thirteen years old, and Arling, seventeen, were busy cleaning and restocking, as they did every Saturday night. Diagonally across West Temple, at the corner of Eighth South, was a tall billboard under which, the police believed, two men could have been lurking and watching until the grocery was empty of customers.

By nine-forty-five, the store's last customer, the meat cutter from next door, had departed through the tall front double doors. John Morrison was dragging a gunnysack of potatoes into the aisle dividing the gleaming glass showcase that extended the length of the right side of the long, narrow store. Along the entire wall behind him were floor-to-ceiling shelves crammed with canned goods. Across the room from John, Arling was sweeping the floor between the woodstove and the cash register, near the scales perched on the wooden counter running down the entire left-hand side of the room. Within a few steps' reach of the diminutive Arling—he stood five feet four—and behind the cash register was an icebox, in the upper portion of which was stashed John's loaded six-shooter, a Colt .38. Merlin, meanwhile, was in the back of the store, either inside the storage room or near its door, beside a tall pile of bins.

Suddenly, two men burst into the store. Masked with red bandannas to conceal their faces from nose to chin, they pointed their pistols at John Morrison. *"We've got you now!"* they shouted in unison. They moved in close. A shot rang out; the bullet hit John in the right side of the chest, staggering and then felling him. One of the men fired another shot; it lodged in the wall behind where John had stood. Arling turned and grabbed the revolver from the ice chest. As he attempted to squeeze off a shot, the assailants shot him three times, twice in the back. He was killed instantly.

John Holt catapulted from his reading chair at the sound of the gunfire. Rushing to his front door, he saw two men bolt from Morrison's store and cross Eighth South Street before disappearing down an alley. The alley, between Eighth South and Ninth South, extended behind J. P. Mahan's house, diagonally across Eighth South from the store. Mahan, too, heard the shots and ran to a side window, from which he saw one of the men, apparently wounded and clutching his chest, crossing Eighth South toward the alley. "The one I saw was stooping over and was running very slow," Mahan said later that night.

Merlin ran first to his father. He was "lying on his face . . . alive," Merlin would later testify. "He spoke to me." Merlin then went to his brother, who was dead behind the wooden counter. In or near Arling's outstretched hand lay the revolver. "I picked up the gun and laid it on the cheese case," Merlin said. The boy telephoned the police, telling a Captain Roberts in "a hysterical, high-pitched voice" that his father and brother were dead. Both Mahan and Holt ran to the store, where they found John Morrison splayed on the floor near the center of the room. "I tried to get him to tell me about the shooting and what the men looked like," Holt said. But it was too late. The grocer was unconscious; within a few minutes he would be dead. As the neighbors attended to John and a crowd gathered outside, four police officers hurried in. They found Merlin near the front door, sobbing. "They got both of them," he said.

AT TWENTY MINUTES PAST ELEVEN, about ninety minutes after the murders, a fifty-six-year-old machinist named Peter Rhengreen left his Westside home on foot for his overnight shift at the shops of the Denver & Rio Grande Railroad. Five minutes later he approached the corner of Eighth South and Eighth West streets, where he noticed two men standing on the sidewalk along Eighth West, about halfway up the block. One was about six feet tall, Rhengreen thought, the other shorter. As Rhengreen neared, the pair split up: the shorter one walked north; the taller, south, toward Rhengreen. At first Rhengreen made him for a footpad—a robber. Rhengreen tensed. He considered picking up his pace and crossing the street. By then, though, it was too late: their paths were about to cross. That's when the tall, rawboned man startled him: he lay down (or collapsed) on the snowy sidewalk. He was not obviously wounded, but he shut his eyes and began moaning, almost as if he were howling at the full, resplendent moon.

"I stopped and looked at him for a minute; I didn't know what to do," Rhengreen recalled six months later in a courtroom. "I didn't say anything, he didn't say anything." The odd standoff lasted maybe a minute, and Rhengreen went on his way. As Rhengreen crossed the street, the fellow stood and followed him. Just as Rhengreen felt him on his heels, the man boarded a passing streetcar. WAS STRANGE MAN WHO BOARDED CAR ONE OF BANDITS? the *Herald-Republican* asked.

This much the police knew: if he was one of the bandits, if he had killed John or Arling Morrison, whatever the reason, he had not been intent on robbery. The perpetrators had taken not a penny from the cash register; nor had they even attempted to. *"We've got you now!"* the thirteen-year-old Merlin Morrison had heard one or both of the gunmen shout as they closed in on his father. "It was a premeditated murder," Salt Lake City police inspector Carl Carlson announced, his theory being that the crime was probably the result of an old grudge between John Morrison and his killers. The next morning's *Tribune* included a scoop that seemed to substantiate Inspector Carlson's premise: the six bullet slugs the police said they had found on the floor of the store, all of which had come from an automatic pistol, matched those found at the scene of Morrison's gunfight on the street near his house four months earlier.

Chief of Police Brigham Grant dispatched his entire available force, forty officers, to the scene. They fanned out, canvassing the neighborhood, combing the rail yards, banging on flophouse doors, rousting ne'er-do-wells from bar stools. Based on Merlin's initial description of the gunmen, the authorities were looking for, and immediately warned other jurisdictions to watch for, a pair who both weighed about 155 pounds and were five feet nine inches tall. Also, Merlin said, both had been masked with red bandannas, and both had worn dark clothing with long overcoats and dark slouch hats. But hardly had police issued the advisory before conflicting reports emerged about the killers' physical description. Was one taller than five feet nine? Were *both* taller? Had one worn a light gray coat and a dark gray hat? By Sunday evening the police would admit that the "descriptions of the two bandits . . . are not only incomplete as regards color and style of clothing, but as to height and possibly weight, as well."

The terrified thirteen-year-old boy, the only surviving witness, might well have heard more than he saw of the shootings. Had Merlin been in the back room when the shots had rung out, as was first reported, and "opened the intervening door" just in time to see the assailants flee through the front door? Or had he peered out from "behind some shelves" in the rear of the main room and witnessed the grisly scene in its entirety, as was later reported and as he would tell it in court?

Frank and Phoebe Seeley, the pedestrians whose moonlit path homeward from the Empress had crossed with that of two toughs near the Morrison store about ten minutes before the murders, provided the other description upon which the authorities would come to lean. The Seeleys' initial account, as recorded in the sheriff's office, said that the taller of the men who had refused to yield the sidewalk had been five feet nine, had weighed around 160 pounds, and (under his dark gray hat) had had a head of bushy, light brown hair. That description, however, was wholly incompatible with the features of the man who would come to be on trial for his life.

FROM THEIR FIRST INTERVIEWS with Merlin Morrison and the neighbors, the police believed this was a revenge killing, not a botched robbery. And right from the beginning, they believed that one of the two perpetrators had been shot by Arling Morrison in the moment before Arling was killed. Merlin told the police he *thought* so—he was not certain—and J. P. Mahan, the observant neighbor, and his daughter reported seeing one of the fleeing men bent double and clutching himself as if he was wounded. Mahan's daughter also said she had heard the distressed man wail, "Hold on Bob, I'm shot." And yet another neighbor said she had heard someone outside her house yelp, "Oh, Bob." Also, one of the six chambers in the gun in or near Arling's hand when he had died lacked a bullet. This was either because he had managed to squeeze off a shot in his final moments, as the neighbors' testimony would suggest, or because his father, the former police officer, had left empty one chamber of his six-shooter, as was Salt Lake City police custom. Further, if Arling had fired a shot, where was it? A meticulous search of the store turned up no trace of the bullet, a fact from which police deduced that one of the perpetrators had indeed been hit. Curiously, however, police detected not one drop of blood inside the store that came from anyone but the Morrisons, nor did they find any blood just outside the entrance. The marauders *had* disappeared in a flash, but so fast as to avoid spilling any blood had one of them been shot? Perhaps, then, Arling had failed to get a shot off, or maybe he had succeeded: maybe a gunshot victim of indeterminate height, weight, and dress was walking around Salt Lake City with Arling's bullet lodged within—irrefutable .38-caliber proof of guilt.

3.

A Prime Suspect

On the morning after the killings, Salt Lake City awoke to sensational headlines: FATHER AND SON SLAIN BY MASKED MURDERERS, the *Herald-Republican* bannered across the full width of page one. The subhead implied motive: a revenge killing. NO CHANCE TO SUBMIT GIVEN BY INTRUDERS TO JOHN G. MORRISON; THEY SHOOT ON SIGHT; BOY REPLIES. A one-column drop spelled out Arling Morrison's "reply": BELIEVED BULLET OF MURDERED LAD REACHED ITS MARK.

The *Tribune*'s headline stretched across all seven columns of its front page—and well beyond the *Herald-Republican*'s mere implication of motive. HOLDUPS KILL FATHER AND SON FOR REVENGE, the *Tribune* announced above a subhead explicitly linking Morrison's previous shoot-outs to his murder: TWICE VICTOR IN BATTLES WITH BANDITS, GROCER SHOT TO DEATH IN THIRD ENCOUNTER. The Monday edition of the *Deseret Evening News* (the church-owned paper did not publish on Sundays) claimed the middle ground: MOTIVE PROBABLY REVENGE. "The generally accepted theory," the *News* declared, "is that the highwaymen who were routed by J.G. Morrison on two occasions within the past 10 years . . . returned to the Morrison store and killed the proprietor through revenge." And the Monday *Salt Lake Evening Telegram* carried a titillating sidebar that seemed to confirm the revenge theory. Following Morrison's September 1913 shoot-out, the *Telegram*'s police reporter had called on the grocer for his version of events. The reporter, Hardy K. Downing, had agreed to the grocer's request that he withhold from publication certain details, principally Morrison's assertion that he was acquainted with one of his assailants. Upon Morrison's death, Downing released himself from the confidence. Under the headline

56

MORRISON KNEW ENEMY WANTED TO MURDER HIM, Downing quoted the deceased as having told him four months earlier that the perpetrator "did not want my money, he wanted my life."

"ALMOST IMMEDIATELY" after the shootings, the police had a suspect in mind: a career criminal they knew as Frank Z. Wilson. Wilson had served sixteen months in the Utah State Penitentiary for burglary. He was known to have left town upon his release a little over a year earlier, on Christmas Day, 1912, and was also known to have come and gone more than once since. After an absence of several weeks, according to the *Tribune*, Wilson had been seen a few days before the murders and again, by a state prison guard, that very afternoon. Even before the Morrisons had been murdered, detectives had sought Wilson for questioning in another matter. Nor was Salt Lake the only jurisdiction looking for Wilson: he was wanted in at least two other proximate towns.

Did Frank Z. Wilson hold a grudge against John Morrison? Had he harbored it since Morrison's brief tenure as a police officer back in 1906 and 1907? Or did Wilson's rancor stretch back even longer: was he one of the armed robbers against whom Morrison had returned fire inside his original store in 1903? Police considered both of those scenarios, but it seemed likelier that if Wilson had murdered Morrison, he had done so as retribution for a fresher affront: the gunfight on the street near Morrison's home four months earlier, on September 20, 1913—another Saturday night just after closing time.

Whether Frank Z. Wilson and John G. Morrison shared a past, and whether Wilson murdered Morrison, can only be conjectured; there was no physical evidence definitively connecting them. The fact that Wilson was the initial prime suspect and that he had been in the vicinity of the crime scene within hours of the murders would seem to have warranted as thorough as possible a study of his criminal record, his character, and his movements in the days and weeks prior to the murders. And yet this was never undertaken—not by the Salt Lake police in the immediate aftermath of the Morrison murders, nor by any of the many journalists and historians who have since written about the case.

I looked into Wilson because the mystery of why police had dismissed him as a suspect got the best of me, and because it seemed derelict not to. The one local newspaper story I could find about him in the weeks after Hill's arrest only deepened the mystery; it reported, without

Left, Magnus Olson, alias Frank Z. Wilson, Salt Lake County Jail, August 1911, and right, as James Franklin, Folsom State Prison, California, 1905. (Left: courtesy Salt Lake City Police Museum; right: courtesy California State Archives)

elaboration, that detectives had released Wilson because he had "convinced" the department that "he had not been involved in the Morrison murders." The story also added another piece of information that begged for further inquiry. It reported that police had turned Wilson over to the sheriff of Elko County, Nevada, where he was wanted on suspicion of burglary of a boxcar—a crime to which, curiously enough, he had confessed to Salt Lake detectives.

I went to Elko, an old railroad, ranching, and gold-mining town in the high desert of northeastern Nevada, to look up the court documents in the district clerk's office and to see whether there was reference to Frank Z. Wilson in the town's two newspapers. I could find no reference to Wilson in the courthouse, but I did find the case of a defendant named James Morton. From the facts and the chronology, it was obvious that "Morton" was Wilson's alias. At least I thought so. But one of the newspapers, the *Elko Independent*, referred to him as neither Wilson nor Morton; it called him "F.Z. Wheeler," adding, helpfully, that he "sails under that name and several others." The paper reported that Wheeler led "a gang of box car thieves that have operated on the Western Pacific [Railroad] for over a year." The *Elko Daily Free Press*, meanwhile, went with the name he used at trial, James Morton. Both papers said he was a repeat offender, although they differed as to certain biographical details.

Clearly this was a man with a sketchy past, and a penchant for hiding it. What was the extent and nature of his criminal record? Was it violent? Was he capable of murder? What patterns might it reveal? Where and for how long had he been in prison? And if it was true that he had

Left, Magnus Olson, alias James Farmer, Nevada State Penitentiary, 1908, and right, as James Morton, Nevada State Penitentiary, 1914. (Both courtesy Nevada State Library and Archives)

been on the run for a year with a gang of boxcar thieves in the region, was there any evidence that he had operated in Salt Lake City? Could he be placed there on or around September 20, 1913, the night John Morrison fired his revolver at his would-be assailants?

Trying to stay on Wilson's trail, I ran into countless dead ends and skidded off on detours to nowhere. But every so often, another clue turned up. For instance, a small-town librarian in Northern California called two months after we had last spoken to tell me he had run across a 1905 newspaper story about an armed robbery that I might find of interest; that information, in turn, provided the dates (and the alias) I needed to request certain incarceration records. And an open-records request in Illinois revealed Wilson's juvenile record, which listed his next of kin, which gave me names to search for in city directories, census reports, local newspapers, immigration and naturalization records, and so on.

Before long, I understood that one reason no one had drawn the contours of Wilson's life was his lifelong devotion to obscuring them. He falsified countless documents and changed his name like a snake sheds its skin: by climbing out and leaving it behind. He lied under oath about other basic facts of his identity, wrote a completely fabricated autobiographical account (under a false name) in 1909 as a plea to one state for leniency, and issued another inventive memoir (under another alias) forty years later. In the latter one, published as a three-part serial in the *Saturday Evening Post*, Wilson acknowledged lying habitually to the authorities over the years, but in that mea culpa he papered over many of those lies with yet more lies—even when he claimed to be setting the record straight.

Peel away the decades of deceit, and what is revealed is Wilson's startlingly violent and lengthy criminal career—a career that he took up as a teenager in and around Chicago in 1900 and that he would pursue with pathological resolve for fully fifty years. Over the course of that career, he would, by his own accounting, rob "post offices and stores" in every one of the lower forty-eight states save for those in New England and three in the Deep South. "The cops still haven't caught up to me on most of the jobs I pulled," he wrote (under the pseudonym James Morton) in the *Saturday Evening Post* in 1950, near the end of his career. He served time in no fewer than nine states. He burglarized homes, retail stores, and boxcars; he blew safes, robbed banks, stole cars, committed assault and arson, attempted murder, and, in all likelihood, committed murder. In his late forties, when he was back home in Chicago wreaking havoc, he worked for Al Capone. A relative called him a "henchman" for the famous gangster and bootlegger; Wilson allowed only that he had been on Capone's payroll "for a while" and that he had served, variously, as bodyguard, bill collector, and assistant foreman for the gang's rackets on the city's North Side. But it is known that Wilson played a role in the notorious St. Valentine's Day massacre of 1929, which left seven men dead in a North Side garage: he owned the getaway black Cadillac that the killers drove from the scene.

AT THE TIME of the Morrison murders, in 1914, Frank Z. Wilson was thirty-two years old. He had shuttled in and out of jails and prisons for the whole of the young century—had, in fact, been incarcerated for at least part of every one of those years but two. That Wilson was unconfined and at large on the streets of Salt Lake on the night of the murders was due partly to his skill in concealing from the authorities his real name. (This was the era just prior to systematic fingerprint identification; law enforcement authorities generally used the Bertillon system, an imprecise, unreliable, and cumbersome means of identification that required taking measurements of the head and various body parts.)

As Wilson's name changed, the psychological forces that impelled his recidivism remained constant. To excavate and piece together his crimes— their chronology, location, nature, outcome, and aftermath—is, if not to discern those psychological forces, to see emerge from his deeds certain behavioral traits, or patterns. And when one considers those patterns together with his modus operandi—the means by which he carried out his crimes—and alongside newly discovered evidence of Wilson's rampaging criminal itinerary throughout the fall of 1913 and the first weeks of 1914, one sees a man who not only could have killed Morrison but also fits the profile of Morrison's killer: a sociopath possessed of uncontrolled anger and aggression, a habit of murderous vengeance in the wake of failure, and an extraordinary amorality. This, of course, should not be construed as evidence that Wilson killed Morrison. What it does suggest, and what the new findings support, is that the circumstantial case made against the man who ultimately was executed for the crime was nowhere near as convincing as the one that could and should have been made against Wilson.

During the sixteen weeks from the middle of September 1913 through the middle of the following January—a period that included both Morrison's shoot-out on the street with his unknown assailants and his and his son's murders—Wilson led a brazen crew on a spree of violent crime in Utah and neighboring Nevada. They specialized in boxcar burglary and armed robbery in railroad towns and depots along the Western Pacific and Southern Pacific freight and passenger lines that stretched from the terminus in Ogden, Utah, through Salt Lake, thirty-five miles south, and from there some two hundred miles west across the salt flats and high desert to Elko. It is further known, and also heretofore untold, that on September 20, 1913, the very day that highwaymen attacked Morrison, lawmen in both Elko and Ogden attempted to obtain copies of Wilson's criminal record, and that he apparently was wanted for questioning in both those jurisdictions about a series of recent felonies.

In separate queries sent that day to the superintendent of the Nevada State Prison—where Wilson had served two and a half years for grand larceny of a Western Pacific boxcar in 1908—the lawmen requested his record, mug shots, and description. They knew him not as Frank Z. Wilson, or Wheeler, or James Morton, but as James Farmer, or, as the Ogden officer specified, "James Farmer alias James Franklin." The state prison superintendent promptly provided this description:

American, age 30 years.
6 ft. ½ inch. 158 lbs.
Slim build, blue eyes,
Light complexion,
Medium chestnut hair.
Home, Hastings, Neb.
Has a small mole below right ear.

Only the physical description was accurate. Regarding the biographical information—James Farmer's nationality, age, hometown, and, of course, name—the prison record was incorrect on all counts. Who was he? Where had he come from? And what did the totality of his record reveal about his operating procedure?

His birth name was not even close to those he proffered. It was not Frank Wilson or James Farmer or James Franklin. Nor was it any of the variations on those names by which he sometimes went: F. Z. Wheeler, James Framer, James Franklyn. Nor was his birth name any of those he would wear and discard after the Morrison murders: James Morton, James Martin, George Moore, George Lawrence Moore, Lawrence George Moore, George Lawrence, James Herbert Morgan, Harry Fuller, Joe Murray. Nor was he Madmus Morton, nor Magnus Morton, nor Magnus Moran, nor Magnus Morran, nor Magnus Osburg, although those latter aliases were within walking distance of his actual birth name: Magnus Olson.

The facts are these: Magnus Olson was born in April of 1881 in Norway, in or near the city of Tromsø, the youngest of five children to Otto Olson, a carpenter, and his wife, Emma. Just after Magnus's third birthday, the Olsons immigrated to Evanston, Illinois, a leafy suburb on Lake Michigan about twenty miles north of Chicago where Emma had family. Before Magnus's tenth birthday, both his parents were dead. One of his mother's brothers, who owned a steam laundry in Evanston, took in Magnus and his siblings. Writing in 1950, he recalled growing up without want, but without discipline, too. "I sensed that my uncle felt that if he punished me I might feel that I wasn't wanted [so] I'd stay out late, play hooky from school . . . knowing I'd get away with it."

He didn't get away with it for all that long. By early 1900, Olson belonged to "an organized band of thieves," as the Evanston police put it. The gang operated out of a cave, but from their crude headquarters the members kept up, to some extent, with world affairs: the twenty youthful gangsters, mysteriously enough, "dress[ed] and act[ed] as Filipinos." But while their counterparts in the Philippines were busy resisting American occupation, the activities of the Evanston boys were, it may be said, less ennobling: they engaged in "burglary, larceny, and malicious mischief," according to a newspaper account.

In February of 1900, Evanston police arrested Magnus Olson and three of his fellow ersatz Filipinos for stealing brass and copper from a junk dealer's barn. The disposition of their cases is unclear, but from those relatively harmless beginnings the gang graduated to rather more grandiose and, indeed, malicious thievery of the sort for which Olson would make his name(s). The gang advanced to knocking off railroad cars. From freight trains and passenger cars they stole more of their favored commodity: precious metals. They filched brass journals—boxes that protected the axles and ensured proper lubrication—lead pipes, portions of air brakes, and other fixtures that if missing or damaged could endanger the lives of workers and passengers alike.

Police routed the gang in the middle of April 1900. Olson, who had just turned nineteen, was convicted of burglary and sentenced to a minimum of one year and a maximum of twenty in the Illinois Boys' State Reformatory, in Pontiac. He benefited from the fact that the state's penal institutions were in the hands of Progressive Era reformers who emphasized rehabilitation over punishment. Sixteen months into his stretch at Pontiac, Olson was paroled.

Paroled, but hardly rehabilitated. For perhaps a few months he heeded his uncle's plea that he "stay away from bad company." But no more than six months into his post-reformatory life, Chicago detectives arrested him and another young man on suspicion of committing "a score of small burglaries." Rather than wait for the authorities to learn that he was a parole violator, Olson left town in a hurry, not even stopping "to say goodbye to anybody or even to pack my clothes" before catching a westbound freight train. He bummed through Montana and North Dakota, working briefly as a circus roustabout, following the harvest, rubbing sprouts off potatoes in a hotel keeper's root cellar. He "drifted to a dozen other places." Sometimes he slept on the ground; often he was hungry. After ten months on the road, Olson headed home to Chicago. Unfortunately for him, an adversary notified the parole board that Olson was back in town. He was picked up and taken back to the boys' reformatory in Pontiac.

The boys' reformatory could not hold Olson for long, though: seventeen months later he escaped. He and a fellow fugitive, John Ross, went west, dreaming of gold fields in Alaska. They got as far north as Seattle, but when they couldn't get a boat to Alaska, they "rambled down" to California. On Christmas Eve of 1904, Olson and Ross broke into a hardware store in rural Tehama County, about halfway between the Oregon border and Sacramento. They stuck to pilfering staples: pocketknives, revolvers, and cartridges. Within an hour they were arrested. At trial, Olson gave himself a new name, James Franklin. The superior court judge gave him five years in Folsom State Prison.

If Olson reconsidered his career path during his three and a half years in Folsom before winning parole, the thought must have been fleeting. For one thing, he made at least one acquaintance there, a veteran safe blower, from whom he learned "the essentials of the stealing trade" and with whom he would later partner in crime; for another, within a few months of his release he again drifted back to Chicago, where he eagerly resumed his craft. If Olson, at twenty-three, had entered Folsom a prospect for rehabilitation, he had exited a Progressive reformer's nightmare: a hardened, angry criminal with a temper as deep and dark and combustible as a coal seam.

FROM THEN ON, his career was marked with episodes of escalating violence and murderous rage. On a fall night in 1907, in front of a West Side Chicago saloon, Olson beat up a passerby, a stranger to him, for no apparent reason. The victim, who required hospitalization and who pressed charges, said that Olson had not robbed him and that he had no idea why Olson had attacked him. The jury found Olson guilty of assault. He was sentenced to a short stay in the city jail and fined a hundred dollars.

Three weeks later, Olson was arrested on suspicion of murder as he boarded an elevated train at three-thirty in the morning. Police said he "answer[ed] closely to the description" of an intruder who had shot and killed a man fifteen minutes earlier during a burglary attempt at a house near the train station. (The murder case went unsolved; neither Olson nor anyone else was prosecuted.)

Regardless of whether he committed murder that morning, Magnus Olson soon proved he was *capable* of murder, even mass murder. Three weeks later, at the end of December 1907, he slipped into an apartment in a three-story brick tenement. While the occupants dined in another room, Olson pried open a trunk in the front room and extracted what he believed to be six hundred dollars in postal money orders. He apparently could have snuck out with the loot as quietly as he had entered. Instead, he acted with spectacular malice: he poured the oil from an oil lamp on the furniture and carpet and struck a match. As he escaped the blaze, a wind gust slammed the door behind him. The family heard the noise and snuffed the fire before it could spread beyond their apartment.

Olson was arrested at a saloon a short time later, when he tried to pay for a drink with one of the money orders. Only it wasn't a money order; it was a *receipt* for a money order. (Indeed, his entire take was nothing but receipts.) He was charged (as Magnus Osburg) with burglary and "incendiarism," pleaded guilty to a lesser charge of "receiving stolen property," and was sentenced to a mere thirty days in the Cook County jail.

He retraced his well-worn path westward, eventually to Reno, where in the summer of 1908 he fell in with four other ex-cons. One was William Cronin, a fifty-four-year-old, five-foot-two-inch safe blower who himself had a half dozen aliases and who was best known as Frisco Mickey. Olson knew Cronin from inside Folsom, and it was he who had taught Olson how to use "soup"—nitroglycerin—for blowing safes. Olson, Cronin, and the others made a specialty of looting Southern Pacific boxcars. One night they were caught in the act. All were convicted of grand larceny and sentenced to the Nevada State Prison in Carson City.

Thirteen months into his three-year term, Magnus Olson—the Nevada authorities knew him as James Farmer—formally applied to the state pardons board for leniency. He framed his appeal for justice around an entirely fictional autobiographical sketch, the "Brief History of My Life." He said he was born in 1884 in Hastings, Nebraska (rather than in 1881 in Norway). He said his father was a stonemason, "which Trade I follow, and still follow, when at Liberty." He said he left Nebraska at the time of the San Francisco earthquake, in April of 1906 (he was in Folsom Prison—as James Franklin—from January of 1905 through August of 1906). "I thought it would be a good opening, for me and left home, and came to Oakland," he wrote. He said he worked there for a construction company for eighteen months before leaving "to do a few small jobs . . . for myself." He then returned to the construction firm and stayed for three months, he wrote, before "I was attracted to Nevada, by work." He chronicled for the pardons board the unlucky night of his arrest in Reno and his unhappy day in court, made his pitch for "either a Commutation of Sentence, or a Parole," and signed the letter "Your Humble Servant, James Farmer."

The board was unmoved; Olson served all but five months of his three-year sentence. He was released on April 18, 1911. By the middle of August he was again behind bars, again for burglary, this time in Salt Lake—as Frank Z. Wilson. In the days after John Morrison's murder, in January of 1914, the Salt Lake press would report that Olson, or "Wilson," had only recently been released from prison, and that it was Morrison, during his tenure as a Salt Lake police officer, who had put him there. Though that tidy scenario provided Olson with a motive, and though most authors who later wrote about the case accepted it as gospel, it was, in a word, false. Morrison had resigned as a cop four years before Olson's latest transgression: the theft of five hundred dollars' worth of silks and furs from a rooming house. He and three partners were just leaving when Patrolman Richard Beynon happened by. They took off running. With Beynon in hot pursuit, Olson and one of his co-conspirators dashed into a hotel, sprinted up a flight of stairs, and leaped through an open second-story window. They landed on a flimsy tin-roofed shed. The roof gave way, and the thieves literally fell into the arms of their arresting officer. After serving sixteen months of an eighteen-month sentence in the Utah State Penitentiary, Olson was freed on Christmas Day of 1912—thirteen months before Morrison was killed. Had Olson sought revenge for that prison stay, it seems likely that Patrolman Beynon would have been his target. And even if Olson and Morrison *had* clashed during Morrison's brief tenure as a cop in 1906 and 1907, it seems implausible that the hotheaded Olson would have waited seven or eight years to exact revenge. Self-control was not among his gifts; he lived by impulse, and for immediate gratification.

WESTERN RAILROAD TOWNS were renowned for their red-light districts; some, such as Salt Lake City and Elko, regulated the brothels, or at least herded them into a segregated quarter close to—but not in plain sight of—the town's more "respectable" commercial enterprises. The sort of immediate gratification offered by those districts was not the sort that attracted Magnus Olson. As with the women who lived and worked in the brothels, Olson's primary interest was financial rather than sexual.

It was early on the morning of September 4, 1913, and Elko's annual rodeo, a major tourist attraction, had closed only hours earlier. The city's houses of prostitution had benefited from the tourist trade and were said to be flush with profits. At one such establishment, across the street from the Western Pacific depot, two of the female residents discovered a torn window screen in one of the bedrooms, and under the bed, hiding, a man named Milton Abbey. Though he claimed he was drunk and just wanted a place to sleep, the women reported cash and property missing, and the police held him on suspicion for attempted burglary.

Twelve days later, a man whom the *Elko Independent* referred to as Abbey's "pal" and whom the local constable apparently suspected was "James Farmer"—the name Olson had used in Nevada five years earlier—visited the same brothel. In the madam's bedroom he found a jar filled with diamonds pickling in alcohol—her method of cleaning them. The burglar stowed the jar (and presumably himself) under her bed until he could steal away unseen, but the vigilant madam soon discovered the missing jewelry. He escaped ahead of the police, but without the pickled diamonds, which were valued at a thousand dollars.

That was on September 16, a Tuesday. At three o'clock on the morning of Thursday, September 18, when the house was closed for business and the madam and her employees were thought to be asleep, someone leaned a ladder against the exterior wall on the south side, climbed through a second-floor window into a vacant bedroom, and set the bed on fire. At about the same time, that person or an accomplice set fire to the north side of the house. The setting of the fires on opposite ends of the building left no doubt that the arsonist wanted to "burn it down and roast [the madam] to death in revenge for the jailing of his pal," the *Independent* wrote.

When the smoke had cleared, the local constable wired the superintendent of the Nevada State Prison for information regarding a former prisoner, "James Farmer." The constable sent the telegram on the morning of Saturday, September 20, 1913, and the superintendent replied the same day. But the suspect had already skipped town, probably on the first eastbound train he could catch. He must have hopped off at Ogden, Utah, where his presence provoked yet another inquiry to the Nevada State Prison. "Will you please send me photograph and description of James Farmer alias James Franklin," the Southern Pacific Railroad's special agent in Ogden asked the superintendent. He, too, was writing on Saturday, September 20. Did Olson stay in Ogden that Saturday night, or was he on the move again? Had he made the quick train trip to Salt Lake? Was he one of the armed robbers who shortly before eleven P.M. waged a gun battle on the street with the cantankerous John Morrison, whose quick-triggered defiance forced his attackers' hasty retreat?

Consider that in the nearly four months between Morrison's holdup and his and his son Arling's murders, there were no fewer than five crimes—two burglaries and three armed robberies—committed in either Elko or Ogden that seemed to bear Olson's figurative fingerprints. Five nights after the Morrison stickup, "professional" burglars broke into seven Western Pacific boxcars in Elko. And in the middle of December, two masked and armed robbers held up an Ogden saloon just before closing time on a Thursday night. "In a business-like manner," the *Ogden Examiner* reported, one gunman covered the half dozen customers seated at the bar while the other marched the proprietor into the front office and demanded that he open the safe. All told, the bandits got away with 250 dollars in cash and a diamond stud. They worked so efficiently that the victims never got a good look at them. "The usual description of the tall and short man was about as far as the victims could inform the police," the *Examiner* lamented. They were last seen running north, toward the freight depot, a distance of less than two blocks.

Back in Elko two nights later, thieves broke into the home of the

Western Pacific pumpman. Olson was not arrested, but he was well acquainted with at least one of the three burglars who were convicted and sentenced to Nevada State Prison. When the state paroled the man, who went by the name J. D. Higgins, it notified Higgins that he was entitled to the customary "final discharge allowance" of ten dollars. Higgins declined the payment. In a note he wrote on the letterhead of a Salt Lake City hotel, he instead instructed the state to forward it to "James Morton"—Magnus Olson's current guise.

A week after the break-in at the pumpman's house, two men, armed but not masked, held up the Depot Saloon in Elko, just across the street from the Western Pacific depot. It was nine-thirty at night on the Saturday before Christmas, three weeks to the day and nearly to the hour before the Morrison murders. Only the proprietor was inside the saloon. One robber stuck a gun in his ribs and ordered him to turn his face to the wall and "shove his hands skyward." The intruders worked quickly. They relieved the proprietor of thirty-five dollars and ran out just in time to hop a westbound freight train. The victim described one of his assailants as wearing about a week's growth of beard, "not very black," and a "dark suit much-worn." The Elko authorities conceded there was little hope of catching the offenders. Perhaps they zigzagged back to Ogden, where three nights later, on Christmas Eve, burglars broke into a sporting-goods store and helped themselves to a substantial arsenal: two shotguns and thirty-five revolvers. At year's end, the rolling crime wave was undiminished. "It would seem that an organized gang of thieves is at work," the *Elko Independent* concluded.

THE SALT LAKE POLICE, though, knew nothing of the criminal exploits of the man they considered their prime suspect in the Morrison case—nothing, that is, beyond the burglary attempt in Salt Lake City for which he had served sixteen months in the state penitentiary in 1911 and 1912 as Frank Z. Wilson. But even before the Morrisons were murdered, a police detective was looking for "Wilson" in connection with another local crime. And on the night of the murders, Olson practically announced himself as an obvious suspect.

At eleven-thirty, about an hour and forty-five minutes after the killings, a streetcar conductor, James R. Usher, stopped his inbound car to pick up a peculiar man near the corner of Eighth West and Seventh South. Usher considered him "suspicious-acting"; he boarded the car on the left-hand side—the exit side—rather than through the usual entrance on the right-hand side. Usher thought he might have a drunk on his hands, but when the man stepped within a foot of Usher to pay his fare, the driver changed his mind. "I couldn't smell any booze on him," Usher later testified. His description matched that of the machinist Peter Rhengreen, who only moments earlier had had the strangest of encounters with the man on the street. Both Rhengreen and Usher described him as tall, about six feet one, and rawboned. Usher added that the man wore a dark slouch hat and a dark suit "rather worse from wear"—an echo of the Elko barkeep who three weeks earlier had described one of his assailants as wearing a "dark suit much-worn." The man rode the car all the way downtown, exiting near the end of the line at Second South and Main.

Around one A.M. on Sunday, police picked up the same man on the street in front of Morrison's store. He was coatless by then and shivering in the subfreezing air. He claimed to be taking a walk before bedtime. He gave his name as W. J. Williams or W. Z. Williams. (Newspaper accounts varied.) He said he worked in a restaurant and lived at the Salvation Army boardinghouse. Both statements were as false as his name. Police made a cursory search of his person. They found nothing incriminating. Nevertheless, they detained him for further questioning. Later on Sunday they searched him again. That time they found a bloody handkerchief.

On Monday morning, the police summoned James Usher to the station to examine a rogues' gallery of mug shots. His eyes alighted on one: Magnus Olson, the man Salt Lake City police knew as Frank Z. Wilson. Whether he was still in custody is unclear.

But this was not the man whom police arrested for murder a day later. That man had no history of crime (save for a vagrancy charge). He did, however, have a fresh gunshot wound, and he looked so much like Frank Z. Wilson that police assumed he was lying when he gave his name as Joseph Hill.

4.

A Deadly Certainty

Sometime between eleven o'clock and eleven-fifty on the night of the murders, the second Saturday of 1914, a young physician awoke to the chimes of his doorbell. He lived in suburban Murray City, at Fourteenth South and State streets, five miles south of the Morrison grocery. The doctor threw on his bathrobe, stepped into his slippers—he had just nodded off—and padded toward the front room, his medical-examination office. In the darkness, Frank M. McHugh could make out a silhouetted form already inside the doorway.

"Is that you, doctor?" a man cried.

"Yes, what is it?"

"I've been shot, doc, and want you to do something for me."

McHugh recognized his patient, whom he knew as the songwriter and IWW member Joe Hill. They had met at the home of the Eselius family, where Hill was boarding and where McHugh had recently treated a family member for pneumonia. McHugh was a prominent Socialist in town (Murray was a Socialist-led municipality), and he and Hill had also crossed paths at one or more political forums.

McHugh guided the woozy Hill through his office and onto a couch in the dining room, where the evening fire was still aglow. He helped his patient strip to the waist, peeling off his blood-soaked overcoat and vest, his shirt and undershirt. Blood continued to spurt, a sure sign, McHugh would say later, of a "fresh" wound. The bullet, apparently of large caliber, had pierced the breast just below Hill's left nipple. But Hill was lucky: it had missed his heart by less than an inch before tearing through his lower left lung, turning slightly upward, and exiting below his left shoulder blade.

McHugh asked Hill how he had come to be shot. Hill told him he had quarreled over a woman who lived in Murray: "I got into a stew with a friend of mine," Hill said. "I knocked him down, but he got up and pulled a gun on me and shot me." Hill told the doctor that he "was as much to blame in the affair as the other man" and that he wished it to be kept quiet, McHugh would testify six months later. "I want to have nothing said about it," Hill said, according to McHugh. "If there's a chance to get over it, it will be OK with my friend." Hill asked to be taken to the Eseliuses' house, a plan McHugh deemed "perfectly safe." Though Hill "suffered lots of pain" and was "spitting blood," McHugh concluded that his patient was not wounded "seriously" enough to require hospitalization. "When a man has walked to a doctor's office with a bullet wound through his lung and there is no serious hemorrhage, he is in pretty good condition and is able to stand a lot of pain," McHugh would later explain.

Around midnight, a friend of McHugh's, a fellow physician named Arthur Bird, was motoring by on his way home from a house call when he noticed a light in McHugh's window. He decided to drop in on his younger colleague—Bird was ten years older than McHugh—for a chat and maybe a bite or a smoke, as he did from time to time.

Whether Bird arrived in time to help dress Hill's wound is uncertain; both doctors told different stories on different occasions. Press accounts, too, were contradictory. The newspapers variously placed Bird's arrival anywhere from "immediately after" McHugh's "promise to examine the wound" to "immediately after he had examined the wound" to after McHugh had "finished dressing the wound." (Many years later, McHugh himself recollected that he had been "about through dressing" Hill when Bird had showed up.)

The sequence of events mattered because at some point during the procedure McHugh helped Hill remove a shoulder strap that holstered a "large automatic revolver." McHugh glimpsed only the handle of the gun; he could not, he would later testify, identify its make or caliber, only that he thought it larger than a .32. Bird, however, would swear he got a good look at the entire gun. He insisted it was a .38-caliber Colt automatic pistol—the make and model used to kill the Morrisons earlier that evening.

Bird agreed to give Hill a lift to his friends' house, some three miles distant. Sometime between one and one-thirty on Sunday morning, the pair appeared at the Eseliuses' kitchen door.

The large family—there were twelve children in all—had emigrated from their Swedish farmstead (land granted by the government in return for military service) in a rural area called Guttebol in the parish of Rudskoga, in the province of Värmland. Guttebol was remote, but not so remote as to be untouched by the long arm of Mormonism. The Mormon church had been dispatching missionaries from the United States to Sweden as early as 1850. (Its first, a Swedish citizen named John Forsgren, had been born two hundred yards from the house where Joe Hill had grown up.) And as early as 1850, partisans of the territorial Lutheran church—the state religion—had greeted Mormon missionaries and converts with stones and beatings. "To join the Mormons was to have one's windows broken," went a common refrain. Yet victims of mere vandalism were the lucky ones. As one diarist writing in 1883 in southern Sweden succinctly described life for herself and other Mormon proselytes, "Everyone that joined was hunted like wild beasts to be destroyed."

Those early converts and missionaries, like the Mormon pioneers in America, were ferociously tenacious. And despite the shattered windows and the violent Lutheran mobs hell-bent on driving them straight back to Utah—Forsgren, for one, was jailed and later deported—the missionaries left with their fair share of emigrants: thirty thousand Scandinavians in the last half of the nineteenth century, among them Carl Eselius and his wife, Emma.

The Eselius family left the farmstead in stages. Beata, or Betty, the eldest sibling, her husband, and her brother Victor were the first to emigrate. They left home in 1886, bound for Verona, a farming village in southwest Missouri with an established Swedish community. Other family members soon followed, and sometime before 1910 the Eseliuses picked up and moved across the plains to the central Salt Lake Valley, to the little boomtown of Murray City, Smeltertown USA.

On the night of Saturday, January 10, 1914, John and Ed Eselius took their nephews Bob and Oliver Erickson (two of Betty's four children) to a local stock troupe's performance of *The Escape*, at the Utah Theatre in Salt Lake, after which they stopped by a Commercial Street saloon for a nightcap and tamales. They arrived home shortly after midnight and were in the kitchen enjoying a bit more to eat when Dr. Bird and a pained Joe Hill announced themselves at the kitchen door.

"What's the matter, Joe?" John asked.

"Oh, some son of a gun shot me."

*   *   *

WHO WAS THE "SON OF A GUN," and why did Hill remain mute on the circumstances of the shooting? The questions bedeviled reporters who covered his earliest legal proceedings—he "still maintains his sullen and morose silence," one observed at Hill's arraignment—as well as generations of researchers who would examine the case. At the time, Hill's supporters believed that the shooter was the man whom his adversaries were calling Hill's accomplice in the murders: Otto Appelquist. But because Hill would never explain, and because Appelquist could never be found, there was nobody to make that case. He "clings to his story that he was wounded in a quarrel over a woman," the *Deseret Evening News* complained. "He still refuses, however, to divulge the name of either the woman or his assailant."

For years, I was mystified by those questions. Because my initial reporting was based on reading much of the same well-thumbed evidence available to past students of the case—newspaper accounts, the incomplete trial transcript, Hill's published letters—I concluded as others have: if Arling Morrison did not shoot Hill, then probably Appelquist did. But "probably" is not very satisfying. So I looked everywhere for traces of Appelquist. I found a few: in the church records of his Swedish birthplace, the port city of Helsingborg; in ship manifests (he worked as a fireman) on the East Coast after he left Salt Lake; his draft registration card for World War I. But not much else. I was especially interested in seeing if I could place him in Buffalo, New York, in 1915, while Hill was alive. With Hill's execution date about a month away, someone in Buffalo sent an anonymous letter to a key supporter of Hill's that suggested direct knowledge of the circumstances of Hill's shooting. But I couldn't put Appelquist in or near Buffalo, could not attach his name to that letter.

Then I got lucky. I found another letter, the one written by Hilda Erickson that fills in the unknown details of Hill's shooting. We'll come to the full particulars of Hilda's letter later. For now, though, it should be said that it corroborates Hill's own explanation of how and why he was wounded: it states that Appelquist shot him in a row over Hilda herself.

Both men had designs on Hilda, a fair-haired twenty-year-old whose uncles were the Eselius brothers. Appelquist had met and wooed her first, when he had moved in with the family before Hill arrived in Utah. (Hilda, though, did not live at the family's crowded house in Murray. She boarded in Salt Lake, where she worked as a domestic.) Hill came to stay with the Eseliuses around the middle of August; by year's end, he, too, had moved in on Hilda.

Appelquist won her hand. On Christmas Eve of 1913, Hilda's mother, Betty, introduced Appelquist to a friend of hers as her future son-in-law. Within the first few days of the new year, however, Hilda broke the engagement, as she wrote in the letter many years later. Whether Hill prompted her change of heart cannot be said, but Appelquist certainly thought so. He "got very angry and asked me if I liked Joe better than him," Hilda recalled. She told Appelquist no, but the denial did not placate her jilted suitor. Nor did the taunting he took from Hill. Hilda overheard Hill "tease" Appelquist "that he was going to take me away from him."

And yet their friendship remained intact. Hill and Appelquist roomed together that first week of the new year in a Salt Lake boardinghouse. On Thursday, January 8, they returned to the Eseliuses, where they shared the guest cot in the parlor for a couple of nights. And on Saturday, January 10, the two spent the entire day together, until at least six P.M., tinkering with a motorcycle in the yard.

Then, briefly it seems, they went their separate ways that evening. Appelquist met up with Hilda and her friend and next-door neighbor, Christine Larson. The three decided to attend the seven-thirty P.M. vaudeville show at the Empress Theater. (In the same audience were Frank and Phoebe Seeley, who after the show would encounter the two rude men on the sidewalk near John Morrison's store minutes before the murders were committed.) Some time before the show, Hill's friends apparently

Hilda Erickson, 1915. (Special Collections Department, J. Willard Marriott Library, University of Utah)

returned to the Eseliuses' house, but Hill had left. Later he found their note:

Hilda and I and Christine were here.
We went to the Empress. Tried to find you.
OTTO.

Hill made it to the theater, according to Hilda, but was unable to sit with his friends. "We found Joe in a back seat when we were going out of the show," she recounted in her letter.

WHEN DR. BIRD BROUGHT Hill to the Eseliuses' house from Dr. McHugh's office around one A.M., they found the cot occupied—by a snoozing Appelquist. The Eselius brothers roused him, and he ceded the cot to Hill. Dr. Bird departed, the brothers returned to the kitchen, and Hill and Appelquist, left alone, spoke for a few minutes. At about two A.M., Appelquist said he was leaving to catch the final streetcar to Salt Lake. He needed to find work, he said, and despite the Eselius brothers' protestations that two o'clock on a Sunday morning—a bone-chilling one at that—was not an ideal time to search for a job, Appelquist was resolute. He left at once.

On Sunday afternoon, Hilda came home to Murray to find Hill on the cot in obvious distress. In her letter, she recounts their conversation. If she had told the same story at the time of Hill's legal proceedings, and if it had been proved true, he would have been exonerated.

"What's the matter?" she asked.

"Nothing much," he replied.

Hilda pressed for an answer, and he "finally told me that Otto shot him in a fit of anger," she recalled, adding that Otto "was sorry right after, and carried him to Dr. McHugh's office."

On Monday, all four Salt Lake newspapers carried Governor William Spry's proclamation of a reward of five hundred dollars for information leading to the capture and conviction of the killers of John and Arling Morrison. The offer was to go into effect at noon that day. Sometime after noon, the chief law enforcer of Murray, Marshal Fred Peters, received a telephone call from McHugh. The two knew each other from political circles; like McHugh and many of Murray's civic leaders, Peters was a Socialist. McHugh told Peters that late on Saturday night a man named Joe Hill, with a fresh, large-caliber gunshot wound to his chest, staggered through his examining-room door. McHugh reported that Hill had told him he had been shot by an unnamed friend in a row over a woman, and that he had asked the doctor to keep mum about the incident. When he had treated Hill, of course, McHugh had known nothing of the grisly crimes committed two hours earlier and five miles distant; he would hardly have had reason to suspect his patient of anything but poor judgment and bad luck.

By the time McHugh called Marshal Peters on Monday afternoon, though, more than twenty-four hours had passed since news of the double murder had commandeered the front pages. Why, with killers on the loose and the supposition that one of them had a large-caliber bullet wound being widely reported, did McHugh (and Dr. Bird, for that matter) delay informing the authorities of his suspicions until the governor's reward took effect? Was McHugh simply in the dark until then, as he himself reportedly told a historian in 1946, more than three decades later? On the Sunday after the murders, McHugh was "out in the country" on a house call and missed the day's headlines, writes Professor Vernon Jensen of Cornell University. Jensen adds that McHugh "did not get an opportunity to see the newspapers until the following [Monday] morning." (Curiously, Bird also pleaded ignorance of the Morrison murders until Monday.)

It is uncertain whether McHugh attended to Hill on Monday evening. In a letter he wrote to Professor Jensen in 1948, McHugh made a mind-blowing, if incredible, claim: that Joe Hill, presumably on that Monday night, had *confessed to murdering both Morrisons*. "I do not remember the exact words of Hillstrom," McHugh wrote, "but I think he said: 'The older man reached for the gun and I shot him and the younger boy grabbed the gun and shot me and I shot him to save my own life.'"*

The claim of confession has to be summarily dismissed. After all,

---

* Jensen excerpted the letter in an article he published in an academic journal in 1951, three years after McHugh's death. Most curiously, the published version contains words that Jensen attributes to McHugh's letter but that do not appear in the original, unpublished letter. The published article, for instance, has McHugh recalling that Hill told him, "I'm not such a bad fellow as you think. I shot in self-defense." Jensen also inserts in McHugh's mouth a sentence at odds with the fundamental, theretofore undisputed theory of the case: that it was a revenge killing. (It will be recalled that the perpetrators made no robbery attempt before closing in on the elder Morrison with the last words he heard: "We've got you now!") Jensen writes that McHugh recounted that Hill was intent simply on robbery. "I wanted some money to get out of town" is how Jensen quotes McHugh's recollection of Hill's explanation for the murders.

McHugh never relayed this information to the police, nor did he disclose it while under oath during two appearances on the witness stand in 1914. Those many years later, the doctor defended his discretion while Hill was alive, telling Jensen that he considered Hill's confession "confidential and privileged" and that he "would not have divulged it in a manner to harm him, under any condition."

But Frank McHugh's principled posture regarding the sanctity of

DR. FRANK M. McHUGH
SOUTHWEST CORNER 14TH SOUTH AND STATE STREETS
SALT LAKE CITY, UTAH

Dec. 7ᵗʰ 1915.

Hon.Wm.Spry,Gov.of Utah,
Salt Lake City Utah,

Dear Governor Spry:-
          Sometime ago I called on you at your office in
the City and County Building and presented my claim to the five hun
dred dollars reward offered for the capture of the murderer of J. G
Morrison and his son Arlin.. At that time you told me to write you
a letter setting forth my claims for this reward. I did as you
directed but as yet have received no acknowledgement of this commu-
nication and I feel that it was probably not brought to your attention
I visited your office yesterday afternoon and this morning but owing
to the rush of business there was unable to obtain an interview with
you. If you failed to receive my letter I hereby make claim for the
reward.. If details are desired I will furnish a statement. If you
did received my letter I again urge my claim and ask that you kindly
let me hear from you in regard to it.
     I am,Sir,
          Yours very truly,
          F. M. McHugh

Despite McHugh's persistence, it does not appear that he (or anyone else) received the reward money. (Used by permission, Utah State Historical Society, all rights reserved)

patient-doctor confidentiality could fairly be described as elastic; perhaps in the long years stretching back to Hill's death in 1915, and to when
McHugh was a young, politically ambitious physician—he would be the
Socialist Party's nominee for governor in 1916*—his stance changed or
his mind slipped. For the reality was that McHugh kept mum about Hill's
wound only until he, McHugh, got wind of the governor's reward.
Then he bolted to the head of the line for the five-hundred-dollar bounty.
"Dear Governor Spry," McHugh would write three weeks after the final
disposition of the case, and after several unsuccessful attempts to appeal
for the money in person, "I hereby make claim for the reward. If details
are desired I will furnish a statement."

McHUGH·CALLED ON his patient on Tuesday night. He did so as both
physician and adjunct of the Murray police, who had told McHugh they
planned to arrest Hill later that night for the murder of John Morrison.
For the first time in four days of medical treatment, McHugh gave Hill
a painkiller, injecting him with half a grain of morphine. He did so not
to relieve his patient's pain but, as he would testify, "to make him drowsy"
so that Hill "might be arrested without hurting himself or anybody
else." But McHugh also tipped police that Hill was armed with a large-
caliber gun, thereby negating his own wish for peaceful resolution.

Sometime between midnight and two o'clock on Wednesday morning, Hill was awakened by a knock at the door, a searchlight in his eyes,
and three police officers—Fred Peters and two of his deputies—pointing
revolvers at his face. Drugged, dazed, and maimed by the bullet wound
in his left lung, Hill posed little threat to the officers. Maybe he "leaped
from his bed and made a dash for the corner of the room," as the *Herald-
Republican* first reported, or maybe he reached under his pillow "as if for
a hidden weapon," as it later reported. More likely, though, given his
stupor and wound, he barely moved. But the lawmen took no chances. "I
fired immediately," Peters told the *Herald-Republican*, adding, "I am responsible for the hole in [Hill's] hand. He appeared to be reaching for a
gun when he saw me, and I fired, hitting him in the hand." In fact, as
Hill told it, the bullet grazed his shoulder and tore through his right
hand. The marshal's preemptive bullet and the shot of morphine left Hill
in a "semiconscious condition," and he very nearly died. "The only thing

* He finished a distant third, winning 3 percent of the vote.

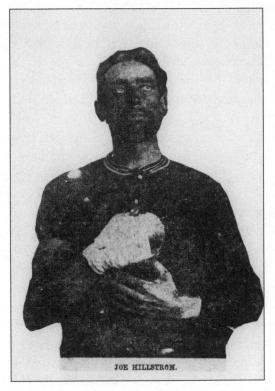

JOE HILLSTROM.

Hill's arresting officer shot him through the hand. (*Deseret Evening News*, January 15, 1914)

that saved my life," he quipped many months later, "was the officer's inefficiency with firearms."

NO SOONER WAS Hill photographed and booked into the Salt Lake County jail than thirteen-year-old Merlin Morrison, the lone witness to the murders of his father and brother, was whisked to the jailhouse to have a look at the alleged perpetrator. From his vantage point in or near the storage room at the rear of the store, what had Merlin seen of the crime? Had he had a clear enough look at the killers to positively identify one or both? The lad's middle-of-the-night visit was arranged for not by the police but by a cheeky newspaper editor. The *Herald-Republican* dispatched a car and driver to the Morrisons' home to pick up Merlin and shepherd him to Hill's cell. Under the headline WOUNDED PRISONER MAY BE BANDIT WHO KILLED MORRISONS, the five A.M. scoop declared that Merlin had "identified" Joe Hill as his "father's slayer." But that assertion promised more than a wavering Merlin had delivered. Despite viewing the suspect from arm's length and in what amounted to a one-man lineup, the youth could only say, "I *believe* that is the man my brother shot." (Emphasis added.)

For the next day's *Tribune*, Merlin was more expansive, but he equivocated as much as he elaborated:

> Hill is about the same size and height as one of the men who entered my father's store Saturday night. As the light was dim, I could not get a lasting impression of the man's features, but Hill appears to be very much the same build as the man who entered the store first and whom I saw fire at my father. After my father had fallen and the murderers saw that my brother intended to fire in return the man whom I think resembles Hill crouched behind the end of the counter and shot my brother.

The ambiguous qualifiers that coated Merlin's language with a film of doubt—"I believe," "about the same size," "appears to be," "I think resembles"—would in time be scrubbed from the boy's vocabulary, replaced by the clear air of certainty that suffused the breaking news coverage. Hill's cell door had barely slammed shut before the press verdict came in. The *Evening Telegram* reported that the authorities "declare" that the evidence "fastens the crime upon Hillstrom without a doubt." The *Tribune*'s account was, if possible, even more categorical: The police, "jubilant" *and* "elated," "now believe that the circumstantial evidence all points with a deadly certainty to the guilt of Hill."

But what of the prime suspect, Frank Z. Wilson? Unlike Hill, Wilson *was* seen in the vicinity of the store after the murders. Not just seen, but seen sprawled on the snowy sidewalk, moaning. And later that frigid night, when police found him on the street in front of Morrison's store without overcoat or credible alibi, he clearly lied about where he worked and lived. As for the bloody handkerchief that police found in his pocket, whatever his explanation, history did not record it.

IT MUST HAVE BEEN of some relief to Marie Morrison, the widowed mother of five minor children, and the thousand mourners who joined her at the funeral that afternoon to know that the murderer was behind bars. Following the two o'clock services at the Eagles Hall conducted by her husband's fraternal organization, the Ancient Order of United

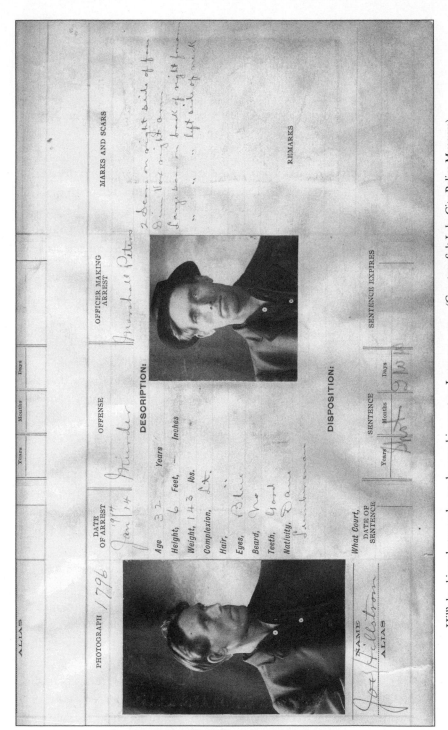

Hill's booking photographs, made upon his arrest on January 14, 1914. (Courtesy Salt Lake City Police Museum)

Workmen , the bodies of John and Arling Morrison were laid to rest in the family plot on a hillside in City Cemetery.

The family knew little of the suspect at that hour beyond that he was "a musician," that he was gravely wounded, that his accomplice remained at large, and that he was not who he claimed to be, according to a police source quoted in both morning papers, the *Tribune* and the *Herald-Republican*. The *Tribune* led with this boldface bulletin:

At an early hour this morning Sergeant Ben Siegfus expressed the belief that Joseph Hill, arrested for the murder of the two Morrisons, is Frank Z. Wilson, a former inmate of the state prison. The description of Hill corresponds closely with that of Wilson. The police have been searching for Wilson ever since the murders.

It is understandable that Sergeant Siegfus confused Joe Hill and Frank Wilson (as the Salt Lake police knew Magnus Olson), for their physical characteristics and ethnicities were strikingly similar. They were about the same age (Hill, thirty-four; Olson, thirty-two) and of similar height and weight (Hill was six feet tall and 143 pounds, a half inch shorter and nine pounds lighter than Olson). Hill had light hair, blue eyes, and good teeth; Olson, light brown hair, blue eyes, and good teeth. Both were Scandinavian: Hill was Swedish; Olson, Norwegian. (Olson's birthplace, Tromsø, is fifty-six miles from the Swedish border.) And each was moving about Salt Lake City within two hours after the murders: at about eleven-thirty, as the conductor James Usher admitted to his in-bound streetcar the "suspicious-acting" passenger he identified as Frank Z. Wilson, Dr. Frank McHugh opened the door of his home in Murray to the freshly wounded Joe Hill.

Magnus Olson was likely long gone from Salt Lake by the time Marshal Fred Peters shot and handcuffed Joe Hill four days after the murders. In that time, the press had pushed the police to hurry it up, pin the murder on someone, and shut down the investigation. Now that the police and the press could point "with a deadly certainty to the guilt of Hill," Olson was of no consequence.

All the police lacked to close the case was Hill's alleged accomplice, Otto Appelquist, who had vanished the night of the murders. Police had obtained his photograph (from the Ogden building contractor for whom he had worked) and circulated it nationwide. And although he never was found, many would-be bounty hunters claimed to have caught sight of him. So frequently was he said to have been glimpsed that one paper coined a verb to describe the "popular pastime": "Applequisting." (The press usually spelled Otto's surname "Applequist" rather than "Appelquist," as he spelled it.)

If Hill's arrest and the hunt for Appelquist withered the curiosity of Salt Lake police detectives concerning the whereabouts of Magnus Olson, authorities elsewhere remained keen to question him. Not forty-eight hours after Hill's capture, a special agent for the Western Pacific Railroad asked the Nevada State Police for help in finding "James Farmer, alias James Franklin." He gave Farmer's Nevada prison number as 1182—the number by which Olson had been admitted to the state prison in 1908 for stealing from a boxcar in Reno. Although the agent's correspondence with the state police does not indicate why he sought "Farmer," it very well could have regarded the most recent known robbery of a Western Pacific car: in Elko on the night of Friday, January 9, 1914—roughly twenty-four hours before the Morrison murders. (The haul included "a barrel of whiskey, several cases of gin, some cigars and underwear," according to the *Elko Daily Free Press*.)

For nearly two weeks after the murders, there was no sign of Olson. Then on January 22, he and a tenderfoot accomplice pulled a brazen job: from a Western Pacific refrigerated car in Elko, they stole a trunk filled with one thousand pairs of U.S.-government-owned buckskin leather gloves, made in New York and bound for San Francisco. The fine gloves aside, though, what Olson and his partner, Thomas Waite, really needed in the high desert in late January were overcoats, an article of clothing neither man seemed to own. (It will be recalled that Olson was coatless when police questioned him on the street near Morrison's store in the aftermath of the murders, despite the subfreezing temperature.) Three days after heisting the gloves, the thieves remedied their wardrobe deficiency by stealing a couple of overcoats on board a passenger train in eastern Elko County. The pair hightailed it off the train at Wells, Nevada, where officers, alerted by a sheriff's telegram, lay in wait. They missed their quarry, however, when the coat crooks boarded an eastbound train for Salt Lake. Once again, the Elko County sheriff wired ahead of their imminent arrival. Olson must have figured as much; he departed the train before it pulled into Salt Lake. Waite, however, stayed aboard; he was arrested as he stepped from the train.

Magnus Olson was caught a day later. It was Wednesday, January 28, eighteen days past the Morrison murders. Joe Hill had been in jail for two weeks, and for two weeks the Salt Lake police and press had been tailoring the ill-fitting circumstantial evidence to him. Perhaps, though, a more accurate metaphor to describe Hill's state, the consensus metaphor at any rate, was constriction: OFFICERS WINDING EVIDENCE ABOUT HILLSTROM, the *Evening Telegram* put it; WINDING THE MESHES ABOUT HILLSTROM, echoed the *Deseret Evening News*; FORGING THE CHAIN AROUND HILLSTROM, the *Tribune* agreed.

With Hill ensnared, whatever residual interest the police and press had in Olson wound down; indeed, his capture merited no news coverage at all. Yet, even as the noose tightened around Hill, Olson must have felt his own jugular closing. That might account for his unprecedented act of repentance: for the first time (as best as can be determined) in his eventful fourteen-year criminal career, he confessed to a crime. He told detectives he had stolen the thousand pairs of gloves from the Western Pacific car a week earlier. While Salt Lake police held Olson until the Elko County sheriff could get there to escort him back to Elko to answer to the boxcar burglary, two detectives questioned him about the Morrison case.

Nothing is known about the interrogation beyond the short, unrevealing article in the *Evening Telegram* that stated Olson "convinced" detectives he "had not been involved." One distinct possibility is that he "convinced" them with cash. The department was rife with grafters; at least one of the two detectives who questioned him was infamous for soliciting bribes in exchange for protection. And as Olson acknowledged long years later, "I bought my way out of at least a half-dozen 'falls' and raps."

Olson agreed to "waive the formality" of an extradition request; he willingly left Utah for Nevada even though he had to know he was facing a lengthy stay in the state prison. Before a state district court judge in Elko, Olson (appearing as James Morton) pleaded guilty to first-degree burglary. He did so because the prosecutor informed Olson that he knew of at least three prior felonies Olson had committed (each under a different name) and that were he to go to trial and be convicted of a fourth, Nevada sentencing guidelines would mandate a term of life in prison. Instead, the judge sentenced Olson to the penitentiary for no less than ten years and no more than eleven.

At Carson City, Olson was a "model prisoner," one so decorous and charming that in short order he became the warden's driver. That relationship provided Olson with the opportunity to meet and ingratiate himself with the warden's patron: Nevada governor Emmet D. Boyle. Olson had learned from his stints in prison that nothing was more valuable than finding an influential "connection"—a crooked lawyer or police official or politician to "fix" the sentence of even a "notorious character" like himself. "Criminals believe in such connections almost like a religion," he later wrote.

Soon enough Olson's faith was rewarded. Whether through bribery or some other means, Governor Boyle warmed to him, too. "My dear Jim," Boyle began one letter to Olson (whom he knew as James Morton). The governor did more for Olson than become his pen pal. He yanked the state's jurisprudential levers to secure Olson's early parole: a mere twenty-six months into his ten- to eleven-year sentence, the Nevada Board of Pardons acceded to the governor's wish. (The pardons board itself seemed bewildered that this violent, recidivist prisoner was to be released. In a letter to a copper-mining executive whom Governor Boyle had personally asked to hire Olson upon his release, the clerk of the board advised the prospective employer that Olson had "spent the last eleven years in various prisons for burglaries committed in California, Nevada and Utah." The clerk continued, "Despite this record, the Sheriff and District Attorney of Elko County recommended his parole."*)

The governor was not the lone Nevadan of influence delighted by Olson's freedom. The editor of the *Elko Daily Free Press* heralded Olson's parole as if welcoming home a heroic native son: "He is a man 30 years of age, fine looking, intelligent, and is known as the 'King of the Box Car Robbers.'" Olson's record, the editor added admiringly, "reads like the detective tales of dime novels."

Olson's twenty-three-year-old accomplice, Thomas Waite, apparently a first-time offender, served thirteen months of a fourteen- to sixteen-month-long sentence.† And his story would warrant no more than a footnote if not for a few suggestive facts in his Nevada State Prison case file. Waite weighed 156 pounds and stood five feet eight and a half, according to the file. It will be recalled that Merlin Morrison's initial

---

* The clerk of the pardons board also suggested the employer would do the parolee "a great favor if he is kept away from intoxicants at all times, and if you can influence him to keep away from evil associates."

† Waite was discharged from prison on March 21, 1915. On his first night of liberty, he slept in a Reno boardinghouse, where he experienced a horrific dream: in a fight with an imaginary foe, Waite fell out of bed, face-first, onto a porcelain cuspidor. He ended the night at the emergency hospital, where he was treated for a lacerated face, a broken nose, and a gashed throat. MAN WITH NIGHTMARE FIGHTS FURNITURE, the next afternoon's newspaper put it.

description of at least one of the murder suspects pegged him at 155 pounds and five feet nine. It will also be recalled that one of the hostile strangers Frank and Phoebe Seeley encountered on the moonlit sidewalk near the Morrisons' store minutes before the murders had a "defection"—a scar—"on the side of his face or neck," as Phoebe would testify. Waite's file indicates he had a pronounced "cut scar": a four-inch-long gash punctuating his face, curving upward and slightly inward from the center of the point of his chin and across the right cheek like an opening parenthesis.

If Salt Lake detectives were ever inclined to investigate Magnus Olson—his long and violent record, his habit of vicious retribution, his movements in the days and weeks before and after the murders and on the day and night of the crime itself—the inclination passed prior to their arresting him as a courtesy to the Elko County sheriff's department on January 28. The Salt Lake authorities had long since been satisfied that Hill was a serviceable culprit. As acting sheriff Atha Williams told the *Herald-Republican*, "I am confident that we will procure a conviction—as confident as I am that Hellstrom is one of the men who in cold blood shot down and killed J.G. Morrison and his son on the night of January 10." (For a week after his arrest, the *Herald-Republican* referred to the accused, whose full, Americanized name was Joseph Hillstrom, as "Hellstrom.")

If the citizens of Salt Lake City needed further proof of the accused's brutishness, rock-solid evidence arrived in the form of a letter to Chief of Police Brigham Grant from a counterpart in Southern California. The detectives who had questioned John and Ed Eselius had learned that the brothers had met Hill and his reputed partner in crime, Otto Appelquist, the previous spring in San Pedro, where they had all worked as longshoremen. Chief Grant had diligently queried police in San Pedro, a semiautonomous district of Los Angeles, and on the morning of January 22, hours before Hill was to be arraigned, that afternoon, came the reply. "They are a bad pair," San Pedro police commander J. A. Smith confirmed. (Smith, it happened, came from an accomplished family in Salt Lake City: his brother was a physician, his nephew a lawyer.) Commander Smith told Chief Grant that Hill and Appelquist had held up a streetcar in San Pedro eight months earlier, in May of 1913, and that they had skipped town the same night. When Hill had returned in June, Smith had collared him. The commander admitted, though, that "neither the car crew nor any of the passengers were able to identify [Hill] as he had his face covered with a black veil." Even so, Smith said he had wrung from Hill a guilty plea—for vagrancy.

AT TWO O'CLOCK on the afternoon of January 22, hours after Chief Grant had received the damning letter from San Pedro (and then passed it on to the press for publication that afternoon), an "unkempt" Hill appeared before a Salt Lake County justice of the peace for a plea hearing. His right hand, the one through which his arresting officer had fired a bullet eight days earlier, was heavily bandaged and cradled in a sling. His hair was long and lank and partly covered his eyes, and his eyelids were "constantly drooped," noted a keenly observant reporter, who yet also ascribed to Hill a "hardened look." He wore a "nondescript" cotton shirt, blue overalls, and tan shoes "only half buttoned," presumably because he was down to one functioning hand. He was so weak and woozy that he could barely shuffle the few steps from his chair to stand before the judge. When he reached the bench, he steadied himself by resting his good hand on it while the judge read aloud the formal complaint of murder in the first degree. The judge told Hill he had twenty-four hours to consider his plea.

"I will enter my pleading now," Hill replied. "It is not guilty."

"Also, you are entitled to counsel," the judge said.

"I have no money to pay counsel," Hill answered. "I will act as my own counsel."

The reporter for the *Herald-Republican* took Hill's declaration that he would represent himself as cockiness, which perhaps it was. But if Hill was cocky, it was not because he was especially "familiar with court procedure," as the reporter stated, or because he was an experienced criminal defendant, as the article implied. If Hill was cocky, it was because he did not yet fathom the seriousness of his predicament. Indeed, he was glad to hear that the preliminary, or probable cause, hearing was on the docket for the following week. He told the judge, in one reporter's words, that he "wished to have the thing over with as soon as possible." He never imagined that the case would go to trial, let alone that he would be convicted and sentenced to die.

It was only that afternoon, after all, that the extent of Hill's supposed past criminality was laid before the public via the release of the letter from the police commander in San Pedro. For besides revealing that Hill and Appelquist were a "bad pair" of highway robbers, Commander Smith's letter outlined another critical piece of evidence against Hill, one more clue to his life of lawlessness. Smith told Chief Grant that Appelquist—who Smith obviously confused with Hill—was guilty of being "somewhat of a musician" and "a writer of songs for the IWW song books." Such a record left no room for doubt; in Smith's mind the case was closed. The commander typed his uppercase congratulations to Chief Grant for a job well done: "YOU HAVE THE RIGHT MAN."

II

FINDING A VOICE

"As yet," cried the stranger . . . "as yet I have done nothing. Were I to vanish from the earth tomorrow . . . not a soul would ask, 'Who was he? Whither did the wanderer go?' But I cannot die till I have achieved my destiny. Then, let Death come! I shall have built my monument!"
—NATHANIEL HAWTHORNE, "THE AMBITIOUS GUEST," 1835

5.

"The Thought for the Day
and the Dream of the Night"

He had an artist's compulsion to create and a propagandist's need to incite. Those urges famously and harmoniously collided in his music. Yet perhaps Joe Hill's greatest creation was that of his role in history: the establishment of his own legend. That accomplishment seems all the more remarkable when one considers the arc of his short life: for all but the last four of his thirty-six years—when he found his voice as the preeminent songwriter for the IWW and when his murder case conferred on him infamy and then worldwide renown—he left few traces of his existence. Partly, his anonymity was related to the times. He had washed up on a swell of almost nine million immigrants to America in the first decade of the twentieth century, 220,000 of them Swedish. And like millions of poor and working-class immigrants, he virtually disappeared upon arrival, as if caught in an undertow beneath the turbulent surface of American society.

In a way, the New World had engulfed him, rendered him invisible. He would not emerge, not fully, for a dozen years. Only when he was tried and imprisoned in Utah did he begin to appear in sharp focus; only then could we see the person he was becoming, and the person he became.

But if the clearest picture of Hill's years in America does not develop until the end of his life, of his beginnings in Sweden one can draw a fairly detailed portrait. It helps the researcher that he lived in one city, and basically in one house, the entire time; it also helps that Sweden, like Utah before statehood, was a theocracy that kept scrupulous records and close track of its citizens.

Also like Utah (and, for that matter, the whole of the American West),

Hill's homeland during the latter half of the nineteenth century was in the midst of an industrial and social revolution. Until then, Sweden had changed sparingly in the three centuries since the governing Church of Sweden had been established. Now, a society at the mercy of the weather and the seasons was rapidly giving way to a society at the mercy of the steel-wheeled whine and chuff of progress: of steam-powered locomotives, sawmills, plows, and ships. In the last thirty years of the century, the proportion of Swedes earning a living from farming fell from three-quarters of the population to one-half. And the number of craft and manufacturing jobs doubled during the same period. While Sweden was still overwhelmingly agrarian by the end of the nineteenth century, the economic and demographic center was shifting: two in ten Swedes lived in cities, twice the percentage of three decades earlier.

Within the numbers that describe the migration from farm to factory is the story of Joe Hill's lineage. Hill's paternal grandfather, Olof Hägglund (pronounced HEG-looned), worked as a *dagkarl*, an agricultural day laborer. He and his wife and their five children lived on a small, isolated tenant farm, or *torp*, in Forsby, a settlement within the rural parish of Hille, in east-central Sweden.

The family had "maybe enough land to grow the essentials," Rolf Hägglund, a grandnephew of Hill's, told me, but perhaps not enough to adequately feed the entire family. In 1860, at the age of fourteen, the oldest child, who was also named Olof, moved in with his grandparents and went to work as a *dräng*—a farmhand. Six years passed. The younger Olof moved south to the neighboring big city of Gävle (pronounced YEV-leh), a bustling seaport on the Baltic coast, a hundred miles north of Stockholm. At eighteen thousand people, Gävle ranked as the fifth-largest of Sweden's cities, but it was growing fast—its population would more than double between 1870 and 1900—and wielded an outsize influence: it was home to the country's largest harbor.

Olof moved into the working-class district on the south side of town known as *Gamla Gefle*—Old Gävle—where he took a room in the small frame cottage of a family named Wennman.

The Wennmans, Johanna and John, had also migrated from Hille to Gävle, where John worked at the harbor hauling steel to the giant shipping scales. The couple had three children. (Four others had died in infancy or early childhood.) The oldest, a daughter, had been born out of wedlock in 1844, the year before the couple married. The odor of that fact did not elude the paternalistic Church of Sweden, which had a bloodhound's nose for moral decay and the authority and responsibility to persecute behavior forbidden to its members—which by law included *every* Swede. Indeed, no sooner were Swedish daughters and sons born to the soil than they were swaddled in the cloth of the Church of Sweden. Founded during the Protestant Reformation, the church was an Evangelical Lutheran denomination over which the Swedish monarchy had reigned since the early sixteenth century. There was no blurry line between church and state; there was no line at all: state and church were one, a tax-supported monopoly. From cradle to grave—from mandatory baptism of each newborn to mandatory confirmation and communion to mandatory church-officiated wedding to mandatory burial in a state-church-owned cemetery—the Church of Sweden demanded strict conformity to doctrine.

In the parish birth register, the state priest marked the newborn Wennman girl as "*oäkta*," or illegitimate, a badge of shame she would wear forever, and the mother, Johanna, with the equivalent of a scarlet letter: "*slampa*"—slut. Johanna and John worked on farms (she as a maid, he as a hand), frequently moving over the course of their daughter's first three years of life. Probably they relocated when and where work could be found, and perhaps also to escape official persecution for their *oäkta* daughter. The name of the "whore's child" (as the church branded those it morally condemned from birth) was Margaretha Catharina Wennman.

Catharina (as she was known) grew to be a talented singer possessed of a "soft and clear soprano." Her love of music was shared by the long-term boarder in her parents' house, Olof Hägglund, himself a skilled organist. When Catharina's father died in 1869, three years after Olof moved in, Olof assumed the role of "man of the house," a duty that was officially recognized on October 10, 1873, the day he and Catharina were married. At twenty-nine, two years Olof's senior, Catharina had blue eyes and long blond hair she wore pulled back in a bun. He was wide-eyed, with curly dark hair and a bird's-nest beard. The newlyweds stayed on in the house now owned by Catharina's widowed mother, Johanna.

Nine months to the day from her wedding, Catharina gave birth to the first of nine children, Elisabeth Catharina, who died at the age of eighteen months. Olof Efraim was born in 1875 and another, Paul Elias, in 1877; both would reach adulthood. A third son, Joel Samuel, born in 1878, lived only sixteen days. The Hägglunds also named their fourth son Joel—Joel Emanuel. He was born on October 7, 1879. (In America, he would rechristen himself Joe Hillstrom, but for the duration of this chapter, I'll call him Joel, the name he went by in Sweden.) The next born to Catharina and Olof was Judith Elisabeth, who died in infancy in 1882. She was followed by Judith Catharina, born in 1883, Ruben Andreas, born in 1885, and Ester Elisabeth, born in 1887, all of whom lived into adulthood.

AT THE END OF 1880, when Joel was fourteen months old, the family—Olof and Catharina, Joel and his two older brothers—moved from the house owned by Catharina's mother into a home of their own nearby: a two-story frame cottage at Nedre Bergsgatan 28. (The name of the narrow, cobblestoned street offers a clue, perhaps, to the derivation of Joel's future pen name: it translates to Lower Hill.*) The house was located within easy walking distance of Olof's employer and a mere three hundred meters from the family's church, the Reverend Paul Peter Waldenström's gleaming new Bethlehem Chapel.

Olof paid two thousand crowns for the house—more than twice the nine hundred crowns he earned yearly as a conductor on the Gävle-Dala Railway, the line that carried minerals and workers from the mining belt of north-central Sweden to the port at Gävle. But his was a steady job in a robust industry, and the *sparbank*—people's savings bank—from which he probably obtained his mortgage loan would have considered him a low-risk customer. Still, the family could afford the house only by cramming into the downstairs flat and renting the two flats upstairs to boarders.

The house was no less than a hundred years old—and showing its age. It lacked plumbing. A draft routed any insulation; in the wintertime it was so cold that before the children went to sleep, Catharina tied mittens on their hands—"so that they should not freeze at night," Joel's youngest sibling, Ester Hägglund Dahl, told an interviewer many years later. It helped that Olof was both handy and energetic. Laboring early in the morning, before dressing in his conductor's uniform and leaving for a long day on the job, he took on project after project. He installed water pipes and a drainage system, built all the furniture and the four-octave pump organ around which the family frequently gathered, and for Cath-

* Another theory is that he chose his full "Americanized" name, Joseph Hillstrom, as an homage to his father's birth parish, Hille, and village, Forsby, the first syllable of which translates to "torrent" or "stream" and is a synonym for *ström*.

arina made a *vevmangel*—a hand-cranked press that dried and ironed clothes wet from washing.

FARMING VILLAGES were losing people like Olof not only to the cities but to the New World as well. Whether those who left felt they were being pushed off the land or pulled, and whether for economic or religious reasons, it must have been harrowing for them to leave their known world for the unknown. For better and worse, that world had been home, and it would be no more.

By the time Joel was born in 1879, "America fever" had reached pandemic proportions. Though there had been isolated cases of the malady in the 1830s, the first mass outbreak occurred in the late 1840s, among farm families in the southeastern province of Småland. "People of the soil," the novelist Vilhelm Moberg calls them, but the soil could sustain them no longer. It was played out, thin and rocky and overpopulated (Sweden's population would double between 1800 and 1880), and many farmers, facing crop failures and famine, and with irredeemable debt and "no other capital than their hands," as the provincial bishop wrote, saw little choice but to uproot themselves from the land their families had plowed for centuries.* Those Småland farmers prefaced an astonishing exodus: during the course of three waves of emigration over the latter half of the nineteenth and the first decade of the twentieth century, Sweden lost roughly 1.2 million people to America—a quarter of its population.

Not all those bound for the New World were economic refugees. Most of those afflicted earliest with America fever were religious outcasts—followers of another, and therefore illegal, denomination or a breakaway sect—or individuals who simply could no longer abide church governance of virtually every aspect of their spiritual and temporal lives. The state church divided Sweden's local political boundaries into dioceses and again into parishes. To reside in a parish was to belong to its congregation. Mandatory membership fostered a sense of community, but for many the repressive aspects of the church had come to outweigh the sense of security and belonging it provided.

The church brooked no dissent. And no dissent, or at least no sustained

---

* One reason for the population pressure, in Småland and throughout Sweden, was the success of the smallpox vaccine, which had been introduced in Sweden in the mid-1750s and which "dramatically" reduced the country's infant and child mortality rates from the mid-eighteenth century to the mid-nineteenth.

organized dissent, plagued the church for its first three hundred years. By the middle of the nineteenth century, however, advancements in transportation and communications technologies had brought the outside world in. Foreign products and foreign ideas infiltrated the country. The advent of the steamship and the railroad enabled cheap grain from Russia and the United States to enter the Swedish market—another factor driving farmers off the land. And missionaries for other denominations trickled in, flouting the prohibition on competing religions. The state church dealt harshly with proselytizers and converts both, as was illustrated by its hounding of the early Mormons.

Punishment, though, had its own severe repercussions for the church. It triggered in the laity a chain reaction of resentment, excitement, and organization—an awakening that not only touched off a latter-day reformation of the Church of Sweden itself but also set in motion a tide of popular movements—from temperance to labor to suffrage to public education—that would democratize the whole of Swedish society. It began in the 1840s, when there bubbled up from the laity a groundswell of revivalism: an ad hoc movement of evangelical "free" churches.

The Hägglund family's church, Bethlehem Chapel, was at the center of Sweden's free church movement. Its chairman, the Reverend Paul Peter Waldenström, was a "born popular orator" whom one leading historian of Swedish religion regarded as "easily the greatest free-church leader and possibly the greatest religious force" in all of Sweden. He was at the height of his influence during Joel's boyhood. When he held the first services at Bethlehem in 1880, Waldenström was forty-two years old and broadly built, with pursed lips, heavily lidded eyes, and jagged peaks of dark upswept hair turning to white, like a snow-dusted mountain range. His intellect, too, seemed a soaring, serrated force of nature; his was a piercing brilliance paired with a blunt-force personality and a caustic wit. Perhaps the young Joel absorbed the latter trait from his minister; like Waldenström, he knew where to insert the knife.

Waldenström commanded attention and admiration, if not affection. "He was curiously deficient in the graces of human association," as one scholar put it, adding that "more dangerous heretics than Waldenström have been better liked." Waldenström's heresy was that he was an ordained Church of Sweden minister whose loyalty lay closer to the Bible than to institutional orthodoxy. He was dangerous because on crucial points in the Scripture his reading was at odds with Lutheran doctrine, and because no Church of Sweden preacher had greater ability to speak his mind from the pulpit—or less fear of doing so.

Waldenström preached that the essence of faith was not one's adherence to theological orthodoxy but one's personal bond with Christ. "Salvation," he wrote, "depends on the individual's relationship to the savior who God gave to the world." And for Waldenström and those whom he inspired, a life steeped in glorifying Christ was a life dedicated to bettering one's community. It meant acknowledging "the social inequalities that exist" (as he said during the first of his several American tours, in 1889), and it meant serving Christ's mission on earth to seek social justice, or, as the New Testament says, to "release the oppressed."

Ultimately, the free church movement forced the repeal of Swedish monopoly laws that made criminals of non-ministerial Lutheran gospel-spreaders and those who represented or joined any other denomination. Those reforms alone were tribute to the power of organized dissent—a power stirred by a human trait long dormant in Swedes: rebellion in the face of the unendurable.

The great religious awakening redrew the Swedish map of possibility: if at long last a measure of religious liberty was at hand, in what other directions could the multitudes assert their own powerful presence? What other freedoms were within reach? By giving voice and vision and muscle to the laity inside the churchyard, could the free church movement reconceive the world outside, tip the axis of political and cultural life? Beginning in the 1870s, ordinary people created their own popular institutions: workers' clubs and folk schools; trade unions (which the authorities deemed most contemptible); mutual-benefit societies to provide burial insurance; temperance organizations to combat rampant alcohol abuse*; the country's first outposts of the Salvation Army, which was both a charity and a free church; and a political movement, the Social Democrats, a coalition of trade unionists and Socialists inspired by, and allied with, other European Socialist movements. (Among the planks in the party's early platform were a maximum eight-hour workday and universal male suffrage; the right to vote in parliamentary elections was limited to men whose assets met a threshold beyond the reach of virtually all workers and small farmers.)

IN ADDITION to his year-round salary, the Gävle-Dala Railway provided Joel's father, Olof, with a modest pension plan, endowing the Hägglund

---

* It was not uncommon for Swedish workers to be paid in *brännvin*—literally "burn-wine"—which was made with potatoes and grain and consumed by everyone from priests to farmers to factory workers before, during, and after mealtimes.

family with a good deal more stability and security than if he, like so many of his neighbors in Old Gävle and the nearby Brynäs district, had had to resort to seasonal employment at the harbor. (During the long winter, when ice floes closed the harbor and the long arms of the steam cranes stood limp, the only income port workers could hope for was from occasional logging or mill work in the countryside; mainly, though, they tightened their belts and waited for the spring thaw.)

The name Hägglund translates literally as "grove of bird-cherries"— Olof's great-grandfather took the surname in a bow to his natural surroundings—and the family's economic security proved to be as delicate and fleeting as the tree's white-petaled blossoms. Two weeks past Joel's seventh birthday, in October of 1886, Olof was hurt on the job. While at work at the station in Korsnäs, fifty miles west of Gävle, he was knocked from a switching engine and caught underneath the locomotive. His injuries, primarily internal, were not immediately fatal, but the accident foretold the beginning of the end of the family's life together. Olof returned to work, but the pain would not subside. For more than a year, he refused to seek medical treatment, probably owing to the cost (there was no health insurance or workers' compensation) and perhaps also out of shame: he blamed himself for the accident and wanted it forgotten, Ester Hägglund Dahl told Ture Nerman, her brother's first Swedish biographer. Little more than a year later, on December 7, 1887, Olof was in surgery for treatment of a "sickness possibly developed from

Olof Hägglund. (Courtesy Barrie Stavis)

head injury," as recorded in the railroad personnel ledger.* From his sickbed a day earlier, he had sent home a note: "When you go to God in prayer, pray for Pappa."

The prayers were unanswered: Olof died on the operating table. He was forty-one years old; his widow, forty-three, with six children, none older than twelve. At Olof's burial, Catharina sang for him one last time, her warm, vibrant soprano ringing above the December chill of the graveyard: "Now I cast all the sorrow, which burdens my soul, Jesus, up to you." The death notice in the newspaper included a verse from Revelations: "Blessed are the dead who from now on die in the Lord. Yes, says the spirit, they will rest from their labors, for their deeds follow them."

For those Olof left behind, there would be no rest, only mourning and wretchedness. His death was especially hard on his mother, Kajsa (an affectionate name for Catharina), a sturdy woman of sixty-seven with a leathery face, a prominent nose, and eyes of gray that matched her customary scarf and full-length woolen shawl. After her eldest son's death, she became a familiar if solitary figure on Gävle street corners: a Bible-cradling soapboxer lambasting passersby about the wicked and ungodly world filled with "great wrath on the children of men."

There was no reliable safety net to catch a family that lost its breadwinner. The railroad paid Catharina a widow's pension of 225 crowns annually for five years—precisely a quarter of Olof's annual salary. To supplement the rental income and meager pension, she turned the *vev-mangel* to commercial use, taking in ironing. She or one of the children with a free hand cranked it day and night, earning ten *öre* an hour—the equivalent of two cents. Yet ends were not always met. Some days there was nothing to eat: no flour for bread or barley for porridge or milk to drink—a working family's staples. Other days the family would eat only if, as Ester remembered it, one of the children happened upon a sack of old potatoes on the road and dragged it home "as if it were a treasure." "It is hard to describe how it felt for a hungry girl," Ester tearfully told an interviewer nearly a lifetime later, when she was sixty-five.

Catharina refused to seek help from the Poor Relief Board, a municipal panel known for its hostility to supplicants. The "high gents" of the board, as one newspaper termed it, seemed to regard many who appeared before them as freeloading criminals or, as a historian of Gävle

---

* The record also speculated that Olof might have had *"kräfta"*—cancer.

The Hägglund family after Olof died. Catharina and her six children, none older than twelve.
Joel, about eight, stands at far left. (Courtesy Barrie Stavis)

social policy wrote, "lazy and immoral elements [who] tried to live at the
expense of the town." Catharina apparently was one of Gävle's destitute
who preferred starvation to facing the abusive board. "Life was already
full enough of humiliations," as Ester's interviewer, John Takman, assessed Catharina's state of mind.

Still, occasional visits from one or another of the private charities yielded
the family small alms, and the children contributed what they could. Olof
Efraim (who went by Efraim), the oldest, quit technical school to work as
a messenger for the railroad his father had worked for. Paul, the next oldest, followed into that line of work soon after he turned twelve, in 1889.
And at the close of every term, Joel and his siblings of school age traipsed
to the town hall, where each was allotted from one to three crowns
(a crown equaled twenty cents), according to a formula based on age and
report card.

* * *

IN A LIFE weighed down with sorrow and drudgery and deprivation, a saving grace was music. Catharina and Olof's shared love of singing and playing had always helped sustain the family. Music had facilitated the couple's union, and when Olof was alive, the family regularly assembled around his hand-fashioned pump organ. He would start to play, Catharina to sing. The youngest children would take up their mother's voice, Efraim the second voice, Joel the third, and Paul, baritone. Also, almost certainly Olof and Catharina belonged to the Bethlehem Chapel choir, singing Reverend Waldenström's hymns and those of Karolina Sandell, a prolific writer of free church psalms. Lina (as she was popularly known) blended to great effect words and simple but evocative tunes—a technique Joe Hill would one day replicate for his church: the Industrial Workers of the World.

In the uplifted voices of the Bethlehem Chapel choir and in the family's own spirited harmonizing at home, Joel must have begun to feel the transformative power of music: a potent alchemy of word and melody and instrument and voice that brought people together and sometimes shook their very souls. He and all his siblings learned to play the organ "as soon as we could reach the keys," Ester recalled. Joel taught himself the notes, but mostly he played by heart on the organ and on his instrument of choice, a violin that Olof had given him. He practiced so incessantly that at times his music-loving mother could listen no more. Perhaps to the dismay of the neighbors, Catharina shooed him outdoors, where he would recommence, probably without skipping a measure.

The only place Joel did not play was at Gävle Boys School, where the state church curriculum offered no music instruction beyond recitation of the dirgelike hymns. The school was a vital organ of the Church of Sweden—the heart of the church's program of indoctrination. But for Joel and surely for other students—perhaps those, like him, who bent artistically, or whose families belonged to a free church—the indoctrination did not take. His report card for the spring term of 1891, when he was eleven and in "third class," his next-to-last year at Gävle Boys School, describes a modest academic performer. He received no uppercase A (that being the top grade; the bottom, a lowercase c), but did manage lowercase a's in penmanship, attitude, and *flit*—diligence. And he earned a-b's—a notch below lowercase a—in spelling and grammar, geometry, and drawing. Perhaps not surprisingly, given the aversion to organized religion he would later display, among the subjects in which he fared poorest, earning lowercase b's, were biblical history and catechism. Still, the state church was not finished with him. Like all Swedes, at fourteen he was made to enroll in confirmation class. His grade of c in Christian knowledge would appear to have demonstrated a willful, irreverent indifference to authority—a trait all good Wobblies seemed genetically disposed to. At any rate, confirmation class was the last sip of his force-fed Christian education.

TO CROSS JOEL'S PATH around the time he was confirmed, in the early to middle 1890s, was to behold, in Ester's words, a "gangly," "solitary" teenager. A classmate at Gävle Boys School, P. E. Hedblom (whose father had worked with Olof on the railroad), described him similarly: "A little more serious and more introverted than his two older brothers." And Hill himself once remarked, "There is no poetry about my personality." Ester attributed his introversion to birth order: his older brothers "had their common interests and [he] was on the outside. We sisters were younger so that he had no share in our interests either. He kept much to himself and had his own interest and that was mostly music." It was more likely that, as with a lot of creative people, Joel's inner life was as pulsating as his demeanor was reclusive. As Hill would tell a young aspiring musician near the end of his life, "When you know how to play music [you can] never be lonesome." He added that although there was no money "to take music lessons when I was a kid," he had some innate talent. "I've got music in my blood and it just comes natural to me to play any kind of an instrument." On another occasion, he told his young friend that when he was a fatherless boy, even food was a luxury his family could not always afford. But that was all right, he joked, for music provided all the sustenance he needed. "I would rather play the fiddle than eat."

If he had music in his blood, he had satire in his gut. Fifteen years or more before he deployed his acidic and remorselessly funny songs as deadly serious weapons in the American class war, Joel Hägglund wrote and performed send-ups poking gentle fun at his family. At first he sang his "taunting songs," Ester said, but after a while he needed only "to play them on the violin to have the same effect." He also took to "lecturing" from the newspaper—concocting absurdities by extracting a line from one story, pasting it into the text of another, in turn appending those lines to yet another story, and, to great acclaim, reading aloud, surely in a deadpan tone, the resulting mishmash. At the dinner table, he was known to pick exaggeratedly at his food (when there *was* food), spotting in every dish, Ester said, "much more than we could see or imagine": rubber galoshes, moleskin pants, claws, and so on. The humor did not always play well. But it always provoked. "Mamma was angry at times," Ester said, "and at times she had to laugh, too." In a humorless, repressive world, a world of chronic deprivation and daily humiliation, Catharina's third son made her laugh, made them all laugh.

He made them laugh by hitching his wordplay to melodies he appropriated from the hymnbook of none other than the Salvation Army—the worldwide Christian charity that would become one of Joe Hill's greatest musical foils. That as a lad Joel was already tampering with the Army's tunes portended his shift from purely comedic satirist to budding provocateur. The Army founded its Gävle branch in 1888, within months of his father's death. But as desperate as the Hägglunds were for relief—so desperate that some days a found sack of old potatoes was the difference between a meal and nothing to eat—the organization's records do not indicate the family sought its financial assistance. Perhaps the indignity of asking for a handout was greater than Catharina could bear. Or maybe she took exception to the soul-saving guidance the Salvation Army dispensed with its charity. The guidance ran toward "No matter how you starve and suffer here, you will feast in Paradise, that is, if you will follow the directions." The American author Jack London jotted down those words of a Salvation Army adjutant while visiting an Army "feasting hall" in the East End of London in 1902. (He was at work on *The People of the Abyss*, an exposé of slum conditions.) London observed that the famished men in the hall were made first to sit down "not to meat or bread, but to speech, song, and prayer." The Army adjutant's warning of eternal torment was lost on them, London wrote—they were "too inured to hell on earth to be frightened by hell to come."

Joel Hägglund, too, was undaunted by the afterlife. Although he left no record of when and why he lost faith in the church, it is plausible that when he lost his father as a churchgoing boy of eight, he wondered how a compassionate God—the loving God he had grown up knowing in Waldenström's free church—could allow such cruelty. Could it truly be that God intended to use the tragedy of Olof's death and the family's grief and destitution to deepen their faith? Perhaps faith *did* lead to a paradisaical feast, but faith could not ease a boy's privation in this earthly life; faith put no bread on the table that the boy's departed father had built with his own hands. As Hill acerbically expressed it two decades later in "The Preacher and the Slave," he was averse to "long-haired preachers" trying to tell you "what's wrong and what's right" but, "when asked, how 'bout something to eat," advising ("with voices so sweet"), "Work and pray, live on hay, you'll get pie in the sky when you die."

NEAR THE END of his life, Hill told a friend, "I had to go to work at the age of 10, when my father died." But his memory might have betrayed him. Olof passed away shortly after Joel turned eight, and Joel's attendance records from Gävle Boys School indicate that he remained in school through his twelfth birthday. When he did go to work, it was in a rope mill near the harbor. The factory, one of the many local suppliers to the maritime trades, processed flax into rope for rigging on ships. That he chose factory work over the railroad, his brothers' employer, suggests that Efraim and Paul warned him off. "They kept on complaining the pay was bad and the promotions were too slow," Ester recalled.

Joel was entering an increasingly industrial economy. "Gävle was built in the Middle Ages, and in many ways it was stuck there," said Ulf Ivar Nilsson, a historian who has written extensively on nineteenth-century life in the city. (The city was founded in 1446.) Nilsson was describing Gävle prior to a fire in 1869 that destroyed five hundred houses—virtually the entire city north of the Gävle River.* The fire, he told me, enabled the city to reinvent itself as a modern hub of commerce and transport. By 1900, Gävle's population of nearly thirty thousand was double that of 1870, the year after the fire. There were 110 factories operating in and around the harbor, manufacturing everything from candy to coffee to prefabricated houses to tobacco.

Gävle became a magnet for farm dwellers who envisioned industrial jobs as liberation from fickle weather and rural penury. But for many, the living and working conditions in Gävle provided no respite from the harshness of life. As Hjalmar Branting, a framer of Swedish socialism (and winner of the Nobel Peace Prize in 1921), described it in a landmark speech to the Gävle Workers' Federation in 1886, factory workers toiled at least as many hours as farmworkers, and for wages calibrated to the "lowest possible level"—a level designed to meet only workers' "most necessary needs" while "still admit[ting] life and giving birth to the next generation of wage-slaves."

The Gävle Workers' Federation was one of the many popular institu-

---

* The river bisected Gävle, dividing it by class: the working poor lived on the south side in Old Gävle or Brynäs; the more well-to-do—those, generally, whose incomes qualified them as voters—lived north of the bridge.

Gävle, 1903, the year after Hill emigrated. The bridge crosses the Gävle River, which separates the working-class district of Old Town where Hill grew up, to the south, from the business district. (Courtesy Länsmuseet Gävleborg)

tions that had sprouted from seeds sown by the religious revivalists. Founded in 1866, the federation undertook to improve members' material and intellectual well-being. It established mutual health care and burial-fund benefits and several consumer cooperative stores, and it instituted cultural and educational-extension programs, including a lecture club, study circles in reading, math, and English language, and regular musical and theatrical entertainment.

The federation governed itself but was allied with the other workers' federations in Sweden and with emerging socialist and trade union movements across Europe. Workers in Gävle began organizing by industry in 1885. It had been a hard road. To agitate for workers' rights—for the right to negotiate wages, hours, and working conditions; the right to vote; child-labor restrictions—was to court repression. The state church viewed labor leaders as it had free church revivalists and missionaries of other denominations a generation earlier: as "blasphemous." And the authorities dispensed justice reminiscent of that meted out to spiritual subversives; union activists were jailed for "lese-majesty"—essentially, treason—and for "threats against general order."*

---

* A generation later, in 1917, the U.S. government charged hundreds of IWW activists with treason for organizing strikes and slowdowns during wartime.

The authorities had a point: the general order *was* threatened. But unions alone could not reorder Swedish society. Prior to the 1880s, factory owners, backed by civil, and in some cases military, authorities—by "the whole power in society, both courts and bayonets," Branting said—routed most workplace-organizing attempts. Typically, management made examples of union leaders, firing, blacklisting, beating, and jailing them, surveilling them and their families, evicting them if they lived in company housing, and chasing them out of town and, sometimes, out of Sweden altogether. In the spring of 1879, five months before Hill's birth, five thousand sawmill workers in the Sundsvall district, the timber-producing capital of northern Sweden, struck some twenty mills to protest district-wide collusion to lower wages during an economic downturn. Citing the need to restore order, the provincial governor summoned military troops to attack the strikers. The overwhelmed workers returned to the mills; the pay cut stood. Soon after the strike was broken, a radical journalist named Isidor Kjellberg went undercover in the Sundsvall mills to report on conditions. (He would serve two months in prison for overstepping the narrow boundaries of press freedom.) He surfaced with the impression that to not a few of the workers, emigration seemed a better alternative than struggling against the tyranny of the church-industrial state. "If any plan for the future can be called common there," Kjellberg wrote of Sundsvall later in 1879, "it is that of leaving, the sooner the better." He reported that since the strike had ended, as many as two thousand people ("counting wives and children") had already emigrated. "America," Kjellberg observed, "is the thought for the day and the dream of the night."

NOT EVERYONE DREAMED of America as the escape route from their industrial nightmare, though. Just as ruthless persecution against those who had defied the state church awoke the laity to the need for and power of organization, the declaration of war against sawmill workers in Sundsvall inspired some to dream of another great awakening, of a powerful labor movement that fused trade unionism with democratic socialism, direct action with political action. The two divisions would be indivisible, like church and state, or, as the socialist editor Axel Danielsson put it, "like Siamese twins, the life of one dependent upon that of the other."

Hjalmar Branting's address to the Gävle Workers' Federation in 1886 expanded on the theme of how a program of democratic socialism would liberate workers from the shackles of industrial capitalism. He spoke for the larger movement that was sweeping across not only Europe, home to its intellectual forebears, but the world. Branting termed capitalism the "root and source of evil" and said that the nascent Social Democratic Labor movement could settle for nothing less than "complete freedom for the working class from all slavery—political, economical, social and spiritual." (Two decades later, in 1905, Big Bill Haywood would echo those Marxian words in Chicago in his opening remarks to the "Continental Congress of the Working Class," the founding convention of the Industrial Workers of the World; he called for "emancipation of the working class from the slave bondage of capitalism.")

In Gävle, Branting implored workers to direct their ire not so much against individual "bloodsuckers," but toward "the very system which enables these individuals to exist." What good is it, he added, to remove "one despotic *person*" when "the despotism of *the circumstances* still falls as a weight of lead over the suppressed mass?" And Branting reminded the audience that if "tomorrow" they were to win any number of political reforms—"universal suffrage, complete freedom of religion," a "normal workday and state insurance for everyone"— still unresolved would be the core issue: "the unequal distribution of wealth," which "follows large-scale production as the shadow the body."

IN LATE 1896, when Joel was seventeen and working at the rope factory, he had his first brush with death. He developed worrisome splotches on one side of his nose and his right wrist—worrisome because the skin condition showed no sign of healing on its own and because it was symptomatic of an infectious and often fatal disease for which there was no known cure. A visit to the hospital confirmed what he likely had feared: tuberculosis of the skin. Where and how he had caught the disease remains undetermined; heredity could have contributed to his vulnerability, as could have his workplace. One clue is that by the late nineteenth century European epidemiologists had linked the incidence of tuberculosis to certain industrial conditions. It was known, for instance, that fine dust particles prevalent in flax—the raw, organic material for rope—caused lung damage in rope-mill workers, and in turn predisposed them to tuberculosis. (As early as 1700, a pioneering Italian public health physician had posited a causal connection between flax processing and lung disease.*) If Joel was at risk in the dust-choked mill, though, he was also susceptible away from work, where the poverty of inadequate nutrition and poor sanitary conditions was reliably associated with "a tendency to higher tuberculosis rates," as a British public health researcher wrote early in the twentieth century.

As the disease progressed, it rendered Joel unable to work for extended periods, his sister Ester said. He underwent X-ray treatments at the Gävle hospital, to little apparent affect. (The treatments necessitated a large bandage on his right hand—his bow hand—which would have thwarted his violin-practice routine had he not simply and ingeniously attached the bow to the bandage and kept right on playing.) When he could work, it was sporadically, and he drifted from job to job, laboring as a machinist in a box factory and as a fireman, or stoker, at a wood refinery and in a bathhouse on the Gävle River at Stadsträdgården (City Park). But his condition worsened to the point that his local doctor referred him to a specialist in Stockholm, a dermatologist in the vanguard of an experimental "phototherapy" for skin diseases that used concentrated ultraviolet irradiation to stimulate damaged tissues.

Joel bought a one-way train ticket to Stockholm sometime in 1898. He rented a room in Gamla stan, Old Town Stockholm, and took odd jobs as he could, selling newspapers and such. (Old Town dated from the thirteenth century, and while it retained much of its medieval architecture, the six centuries since had been unkind: many structures were in advanced states of decay. And though Joel's room was literally in the shadow of the six-hundred-room royal palace, the neighborhood was unfit for a king; it was, in a word, a slum. Still, Old Town fit Joel's budget and his need: his room was a half mile south of his doctor's clinic.)

Two years of light treatment followed. Joel's letters home never mentioned it, but the light therapy was ineffective: the tuberculosis was spreading to his glands, the inside of his nose, and under his arms. Still, as ill and broke as he was—"hunger and cold" were not infrequent companions, Catharina later heard from P. E. Hedblom, an old Gävle Boys School classmate and friend of Joel's—the notes were darkly funny and exaggeratedly upbeat; they "sparkled with a love of life," Ester said.

On April 15, 1900, Royal Serafimer Hospital in Stockholm admitted

---

* The physician, Bernardini Ramazzini, wrote that "few indeed of these workmen grow old at this occupation," and that he knew of an entire family of flax workers who had "all died miserably worn down by consumption"—tuberculosis.

Joel for emergency surgery. He would remain there in postoperative therapy for six months. Within two weeks of the operation, Hedblom stopped by Serafimer at Catharina's request; he was passing through Stockholm to points south. What he witnessed startled him. "His entire head and arms were wrapped in bandages," Hedblom reported to Catharina, "so I saw only his eyes and mouth." He went on: "Before I left the hospital I asked the head nurse how Joel was doing." She replied that he was "full of tuberculosis in his entire body." Hedblom figured he had seen his lifelong friend for the final time. "I believed then that it was over for him."

Somehow, though, inexplicably, Joel recovered, and Serafimer Hospital discharged him on October 3, 1900. Four days later he turned twenty-one. Any celebration at home, though, was probably muted due to his mother's aching back. Catharina had suffered unrelieved and undiagnosed back pain for years, but like her husband after the train accident, and despite her children's pleas, she had steadfastly refused to see a

Hill at nineteen, about the time he developed a nearly fatal case of tuberculosis. (Courtesy Barrie Stavis)

doctor. "This will pass," she would say, or "That's what one gets when one is old." Yet the pain would not pass; it became unmanageable. At year's end, Catharina finally checked herself into the hospital. She was diagnosed with a fistula—an abnormal passage between organs—according to Ingvar Söderström's Swedish-language biography of Joe Hill. Though no more about her illness is known, the fistula could have developed from a tubercular abscess in her spine, a condition that would compress the spinal cord and thereby cause debilitating back pain. The condition was known medically as Pott's disease and commonly as consumption of the spine. Despite nine operations over the next thirteen months, Catharina never recovered. On January 17, 1902, at the age of fifty-seven, she gave "her body and soul to the Greatest Protector," as her obituary read.

THE SUMMER before Catharina died, Gävle hosted a large exposition celebrating "industry and handicraft." Held just north of the town square, the sprawling, two-month-long expo was at once an industrial trade show, an agricultural fair, an amusement park, and a gathering place for professional societies (of technicians and engineers), sports competitors (sailors, gymnasts, rowers, and shooters), popular organizations (shoemakers' and watchmakers' unions and the temperance society), and entertainers (sword swallowers, among others). The cover of the official expo program portrayed two men shaking hands: one a blacksmith clad in a full-length leather apron and holding a hammer; the other a farmer dressed up in a Swedish folk costume with axe in hand. In the background, centered between the men, a Swedish flag flew atop an ornate cupola. The image romanticized the country's economic past, evoking an agrarian paradise of independent, politically potent craftsmen and crofters united and insulated from the outside world. But the Industrial Revolution had long since reordered the kingdom's economy, altering forever the Swedish people's relationships to their land, their tools, and one another, redefining their place in the world. Though the century-straddling expo stole a last, nostalgia-tinted glance backward, it peered ahead as well: the theme of the 1901 Gävle exposition was "Faith in the Future."

Joel Hägglund had no faith and no future in Gävle. At the time of the expo, his birthplace must have seemed like a dystopian nightmare come alive. Gävle was where he had seen a horrific on-the-job accident and subsequent medical neglect kill his forty-one-year-old father; where his mother during that summer of 1901 lay on her hospital deathbed, worn down and wrung out like a piece of cloth through her *vevmangel*; and where he himself had caught an infectious, poverty-borne disease that had snapped the sinew of his youth and very nearly felled him. Only Catharina's lingering death kept Joel and his siblings at home, the family intact.

Since returning from Stockholm, Joel had hired on at the same large steam crane in the harbor where his brothers Paul and Ruben worked. Mainly, though, he rededicated himself to his music—practicing the violin and the piano, writing, composing, and attending concerts. He also began performing, playing piano occasionally in cafés around town. Most evenings, he and his older brothers could be found at the Workers' Federation house. (Efraim, who had moved across the country to Gothenburg in 1898, had returned temporarily, probably to help care for Catharina.) Joel studied English, painting, and music (composition and performance); Paul joined a quartet; and both Paul and Efraim sang in the chorus. Joel rarely missed an evening concert, according to Ruben Sjödin, a fellow member of the federation. And at least once, Joel himself performed on violin before the federation. Sjödin listened to Joel play "Death of Aase," a spare and somber opus composed by the Norwegian Edvard Grieg for *Peer Gynt*, by the Norwegian playwright Henrik Ibsen. Grieg's plaintive melody (as well as some elements of Ibsen's plot) evidently resonated with Joel. One Ibsen scholar interprets the melody as suggestive of a dying person's last gasps: "Slowly her life flames up and dies down . . . then a long, deep breath, and then the care is over."

Ibsen's Peer Gynt is a lost soul on a bleak, lifelong journey of misadventure. His story parallels Joe Hill's in places. Peer kidnaps his former lover, the bride of another man, on her wedding day. He becomes a fugitive, emerging in act 3 from his forest hideout for a deathbed farewell to Aase, his widowed and worn-out mother. Barely has she taken her last long, deep breath before Peer announces his impending departure. "Give my mother a decent burial," he tells a neighbor, Kari. "I'm going away from here."

"Are you going far?" Kari asks.

"To the sea."

"So far?"

"Yes," he replies, "and farther still."

WITH THEIR MOTHER DEAD and properly buried in January of 1902, the six Hägglund siblings had no compelling reason to stay in Gävle. They sold the house, divided the proceeds, and paired off or went their separate ways: Joel and Paul to the sea, and farther still, to America; Efraim back to Gothenburg; Judith to a teaching job in Högvålen, not far from the Norwegian border in northern Sweden, with Ester soon to follow; Ruben to Stockholm. One might guess that the idea of crossing the ocean first scratched Joel's imagination after his father died and during his days as an irreverent, indifferent student, and that he had developed full-blown America fever by the time he returned to Gävle from Stockholm. He had reached his majority, and as a grown man reflecting on his parents' sad fate, he must have asked himself what he could look forward to in Gävle other than a lifetime of grueling, dangerous work with nothing to show for it but ill health and little money. As for Paul, the choice to leave home might have been complicated. He was a husband and the father of a two-year-old son. And not only was Paul grieving the death of his mother; he was also bereft over another loss: that of his infant daughter Greta, not quite three months old, who had died in April. Six months later, he abandoned his wife and son, never to return.

IN AMERICA, the work might be as hard and unyielding as at home, but there an unskilled laborer stood a chance to prosper—or so one would gather from the propaganda copiously circulated throughout Sweden. And if not, well, it would be an adventure, something to see besides "the bed and the cupboard," in one emigrant's words. The leading circulators of material and men promoting the New World were transportation concerns, mainly European steamship companies and American railroads, both of which employed networks of agents in Swedish cities and subagents in the remotest hinterland as commissioned ticket sellers. (Besides passengers, the railroads were recruiting Swedish laborers, whose workhorse reputation preceded them. As James J. Hill, the baron of the Great Northern Railway, reportedly said, "Give me Swedes, snuff and whiskey, and I'll build a railroad to hell!") Individual American states also trolled for immigrants. Copies of pamphlets such as *Minnesota, Its Advantages to Settlers* were distributed by the tens of thousands. Nor was Minnesota, rich in farmland but scarce in population, the only such state in the upper Midwest to dispatch prosperous Swedish émigrés to beckon their former countrymen to come and gape for themselves at the economic rainbow in the big Midwestern sky. And there were the jolly and prideful letters emigrants sent home—letters omitting misgivings about leaving Sweden and descriptions of hardships in America. Those letters, as H. Arnold Barton, a historian of Swedish

America, chronicles, "were eagerly received, read aloud at every opportunity, passed from hand to hand, copied and recopied, and not infre-
quently printed in local newspapers." Said one wistful emigrant of the
deceptively cheery correspondence, "There are many who are blinded
by that and in that way many have been lured . . . I speak from my own
experience."

PROBABLY IN THE SECOND WEEK of October 1902, Joel and Paul bid
farewell to family and friends in Gävle, and to the home where they had
studied Scripture and sung harmony with their parents, and where, too,
they had endured heartache and hunger, humiliation and illness. They
traveled by train to Gothenburg, where they said good-bye to Efraim,
who saw them off on the well-worn path to America. (In 1902 alone,
thirty-three thousand Swedes immigrated to the United States, a majority of whom embarked from Gothenburg.) Paul and Joel last saw their
homeland from aboard a Wilson liner steaming across the North Sea.
The steamer was headed to the port of Hull, on the east coast of England,
the primary transfer point for Scandinavian emigrants. In Hull, they
waited in the train station (in a waiting room built especially to accommodate the masses of Scandinavian through-travelers) for transport to
the west-coast port of Liverpool, a terminus for transatlantic traffic.

Joel, seated, Paul, left, and Efraim, right, in the port city of Gothenburg in October 1902,
shortly before Joel and Paul left for America. (Courtesy Rolf Hägglund)

On October 18, 1902, they embarked on the *Saxonia*, the queen of the Cunard Line. (It was then the largest, latest model of the Cunard fleet, spanning six hundred feet in length and accommodating nearly two thousand passengers; its maiden crossing had been two years earlier.)

The sale of the family house had unmoored Joel and Paul from everything and everyone they knew. It had afforded them transatlantic passage, a ten-day refuge between the known and the unknown, between what had been and what would be. After the voyage, after they passed through the portals of New York Harbor into the confounding and wondrous New World, the brothers wandered together for at least one hard year. As Paul wrote to his sisters, he and Joel lived "a dog's life" that first year in America. Soon thereafter, the brothers' paths diverged. Joel's transformation from Swedish wage slave to Swedish American wage slave occasioned snipping his given name to Joe and changing his family name to Hillstrom. Paul, too, changed his surname, to Hedlund. He married an American, Lucile White (although he never divorced his Swedish wife). They settled in Lucile's hometown of Albion, in northwesternmost Pennsylvania near the shores of Lake Erie. Paul and Lucile had a son, Wells, and Paul found a job on the Bessemer and Lake Erie Railroad—the line of work he had first entered at the age of twelve. Later in life he worked as a night watchman at an industrial-trailer manufacturing company. He was still working in 1955, at the age of seventy-seven, when he fell on the job, fractured his skull, and died. It is not known whether Paul and Joe saw one another in the dozen years after they split up in America. Paul may never have left Albion; his grandchildren, who were young when he died, told me they knew of no extended trips.

As for Joe, he never stayed put very long. He tramped across the continent, ever searching for work, of course, but also for something more: for his place in the world, a new home, an identity, a mooring. In time, in the Wobblies, he would find what he was looking for.

6.

"Hallelujah, I'm a Bum!"

If the ten-day passage was arduous, Joel and Paul did not let on. "Coming to America tomorrow after the nicest crossing you can imagine," the brothers Hägglund wrote in Swedish to Efraim in Gothenburg the day before the *Saxonia* steamed into New York Harbor. "The finest Atlantic crossing you can imagine," they repeated. "Singing, music, strolls and food, and food and strolls and music and singing all day long." Joel and, apparently, Paul were nothing if not jesters. And Efraim would hardly have had to read between the storm-tossed lines to discern the flippancy therein. "Suddenly, while lounging around with some nice English and American women, it's Ulrik right and Ulrik left and that is really funny.* Even if the waves are no bigger than in a bigger washbowl." After further seasickness discourse and a promise to write again in two weeks, Paul's postscript noted that he and Joel would "perform at a . . . concert aboard this barge. Duet for violin and piano."

Adopting his first pseudonym, Joel took the last word: "I agree with former speaker on all counts. Your brother, James Browning, New York."

He might as well have been James Browning. Besides Paul, nobody in the New World knew him as Joel Hägglund—or knew him, period. He had no identity, no voice, no community in which he was known and which was known to him. In the tumult of America, in its raw, unsettled economy, in its roiling, chaotic cities, and in the vast, newly industrializing West, he was an interchangeable commodity: another immigrant whose speech was clumsy, whose job skills were limited, whose education

---

* *Ulrik* is Scandinavian slang for "vomit."

was meager, but whose able body could dig or saw or thresh or pick from dawn to dark. And when that body could no longer, or would no longer, do the work, another would always be waiting in line. Soon enough he would pick a new name, one easier on the American tongue, and gradually, over the course of a decade spent adrift in the labor camps and on the long wharves and in the hobo jungles of the West, he would perfect his language skills, shed his anonymity, and find his voice—a voice that in time would deepen into a pitch-perfect instrument of the dispossessed.

The letter Joel and Paul sent Efraim was dated October 27, 1902. A day later, the brothers descended the *Saxonia*'s steep, wooden gangplank and soon disappeared into the racket and roar of New York. They spent their first night in the city at the Swedish Lutheran Home for Immigrants, at 5 Water Street, a four-story brick building a short walk from the docks. (It was common for enterprising lodging agents to meet arriving countrymen at the dock and steer them to their establishments.) How long the brothers remained there and where they went next are questions to which no answers have been found. Indeed, regarding the time span between the day Joel Hägglund regained his land legs in New York and the night a dozen years later when, as Joe Hill, he staggered into a doctor's office in Salt Lake City with a gunshot wound, the rumors of his whereabouts are plentiful, the verifiable facts scattered across the continent like a century-old trail of crumbs.

There are snapshots of Joe Hill's early years in America—his published essays, poems, letters, and cartoons; postcards he wrote, illustrated, and sent to family and friends; recollections of others in private and published correspondence; and most important, his songs. But the images are fleeting and blurry; there are few details as to his likeness. He was a moving target, and in that regard he was like hundreds of thousands of unskilled immigrants. His was an itinerant, uncertain life, the only constant the hunt for another job, a meal, a bed, a toehold in industrializing America. It is said that between the fall of 1902 and the spring of 1906 he swept the floors of Bowery bars; he consorted with the radical writer John Reed in Philadelphia; he tried to organize a union in a Chicago machine shop and for his efforts was fired and blacklisted in that city before winding his way out West; he stacked wheat in North Dakota; he worked in Colorado mines and on Wyoming ranches and on the railroad in Nevada and in orchards in California. Some or all of those yarns could be true—most were spun by a single source, a drunken Swedish sailor who claimed to be a cousin of Hill's named John Holland (which conceivably could have been Paul's nom de saloon)

Industrial Worker, April 23, 1910.

and who late one night in a Cleveland bar regaled a rapt IWW editor, who took it all down "word by word and drink by drink."

Whenever Hill did finally head westward, he would have admired the propaganda skills of the promoters for the states and railroads and steamship companies that lured unsuspecting immigrants to the region with promises of plenty. Instead, what he and hundreds of thousands of other newcomers found was the underside of the American dream: exploitative and dangerous living and working conditions; seasonal and cyclical unemployment that kept workers on the road, in debt, disenfranchised, and uneducated. And yet those appalling circumstances ignited in some of those workers a fighting spirit and fostered a sense of class solidarity that eventually led to the founding of the Industrial Workers of the World. And just as the IWW tapped into the anger and frustration of Western workers, turned mass alienation into mass organization, Joe Hill tapped into the IWW. His songs gave voice to the voiceless, himself included; he helped as much as anyone to weld together those Western workstiffs and bindlebums, helped them see the forces they were up against—and what they could do to overcome them. And as he helped craft the image of the IWW, he crafted his own identity, too. It obviously cannot be said who Joel Hägglund would have become without the IWW—only that he would not have become "Joe Hill."

* * *

OF HILL'S FIRST FEW YEARS in America, all that can be confirmed is that in December of 1905 he mailed a Christmas card from Cleveland to his sisters in Högvålen, Sweden, and that the following April, he and a former classmate at Gävle Boys School happened to be in San Francisco during the great earthquake and fire. The source, for once, is authoritative: Hill himself, whose first known published work is a vivid, first-person account of the quake. The story appeared in Hill's hometown daily, *Gefle Dägblad*, under the headline THE CATASTROPHE IN SAN FRANCISCO—A RESIDENT OF GÄVLE TELLS THE STORY.

The article warrants our attention. It is telling that he wrote it at all—that he figured he had something noteworthy to say to the folks back home. At twenty-six, he had been absent from Gävle for almost four years, yet felt connected—and prideful—enough that he wanted people to know he had been present and accounted for during a historic event in America. His prose is clear and harrowing but, true to his later style, leavened with humor and laced with political commentary. It captures Hill at a number of transitional moments: between life and what he thought was imminent death, when he found comfort in singing an old Sunday school hymn; between his period as an anonymous hobo and his immersion in the IWW; between writing in his native tongue and becoming adept in the English language; and between being capable of writing a crass, intolerant remark and, as a Wobbly, discovering his voice and passion for social justice and equality. The article is also of note for Hill's already jaded view of law enforcement. Apparently he had seen and suffered enough police misconduct during his hobo years to recognize that not only was he lucky to survive the quake but he was also fortunate to live through a subsequent shakedown attempt by a corrupt San Francisco officer.

An editor's note introduced the piece: "From a former resident of Gävle, Joel Hägglund, who was present at the terrible catastrophe in San Francisco, we received a letter [that] . . . gives you some idea of what they had to go through there. He writes among other things:"

> I woke up on the morning of Wednesday, April 18, at 5:13 by being thrown out of bed. I stood up by grabbing the door handle which I got hold of by accident, and after opening the door, I managed to reach the stairway after much scuffling. How I managed to get down the stairs I can't really tell, but I went fast. I had come halfway down the third and last flight and began to hope I would

make it, when suddenly the stairway fell in and I fell straight through the floor down into the basement.

I thought that my last moment had come, so I tried to recite one of the old hymns I had learned in Sunday School in Gävle. Then I closed my eyes and waited for my fate.

But then the shakings became weaker and weaker and finally they were completely still. I was pinned between some boards, but managed after some effort to get loose. I moved my arms and legs and found them still working. With the exception of some bruises on my right side and arm, I was completely unhurt. I heard voices and shouts and crept up until I saw a hole large enough for a man to crawl through. In a moment I was out in the street only to meet a sight still worse than was in the basement.

A large six story house on the other side of the street was flat as a pancake on the ground, and men, women and children were running around in complete disorder. Some had some clothing on, some had not more on than a newborn child, and to tell the truth, I wouldn't have taken a walk on main street in the suit I was wearing.

I got hold of a pair of trousers which fit me about as well as a pair of Swedish soldier's pants, and I went up to an opening where I had a good view of the city. It was a terrible sight to see the large houses, some in ruins, some similar to the leaning tower of Pisa. The ground was full of cracks, some nearly three feet wide, and here and there a dark smoke pillar came out of the ruins, which was the first indication of the terrible fire that later hit San Francisco. It didn't take long before red flames were seen in several places and as all the water pipes had broken and not a drop of water could be had, these spread with terrible speed and the city was changed within a few hours into one single lake of fire.

I saw many moving and heart rending scenes. Half-naked women carrying small children were driven from their homes. Some refused to leave their old homes, and were seized and bound to keep them from going back into the flames. So-called "martial law" was proclaimed immediately—that means momentary death for the least criminal act or disobedience. Two soldiers came and gave me an axe and put a large steel hat on me, and before I knew what it was all about, I was employed as a fireman in the San Francisco Fire Department. I worked for thirty-six hours without food or drink before I was released. My work consisted of helping old people

from the fire, carrying out sick from the hospitals, saving valu-
ables, etc. The officer who released me first wrote down my name,
then he looked into my pockets for loot. If he had found any, I
would have received an extra buttonhole in the vest for all my
work and would probably have never written this letter.

Many tried to make money on this calamity and charge sense-
lessly for food. A grocer who sold crackers, small cookies about ⅕ of
a cent piece, for ten cents apiece and eggs for two dollars a dozen
made money by the barrels. But then the police were told. They
came and gave away all he had to the people outside. Then they
brought him out into the street, bound him to a pole and placed a
sign over his head with the following inscription: THE MAN WHO
SOLD CRACKERS FOR TEN CENTS APIECE. SPIT ON HIM. All those
who passed spit on him, and I couldn't resist the temptation to go
forward and aim at his very long nose. It is hardly necessary here to
say that he was a Jew.

My companion, Oscar Westergren, a well known person from
Gävle, I have not seen since the day before the earthquake. I know
not whether he is dead or alive, but I am hoping for the best. He
may have received some kind of "forced labor."

The fire is not out everywhere and the formerly rich San Francisco
is now only a smoking ruin. About a hundred frame houses are all
that is left of the "Proud Queen on the Shores of the Pacific Ocean."*

Oscar Westergren was not Hill's only boyhood friend in San Francisco. Shortly before the quake, Hill bumped into another classmate
from Gävle, Karl Rudberg. He was a seaman who no longer wished to be
one: he had jumped ship in the San Francisco harbor and swum ashore
with no money, only the clothes on his back and a pair of shoes strung
around his neck. The shoes sank, leaving Rudberg trudging barefoot up
Market Street when who should come along but his old friend Joel
Hägglund, as Rudberg knew him. Lucky for Rudberg, his friend Joel
knew his way around the city and seemed to have some connections.
"Come with me," Hill told Rudberg, taking him to the Sailors' Union
Hall, on the waterfront at Mission and East streets. "I'll get you some
shoes."

---

* His Swedish biographer, Ture Nerman, first reprinted the letter in his 1951 book
Arbetarsångaren Joe Hill, mördare eller martyr? (Folksinger Joe Hill, murderer or martyr?).
An English translation, which I relied on, appears in Gibbs M. Smith's 1969 book *Joe Hill*.

With San Francisco a smoking ruin, Hill and Rudberg rode the rails north to Portland, Oregon. Along the way, they earned meal money by betting some railroad workers that they could hoist a water tank onto a water tower. The railroad men hadn't been able to do it, but the Gävle boys succeeded by dousing the pulley rope with water, a trick that evidently facilitated the hoist, and that Hill had probably learned on his very first job—at the Gävle rope factory. It is likely the pair found work in Portland, probably on the docks. There was "exceptional demand for labor of all kinds," an IWW pamphleteer wrote. By early 1907, the union had organized its first Portland local, No. 92. On March 1, the local led twenty-five hundred sawmill workers out on strike, idling the city's four largest mills. They struck for a nine-hour day and a seventy-five-cent wage increase, to two dollars and fifty cents a day. Within a week, workers in most of the smaller mills had joined the strike; those who had yet to were visited by delegations of strikers. According to the *Oregonian* newspaper, one such delegation of two hundred Wobblies induced forty-seven workers on the night shift at one mill to leave the yards on the spot. "A procession was formed and the new recruits were marched to the union headquarters . . . where they signed the membership roll of the Industrial Workers of the World."

Joe Hill was one of the IWW's new recruits. It is not known when he joined Local 92—there are no membership records extant—or where in Portland he was working at the time. It is plausible that he was among the longshoremen who responded during the strike to the IWW's city-wide appeal for solidarity. Regardless, it is evident from his first article for the union's Western weekly, the *Industrial Worker*, that he took out a red card in Portland. The 1910 story carried the byline JOE HILL, PORT-LAND LOCAL, NO. 92.

The sawmill strike lasted forty days, during which the union opened a free employment agency and soup kitchen for striking workers. Although most of the strikers did not return to the mills—the union said it placed them in other jobs—the IWW claimed victory. It said that the mill owners were "forced indirectly to raise wages and improve conditions." An IWW historian observed that the strike marked the union's "first west coast progress." And an admiring story in the *Oregon Sunday Journal* hailed the strike as emblematic of "a new and strange form of unionism which is taking root in every section of the United States, especially in the West." The author went on: "The suddenness of the strike and the completeness of the tie-up are things quite unprecedented in this part of the country . . . Wherever the Industrial Workers of the

World are organized they can paralyze industry at almost the snap of a finger. It is the way they work."*

THE STRIKE OCCURRED during a boom-and-bust period for the IWW. At its third annual convention, in September of 1907, the union boasted that during the previous twelve months it had chartered 118 locals, and that there were 200 locals in all. Concurrently, however, the union had suffered a tremendous net loss of dues payers: the entire Mining Department, composed of twenty-seven thousand members of the Western Federation of Miners, had seceded that spring. And within a few weeks of the convention, the enormity of that setback was dwarfed by worse news: a nationwide economic depression that came to be known as the Panic of 1907. Mass layoffs and wage cuts were rampant, and while all unions suffered, the IWW and its predominantly unskilled membership were probably hit hardest. "The IWW was nearly wiped out of existence," Paul Brissenden, a professor of economics at Columbia University, writes in his 1919 book *The IWW: A Study of American Syndicalism*, the first scholarly account of the IWW. Brissenden cites an IWW article reporting that "locals dissolved by the dozens and the general headquarters at Chicago was only maintained by terrific sacrifice and determination."

The panic was triggered in part by an economic chain reaction set off by the San Francisco earthquake, which led to a tightening of credit and capital on Wall Street. But the immediate precipitating event was another disaster out West, albeit an unnatural one: a war of Montana copper kings. In October, one of them, a Brooklyn-born speculator named Fritz Augustus Heinze, tried and failed to corner the copper market. The scheme led to a run on banks he owned in Montana and New York, and ultimately on practically all financial institutions in New York.

Working conditions were harsh, and made harsher by the Panic. As production orders dwindled nationally, the extractive industries of the West—on which most Wobblies depended for their meager livelihoods—lengthened the workday and cut wages, either because they believed they had to or because the financial crisis provided convenient cover for doing so. The owners of a logging camp in Idaho fired the entire

---

* The author of the story, John Kenneth Turner, went on, in 1910, to publish *Barbarous Mexico*, his muckraking classic about oppression under the dictatorial rule of Mexican president Porfirio Díaz.

workforce—and promptly rehired those who capitulated at a lower wage scale and charged them more for board, the *Spokesman-Review* of Spokane, Washington, reported, adding that there were plenty of men available to "take the places of those who decline to work under the new schedule." Living conditions compounded the misery. Farmworkers slept in barns or open fields; loggers, in crude bunkhouses; construction crews and miners, in tent camps. Nutritious food was scarce, vermin abundant. "In many camps," a magazine journalist reported, "the men are engaged in a perpetual warfare against lice."

As damnable as conditions were in the camps and fields, many migratory workers had no job at all once the Panic set in. Virtually overnight, the lumber camps of the Northwest emptied. Thousand of loggers who needed to earn a "stake"—money enough to tide them over in town during the idle winter months—were instead drafted into "a penniless and homeless army," a Wobbly later wrote. Most had been paid off in "scrip paper," legal tender at the lumber camp that no outside merchant or bank would accept without a nearly 50 percent surcharge. One man complained that it cost him eight dollars to cash his paycheck of seventeen dollars and fifty cents. Others said they could not sell their checks at any price. While IWW halls were desolate—the Seattle branch fell to only sixty-eight members in 1908 from a peak in 1907 of eight hundred—the roads, a Wobbly recalled, "were black with jobless men."

The Panic had touched down like a twister, demolishing most signs of the IWW's progress in the West. Still in its infancy, it is a wonder the union survived. Bill Haywood had chaired its founding convention only two summers earlier. But Haywood had since spent eighteen months in prison on a charge of conspiring to murder a former governor of Idaho. (He was acquitted in July of 1907.) And Haywood's original union, the once-radical Western Federation of Miners, for which he had served as secretary-treasurer and which had merged with the IWW at the latter's founding convention, had, in Haywood's absence and with new leadership, grown conservative and increasingly hostile to the IWW's revolutionary ideology and rhetoric.* In May of 1907, the WFM pulled out of the union it had helped create. The split left the IWW with no more than ten thousand dues-paying members, half of whom shuttled

---

* Another ruinous internal dispute involved the Socialist Labor Party (as opposed to the Socialist Party) theorist Daniel DeLeon, who split from the One Big Union only to start his own Detroit-based IWW. DeLeon disagreed with the original IWW's use of direct action and disdain for political action.

in and out of the union and perhaps were counted twice, Melvyn Dubofsky observed in his 1969 book *We Shall Be All*, the authoritative volume of IWW history.

With its local unions shrinking (or disappearing altogether), and with the WFM's defection, by the close of 1907 the IWW's dues income had shriveled to almost nothing. The loss of revenue was so severe that the general executive board laid off the union's field organizers. The organizers were told to fund themselves through the commissioned sale of union literature. But even *that* was hard to come by: as the printing bills piled up, the *Industrial Union Bulletin*, the IWW's weekly newsletter, became a biweekly.

THE FINANCIAL PANIC helped heighten labor tensions in the West to the flash point, and no Western city was more combustible than Spokane. Spokane was the "Hub of the Inland Empire," an expansive region that included eastern Washington and portions of bordering Oregon and Idaho as well as Montana and southern British Columbia. From 1900 to 1910, the city's population would nearly triple, to just over a hundred thousand. Its growth coincided with its emergence as a railroad center—regional freight lines and half a dozen transcontinental routes crisscrossed the city. Spokane itself had little industry; it was primarily a financial and distribution center for the natural resources wrested from the fertile hinterland. And Spokane was a distribution center for those who did the wresting—the harvest stiffs, pick-and-shovel artists, and lumberjacks who comprised the large, rootless army of migratory workers known as "floaters."

The IWW was a forceful presence in Spokane—or had been, prior to the Panic. Its local hall, like the one in Seattle, was moribund in early 1908, as dilapidated as the skid road flophouses that surrounded it. Then in February or March, John "Jack" H. Walsh, a national organizer down from Alaska, arrived on the scene. Vowing to rebuild the membership and to move the branch headquarters into a "more commodious hall" (complete with library, baggage room, and employment office), Walsh took to the soapbox with a fervor and at a volume unheard on the streets of Spokane since the Panic had paralyzed all Wobbly movement. He was signaling to workers and city officials alike that the IWW was coming back, and that it was spoiling for a fight. Walsh and the union wanted to take on every floater's worst adversary: predatory employment agencies, or "labor sharks," as the IWW called them. The sharks fed on job-placement fees from migratory workers in exchange for nonexistent jobs, often in collusion with employers. Spokane was rife with such outfits, as were other centers of Western commerce and industry. The Wobblies' decision to go up against the agencies and the city (which sanctioned the agencies' conduct and banned IWW street meetings) would turn out to be not so much a test case for free speech as a test conflagration—the first of several in the West over the next few years. In Spokane, as elsewhere, the IWW struck the match, but the city supplied the kindling and the kerosene. And Joe Hill, who fanned his first musical flames in Spokane, would go on to set tuneful blazes of discontent all across the country.

THERE WERE THIRTY-ONE private employment agencies on Stevens Street, the heart of Spokane's "slave market." In return for a fee of two or three dollars, sometimes more, an agency assigned a floater to a job at an employer somewhere in the far-flung Inland Empire. The problem for floaters was that a job promised and paid for was often nothing more than a fraudulent enticement—a means of separating a floater from the few dollars he had saved to buy a job. Legion were the stories of workers who paid their way to a distant job site where they might work for only a day or a week or a month. A Wobbly named Herb Edwards recalled hanging around all winter in Spokane waiting for the sharks to reopen their doors. (Much of the work was seasonal.) "We jungled up in the flops to wait for something to open up when the weather broke," Edwards said. "You'd burn up your road stake getting, booming over to the job, and then you'd be on the job thirty days, for a month, get paid and laid off." Or, worse yet, a stiff would arrive at an isolated camp, having fed the shark his last dollar, only to learn that there was no job at all. The *Industrial Worker* reported, "If an employment shark gets an order for thirty men he will often hang out a sign: 'WANTED. 300 MEN.'" Or if there was a job, the shark had misleadingly described it. "Not one in fifty who ships out from an employment office ever gets the job he paid for," the paper noted.

The inexhaustible labor supply allowed a foreman, or "straw boss," to keep the hours long and the wages low, and to weed his camp of any rabble who would rouse the workers to organize. And the harsh conditions ensured rapid employee turnover, a pleasing situation for the many employers in the Inland Empire who helped themselves to a "rake-off"—a cut—of one-third of the fees paid by new hires to employment agencies. The cycle went like this: the more men hired, the more fees generated; the more men fired, the more hired. And so on. And although employment agents were known to be slapdash bookkeepers—their records "are not merely inadequate; they are a joke," noted an academic observer of hobo life—Wobblies nevertheless credited the sharks for proving the mathematical theorem of "perpetual motion": "You got one guy going to the job, one on the job, and one coming back to town," Herb Edwards explained it.

The guy coming back to Spokane invariably wound up talking to Jack Walsh at the IWW hall. The *Industrial Worker* reported that no fewer than a dozen men in a day and sometimes as many as fifty would come by the hall to complain that they had been "robbed" and to ask the union to recover their money. It would have been futile and counterproductive for the Spokane branch to take on individual cases of fraud; in 1908, one Spokane agency alone, Peerless, sold *eighty thousand* jobs—whether "real or imaginary," as the *Industrial Worker* dryly noted. Nor was it fruitful to appeal to the Spokane authorities to prosecute. Although there had been a city ordinance barring employment agents from making "willful misrepresentations to any person seeking employment and charging a fee for such employment," in March of 1908 a superior court judge had abolished the ordinance. The judge held that the city had no regulatory authority over employment agencies because the industry did not "affect the public health" or "disturb the good order" of Spokane. Furthermore and to the contrary, the court embraced the industry as "beneficial and necessary." "By finding work for the unemployed," the judge opined, "it aids in removing idleness, which is productive of disease and disorder."

ALLIED WITH THE LABOR SHARKS and the legal establishment against the IWW was the Salvation Army. Walsh and his fellow soapboxers had been crowding out the Army, whose own street preachers sought to save the same beaten-down workers' souls. But on Stevens Street in Spokane, as on other Western cities' skid roads, the Salvation Army had an attention-commanding advantage over the IWW and the many other groups— Socialists, currency reformers, diet faddists, single taxers, suffragists, and so forth—that would claim the open air to propagandize. The Army had its loud and smartly uniformed brass band.

In the weeks after the court had upheld the employment agencies' fraudulent practices, Walsh had taken to verbally shaking the mackinaw lapels of the two thousand or so floaters who assembled nightly on Stevens Street, urging them to "wake up" and refuse "to permit organized monopoly to grind you under its heel." Occasionally, a plant from an employment agency would heckle him:

"Mr. Speaker, when and where did you last do any work?"

"Why," Walsh would reply, "I'm working now. Trying to show these workers what suckers they are to buy jobs from robbers like you." Walsh would then invite his antagonist to take the soapbox to make his case.

"Come on now," he would say, "and defend yourself. These men won't hurt you—although they have good cause to give you your lumps. They'll listen to you with attention, for they believe in free speech, even for robbers like you. They want to hear your defense of your evil practices. Come on, hop up here and let's have your story."

The ease and polish with which Walsh dispensed with his hecklers—none accepted his dare—demanded of his foes a more aggressive tack. One April night as he was soapboxing, the Salvation Army struck up its band, inflicting its tambourines and trumpets and bass drum on the proceedings. The "band's noise triumphed" in the telling of the next day's *Spokesman-Review*, and Walsh's "eagerly listening assemblage" metamorphosed into a "mob." It took the night platoon of twenty police officers in concert with the afternoon squad to "bear down" on the mob and restore order.

TO WALSH, the Salvation Army's musical blitz was maddening, but it was also a call to arms—and a revelation: he got the bright idea to give the Army some competition by forming an IWW band. Richard Brazier, a Canadian-born miner who would later serve on the general executive board of the union, recalled Walsh's declaration:

> We have as many tunes and songs as they have hymns; and while we may borrow a hymn tune from them, we will use our own words. If they do not quiet down a little we will add some bagpipes to the band, and that will quiet them. We do not object to religious bodies, as such, but when they try to hog the streets for their own use we do object—and most vigorously so.

Out of the idea for the band came the idea for a book of IWW songs. As Walsh envisioned it, the book would have a distinctive red cover adorned with the union label: "Industrial Workers of the World" encircling the northern half of the globe and the initials I-W-W interspersed with three stars, one each for Emancipation, Education, and Organization. Brazier later distilled Walsh's guidelines for the songs that would comprise what would come to be titled, simply, *The Little Red Songbook*:

> We will have songs of anger and protest, songs which shall call to judgment our oppressors and the Profit System they have devised. Songs of battles won (but never any songs of despair), songs that hold up flaunted wealth and thread-bare morality to scorn, songs that lampoon our masters and the parasitic vermin, such as the employment-sharks and their kind, who bedevil the workers. These songs will deal with every aspect of the workers' lives. They will bring hope to them, and courage to wage the good fight. They will be songs sowing the seeds of discontent and rebellion. We want our songs to stir the workers into action, to awaken them from an apathy and complacency that has made them accept their servitude as though it had been divinely ordained. We are sure that the power of song will exalt the spirit of Rebellion.

Brazier himself was one of the first Wobblies to take up Walsh's challenge to write topical lyrics to familiar tunes. Unsurprisingly, one of his earliest efforts, "Good-Bye Dollars; I Must Leave You," describes a floater's encounter with a shark. The song parodies "Good-Bye Dolly Gray," a tune written in 1900 about a soldier leaving his sweetheart for the battlefield. This is Brazier's chorus:

> *Good-bye dollars; I must leave you,*
> *For a job with you I've got to buy.*
> *Something tells me I will need you.*
> *When I'm hungry and get dry.*
> *Hark, the employment shark is bawling,*
> *For that job he wants his pay.*
> *Soon to the boss I will be crawling.*
> *To make wealth for him each day.*

The shark gets the best of Brazier's working stiff in that song, but in a subsequent number, the character is determined to settle the score—violently, if necessary. In "I'll Remember You," Brazier's stiff buys his job, pays his way out to the camp, and works "hard for a day or two" before he is fired and has to "beat his way back into town." He then buys a piece of pipe from a plumber and lies in wait.

> *I remember you, I remember you;*
> *Mr. Shark, you grafter;*
> *You're the feller I am after,*
> *For I mean to comb your hair with this piece of pipe.*
> *Oh I remember you, and you'll remember me.*
> *See the shark to me is walking,*
> *Soon this gaspipe will be talking,*
> *Then he'll remember me.*

BY THE TIME of Jack Walsh's brainstorm in mid-April of 1908, Joe Hill had arrived in Spokane. It is not known if Hill had come directly from Portland, or how long he had been in Spokane, or how long he stayed, or why he had come. (One possible reason is that he had met the charismatic Walsh in Portland, where Walsh had organized after coming to the States from Alaska and before his Spokane assignment.) But it is known that Hill, like Dick Brazier, was one of a handful of Wobblies who were responsible for the IWW's first foray into musical parody, and to whom Walsh referred when he wrote, in the *Industrial Union Bulletin*, of the "idle men . . . around the headquarters [who] have little to do but study the question, compose poetry and word up songs for old tunes."

Walsh did not take credit for the idea to pluck the tunes from the Christian hymnal of their street corner rival. (And indeed, it may not have been his idea alone; Hill, after all, had concocted his own parodies of the Swedish Salvation Army *psalmbok* a decade or so earlier.) As the IWW in-house historian and editor, Fred Thompson, heard it from a Spokane soapboxer named Pat Carmody, "some of the boys cooked up the idea of making parodies to the favorite Salvation Army songs, making copies of them, and singing them to the Salvation Army music."

Though Walsh's article mentioned no songwriters by name, both Carmody and Charles L. Anderson, another Wobbly who was in Spokane at the time, remembered Hill's contributions. In a 1947 letter, Anderson said that Hill had been among the "group of fellow workers sitting around the table on the speakers' platform, making songs." Anderson said he had been introduced to Hill by James Wilson, who in 1909 would become the first editor of the Spokane-based *Industrial Worker*. Anderson, a Swede, said that Wilson had introduced Hill to him as a "clear-thinking" countryman—meaning, Anderson explained, that Hill was clear on the day's "hotly-debated" political issues.

Carmody recalled that he, Walsh, Wilson, and Hill had jointly written three songs: "Hellelujah (I'm a Bum)" (later changed to "Hallelujah"), "My Wandering Boy," and "Long Haired Preachers."* Carmody remembered typing the songs himself with as many sheets of carbon paper as he could roll under the carriage of an old Oliver typewriter, and that the same night, they "used them effectively when the SA [Salvation Army] music interfered with the IWW meeting."

That summer of 1908, Walsh took the songs on the road. With musicians from Spokane and Portland, he formed a twenty-piece traveling band of "pesky go-abouts," dubbed it the Industrial Union Singing Club, and dressed the members in blue denim overalls and (in a sartorial nod to the IWW's colors) black shirts and scarlet ties. Walsh's "Overalls Brigade," as it became known, traveled by boxcar—the "Red Special"—from the Pacific Northwest to Chicago for the IWW's fourth annual convention, in late September. In towns and cities along the way, the brigade sang, beat the drum, and passed the hat for industrial unionism. To finance the tour, at every stop they peddled Wobbly propaganda and, for ten cents, a red "songcard" with the lyrics to the numbers the "boys" in Spokane had "cooked up." In a dispatch from Missoula, Montana, Walsh said that the brigade "packed the streets from one side to the other" and that the songcards "sold like hotcakes." One of the songs, "Hallelujah (I'm a Bum)," set to the gospel hymn "Revive Us Again," became the brigade's theme song.†

> *O, why don't you work*
> *As other men do?*
> *How in hell can I work*
> *When there's no work to do?*

---

* Carmody was almost certainly mistaken about the genesis of "Long Haired Preachers" (the original title of Hill's "The Preacher and the Slave"). It was not published in *The Little Red Songbook* until its fourth edition, in 1911 (and when it was, curiously enough, it was credited to one F. B. Brechler). In all later editions, the song was attributed to Hill.
† Scholars disagree as to who wrote "Hallelujah" and when. For a brief summary of the arguments, see the endnotes.

CHORUS
Hallelujah, I'm a bum!
Hallelujah, bum again!
Hallelujah, give us a handout—
To revive us again.

O, why don't you save
All the money you earn?
If I did not eat,
I'd have money to burn!

O, I like my boss
He's a good friend of mine.
That's why I am starving
Out in the breul-line.

I can't buy a job
For I ain't got the dough;
So I ride in a boxcar,
For I'm a hobo.

Whenever I get
All the money I earn,
The boss will be broke,
And to work he must turn!

CHORUS
Hallelujah, I'm a bum!
Hallelujah, bum again!
Hallelujah, give us a handout—
To revive us again.

NOT LONG AFTER Jack Walsh returned to Spokane in the fall of 1908, the IWW hoisted a DON'T BUY JOBS banner. The economy in the Pacific Northwest was reviving again, or at least a floater new in town might have thought so from seeing all the stiffs on Stevens Street crowded around the chalkboards filled with job postings outside employment agency offices. But the IWW called for workers to boycott the agencies;

its objective was to abolish the job-shark system and replace it with a union-operated hiring hall.

Walsh took the fight to Stevens Street, directly in front of the storefronts of the most egregious sharks. He and other soapboxers drew large, appreciative crowds: thousands of hungry, homeless, jobless, and angry workers, many of whom asserted that they had been robbed of their last dollar for a nonexistent job. These were not mere protest demonstrations. The soapboxers named names, and not only names but specifics of the sharks' shady practices: who had been fleeced, for how much, and when and where the crimes had taken place.

The street meetings were a form of direct action—the IWW's all-purpose term for organized agitation. The *Industrial Worker* once defined direct action as "any effort made directly for getting more of the goods from the boss." The *Worker*'s Eastern counterpart, *Solidarity*, explained it as "dealing directly with the boss through your labor union," adding, "The strike in its different forms, is the best known example of direct action."*

Around Spokane, though, strikes were generally out of the question; the IWW had no means to organize workplaces scattered about parts of four states and southern British Columbia. But the Wobblies were masters of improvisation. "We learn to fight by *fighting*," wrote one pamphleteer. Another emphasized the need to precisely aim their blows: "to hit the employer in his vital spot, his heart and soul, or in other words his pocketbook."

The Don't Buy Jobs campaign was beginning to hit the employment agencies where it counted, and the sharks fought back. They organized the Associated Agencies of Spokane, and in December of 1908 the group convinced the city council to ban street meetings downtown. The *Industrial Worker* took the ordinance as a hopeful sign. "All this shows the shoe is beginning to pinch," it wrote, adding that there was much work to be done. "If we are to control the outside jobs and force better conditions—something besides lousy tents and bunk-houses and swill-house grub, we must get busy!"

The campaign breathed new life into the Spokane IWW. More than a thousand members joined within a few months—many, like Dick Brazier, drawn by the music. "What first attracted me to the IWW was its

---

* *Solidarity* also distinguished between direct action and electoral, or "parliamentary," action, which amounted, it said, to workers fruitlessly "begging capitalist lawmakers" to enact capitalist laws.

songs and the gusto with which its members sang them," Brazier would write later, adding that the songs were "good propaganda" and that singing them "held the crowd for Wobbly speakers who followed."

JOE HILL wrote two songs about labor sharks, both from the perspective of a hapless floater. Although it is unlikely he wrote either of them in Spokane—"Coffee An'" was first published in *The Little Red Songbook* in 1912, "Nearer My Job to Thee" in 1913—both seem informed by his time in the city. In both songs, a shark takes the floater's money and pays his fare to a supposed job in the hinterland. In one song, the job lasts all of a week; in the other, there is no job. The songs are different in tone and outcome. In "Coffee An'," the beleaguered fellow finds salvation in joining the "union grand"—the usual antidote to wretchedness in Hill's (and all Wobblies') songs. In "Nearer My Job," though, Hill's floater is more militant: like the stiff in Brazier's "I'll Remember You," he vows to take his grievance with the shark into his own hands.

Hill set "Coffee An'" to the tune of the gospel hymn "Count Your Blessings." (His title was floater shorthand for one of the few meals affordable to the unemployed: coffee and doughnuts.)

> *An employment shark the other day I went to see,*
> *And he said come in and buy a job from me,*
> *Just a couple of dollars, for the office fee,*
> *The job is steady and the fare is free.*
>
> CHORUS
> *Count your pennies, count them, count them one by one,*
> *Then you plainly see how you are done,*
> *Count your pennies; take them in your hand,*
> *Sneak into a Jap's and get your coffee an'.**
>
> *I shipped out and worked and slept in lousy bunks,*
> *And the grub it stunk as bad as forty-'leven skunks,*
> *When I slaved a week the boss he said one day,*
> *You're too tired, you are fired, go and get your pay.*

---

* Often, note the editors of *The Big Red Songbook*, a recently published book in which the song is reprinted, "itinerants first met Asian workers in skid-road cafes."

When the clerk commenced to count, Oh holy gee!
Road, school and poll tax and hospital fee.
Then I fainted, and I nearly lost my sense
When the clerk he said: "You owe me fifty cents."

When I got back to town with blisters on my feet,
There I heard a fellow speaking on the street.
And he said: "It is the workers' own mistake.
If they stick together they get all they make."

And he said: "Come and join our union grand.
Who will be a member of this fighting band?"
"Write me out a card," says I, "By Gee!
The Industrial Workers is the dope for me."

CHORUS
Count your workers, count them; count them one by one,
Join our union and we'll show you how it's done.
Stand together, workers, hand in hand,
Then you will never have to live on coffee an'.

"Nearer My Job to Thee" was obviously a play on the hymn "Nearer, My God, to Thee," a Salvation Army standard.

Nearer my job to thee,
Nearer with glee,
Three plunks for the office fee,
But my fare is free.
My train is running fast,
I've got a job at last.
Nearer my job to thee,
Nearer to thee.

Arrived where my job should be,
Nothing in sight I see,
Nothing but sand, by gee,
Job went up a tree.
No place to eat or sleep,
Snakes in the sage brush creep.
Nero a saint would be,
Shark, compared to thee.

Nearer to town! each day
(Hiked all the way),
Nearer that agency,
Where I paid my fee,
And when that shark I see,
You'll bet your boots that he
Nearer his god shall be.
Leave that to me.

Hill also devoted a verse of his popular 1913 song "Mr. Block" to the shark problem. Of his lumber-headed antihero, Hill wrote,

Yes, Mr. Block is lucky; he found a job, by gee!
The sharks got seven dollars, for job and fare and fee.
They shipped him to a desert and dumped him with his truck,
But when he tried to find his job, he sure was out of luck.

THE SPOKANE STREET-MEETING ordinance took effect on January 1, 1909, and for at least a couple of weeks, the IWW abided by it. Indeed, when one morning two weeks after it took effect a "noisy mob" of fifty "idle workers" smashed the storefront windows of the Red Cross Employment Agency, it was Jack Walsh who jumped on a chair and "stemmed the rising tide of riot and pacified the multitude," according to the *Spokesman-Review*. Walsh later warned that the crowd was crawling with "hired Pinkertons"—undercover private detectives—who "wanted you fellows . . . to start something and then they would have an excuse for shooting you down or smashing your heads in."

In its zeal and haste to stifle the Wobblies, the city council had passed a law written so broadly that it inadvertently silenced *all* soapboxers— including the "long-haired preachers" of the Salvation Army. So the council revised the law, amending it to exempt religious organizations. But then the city's discriminatory intent was transparent; the ordinance had nothing to do with the stated pretext of curtailing traffic congestion downtown, and everything to do with curtailing the civil liberties of dissidents.

The IWW needed the streets of Spokane. There was no better way to spread its message across the Inland Empire's numerous and remote mines and fields and forests. To reclaim the streets, the IWW decided to test the constitutionality of the ordinance. On October 25, 1909, a Wobbly organizer named James "Big Jim" P. Thompson mounted the soapbox with the intent of getting collared. The Spokane police obliged, and Thompson was convicted in city police court—just in time for that week's edition of the *Industrial Worker* to publish the call for a Wobbly invasion. WANTED, the headline read, MEN TO FILL THE JAILS OF SPOKANE.

Fill them they did. In what would form a blueprint for some thirty IWW free speech fights across the country (most of them in the West) over the course of the next seven years (not to mention countless civil rights and antiwar movement protests and sit-ins a half century later), footloose Wobblies came by boxcar to speak on the street, go to jail, and demand individual trials by jury. As Stewart Holbrook wrote in a *True* magazine article titled "The Wild, Wild Wobblies," "Harvest hands in Manitoba, miners in Utah, loggers in Oregon, all got the word incredibly fast by the jungle telegraph. And hundreds of them hopped rattlers for Spokane. The town clowns—police to you—were frantic."

During November alone, more than six hundred wild Wobblies were jailed and "disciplined" for street-speaking. In fact, most spoke hardly a full sentence before the police yanked them down, one after another, and locked them up for thirty days. There was, however, one unfortunate floater who took the box, offered the customary greeting, "Fellow workers and friends," and then, anticipating his imminent arrest, stood silent. Just then, however, no officer was available, leaving the would-be offender stage-frightened and exasperated. *"Where are the cops?"* he finally shouted. The police were occupied beating those who had come before him with clubs, or jamming ten to twelve others into a cell built for a maximum of four prisoners (a space so confined that the men could not sit down, let alone lie down), or feeding them twice-daily rations of water and two ounces of bread. "The misery in those cells was something never to be forgotten—sore, sleepy, and stomach sick and the air foul," one prisoner recalled. Another described in his diary seeing fellow Wobblies' "teeth kicked out, eyes blackened, and clothes torn." He wrote that Thanksgiving turkey in jail was "the work of a fellow-worker artist who drew it on the blackboard." (He was among prisoners housed in the abandoned, unheated Franklin School, which the police had appropriated to accommodate the overflow.)

Still the IWW refused to surrender. Even after police raided its hall, arrested four members on conspiracy charges, and shut down the *Industrial Worker* (which promptly resumed publishing from Seattle), members poured into Spokane, intent only on getting themselves heaved into jail. By March of 1910, "howling, singing" Wobblies had so clogged the jails, created such a logjam in the courts, and cost Spokane taxpayers so much money—a thousand dollars a week—that the city conceded defeat. The combination of passive resistance and direct action got the goods: the jails were cleared of all free speech defendants; the city council repealed the street-speaking ordinance, revoked the business licenses of nineteen of the most flagrant sharks, and even repaid some of the defrauded workers. And though it would take another five years, the Washington legislature acted to regulate employment agencies in the state.

NO CONCLUSIVE RECORD can be found as to whether Joe Hill remained in Spokane during the free speech fight. One problem with seeking confirmation is that many if not most of the hundreds of Wobblies arrested between November of 1909 and March of 1910 gave phony names to the police. I am aware of only one near-contemporaneous claim of Hill's presence in Spokane during at least part of the campaign. Some four and a half years after the free speech fight had ended, during a rally in London to demand Hill's "unconditional release" from the Utah State Penitentiary, an English Wobbly named Ted Fraser said he had "fought" with Hill in Spokane. Then again, the songwriter Dick Brazier doubted that Hill (or Fraser, for that matter) had been in Spokane then, although Brazier conceded he could not have met everyone who had joined the fight. "All I can say for sure," Brazier wrote of Hill many years later, "is that he was not in the Franklin Schoolhouse Emergency Jail where I was confined."

It is plausible that Hill was in Spokane for the early months of 1910. Then again, all I know regarding where he was that year, and when, is limited to two dates, one in April, the other in August. On April 16, a U.S. Census enumerator found him (as "Joel Hill") in San Pedro, California. He was living in a rooming house with Oscar Westergren, his former Gävle classmate, and working at "odd jobs." (They had reunited after losing track of one another in San Francisco during the quake four years earlier.)

By August, Hill was back in the Pacific Northwest. In an article datelined ON THE ROAD, AUGUST 11TH, 1910, he describes his encounter with a woeful floater in the rail yards in Pendleton, Oregon, a wheat-farming town halfway between Spokane and Portland. Published on August 27, this was his first bylined article for the *Industrial Worker* (the piece he signed JOE HILL, PORTLAND LOCAL, NO. 92). Like many of the songs he would go on to write, the article, ANOTHER VICTIM OF THE UNIFORMED THUGS, strikes twin chords of misery and redemption. He meets a forlorn

Hill's undated pen-and-ink sketch seems informed by his encounter with the fellow he met in Pendleton. (Walter P. Reuther Library, Wayne State University)

fellow with a heavily bandaged hand who tells Hill that a railroad bull shot him in Northern California. Of the officer, Hill writes, "His intentions were, of course, the very best, but being a poor shot he only succeeded in crushing the man's hand."* Hill adds that the bull, "not being satisfied with disabling the man for life," beat him severely and threw him in the "tank" for the night. The next morning the floater "got a couple of kicks for breakfast" and an early train out of town in exchange for never returning, or else "it would be the grave yard for him." There is, at the end of this grim but darkly funny narrative, as in "Coffee An'" and in nearly all of the prose and poetry and cartoons and songs that Hill "scribbled," a curative tonic—the one and only way, he writes, to stop "those hired murderers, whose chief delight is to see human blood flowing in streams"—and that is "to unite on the industrial field."

Unity, or class solidarity, was the marrow of IWW doctrine. Hill came to see and feel that during his time in Portland and Spokane. And he had known all along—had known since he was a small boy singing and playing around the family pump organ—that nothing glued people

---

* Hill sounded a similar note five years later in describing the bullet wound he himself had received on the morning of his arrest in Murray, Utah. On that occasion, it will be recalled, Marshal Fred Peters, the "Socialist bull" of Murray, shot Hill in the hand. "The only thing that saved my life," Hill wrote, "was the officer's inefficiency with firearms."

together like song. *"I've got music in my blood,"* he would say. As he once pointed out, for many of his fellow workers (and perhaps for himself), reading a dense pamphlet or following the finer points of a lecture could be a chore. But singing was a joy, and singing together, as he witnessed in Spokane, could be a finely tuned instrument for building solidarity. As Hill articulated it, the secret was to throw "a cloak of humor" over "a few cold, common sense facts" and add catchy, familiar tunes. Next, as Jack Walsh had conceived it, print the songs in a pocket-size *Little Red Songbook* and make it available to anyone with a dime "on the road, in the jungles and in the shops." Then take heed, as one journalist of the day did, of "the curious lift, the strange sudden fire, of the mingled nationalities" when they break "into the universal language of song."

Hill turned thirty-one in October of 1910. He had five years to live. Not immediately, but by the time of his next birthday, he was writing so prolifically that it was as if he recognized that his time would be cut short. He was beginning to shed his anonymity, starting to grow into the role for which he would become celebrated: that of an artist who painted with the slang of the job and jungle, and whose canvas was his fellow workers' everyday struggle for survival.

7.

A Suburb of Hell

By the middle of December 1910, Hill had made his way back down the Pacific coast and inland to a small town near Fresno, California, where the Industrial Workers of the World was already in the thick of another epic free speech battle, and where Hill would resume writing. Over the course of the coming year, 1911, he would grow more fully into his role as a songwriter and receive encouragement from the *Industrial Worker*, which would feature his work on its front page and advertise his songs as forthcoming in successive editions of *The Little Red Songbook*.

In a way, his development mirrored that of the IWW. In the West especially, the union had gained some recognition—and notoriety. Through 1911 and into 1912, the IWW remained consumed with upholding its right to free speech; soapboxing and open-air meetings remained its primary means of recruiting members. Strong voices were needed at the barricades, and Hill's, primarily but not entirely through his music, was a steadily rising and invaluable presence. Yet it would not be until early in 1912 that the IWW's two overlapping and electrifying organizing campaigns on opposite sides of the country—one in San Diego, one in Lawrence, Massachusetts—would rocket the union into the national consciousness. By then, too, Hill would have emerged as the IWW's most prominent songwriter. More important and gratifying to him, though, was his chance in 1911 to realize his dream: to engage not just in the rhetoric of class struggle, but in the *practice* of genuine revolutionary warfare. By the time Hill returned to California in late 1910, the portion of Mexico that shared a border with the state was a cauldron nearing the boiling point; within months, he and hundreds of other Wobblies would leap in.

* * *

Harrison Gray Otis wore his antiunion views as proudly as he did his epaulets. (Courtesy of the Bancroft Library, University of California, Berkeley)

THE CALIFORNIA OF LATE 1910 to which Hill returned was itself a battleground. It was a place storied for its bountiful natural resources, and ironfisted capitalist interests lorded and clashed over those resources, and the people who lived and worked among them, like so many sovereign rulers. One leading interest was industrial agriculture, which depended then, as ever, on cheap, unskilled labor—the core constituency of the IWW. Another power player was the press, and no newspaper was more powerful or influential or antiunion than the *Los Angeles Times*. One man embodied the *Times*: Harrison Gray Otis, its president, general manager, and editor-in-chief.

A Civil War veteran from Ohio, Otis, at seventy-three, looked like a cross between Buffalo Bill and a walrus, and he sounded, said one contemporary, like "a game-warden roaring at seal-poachers." He bestrode his newsroom, and indeed all of Los Angeles, like the military commander he once was. Half a century removed from a wound he had suffered at Antietam, "General" Otis (as he referred to himself) was ever battle-ready: he stored fifty rifles in a turret within the *Times* building—he called it "the Fortress"—and a crate of "loaded shotguns" in the newsroom, where he conducted military drills for employees.*

---

* He had actually been discharged in 1865 from the Union Army a captain but had since used his connections to two presidents—both Rutherford B. Hayes and William McKinley were army pals—to wheedle his rank up to brigadier general.

The "general" had reason to be well fortified. He was known as the most belligerent critic of organized labor in the most antiunion of all American cities, a title he cultivated and wore as proudly as his military sash. His Los Angeles was the "citadel of the open shop" and the "cradle of industrial liberty"—that is, liberty from requisite union membership and the liberty of employers to fire workers who dared to join unions. (He would mock San Francisco, his city's economic archrival and a union stronghold, by declaring that he, too, supported the "closed shop"—closed, that was, to union members.)

By 1910, Otis had been at war with labor for two decades. In 1890, he locked out the *Times*'s printers' union when it declined his take-it-or-leave-it offer of a 20 percent wage cut. That precipitated the union's call to boycott the newspaper and, most significantly, its advertisers. The lockout inspired an unprecedented degree of solidarity on both sides: unions citywide endorsed the boycott, and business owners joined Otis in forming an employers' union: the Merchants and Manufacturers Association of Los Angeles.

Throughout the summer of 1910 and into the fall, Otis was again locked in combat with organized labor. On June 1, fifteen hundred metal-trades workers, seeking to achieve parity with their brethren in San Francisco, struck for an eight-hour day. It was the largest walkout in the city's history, and the *Times*, of course, attacked the strikers—"these labor union wolves" and "their lawlessness and their murderous practices"—with unabated editorial histrionics. Then, before dawn on October 1, a catastrophic explosion blew the roof off the *Times* building. The blast killed twenty-one men. Within a few hours, that day's edition of the *Times* was on the street—it had been published from an auxiliary plant—with a headlined accusation of guilt impersonating fact: UNIONIST BOMBS WRECK THE TIMES.

The unions disavowed any bomb, conjecturing that a gas leak could have ignited the blast. (*Times* employees had complained of gas fumes as recently as the night of the explosion.) Whatever the truth, Otis used the disaster to further his campaign against labor.

JOE HILL AND his fellow workers did not have the reach of Otis's *Times*; they had the *Industrial Worker*. The IWW's organ for Western workers had been founded in Spokane in March of 1909 and had played a crucial role in recruiting footloose Wobblies to fill that city's jails during the free speech fight that had begun that fall. (It covered the activities of

Eastern Wobblies as well, although the weekly *Solidarity*, which had been started by locals in the mining district of New Castle, Pennsylvania, at the end of 1909, was the union's official Eastern publication.) The *Industrial Worker*, to which Hill would begin contributing regularly, also carried news of IWW and other radical movements the world over, especially, in 1910 and 1911, the tempest brewing in the Mexican borderlands. Issues generally ran four pages (special editions ran eight), and in 1911, the *Worker* circulated an average of four thousand copies per issue. In addition to its news coverage, the paper published letters, editorials, and editorial cartoons; songs, of course, and poetry; and announcements of speaking tours, fund-raising appeals, and advertisements for IWW merchandise: subscriptions to the *Worker*, bulk sales of *The Little Red Songbook*, pamphlets on sabotage and direct action, stickerettes, and so on. The paper also accepted display and classified advertising from commercial enterprises, most of it from the likes of skid road lodging houses ("THE OWL" CLEAN IRON BEDS 15¢, CHEAPER THAN THE JUNGLES), pawn shops (O.K. LOAN OFFICE—JEWELRY, REVOLVERS AND ALL KINDS OF MUSICAL INSTRUMENTS . . .), and cafés (THE BEST WORKINGMAN'S MEAL IN THE CITY FOR 25¢ AT THE BON TON RESTAURANT). Some editions carried requests from family members for

Wobblies did not have the reach of Otis's *Times*; they had the *Industrial Worker*. (Labadie Collection, University of Michigan)

information about long-lost relatives, and most issues provided "grape-vine" information about working conditions and wages in various lo-cales. This terse and typical advisory, published in 1910, was courtesy of a member of Local 322 in Vancouver, British Columbia, who worked at a horse-racing track:

> Wages, $2.70 for nine hours. Pay every week. Grub rotten. IWW members can no longer secure work there. Sleep in a stable. Hires from employment shark. Bad slave driver.

Once the Spokane free speech battle was won, in March of 1910, the paper shifted its attention to California. In the previous six months, the IWW had chartered seven locals in the state, and by year's end there would be eleven; there was a Wobbly presence from the Imperial Valley, on the Mexican border, to San Diego and Los Angeles, to the central San Joa-quin Valley, to the San Francisco Bay and the state capital of Sacramento, and way up the north coast to the logging town of Eureka. The *Industrial Worker* took special delight in needling Otis's *Times*, particularly for what the *Worker* considered its false allegations regarding union involvement in the deadly explosion at the *Times* building: "The IWW never had a better organizer than Harrison Gray Otis . . . The workers of Los Angeles are awake and before we get through with [him] and his kind . . . and before they will have their kind of Industrial Freedom, we the workers will es-tablish the kind of Industrial Freedom where men, women and children will be free."

YET IT WAS NOT on Los Angeles—"Otistown"—that the Wobblies ini-tially set their sights in California. It was on the small city of Fresno, two hundred miles north of Los Angeles and the buckle of central Califor-nia's fruit belt. No sooner had the Spokane fight ended than a gaggle of IWW soapboxers, many of them veterans of Spokane, took to the down-town streets of Fresno, this time trying to recruit and organize immi-grant grape-harvest hands. And once again, the capital of a Western agricultural empire (the "Raisin Capital of the World," no less) would apply constitutionally noxious methods to disinfect its streets of the IWW menace—and, in this case, to prevent it from contaminating the vineyards and fruit-drying and -packing houses that drove the regional economy.

For both the growers and the Wobblies, the stakes were high. The

Fresno establishment felt that it could not afford to let the Wobblies gain the foothold they had in Spokane, and the IWW sought to build on the momentum from that victory. *"We have got to win the streets of Fresno!"* stated an unsigned article in the *Industrial Worker* of October 1, 1910, the day the *Los Angeles Times* blew up. *"We've got to show the bosses that we mean business* and unless we make it stick in the Raisin City we are going to have serious trouble in all other California cities."

FRESNO, WITH A POPULATION of twenty-five thousand, was central California's largest city in 1910, a place so prosperous that, a magazine writer of the day gushed, it "[mints] its millionaires and is maintaining them with the prodigality of its productive wealth and the handsome incomes accruing therefrom." Known as "the Queen of the San Joaquin" (in deference to the surrounding river valley), the city was smack in the middle of the state. It was central, too, to California agriculture: the hot, dry summers and cool, wet winters of the San Joaquin Valley were excellent for growing table grapes and wine grapes, of which the region was the state's leading producer, and ideal for producing raisins, of which it was the *world's* largest supplier.

Fresno was also central to the IWW's plans. The union viewed it as the "backbone" of "King capital" in the state. Nearly ten thousand fruit tramps converged on the city at harvest times, and out of the deep pine forests east of Fresno many hundreds of timberbeasts came there to lay up for the winter. "If we break it," the IWW organizer Frank Little said of Fresno, "all California falls to the crimson standard, for we will then systematically proceed to organize."

LIKE THAT OF ANY region largely dependent upon one industry, the establishment in Fresno tended to conflate the private good with the public welfare. As Chester H. Rowell, the editor of the *Fresno Morning Republican*, depicted it in 1909 in a personal letter, "The welfare of this whole community is so bound up in the prosperity of the raisin business . . . that raisin affairs have always been treated, and properly treated, as public affairs." (Rowell himself exemplified that indivisibility. He was the mayor's nephew and namesake, as well as a cofounder of the powerful California Raisin Growers Association.) It was in that spirit of mutual assistance that at the outset of the IWW's campaign to organize raisin pickers, Chief of Police William Shaw laid down the law of the

San Joaquin to the union. "We have a large fruit crop on our hands, and it must be cheaply handled. If you undertake to organize common labor, we will run you out of town."

One night in late August of 1910, police officers arrested Frank Little and two fellow workers for "creating a disturbance"—they were "talking socialism"—on the street in front of the Fresno Beer Hall. Little, who was thirty-two, was a seemingly omnipresent IWW agitator, one of those for whom the mix of direct action and passive resistance was a way of life. He had been raised in Indian Territory (later Oklahoma), and as his fellow Wobblies liked to say, he was "half Indian, half white man, all IWW." Little had been in the thick of the free speech battle in Spokane as well as in earlier scrapes in Goldfield, Nevada, and Missoula, Montana. He got twenty-five days in jail in Fresno, a sentence he attributed to "a perjured jury" of "bourgeois cockroaches and real estate grafters." At one point, the sheriff tossed Little in "the Tanks"—solitary confinement—for refusing a work order. "Your jails and dungeons have no terrors for me," Little said, and proceeded to serve out his time in solitary by singing song after IWW song. "Evidently," the *Morning Republican* marveled, "the dark cell does not bother Little as he began to sing and kept it up all day."*

And if the authorities believed that the harshness of Little's incarceration would cause his fellow stiffs to roll their bindles and hop the first rattler out of town, either they had missed the extensive wire service coverage of the protracted Spokane fight—articles the Fresno papers had prominently displayed as recently as six months earlier—or they were delusional about the strength and depth of the IWW's convictions. The Wobblies were rolling nowhere; to the contrary, they were whistling for

---

* On another occasion, Little told a Fresno jury he could handle whatever sentence it wished to impose. "If a noose were dangling in front of my face, I would laugh at it," he said. Seven summers later, in the predawn darkness of August 1, 1917, Little would get his chance: a mob hanged him in Butte, Montana. But then again, the six vigilantes who hauled Little out of his boardinghouse bed gave him no chance to dress or gather the crutches he used. They beat him, roped him to a car, and dragged him through the streets before hanging him from a railroad trestle at the edge of town. The epitaph on his gravestone at Mountain View Cemetery in Butte reads, SLAIN BY CAPITALIST INTERESTS FOR ORGANIZING AND INSPIRING HIS FELLOW MEN. None was ever charged for the murder. The detective novelist Dashiell Hammett, who as a young man was employed by the Pinkerton Agency as a strikebreaker in Butte, later claimed he had spurned a five-thousand-dollar offer to kill Little. Hammett's lover, Lillian Hellman, said that Little's gruesome death must have been "an abiding horror" for Hammett, and Hammett's biographer wrote that the incident would forever "permeate his life and work."

reinforcements. After Frank Little's verdict came in, the *Industrial Worker* virtually herded its readers into boxcars: ALL ABOARD FOR FRESNO! FREE SPEECH FIGHT ON!

The free speech fight was on from late August of 1910 until early March of 1911. Joe Hill was in Fresno during some of that time—or, to be as precise as possible, he was in Fresno *County*—but it is unclear how, or when, or even if, he participated. Whether he was one of the hundreds of Wobblies who went to jail cannot be determined; as in Spokane and elsewhere, many assumed prison aliases. Among those in the Fresno lockup, for example, were "Samuel Gompers," "Sam Gompers," and "S. Gompers"; also "Harrison Gray Otis," "H. G. Otis," and "John L. Sullivan" (the bare-knuckle boxing champion), to say nothing of the handful of "John Doe's."

But there were two names—or presumably pseudonyms—that caught my eye: "Joe Dock" and "Ah Sam." In the night jailer's ledger book for Saturday, November 19, 1910, those names were listed consecutively, two of the twenty-four free speech offenders admitted that night. Was Joe Dock really Joe Hill, the dock walloper? Could Ah Sam have been Sam Murray, Hill's close friend in the IWW?

What is certain is that by the middle of December, Hill was working in Coalinga, a thriving little railroad, coal-mining, and oil field town (population: five thousand) in southwestern Fresno County, about sixty miles from Fresno. He had perhaps heard about Coalinga from Frank Little, who had gone there in October upon his release from jail, to see if the IWW might assist striking metal workers in the oil fields. The Coalinga workers belonged to a local affiliated with the American Federation of Labor, but their grievances—little pay and long hours—were awfully familiar. Further, they were under free speech restrictions similar to those imposed in Fresno. Little took their complaints as an opportunity to start an IWW local in Coalinga.

One of the Wobblies who went to Coalinga to organize was Sam Murray. Murray was there by at least October, when he wrote in the *Industrial Worker* that the strikers "[are] tired of the conservative AF of L and want some real action," adding, "Some IWW men from Fresno are coming to help out in the struggle."

The guess here is that Hill was one of those men—that he went to Coalinga at Murray's behest. (A few months later, Murray and Hill would together join a platoon of rebel troops fighting in Mexico.) He stayed at least six weeks and worked, as he vaguely put it, "on a building." In an advisory published in the *Industrial Worker* in early January of 1911 (but written before the turn of the year), Hill described the conditions:

Wages fair ($3 for 8 hours common labor), but "hash" and "slops" are away out of reach. There will be some street work here after New Years, but I would not advise anybody to come over here unless they've got something rattling in their pockets!

Yours for freedom,

HILL, L.U. [Local Union] No. 92.

During his stay in Coalinga, Hill contributed at least one cartoon and most probably a poem as well to the *Industrial Worker*. Only the cartoon was bylined, but both evoke his style, and they contribute a bit more detail to the portrait of Hill as a workingman who was also an artist. The poem is an ode to William Shaw, the Fresno chief of police. It was published on February 2 and must have been inspired by a *Worker* article, "Der Chief," that had run two weeks earlier. The story "praised" Shaw for "bravely pushing his vagrancy charges" on any and all Wobblies—there were ninety in jail at the time.

In the poem, "Der Chief, of Fresno," Hill's cutting, funny, and intermittently crude voice is discernible in the way that it slices straight to the bone of the matter. And, too, its ending is reminiscent of his song "Nearer My Job to Thee," in which the floater threatens to kill the labor shark who deceived him. In each of the ten three-line verses in "Der Chief," the poet poses a call-and-response question that frames an issue or encapsulates an event of the free speech fight, and to which the called-for response is invariable. The verse may be pure doggerel—not a few words are shoehorned into ill-fitting rhymes—but, more important, it is *participatory* doggerel: like most of the Wobbly canon, "Der Chief" was written for recitation, not preservation.

> *Who is the freak that had the cheek,*
> *The crawling, slimy, cringing sneak,*
> *That prohibits us the right to speak?*
> *Der Chief.*
>
> *Who gave the workers the loud Ha! Ha!*
> *Who tried to trample down the law?*
> *Who handed us the deal so raw?*
> *Der Chief.*
>
> *Who is the most notorious liar?*
> *Who had stool pigeons in his hire?*

Who mobbed our speakers, camp did fire?
  Der Chief.

Who is this grey-haired guy so wise?
Who winks and blinks his bleary eyes?
Thinks he has the workers hypnotized?
  Der Chief.

Who was the czar with haughty frown?
Who gave us floaters out of town?
And was surprised when we turned him down?
  Der Chief.

Who recommended the cat-o'-nine
And wished to have it soaked in brine,
To make the workers fall in line?
  Der Chief.

Who said the working men were scum?
That we were tramps and on the bum?
And that he had us on the run?
  Der Chief.

Who was the despot who used his might?
Who broke the backbone of our fight?
Vagged all our leaders in one night?
  Der Chief.

Who wears that worried look of pain,
When he finds the fight is on again?
Leaders coming on every train.
  Der Chief.

Who is the mutt with shiny pate,
Who tried to chase us from this state,
And is surely going to meet his fate?
  Der Chief.

Whatever else Fresno County did for Hill, it seemed to arouse in him both creativity and lust. The week before the *Industrial Worker* published

"Der Chief, of Fresno," the paper ran Hill's cartoon on the front page. Titled "Two Victims of Society," the two-panel drawing (signed "J. Hill") portrays a frowning, bent-back stiff saddled with an enormous bindle who leans on a cane as he crosses a railroad tie. "Gee, my feet are sore," he says. In the opposite panel a prostitute beckons: "Come inside, kid!" The caption reads, "He can't afford to have a home. She never had a chance. That's why they are both selling themselves to the highest bidder."

Two days before the cartoon was published, in the January 26, 1911, edition, Hill mailed a thematically similar cartoon postcard to Karl Rudberg, his friend from Gävle whom he had bumped into in San Francisco in 1906, shortly after the quake, and with whom he had hoboed to Portland not long thereafter. Rudberg, too, had since returned to California. He was working on the docks at the Los Angeles Harbor, in San Pedro, where Hill himself would soon gravitate to. On the postcard, postmarked "Coalinga, Cal." and addressed to Rudberg at the Sailors' Rest Mission in San Pedro, Hill drew a skinny, bug-eyed passerby, presumably a caricature of Rudberg, whose hat flies off and whose hair stands up at the sight of a burlesque dancer in a storefront window. The woman is clad in little more than a rose stem in her left hand and an accordion fan in her right. Above her are the words BIG SHOW; below, TONIGHT. The man needs no further enticing. In the next panel, under the phrase DOINGS OF VARAN KALLE— "our Karl"—he makes a beeline for the entrance.

THOUGH THEY NEVER BLEW into town with the gale force that had announced their arrival in Spokane, enough Wobblies drifted into Fresno over the course of late 1910 and early 1911 to periodically fill the jail and to credibly warn of many more to come. As one of their songs had it,

> There is one thing I can tell you
> And it makes the bosses sore.
> As fast as they can pinch us,
> We can always get some more.

Almost every week during that period, the Fresno papers carried alarmist reports of an imminent Spokane-like plague of Wobblies; a *Morning Republican* article on a Wednesday in mid-October advised that the police had gotten word of a "squad" of 175 "agitators" advancing from the Northwest and expected to make Fresno by nightfall Saturday. Chester Rowell, the *Republican* editor and raisin-industry publicist, stole a look at the advancing cloud of pests intent on destruction, then glanced at the U.S. Constitution, perhaps too hastily, and offered a primer for the Wobblies on the boundaries of free speech: "One may not . . . use any form of speech which is in itself disorderly, or which tends to incite others to disorder" or is otherwise spoken "unpeacefully" or "without permit" in a "suitable place for public speaking." To exceed those limits, Rowell warned, was to invite municipal wrath. The paper greeted the approaching swarm with the declaration that if it was war the IWW wanted, "they can doubtless be accommodated." The city closed ranks. In early October, Local 66 was evicted from its downtown hall and could find no other willing landlord. The IWW resorted to renting a large tent and raising it on a vacant lot, owned by a sympathetic Socialist, just outside the city limits. The tent served as union hall, dining hall, and shelter for arriving members and those taking a breather between terms in jail. By mid-October, the jail's bull pen—a stone-floored, purportedly temporary holding cell—swelled with three dozen IWW "disturbers of the peace" and "vagrants," the former classification including anyone who so much as stood on a soapbox in downtown Fresno or tried to peddle IWW literature; the latter an elastic category of criminal the police stretched to snare *any* unemployed man, whether or not he carried a red card. ("Everyone is a vag[rant] with the capitalist sluggers when all other laws fail," the *Industrial Worker* explained.)

The mass arrests (nineteen during one street meeting) coupled with a barrage of sensational headlines—IWW PLANS TO WAGE WAR ON POLICE; ARMED GUARDS ON DUTY TO PREVENT ESCAPE FROM JAIL—only drew more stiffs and gawkers to the Wobblies' outdoor gatherings. Crowds of fifteen hundred were jamming the corner of Mariposa and I streets for the nightly spectacle, a rough, rhythmic cops-and-tramps ballet. The choreography went like this: the chief of police hauled a speaker off the soapbox (as in Spokane, most speakers got—and expected to get—no further into their remarks than the "four-word speech": "Fellow workers and friends"), and as he passed the offender forward to his lieutenants with one hand, he pirouetted and reached back for the next speaker with his free hand. Though as one Wobbly described the musical score, it sounded nothing like a ballet suite. "Each forward and backward movement of the hands was accompanied by thunderous applause, swelling in volume . . . until it became a fierce, wild yell."

Some of influential voice in Fresno believed that warehousing Wobblies in jail, where they begged to be, where they traveled long distances to be, and from which they commanded national attention, was an ill-conceived strategy—one that served only the IWW. As one cheerful jailbird answered a reporter's question, "Afraid of getting arrested? Hardly! We want to get arrested. We'll flood the jail . . . and any other place they want to send us to." Flooding the Fresno jail soaked taxpayers, swamped the police, and engulfed the courts with demands for separate trials by jury. And the attendant coverage alerted Wobblies everywhere to the genuine need for reinforcements and the real possibility of succeeding in Fresno as they had in Spokane: forcing the city, through civil disobedience, nonviolent resistance, and overwhelming strength in numbers, to comply with the Constitution. Instead of jailing the pests, then, one newspaper urged citizens to take matters into their own hands. In an editorial that read like a license to practice vigilante law, the *Fresno Herald and Democrat* wrote, "For men to come here with the express purpose of creating trouble, a whipping post and a cat-o'-nine-tails well seasoned by being soaked in salt water is none too harsh a treatment for peace breakers. Indeed, such a punishment would prove more efficacious than a term in a dark cell."

Within days of that diatribe, and with chatter gleaned from Southern Pacific Railroad employees of a brigade of 75 or 100 Wobblies advancing on Fresno from the south and another army of 175 en route from the north, a committee of merchants and growers took up the editorialist's gauntlet. The group met to "devise means to rid the city of these undesirable characters." "In the near future if the trouble continues," the committee announced, it would call for a "mass meeting of citizens"—a mob—"to drive these men from Fresno."

The "trouble" not only continued; it deepened. During the next month, Wobbly volunteers for jail were arrested nearly every day, usually a handful at a time and always without incident. All faced either the misdemeanor charge of vagrancy or that of violating the city ordinance prohibiting public speaking on the streets without a permit. And all pleaded not guilty. The police court judge rejected their demands for individual jury trials on the constitutionally shaky ground that defendants charged with mere misdemeanors were not so entitled. (And yet the judge set each man's bail at an unreachable 250 dollars.*) Instead, he granted a jury trial to one and only one IWW defendant: Frank Little, "the chief agitator of the bunch," in the jailer's words. The judge announced that Little's trial was to serve as a test case: the verdict would bind to all IWW defendants.

---

* At the going wage rate of a dollar and fifty cents a day for white, native-born, male fruit pickers—and about twenty-five cents less for women, children, and most immigrants—it would take six months of work to make bail.

On December 8, 1910, the day of Little's trial, the Fresno jail held eighty-five troublesome Wobblies, fifty-five charged with disturbing the peace, thirty with vagrancy. Some had been locked up for nearly two months, their constitutional right to reasonable bail and a speedy trial effectively nullified by the coordinated campaign of the city, the press, and the growers ("raisin affairs," after all, *were* "public affairs") to wipe them out like fruit flies on a grapevine. And it was not only the excessive bail imposed, or the prolonged period of pretrial incarceration, but also—as is vividly evidenced in one Wobbly's diary—the degrading and sadistic jail conditions that mocked the constitutional prohibition against cruel and unusual punishment. (Although the authorities employed one particularly cruel punishment so often that it could hardly have been considered unusual: a steam-powered fire hose, known as the "water cure," of such tremendous force—150 pounds per square inch of water pressure—that it could knock a man down or lift him off his feet.)*

For four and a half months, beginning on the night of his arrest in mid-October of 1910, a free speech fighter named H. Minderman meticulously chronicled those appalling jail conditions in his diary. Composed of nearly daily entries and later published by the U.S. Commission on Industrial Relations, Minderman's mostly first-person-plural narrative ("We are not allowed to wash ourselves or use the toilet") is remarkable for its detail ("Cells are 7 feet 2 inches by 6 feet 9 inches and 8 feet 4 inches high") and for its prosaic, economical prose that bestows on the diary a matter-of-fact eloquence and authenticity. "Seventeen beds for thirty-four men," Minderman writes on October 22, during a stint in the jail's bull pen. After a water cure he notes, "We get fifteen dry blankets for eighty-one men." He documents meals ("At four o'clock P.M. we got . . . beans and punk"), underwear rations, and a visit from Salvation Army officials. The specifics of that encounter are unknown, but assumably some sort of dustup occurred. Asked by some Wobblies for a donation of old clothes a few weeks later, the Army captain turned them away. He disapproved, he said, of the IWW's "'shocking' and unpatriotic 'utterances.'"

No matter how un-American or otherwise ear-bruising the Salvation

---

* The *Los Angeles Times* was giddy about the water cure. DOUCHE FOR INDUSTRIALS, it reported on Christmas Eve of 1910. FREE BATHS, a subhead gibed. The *Times* paid particularly close attention for fear that the "Fresno bunch" of "union labor ruffians" had imminent plans for Los Angeles. The paper warned that the police department was beefing up its "hobo squad" and that "anyone caught in the disreputable resorts east of Main Street will be picked up and adorned with a ball and chain."

Army officer found the Wobblies' language, nothing they uttered could have been more shocking than the bombshell Frank Little dropped on his prosecutors at the opening of his test-case trial. In a courtroom "packed to the doors," Little, who represented himself, told the judge that he could not have violated the ordinance against street-speaking for a simple reason: *Fresno had no such ordinance.* That sent the judge scurrying for the seven-volume Fresno City Ordinances, his perusal of which confirmed the inconvenient fact that the IWW men were being held unlawfully. He returned to the bench long enough to dismiss the charges: Little and his fifty-four codefendants charged with disturbing the peace were freed. (The thirty Wobblies who were in jail for vagrancy, including the diarist Minderman, remained in the lockup.) By nightfall, Little was back on a soapbox at the corner of Mariposa and I.

Until the city trustees could convene to pass a street-speaking ordinance, Little and the IWW's other verbal sluggers pounded away nightly at the municipal gut. Chief of Police William Shaw was powerless: he was ordered to direct his officers not to arrest or otherwise interfere with IWW soapboxers. The chief, however, made it plain that his directive did not extend to civilians—not, for instance, to the merchants' committee, the group that eight weeks earlier had called for a "mass meeting of citizens" in the event of further IWW trouble. In a story headlined DRIVE OUT LOAFERS, the *Los Angeles Times* reported Chief Shaw's suggestion that "the citizens might do as they wished."

The citizens of Fresno, hundreds of them—estimates ranged from three hundred to five hundred—wished to assemble at the corner of Mariposa and I streets at around seven o'clock on the night of Friday, December 9. It was no spontaneous gathering. They were there to do to the Wobblies what the incapacitated police could not: inflict bodily harm and engage in rank, uncivil disobedience. All that day, and for the previous few days, "reports were rife of what was to occur," the *Morning Republican* recounted. The paper said that an informant had called the newsroom on Friday afternoon to say that he had been told that "the police were going to let the firemen and citizens handle the IWWs" that night, and that the word on the streetcars was "that the IWW speakers were to be tarred and feathered."

The first IWW speaker had barely uttered a single unpatriotic word before a former prizefighter turned firefighter knocked him down and beat him up. Though no one was tarred and feathered, vigilantes knuckled or clubbed anyone suspected of Wobbly tendencies. Where were the authorities? The police, evidently, had taken solemnly their pledge against interference: they were nowhere to be seen. The sheriff and the mayor would both claim ignorance. They were out of town for the day, they said later, well out of earshot of the widely heard call for uncivil disobedience.

When there were no more Wobblies downtown to batter, the vigilante storm surged toward the IWW tent camp at the northwestern city limits, a mile and a half distant. The mere sight of the large scarlet-and-black flag flying over the camp "aroused the mob to uncontrollable fury," the *Morning Republican* reported. Some shredded the flag to ribbons, passing the remnants around as keepsakes. Others swarmed the big tent, even as the few Wobbly stragglers fled, some clad only in their undergarments. Everything left behind—clothing, food, supplies—was gathered into a huge pile fit for a bonfire. Someone applied a torch, and as they watched the camp reduced to ashes, the lurid blaze illuminating their faces, the arsonists "howled with delight."

And yet the IWW would not desist. Letters protesting police brutality poured in from all over. Representative was the call from Detroit Local 62 for an immediate end to "the abominable outrages perpetrated . . . in that suburb of hell called Fresno."

The morning after the attack, the union's general secretary-treasurer, Vincent St. John, telegraphed this message:

MAYOR, FRESNO, CAL. ACTION OF "RESPECTABLE MOB" WILL NOT DETER THIS ORGANIZATION. FULL AND COMPLETE REPARATION WILL BE EXACTED. FREE SPEECH WILL BE ESTABLISHED IN FRESNO IF IT TAKES TWENTY YEARS.

It would take only three months. By the light of day, it was evident that the body blows sustained by Wobblies were slight in comparison to the black eye on Fresno's image: overnight, the Raisin Capital had become the Riot Capital. Newspapers throughout the land—from Syracuse, New York, to Centralia, Washington—played the wire story on the front page of their Saturday edition. POLICE LET RIOTERS RUN THE CITY and MOB RULE IN FRESNO were not the sort of headlines the Fresno Chamber of Commerce was likely to append to promotional brochures.

For the local press, the vigilante attack posed a quandary. It could neither condone the "respectable mob" nor commiserate with the beat-up and burned-out revolutionaries. The *Morning Republican* met the challenge with a demagogic flourish: "This thing of meeting lawless speech with more lawless acts is bad business," its morning-after editorial began, trampling the salient fact that the IWW speakers had violated no law. The paper grumbled that "Fresno is disgraced by last night's action of its own citizens," but it grieved less for the carnage to civil liberties than for the "strategic advantage" that the IWW ("a gang of irresponsible toughs" led by "fanatical anarchists") had gained. And it grudgingly acknowledged the irony that the capitalist press had facilitated the IWW's cause. "Until yesterday the invaders had to recruit their numbers as best they could, by passing around the invitation in their own newspaper," the editorial lamented. "Today, the Associated Press has carried to all the world the news that there is a fight on in Fresno, and every irresponsible vagrant who is looking for such a fight now knows where to find it."

By early February of 1911, the county jail, built for a capacity of one hundred prisoners, teemed with 174 irrepressibly "irresponsible vagrants" who, when they were not conducting the business of Local 66, sang, chanted, jeered, harangued, and banged on the bars of the cells and the psyches of the jailers—and who were merely the advance guard for hundreds more red-card-carrying reprobates lining up to join them. "What we want is to fill Fresno with VAG[RANT]s," the *Industrial Worker* reiterated. As further incentive to fellow workers who were jungled up in wintry climes, the paper frequently extolled the region's Mediterranean weather. "Fresno has an ideal climate. Better," the *Worker* counseled, to "be a vag[rant] there than anywhere else."*

From everywhere else—or so it must have seemed to the beleaguered, deafened sheriff's deputies—Wobblies were on the march: from St. Louis and Kansas City and Denver, from up and down the California coast, and from the Pacific Northwest, where Southern Pacific bulls derailed the plans of 170 Fresno-bound men. Ousted from a freight train and stranded in a snowstorm in the mountains south of Ashland, Oregon, near the California state line, the intrepid Wobblies took off on foot—uphill and into a blizzard. They were trying to make it to the next train layover, at Steinman, ten miles distant. One of the hikers, E. M. Clyde, a member of the Seattle local, kept a journal: "The snow kept getting deeper and when we finally arrived . . . at 4:30 P.M. we found ourselves wet, cold and hungry, with 18" of snow on the ground and no chance to get food or shelter for the night." At nine P.M., Clyde wrote again: "As the boys were now

---

* Naturally enough, local boosters and land speculators similarly lauded the idyllic climate in promotional literature: "Fresno County. A Wonderfully Prosperous District in California. The Land of Sunshine, Fruits, and Flowers. No Ice. No Snow. No Blizzards. No Cyclones."

Boxcar-riding Wobblies in Ashland, Oregon, shortly before hiking through a blizzard over Siskiyou Pass en route to Fresno. (Southern Oregon Historical Society #5267)

suffering terribly from the exposure, wet, hunger, cold and loss of sleep, and knowing there would be no more trains that night, and knowing also there was no food to be had at this place for breakfast should we remain here, it looked for a time like dissolution was sure to take place." At four A.M., following a few hours of rest interrupted by a pair of "business meetings," the boys resolved to keep going. Their perseverance, their willingness to endure hunger and cold and exhaustion when they knew that all that awaited them at the end of their perilous journey were a welcome-to-Fresno nightstick and an overcrowded cell, confounded some observers. "It is one of those strange situations which crop up suddenly and are hard to understand," noted the police-beat reporter for the daily *San Francisco Call*. "Some thousands of men, whose business is to work with their hands, tramping and stealing rides, suffering hardships and facing dangers—to get into jail. And to get into that one particular jail in a town of which they had never heard before, in which they have no direct interest."

With the front-page news that the band of 170 Wobblies from the Pacific Northwest had somehow hiked over the Siskiyou Pass, through snowdrifts as high as three feet, and were again riding a boxcar special to Fresno, and with his jail already bursting, the newly elected sheriff, Walter McSwain, reached his own breaking point. A reformer (he had reduced his deputies' workday to eight hours from twelve and hired the county's first female deputy), McSwain determined to clean up the mess inherited from his predecessor. The new sheriff saw the futility of fighting an enemy with nothing to lose—no job, no home, no money, no future—and who showed every sign of making good on Vincent St. John's vow that the Wobblies would struggle for twenty years, if it took that long, to exercise their constitutional right to speak freely on the streets of Fresno.

On the morning of February 21, Sheriff McSwain advised the mayor that he would no longer accept the city's prisoners. "Jail is full," he said, before adding the candid double entendre that he could "take no more." Nine days later, faced with daily press reports of the ever-advancing hobo armies, and having proposed a compromise (you get out of jail; we restrict you to a free speech zone) to the uncompromising prisoners, Fresno surrendered. The city rescinded the ban on street-speaking and unconditionally released every last Wobbly prisoner. In a March 6 telegram to the *Industrial Worker*, Local 66 announced the news: THE FREE SPEECH FIGHT IS OVER, AND WON . . . TERMS ARE SATISFACTORY. COMPLETE VICTORY.

8.

Chicken Thieves and Outlaws

Despite an editorial in Harrison Gray Otis's *Los Angeles Times* that cheerfully called for their death, the free speech fighters made it out of Fresno alive.* When Sheriff Walter McSwain liberated the prisoners in early March of 1911, he found the walls of the bull pen chockablock with skillfully drawn, if unflattering, caricatures of local and national personages, as well as the chiseled text of the IWW preamble ("It is the historic mission of the working class to do away with capitalism . . .). No sooner had his dozens of guests departed than the sheriff ordered the bull pen restored to its pre-IWW white-walled austerity. Even as the jail trusties commenced scrubbing and spackling, so many Wobblies were crowding onto departing trains that "accommodations on top of the coaches were inadequate to handle the exodus," one railroad bull noted. Some free speech fighters were returning to the Pacific Northwest or the Midwest. Most, like Joe Hill, were heading the two hundred miles south to IWW halls in Los Angeles or San Pedro, and from there, farther still: to the borderlands of the Mexican peninsula of Baja California. In the early months of 1911, the class struggle was in full swing there, and the workers of the world, or a few hundred revolutionaries anyway, were fulfilling the IWW preamble's directive to "take possession of the earth." And if the preamble was necessarily vague as to which capitalists the earth was to be repossessed from, its

---

* Regarding the five thousand Wobblies reportedly streaming toward Fresno in the days just before the city relented, the *Times* editorialized, "During the visit . . . they will be accorded a night and day guard of honor, composed of citizens armed with rifles. The Coroner will be in attendance at his office every day from 8 A.M. to 10 P.M."

framers could hardly have been disappointed: virtually the entirety of the earth in play in the northern district of Baja California, nearly one million acres of prime, irrigable Colorado River delta farmland, belonged to an American syndicate headed by the most bellicose, and, at that moment, surely the most distressed, of all of labor's foes—Harrison Gray Otis of the *Los Angeles Times*.

The story of how the red-white-and-blue-blooded General Otis came to occupy an empire-size tract of Baja California is the story of Mexico during the Porfiriato, the dictatorship of President Porfirio Díaz that spanned parts of five decades and was as spectacularly criminal as it was long-lived. It is the story of how, for a generation, sandbags of American political and financial capital shored up Díaz behind a fraudulent and blood-soaked façade of democracy. But that is a story best told elsewhere. Here, it is most useful as backdrop to the improbable and little-known tale of the heady, tragicomic beginnings of the Mexican Revolution—of what happened when a revolutionary Mexican political party and a revolutionary U.S.-based labor union joined forces to help topple the dictatorship and drive Díaz into exile.

This is a story about convergence: of politics and labor; of radical movements in bordering countries; of revolutionary theory and practice; of local dreams with global ambition. It is also a story of transformation: of bands of indigenous and IWW rebels who suddenly and with hardly any combat training found themselves practicing class warfare—that which they had preached only from soapboxes, on newsprint, and in song lyrics—and who, in the spring of 1911, were not only engaged in armed rebellion but winning at it, no less. For Joe Hill, who fought with the rebel army for six weeks in the spring of 1911, the experience was certainly transformational. For the first time, he cast himself as a true revolutionary, as someone willing to sacrifice his life for a cause. And four years later, in farewell letters written on what he expected would be the last night of his life, he said as much.

Before Hill went to Baja California, he returned to the docks of the Los Angeles Harbor, in San Pedro, where perhaps he thought to reunite with Karl Rudberg, his boyhood friend from Gävle. Since their chance meeting five years earlier in San Francisco in the wake of the earthquake (when Hill found the shoeless Rudberg wandering Market Street) and their subsequent travels together through Northern California into Oregon, the two had stayed in touch. In January, Hill had drawn the bawdy postcard caricature of his friend and mailed it to Rudberg care of the Sailors' Rest Mission in San Pedro. Rudberg had received the card but had since migrated back to San Francisco. In late April, Hill drew Rudberg another whimsical card, this one a self-portrait: a gangly, rubber-limbed gent—with huge hands, splayed fingers, and carrot-shaped, clown-size feet—sitting on a stool and banging away on a piano in the Sailors' Rest Mission. Behind him sits a motley Greek chorus critiquing his performance: "Gidda hook," one pleads; "Rotten," says another; "Punk," a third critic pans. The pianist is yet undeterred by the harsh reviews. "Still Sticking Around Here," the caption says. "I've Got a MISSION to Fill Don't Ye Knauw." He signed it "Jo-EL."

For the time being, though, Hill had had his fill of the Mission. The card was postmarked SAN PEDRO, APRIL 29; a day later he was in San Diego, en route to the new rebel-recruiting station in Tijuana. Along the way, he read a newspaper article about "some smart jink" in New York who had invented a superior voting machine. To Hill, that was bunk. He had absorbed the IWW teaching that the ballot box was useless; improved or not, no voting machine could help workers seize economic power. "The only machine worth while," he wrote in the *Industrial Worker*, "is the one which the capitalists use on us when we ask for more bread for ourselves and our families. The one that works with a trigger. All aboard for Mexico!"

PRESIDENT PORFIRIO DÍAZ had ruled Mexico for thirty-four years—longer than the life expectancy of the country's working poor. Corruption and malfeasance were the oxygen and water of his governance. He gave his favored generals double duty as state governors and leaders of his standing army and established a paramilitary force of uniformed *rurales*—rural police—to ride roughshod over the smallest municipalities. He stocked the congress and courts with cronies and high bidders; he imprisoned or exiled or massacred political enemies, or seduced them with lavish bribes; he enriched himself, his family, his inner circle, and favored American investors by confiscating the natural resources and *ejidos*—communal lands—of the peasantry, of whom millions (five million, by one estimate, fully a third of the population) were forced into peonage and another 750,000 into chattel slavery.

Resistance to the Porfiriato had flared from the outset. During Díaz's first term, when armed supporters of his exiled predecessor attempted a revolt in Veracruz State, Díaz told the governor how to deal with the captured *insurrectos*. "*Matálos en caliente*," he instructed. ("Kill them on the spot.") Other reformers tried to stand up to him from time to time, but even the nonviolent ones Díaz cut off at the legs, sometimes literally. At the turn of the twentieth century, however, a young, frighteningly fearless writer and intellectual named Ricardo Flores Magón attacked the strongman as no one had dared to—with a typewriter. In August of 1900, when Flores Magón was twenty-six, he, along with his younger brother Enrique and another reckless soul, launched *Regeneración*, the "Independent Journal of Combat," a weekly journalistic grenade aimed straight at the head of the body politic. The newspaper unsparingly exposed the atrocities Díaz perpetrated on constitutional rights and liberties in the name of civil order and economic progress. It named names, and called names, too, depicting American investors as bloodsucking "vampires of finances" and slithering "boa constrictors of Wall Street." Over the next four years, the Flores Magón brothers were imprisoned numerous times, convicted of crimes such as "insulting the president" and "ridiculing public officials." *Regeneración* ceased publishing for a time, but the brothers published elsewhere—even after Mexico's Supreme Court of Justice upheld a lower-court decree that made it a crime to publish the brothers' writings in *any* Mexican publication. Eventually, President Díaz told the Flores Magón brothers to choose, in effect, between execution and exile. In 1904, they forded the Río Bravo (Grande) into Texas. The revolution would have to wait, and it would have to be exported from the United States.

ON MARCH 6, 1911, the very day the IWW declared victory in Fresno, the president of the United States, William Howard Taft, met privately in Washington with the U.S. ambassador to Mexico, Henry Lane Wilson. Wilson advised Taft that President Díaz was "on a volcano of popular uprising" and that "a general explosion was probable at any time," in which case, Wilson warned, "the forty thousand or more American residents in Mexico might be assailed, and the very large American investments"—a figure Taft later put at more than a billion dollars—"might be injured or destroyed."

The same day, Wilson's diplomatic counterpart, the Mexican ambassador to the United States, complained to Secretary of State Philander C. Knox that "certain corrupt elements"—he meant IWW members—were "swelling the ranks" of those in Baja California who "propose to turn the territory . . . into a field of action for criminal undertakings." Wobblies were indeed flocking toward IWW halls near the border, in San Diego and Brawley and Holtville, California, where they would receive second-hand rifles and rudimentary training in guerrilla warfare. And the swollen ranks were those of the Partido Liberal Mexicano, or Mexican Liberal Party—the revolutionary organization led by the exiled Ricardo Flores Magón from Los Angeles. Alarmed by the cross-border flow of armed insurgents (the Mexican consul at San Diego had reported the sale of four hundred Springfield rifles in that city over a recent ten-day period), the Mexican ambassador urged the Taft administration, in words befitting a diplomat, to "make a categorical declaration demonstrating the firmness of the friendly relations between the two countries."

That night, Taft made his categorical declaration—of war: he ordered twenty thousand soldiers, *one-quarter of the entire United States Army*, to the border with Mexico in Texas and California. The president also moved thirty-eight hundred marines on four armed cruisers in the Atlantic fleet from northeastern waters to the naval station at Guantánamo, Cuba, and most of the Pacific fleet to San Pedro and San Diego. The morning newspapers called the mobilization "the most extensive movement of troops and war vessels ever executed in this country in time of peace." The White House vainly retailed the exercise as "practice maneuvers" or a "war game." Obviously it was nothing of the sort. As Taft himself confided to his army chief of staff, he hoped the mere threat of overwhelming force would quash the insurrection without the United States' actually having to invade Mexico. Failing that, the military would be ready at a moment's notice to "save American lives and property."

The U.S. troop movement was not solely in response to the incursions of the "Magonistas"—as the Flores Magón–led rebel and IWW forces were known. There was a rival opposition party, better funded and less radical. The Anti-Reelectionist Party was headed by Francisco I. Madero, the scion of a wealthy and prominent ranching family from the northern border state of Coahuila. Madero had traveled and studied in Europe and the United States. When he returned home to manage his family's haciendas, he could see in the misery and destitution of his own peons what the Porfiriato meant for and had done to ordinary Mexicans. In 1910, Madero challenged the president-for-life for the presidency. Two weeks before the election, Díaz's secret police kidnapped and imprisoned Madero and his running mate. Meanwhile, thousands of "Maderistas" in northern Mexico were imprisoned for "insulting the government," and more abandoned their homes or fled across the border to avoid similar fates. On Election Day, Díaz's uniformed soldiers and paramilitary *rurales* patrolled the polls. In what the ballot counters proclaimed was a "practically unanimous" result, the incumbent was reelected for an eighth term.

Pending "free and fair elections," Madero declared himself the "provisional president," and he, too, called for armed rebellion. However, Ricardo Flores Magón's Liberal Party had no intention of supporting a Madero presidency. "The malady that afflicts the Mexican people cannot be cured by removing Díaz and putting in his place another master," *Regeneración* explained. The paper argued instead for a true economic, political, and social revolution. "No government, no matter how good its intents, can declare the abolition of misery," Flores Magón elaborated in a separate essay. "It's the people themselves, the hungry, the dispossessed who must abolish misery, taking, in the first place, possession of the earth which, by natural right, cannot be monopolized by a few, but is the property of every human being."

Yet the Magonistas and the Maderistas were at war with a common oppressor, and they agreed, at first, to cooperate during actual fighting. The rebellion started slowly. For several months beginning in late 1910, the Madero forces were so poorly funded and organized that with the exception of the border state of Chihuahua, where at the turn of the year guerrillas ambushed a federal convoy, their prospects for survival were tenuous. The Liberals were unsteadier still, militarily, financially, and organizationally, and even as the Maderistas gained traction throughout the country in early 1911, the Magonistas could never find their footing.

Until, that is, they joined forces with the Industrial Workers of the World to invade the remote, sparsely populated peninsula of Baja California, the territory nominally owned by Mexico but much closer and more accessible to Los Angeles than to Mexico City, and operated virtually as a wholly owned subsidiary of its principal landowner, Harrison Gray Otis. In fact, Otis and his land syndicate owned nearly the entirety of the Colórado River delta in Mexico: 862,000 silt-laden acres, arranged roughly in a T-shape fifty miles long and two hundred miles wide—about the size of Massachusetts. Otis had paid "a few cents an acre," according to a U.S. Army general's report.

THE LIBERAL FORCES launched their revolt in northern Baja California for reasons both practical and strategic. The leadership, or Organizing Junta, was headquartered in east Los Angeles, in a "dingy" two-story flat near the IWW hall. Its location was common knowledge due to a lengthy piece in the *Los Angeles Times* that amounted to a WANTED notice. The article featured large photographs—basically mug shots—of the Flores

Magón brothers and other junta members, as well as an exterior picture of the apartment in which they lived and worked. Not once or twice but *four times*, the story gave the address of the building. LOS ANGELES INSURRECTIONIST LEADERS, read the cutline under a picture of 519½ East Fourth Street, AND THE PLACE WHERE THEY DO THEIR PLOTTING AND DIRECTING OF OPERATIONS TO MEXICO.

Not only was the Mexican peninsula proximate to Los Angeles, but it was also difficult to defend. Baja California stretched below American California like a gnarled, arthritic index finger for nearly a thousand desolate miles between the Pacific Ocean to the west and the Colorado River and the Gulf of California to the east. The border with American California was lightly guarded at some crossings and unguarded at others, which allowed for virtually unimpeded passage of rebels, guns, and ammunition. Save for residents of the isolated trading outposts strung along the international boundary (from west to east: Tijuana, population 733; Tecate, population 116; and Mexicali, population 462) and the territorial capital at Ensenada (population 2,170), on the Pacific coast south of Tijuana, Baja California was mostly uninhabited. It was also largely unprotected: there were a total of 450 soldiers and a hundred *rurales* posted, equally divided between north and south. (At the southern tip of the peninsula, where the Pacific met the gulf, lay the fishing village of Cabo San Lucas and not much else.*) And the territory's geographical remove from the Mexican mainland ensured the difficulty of sending in reinforcements. Finally, the rebels theorized that the government would be so preoccupied with defending the mainland, where the Madero forces were concentrated, that it would, as it had historically, all but ignore the isolated peninsula, thus leaving it vulnerable to Magonista occupation and ideal as a base for exporting revolution throughout Mexico.

The Magonistas' theory might well have been realized if not for the power and influence of Harrison Gray Otis. Otis was rightly afraid that if the rebels felled Díaz, they would drive him, Otis, out of Mexico. As he wired President Taft, "The socialistic American leaders of the insurrection openly boast that they intend to seize and divide up among themselves the real property of the California-Mexico Land and Cattle Company" (Otis's land syndicate). Otis urged Taft to send in the cavalry. "They are a bad lot, who ought to be exterminated in the interests

---

* The peninsula was later divided into two territories, north and south, and later still into the states of Baja California and Baja California Sur.

of right, peace and order, and for the protection of honest citizens on both sides of the line," Otis wrote. "Should the worst come to the worst, it would be sound and justifiable policy . . . to intervene by force for the protection of American citizens and interests in Mexico and for the sustaining of President Díaz in power."

Whatever the level of the president's concern for Otis and other American investors (including Taft's brother, a Wall Street lawyer whom Díaz had cagily hired as general counsel to the Mexican National Railway), Taft's greater concern, according to an Associated Press correspondent traveling by train with the president, was that "the line between the United States and Lower California is only an imaginary one and a revolutionary government there would be a source of constant worry." In other words, if revolution could be exported to Baja California by a small, underfinanced junta operating from a "dingy" flat in Los Angeles, could it not then be imported? For at some point, all those Wobblies who were taking up arms in Mexico were bound to recross the border. A Justice Department lawyer bluntly voiced the administration's anxiety about that scenario during a U.S. Senate hearing. Speaking of the IWW insurrectionists, the Los Angeles–based prosecutor said, "They have really been fighting to establish a center for some sort of a revolution . . . to break out in a general uprising of the unemployed and the laboring classes of the United States."

THE IWW and the Mexican Liberal Party were natural ideological allies. The Liberal Party had been founded four years before the IWW, in 1901. For its time and place, the party had been radical—at its founding congress, Ricardo Flores Magón had branded the administration of Porfirio Díaz "a den of thieves"—but it had not at the outset been revolutionary. The Liberals pushed for enforcement of the constitutional guarantees of freedom of press, speech, assembly, and education, and against what they considered to be the unholy influence of the Roman Catholic Church in secular affairs. It was not until September of 1905, and from the relative safety of St. Louis, Missouri, that the exiled Liberal Party leaders issued their revolutionary *Manifesto to the Nation*. The party declared it was forming a seven-member Organizing Junta, with Flores Magón as president, to unify and mobilize party members into a guerrilla army for the avowed purpose of ousting Díaz. The manifesto encouraged the establishment of Liberal Party clubs and newspapers as well as underground cells, the latter to be activated as events warranted.

The invasion of Baja California in 1911 was not the first time the IWW and the Mexican Liberal Party had collaborated. Back in 1905 and 1906, the Western Federation of Miners, the IWW's largest department (until the WFM seceded in 1907), was organizing Mexican and American copper miners in southern Arizona. At the same time, just across the Mexican border in Sonora State, the Mexican Liberal Party was trying to organize miners in the company town of Cananea. Arizona Wobblies crossed over to help the Liberals circulate *Regeneración* and other propaganda and to campaign for a nationwide Mexican miners' union under the banner of the Liberal Party. (A company spy reported to the mine owner, an American, that "agitators of the Western Federation had been through the mines inciting the Mexicans.") And though (or maybe because) a brief strike in Cananea ended horrifically for the miners—at least thirty were shot dead on the street, and others, wrote one journalist, "were taken to the cemetery [and] made to dig their own graves"—the strike would prove to be downright epochal in influence. It marked the beginnings of the alliance between the Mexican Liberal Party and organized labor, and it signaled their collective emergence as a genuine threat to the dual sovereignty in Mexico of Porfirio Díaz and American capital. In a conversation with the American ambassador in Mexico City as the strike violence raged, President Díaz seemed to acknowledge as much. "The little party of about twenty revolutionists at Cananea were only a handful of those who hold the same sentiments in other places," he said.

THROUGHOUT THEIR YEARS in exile in the United States, the Flores Magón brothers and other members of the Liberal Party's Organizing Junta were under constant surveillance—by both governments. Díaz's chief of intelligence, Enrique Creel, hired two U.S.-based private detective firms to tail party leaders throughout North America. (One firm, the Pinkerton Agency, would later contract with the state of Utah to spy on Wobblies and provide security for state officials during the culmination of Joe Hill's case.) Despite the fact that the Liberal leaders had been accused of no crime by the United States, not a few U.S. government agencies aided and abetted the Mexican spymaster. The post office, for one, seized the Liberals' mail (as it would later intercept the IWW's), either diverting it to the private detectives tailing the Flores Magóns or forwarding it to Creel in Mexico City. Among the correspondence Creel obtained were lists of dues-paying Liberal Party members and *Regeneración* subscribers in Mexico, people whose names, for obvious security reasons, the party had intended to keep confidential. Creel passed the information to a gaggle of government departments and agencies, as well as private investors, on both sides of the border. For good reason did the Socialist Party leader (and an IWW founder) Eugene V. Debs proclaim that "Uncle Sam is willing to act as a bloodhound of Díaz."

In 1906 and again in 1908, the junta tried on several occasions to launch a revolution. Each time, however, the uprising was aborted, either due to miscommunication between the U.S.-based junta and Liberal fighters on the ground in Mexico, or because Mexican army troops quickly routed pockets of isolated and undermanned rebels, or because junta members were indisposed in the United States—imprisoned for allegedly plotting to "set on foot a military expedition" against Mexico, a violation of the "neutrality laws" of the United States. Ricardo Flores Magón spent the maximum three years in prison for that crime. From behind bars, though, he founded a newspaper, *Tierra y Libertad* (Land and liberty). The paper lasted for only three issues in the spring of 1908, but its title lived on as the slogan of the Liberal Party (and later of the Zapatistas, the southern rebel army headed by Emiliano Zapata).

FLORES MAGÓN GOT OUT of prison in late August of 1910, and within days published an issue of *Regeneración*—the first since his conviction. (Distribution of the newspaper was as problematic as publication. From the printing press in Los Angeles to border towns on the American side, sympathetic railroad employees helped smuggle *Regeneración* into Mexico like the contraband it was, at times resorting to stuffing copies inside hollowed-out Sears catalogs.) "Here we are again in the field," Flores Magón exulted, "the torch of revolution in our right hand and the program of the Liberal Party in the left, and we declare war. We are not whining messengers of peace"—a gibe at the Maderistas, Francisco Madero's reformist Anti-Reelectionist Party—"We are revolutionists. Our ballots will be the bullets issuing from our rifles."

Even with a volunteer army, revolution did not come cheap. The rebels needed money for arms, ammunition, supplies, and food, and they needed leading propagandists to counter the "willful misrepresentations" the American press made of their cause. (Of course, the junta needed soldiers, too, but to recruit overtly in the United States could have again subjected members to prosecution under the neutrality laws.) In the days following the U.S. military's border occupation, Flores Magón appealed for support in a flurry of letters to prominent labor leaders and radicals. He reminded the Socialist Party's Debs that while the Liberal Party appreciated the "sympathy you have always shown, and are still showing . . . sympathy alone will not win victory for what we feel is the common cause of the disinherited." With Samuel Gompers, too, Flores Magón staked out common ground: "The slavery against which we are fighting is the slavery your American Federation of Labor was organized to fight," he wrote. "It is time that the workers of the United States speak out, and it is for you to give the word, promptly and decisively." (Gompers promptly and decisively sidestepped the request.) Of the renowned anarchist Emma Goldman, whom Flores Magón knew from his early days in exile in St. Louis, he asked that she use "the influence" she wielded "over a large section of the American public" to educate them about the fight "for the restoration of millions and millions of acres of land given away to foreign syndicates by the fraudulent connivance of Díaz" and to speak out against the "gigantic money interests" that propped him up and were now "calling the American nation to arms." (Goldman soon visited Los Angeles and San Diego on behalf of the rebels, where large crowds gathered to sing IWW songs and hear her "powerful appeals" for "economic emancipation.")

Flores Magón saved his most impassioned appeal for the IWW. His *Manifesto to the Workers of the World* was a Marxian program that adhered closely to the IWW's own preamble. "Comrades," it began, "For more than four months the Red Flag has flamed on the battle fields of Mexico, carried aloft by emancipated workers whose aspirations are epitomized in the sublime war cry: 'LAND AND LIBERTY!'" The manifesto made clear that the Liberal Party was fighting both Díaz and Madero, that it had no interest in "destroying the dictator" only "to put in his place a new tyrant" who would perpetuate the "continuance of social inequality, the capitalist system, the division of the human family into two classes—that of the exploiters and that of the exploited." Instead, the manifesto explained, the Liberals' "firm purpose" was to "expropriate the land and the means of production and hand them over to the people." To accomplish that would take three things: "worldwide protest against the interference of the powers in Mexican affairs, class-conscious workers . . . and MONEY, MONEY AND MORE MONEY."

IWW locals and other radical organizations and individuals chipped in what they could. Some ordered *Regeneración* subscriptions in bulk ("The paper goes very well," the secretary of the Sacramento local wrote, adding, "It is the real dope all right"). Others volunteered their particular expertise, whether it was a physician offering surgical care for wounded rebels; an inventor "in possession of a secret to manufacture smokeless powder" for "blasting purposes"; or a pair from Chicago who could handle heavy artillery: "[We] understand there is a special demand for men who fully understand how to operate machine guns, and both of us are fully competent to do so." Others simply offered themselves as rebel-army recruits. A member of the IWW local in Brawley, in Imperial County, California, about twenty-five miles north of Mexicali, wrote Flores Magón that his fellow members were "ready and willing to give their services and lives, if necessary, to the cause."

THE REVOLUTION in Baja California began at daybreak on January 29, 1911. Eight members of the rebel army had mustered at the new IWW hall in Holtville, California, ten miles north of the border and slightly east of Mexicali. Commanding the brigade were two Mexicans: one was a Wobbly farmworker and socialist named Simon Berthold, who had worked and organized in the sugar beet fields of Oxnard, sixty miles northwest of Los Angeles; the other, José María Leyva, had been one of the striking copper miners at Cananea five years earlier and more recently belonged to the Hod Carriers Union in Los Angeles. Additionally, both Berthold and Leyva were active in Los Angeles in "labor exertions," as one scholar blandly put it, which is to say, they were activists in the long-standing fight against Harrison Gray Otis. (It had been four months since the *Los Angeles Times* building had exploded during the citywide strike of the metal trades.)

The men from Holtville met six other *insurrectos* a few miles east of Mexicali, handed out old Springfield rifles they had smuggled across the border, and, at dawn, marched into Mexicali. With "astonishing ease," noted a friendly biographer of Flores Magón, the rebels took control of the town. Of the ten *rurales* on patrol, seven fled across the border and three surrendered. The rebels fired a single gunshot the entire day. They had gone to the adobe jail to demand the release of eleven Magonistas confined as political prisoners. The jailer declined to turn over the keys. He reportedly was about to fire on the insurgents when one shot him dead. Though the rebels allowed private citizens to cross the border to Calexico, California, those who stayed were invited to join the ranks. By early afternoon, the rebel army had swelled to forty. Already the wires hummed with the news. Berthold told an Associated Press correspondent that the taking of Mexicali was merely the first step of a carefully planned insurrection throughout northwestern Mexico—and beyond.

The *Los Angeles Times* published the story under this headline: BANDITS SACK MEXICALI, ACROSS STATE LINE; MOTLEY REVOLUTIONIST BAND IN POSSESSION OF MEXICALI . . . INDUSTRIAL WORKERS OF THE WORLD MIXED UP IN THE MOVEMENT.

The sacking of Mexicali—or perhaps Otis's frantic headlines and telegrams to the White House—provoked President Taft to order the War Department to investigate border conditions. The department deployed Brigadier General Tasker H. Bliss, commander of the U.S. Army's Department of California. Bliss confirmed that the region—indeed, the entire state—was teeming with reds. "California is honey-combed with the Socialistic spirit," he reported. "Those forms of so-called 'Labor Unions' which make Socialism their basic principle are strong here. These are the men who are particularly active in their sympathy with the present insurrection." He singled out one so-called union: "The labor organization known as the IWW . . . is especially active in fomenting the present trouble."

Not only was the IWW fomenting trouble, but a day after the rebels took possession of Mexicali, the IWW brought the trouble directly to Otis's doorstep. Simon Berthold (or, as the *Times* hissed, the "notorious Los Angeles socialist agitator") marched his troops, which by then numbered about sixty-five, to a campsite "in the heart of" Otis's ranch. Surely Berthold chose that spot in part to taunt Otis; the men wore "blood red" buttons proclaiming, "Los Angeles to be taken in 1912." But to camp there also made military sense. The location afforded a clear view of the mountain pass from which government soldiers on the road from Ensenada would descend and good visibility toward Mexicali and Calexico, where the U.S. Army had quickly deployed a few dozen troops to the border. Squatting there was strategic, too, because most of the rebels' new recruits (which was to say, most of the rebels) lacked horses, and there were many to choose from on Otis's ranch. Berthold or Leyva provided a ranch manager with receipts for the "borrowed" horses and assurances that the horses would be returned or paid for "when the revolution succeeds."

With the red flag waving above Mexicali and new recruits and guns flooding the town, revolutionary success in Baja California, isolated as it was from the mainland, where Díaz's troops had their hands full with the Maderista rebellion, no longer seemed far-fetched, and Otis must have felt under siege. At home, he was at war with unnamed unionists, otherwise known as "midnight assassins" and "anarchic scum" who he alleged had blown up the *Times* building on October 1, 1910. And on his Mexican ranch, he was battling what his newspaper (in a story headlined HOBOS

AND CRIMINALS FLOCK TO STANDARD OF "INSURGENTS") described as a "chicken thief band" led by "eighteen IWW anarchists." That story appeared on February 2, 1911. Three days later, Liberal Party members and sympathizers held a mass meeting in Los Angeles. The author and Socialist Party member Jack London addressed an open letter to the gathering. "To the dear, brave comrades of the Mexican Revolution," he began,

> We Socialists, anarchists, hobos, chicken thieves, outlaws and undesirable citizens of the United States are with you heart and soul . . . You will notice that we are not respectable. Neither are you. No revolutionary can possibly be respectable in these days of the reign of property. All the names you are being called, we have been called. And when graft and greed get up and begin to call names, honest men, brave men, patriotic men and martyrs can expect nothing else than to be called chicken thieves and outlaws. So be it. But I for one wish there were more chicken thieves and outlaws of the sort that formed the gallant band that took Mexicali . . . I subscribe myself a chicken thief and revolutionist.

By late April, the *insurrectos* had their sights set on Tijuana. They continued to hold Mexicali and, on their way west from there to Tijuana, had taken Tecate, too. Tijuana was important strategically because its proximity to San Diego offered ease of access to potential recruits from the United States and because, relative to other outposts of civilization in Baja California, it was close to Ensenada—which lay sixty miles to the south—and therefore was the preferred base from which to strike the territorial capital. And as word spread of Flores Magón's *Manifesto to the Workers of the World*—as the appeal for solidarity was reprinted throughout April in the *Industrial Worker* and *Appeal to Reason* and Emma Goldman's *Mother Earth*, and as it was translated and republished in an array of languages—hundreds of recruits found their way to the rebels' encampment. As a help-wanted advertisement in the *Industrial Worker* put it, "The rebel recruiting station is at Tijuana . . . and more men are required to fight the battle for liberty. A rifle on the shoulder of a worker would look better than a bundle of lousy blankets." A few recruits were adventurers in search of a thrill; others, mercenaries in search of a war—any war. For most, like Joe Hill, the chance to fight in Baja California represented a chance—the main chance—to live out an ennobling, revolutionary dream.

*   *   *

IN LATE APRIL, Hill traveled by boat with four or five others from San Pedro to San Diego, en route to Tijuana. Most probably he attended a mass meeting in San Diego on the afternoon of April 30. The Wobblies' resident female firebrand in the city, Laura Payne Emerson, was among a trio who soapboxed against the arrests of three union ironworkers who had been indicted a week earlier for murder in connection with the explosion at the *Times* building. Emerson (who in addition to her IWW duties was an accomplished poet) maintained that the explosion had not been triggered by dynamite, as the authorities alleged, and that "conclusive" evidence showed that it had been an accident caused by a leaky gas line. Further, and most provocatively, Emerson charged that Harrison Gray Otis had "laid the catastrophe at the door of the unions" to discredit organized labor as well as to save himself "from heavy damage suits and to save the insurance on the building." And most recently, Emerson might have added, Otis was again using his power and connections to make a scapegoat of labor, this time for the unrest in Mexico.*

Early on the morning of Monday, May 8, 1911, two companies of Liberal troops with a combined 220 soldiers arrived at the edge of Tijuana. They planned to capture the town and then march south to take Ensenada, which would secure a strong grip on the entire northern peninsula. One company was commanded by a Welshman named Carl Rhys Pryce, a soldier of fortune and a veteran of the turn-of-the-century Boer War and other African conflicts. Pryce had taken command after "General" Stanley Williams (or William Stanley) had been killed in battle

---

* A graphic illustration of Otis's power: In mid-October, during a visit to Los Angeles to shore up support for the 1912 election, President Taft granted Otis a private, secret meeting to discuss the case against the ironworkers and the dire implications for all capitalists should they be acquitted. Otis and his lawyer were afraid that corroborative evidence to win convictions was in short supply. Los Angeles prosecutors had tried and failed to obtain a search warrant for the ironworkers' union's headquarters in Indianapolis, where they believed lay the incriminating material they needed. The Indiana authorities had refused to cooperate, and the U.S. Justice Department had declined to intervene, deeming the case a state matter. Over brandy and cigars, Otis and his lawyer convinced the president to order Attorney General George Wickersham to intervene in the case. The next day, Wickersham, Taft's brother's law partner, ordered federal agents to search the ironworkers' hall, the Indiana authorities be damned. Without Taft, the prosecution had had no case. With him, the state eventually secured confessions and guilty pleas. (Although, as some have pointed out, the confessions may not have been truthful; key parts were at odds with some of the critical facts of the alleged crime.) Even so, the long sentences the defendants received were an affront to Otis. "I want those sons-of-bitches to hang!" he said.

in Mexicali on April 8. Williams, a Wobbly, was possibly a Canadian Indian and probably a veteran of both the Spokane free speech fight and the U.S. Army (he was said to have been a sergeant and drill instructor before deserting). Heading the other company was Jack R. Mosby, who had been a private in the U.S. Marines before he deserted in the middle of February; sixty days later, he found himself a commanding general of the Mexican Liberal Army. (Although a federal prosecutor later dismissed Mosby as "an IWW and a ne'er-do-well" who had "learned his soldiering out of yellow-backed dime novels," Mosby himself claimed military-commander bloodlines: his uncle was Confederate Army captain John "Speed" S. Mosby, he said.) Mosby was promoted to general after Simon Berthold died on April 13 or 14 during a sortie in a southern mining village. (The Liberals' other original commander in Baja California, José María Leyva, had since returned to the United States.)

By ten o'clock Tuesday morning, la Bandera Roja—the Red Army— had routed the undermanned *federales* and hoisted the red flag over the

"Tierra y libertad"—Land and liberty—emblazoned on the rebel flag flying over Tijuana. (Labadie Collection, University of Michigan)

Tijuana Customs House. The following day came word that Francisco Madero's Anti-Reelectionists had trounced the *federales* in a decisive battle at Ciudad Juárez, across the Río Bravo from El Paso, Texas. For Porfirio Díaz, the end was near; his last act as president would be to sign a peace agreement negotiated with Madero. He did so on May 25. "The triumph has been complete," Madero declared. "Liberty will spread its broad wings to all Mexicans."

To the Magonistas that was bunk; without land there could be no liberty. As long as all those million-acre estates remained titled to foreign investors with no program for restoring the land to the millions of poor Mexicans from whom it had been seized during the Porfiriato, the Liberals saw no reason to lay down their guns. "Don't believe the Capitalist papers when they tell you there is peace in Mexico because Díaz has resigned," the junta cautioned readers of the *Industrial Worker*. "There will be no peace in Mexico until the Red Flag flies over the working man's country and Capitalism shall have been overthrown."

With the red flag flapping over Mexicali, Tecate, and Tijuana, as well as over smaller settlements scattered about the peninsula, and with as many as five hundred *insurrectos* in Baja California and more arriving daily, the territory seemed destined for true economic revolution. The Liberal junta was so certain of victory that it encouraged supporters to colonize Baja California, touting its agricultural promise and irrigation canal. TAKE POSSESSION OF THE LAND, it invited readers of *Regeneración*.

The old soldier Otis would not surrender without a last stand. With his patron Díaz gone, and with the rebel forces swarming and allegedly threatening to blow up the canal works (which was the sole source of irrigated water for the entire Colorado River delta on both sides of the border), Otis hauled out the heavy artillery: he called on President Taft at the White House. He told the president that the rebels were trying to extort a huge sum of money in return for leaving the canal unharmed, and that the rebels were already responsible for property damage and losses totaling 325,000 dollars—circumstances, he said, that demanded immediate military intervention. Though Taft remained reluctant to order the troops across the line, Otis did wring one concession: the president would consent to Mexican forces crossing into American territory to facilitate passage to Baja California, provided Francisco Madero asked him.

On May 29, Otis's son-in-law and business partner, Harry Chandler, wired Madero: "President Taft advises can move troops . . . if both you and [provisional] President [Francisco León de la] Barra will wire him in making request." Madero took Taft up on the offer, and one of Madero's first acts as de facto commander in chief (he would formally assume the presidency after the fall elections) was to order a thousand federal troops to Baja California via Ciudad Juárez and the United States. (To dodge the neutrality laws of the United States, Secretary of State Philander Knox directed that the Mexican soldiers be unarmed while traveling through New Mexico and Arizona, their weapons to be "shipped as baggage.") To the Mexican Liberals, Madero had become the "new tyrant" about whom Ricardo Flores Magón had warned; now, as Flores Magón had also predicted, the fall of Díaz would "bring face to face the two social classes."

The face-to-face showdown would be brutal and decisive. But it would not occur until nearly a month after Madero had assumed power. In the meantime, Madero floated unacceptable peace proposals to the Liberals. And there was intrigue within the Liberals' own ranks. General Pryce had gone back to the United States, ostensibly to raise funds for the rebels' advance on Ensenada. Instead, he may have cut a deal with one Richard W. Ferris, a charlatan and part-time actor who contrived a farcical scheme to seize the peninsula and, with the dictator's blessing, create an independent "Republic of Díaz." Then, after a suitable period of independence, Ferris would turn around and sell the peninsula to the United States for a tidy profit, to be split with its embattled namesake. Ferris went so far as to declare himself president of the Republic of Díaz, draft a constitution, and display a flag that he had commissioned from a Hollywood prop man.*

Whatever the truth of Pryce's involvement in that odd affair, he was out as a general of the "2nd Division Army" at Tijuana, and Jack Mosby had assumed full command. Since the rebels had captured Tijuana on May 9, there had been little for Mosby's men to do. While they awaited orders from the junta, the troops remained quartered in Tijuana, where they occupied houses that the townspeople had vacated during the battle. For nearly six weeks, Joe Hill bunked with fellow workers from IWW Local 245 in San Pedro. Hill and the others drilled for thirty minutes or so every day, "so that we will be able to plug the federals full of holes when they have recovered enough to show up again," one volunteer explained. Otherwise they did as they pleased. "There was a piano in one of the buildings vacated and the IWWs used to congregate there to sing their favorite songs and

---

* Ferris later claimed he had staged the secessionist plan as an attention getter for the forthcoming San Diego Exposition, which had hired him as a publicity agent. Fair officials were unimpressed; they fired him before the fair opened.

when they did, Joe would be at the piano," Hill's friend Sam Murray recalled. Murray remembered Hill in Mexico as "a quiet man not given to boasting or self-advertising" and as exceptionally even-tempered. "I have known a tough guy to abuse him, whether he hated him because he was a Swede or an IWW, I do not know," Murray said. "Joe could have broken him in two and would have had cause to do so, but he let the guy get it off his chest and paid no attention to him."

At least one of Hill's songs likely dates from his *insurrecto* days. Don't fight, he counsels in "Should I Ever Be A Soldier," but if you must, march only under the workers' flag. The song is in some respects a departure: a sober tune not much leavened by humor, one that seems to underscore the depth of his antiwar feelings and perhaps, too, his transformation from revolutionary writer and theorist to true class warrior. He set the song to "Colleen Bawn," a 1906 Irish tune about a boy gone to war "to fight for love and glory." The song begins,

> *We're spending billions every year*
> *For guns and ammunition,*
> *"Our Army" and "Our Navy" dear*
> *To keep in good condition;*
> *While millions live in misery*
> *And millions die before us,*
> *Don't sing "My Country, 'tis of thee,"*
> *But sing this little chorus:*

> CHORUS
> *Should I ever be a soldier,*
> *'Neath the Red Flag I would fight;*
> *Should the gun I ever shoulder,*
> *It's to crush the tyrant's might.*
> *Join the army of the toilers,*
> *Men and women fall in line,*
> *Wage slaves of the world! Arouse!*
> *Do your duty for the cause,*
> *For Land and Liberty.*

Beneath the red flag, Hill and his compadres fought for the final time on June 22. A heavily armed force of about six hundred *federales* had arrived in Tijuana that morning, after a five-day march from Ensenada. Mosby and his troops, now numbering about 230 and with comparatively

Company B *insurrectos* before the decisive battle, Tijuana, June 22, 1911. (Labadie Collection, University of Michigan)

little firepower, fought tenaciously but were overmatched. Within three hours of fighting, the rebels were forced to retreat; the second Battle of Tijuana was finished. Casualties were heavy: at least thirty rebels and maybe as many as sixty were killed, and unknown numbers wounded. The *federales* acknowledged only three dead and three wounded on their side. Mosby and a hundred or so of the surviving rebels retreated across the border, where they gave themselves up to the U.S. Army. All but the dozen or so rebels whom the army wanted for desertion, like Mosby, were soon released. (Mosby was sentenced to prison, but he served no time. He was killed en route while supposedly trying to escape.)

For the Magonistas, the revolution was over. (In October, Francisco Madero was elected president of Mexico; he remained in office until he was assassinated in 1913.) Ricardo Flores Magón was convicted of flouting the U.S. neutrality laws and given a twenty-three-month prison sentence. In 1918, he was arrested again in the United States on a charge of sedition, convicted of violating the Espionage Act of 1917, and sentenced to twenty-one years and a day in prison. In 1922, at the age of forty-nine, he died in the U.S. penitentiary at Leavenworth, Kansas.

Joe Hill had eluded the U.S. Army. He apparently was one of the very few surviving rebels who was neither injured in battle nor detained upon returning to the United States. Instead, on June 22 he stole over the American border three or four miles east of Tijuana "without being questioned by a United States immigrant inspector," as he later testified

Above, an unidentified rebel soldier stands sentry in front of a Tijuana saloon; below, Hill drew this caricature in one of his last letters to his friend Murray. (Above: Labadie Collection, University of Michigan; below: *Industrial Pioneer* 1, no. 8 [December 1923])

during an immigration hearing. Hill's luck would run out soon enough, though. Three years to the day after the second Battle of Tijuana, the state of Utah rested its successful case against him for first-degree murder. As he sat on a prison cot in Salt Lake City on the eve of his scheduled execution in the fall of 1915, Hill busied himself writing farewell letters. To each of his correspondents he reiterated that he had nothing to repent for, that he had always said he was "going to get a new trial or die trying," and that, as he told a Swedish friend, "I have always tried to do the little that I could to advance Freedom's Banner a little closer to its goal." To that end, he said, he was most grateful for having had "one time the great honor of struggling on the battlefield under the Red Flag." It was a "little pleasure" that "few rebels have had the privilege of having," he reminded Sam Murray, "and I guess I've had my share of the fun after all." With the letter to Murray, Hill enclosed a caricature of his friend during their *insurrecto* days. He drew Murray standing outside a cantina wearing a wide-brimmed sombrero, spurred boots, and two bandoliers crossed over his chest. He is leaning on a bony horse with one hand and on his rifle with the other. The caption reads, HOW THE MEMORY DOTH LINGER.

9.

"More Beast than Man"

After the war, Hill "sojourned for a time" in California's Imperial Valley, where rebel troops had mustered at IWW halls before capturing Mexicali. He returned to the States from those six weeks in Mexico one proud revolutionary, a "true-blue rebel," he told Bill Haywood. He came back, too, with a heightened sense of the role he could and should be playing in the radical labor movement. Before the war, he had dabbled in writing, having contributed sporadically to the pages of the *Industrial Worker*. But his songs had not appeared in any of the three editions of *The Little Red Songbook* that the IWW had already published. That was about to change.

In early July of 1911, two weeks after Hill slipped across the border into California from Mexico, the *Industrial Worker* advertised the union's forthcoming 1911 *Songbook*: "IWW locals should get busy and send in their order at once. Price of song books is $5.00 a hundred or $35.00 a thousand." At the top of the list of new songs was "Long Haired Preachers," Hill's evisceration of hypocrisy in the Christian church, a theme Hill had spent a lifetime considering. (By the time the book was printed, the title had changed to the now-familiar "The Preacher and the Slave.") Hill had not written the song in response to an acute situation—say, a strike of railroad stiffs or textile workers. Those songs were coming soon. "The Preacher and the Slave" addresses the "holy rollers and jumpers" of the Salvation Army, an institution Hill first encountered as a boy in Gävle. Hill became further acquainted with the "Starvation Army" in Spokane, when it deployed its brass band in service to the authorities and "labor sharks" who wanted IWW soapboxers drowned out. To Hill, the army's

"long-haired preachers" made hollow, or "pie in the sky"—a phrase
Hill coined in this song—promises intended to keep workers be-
holden to their capitalist masters. He chose one of the Salvation Army's loveliest and most popular hymns, "Sweet Bye and Bye," as the
melody for "The Preacher and the Slave."

> *Long-haired preachers come out every night,*
> *Try to tell you what's wrong and what's right;*
> *But when asked how 'bout something to eat*
> *They will answer with voices so sweet:*
>
> CHORUS
> *You will eat, bye and bye,*
> *In that glorious land above the sky;*
> *Work and pray, live on hay,*
> *You'll get pie in the sky when you die.*
>
> *The starvation army they play,*
> *They sing and they clap and they pray*
> *Till they get all your coin on the drum,*
> *Then they'll tell you when you're on the bum:*
>
> CHORUS
>
> *Holy rollers and jumpers come out,*
> *They holler, they jump and they shout*
> *Give your money to Jesus they say,*
> *He will cure all diseases today.*
>
> CHORUS
>
> *If you fight hard for children and wife—*
> *Try to get something good in this life—*
> *You're a sinner and bad man, they tell,*
> *When you die you will sure go to hell.*
>
> CHORUS
>
> *Workingmen of all countries unite,*
> *Side by side we for freedom will fight;*
> *When the world and its wealth we have gained*
> *To the grafters we'll sing this refrain:*

FINAL CHORUS
You will eat, bye and bye,
When you've learned how to cook and to fry.
Chop some wood, 'twill do you good.
And you'll eat in the sweet bye and bye.

By the fall of 1911, Hill had returned to the San Pedro waterfront. Because the newly published *Songbook* attributed "The Preacher" to another writer, one F. B. Brechler (which might have been a pseudonym for Hill or perhaps was a clerical error; it was corrected in subsequent editions), at first Hill received little or no recognition for what was not only his first published song but also probably his best and certainly his most enduring. (Many have pronounced it the "signature song" of the IWW and Hill's "masterpiece." The song is routinely included in anthologies of American folk music—see, for example, those edited by Upton Sinclair and Carl Sandburg—and one music writer recently deemed it one of the "50 songs that changed the 20th century.") This is not to suggest that Hill sought acclaim for his work; he does not appear to have done so, and indeed, individual glory was anathema to Wobbly culture. It is only to say that the publication of "The Preacher" and an awareness that Wobblies everywhere were singing it must have been gratifying and encouraging; from then on he wrote steadily, and before very long, within two years, he was nonetheless the most acclaimed, and published, of all IWW songwriters.

The song with which he was first identified (and for which, along with "The Preacher and the Slave," he is best remembered) was "Casey Jones—the Union Scab." He wrote it in San Pedro, shortly after September 30, 1911, the first day of a huge nationwide walkout of railway employees: more than forty thousand shopmen from Seattle to New Orleans and Chicago to Los Angeles. The strikers were not Wobblies, but the IWW supported the walkout because the shopmen were demanding recognition of a single Federation of Shop Employees that would bargain on behalf of their nine individual craft unions—blacksmiths, boilermakers, machinists, etc.—a precursor, as the IWW saw it, to a One Big Union of railway employees.

The strikers' opponents were twofold. In Southern California, where thirteen hundred men walked off the job, they were fighting the Southern Pacific Railroad, which for decades had been the largest landowner and most powerful corporation in the state—its nickname was the "octopus."

(By 1911, the SP belonged to the Harriman Lines, the transcontinental behemoth against which the strike had been called.) But the strikers were also fighting the craft structure of the American Federation of Labor, which divided workers by skill rather than uniting them by industry, and which was precisely what doomed the strike. The craft unions whose members rode the trains—the brakemen, firemen, and engineers—kept the trains running for fear of losing their own jobs. And yet by scabbing on their union brethren in the shops, the trainmen not only put the strikers' livelihoods at greater risk but also jeopardized their own personal safety by relying on untrained or poorly trained nonunion shopmen to maintain and repair the locomotives and the track. As the editor of the shopmen's *Strike Bulletin* wrote, the nonunion workers were not mere scabs but "an aggregation of moral germs [who] know no more about a locomotive and its requirements than the cave dwellers knew about the higher principles of mathematics."

Joe Hill probably knew something about locomotive engines from his father and his older brothers, who had all worked for their hometown railway. And assuredly he knew a lot about industrial solidarity, the subject of "Casey Jones—the Union Scab." Hill's parody inverts the story of the original "Casey Jones," a popular vaudeville song written in 1909 that celebrates the "brave engineer" for the Illinois Central (a Harriman-controlled line) who "stuck to his duty both day and night" but who dies heroically while saving the life of his fireman (Casey's last words are "Jump, Sim, while you have the time") when his train, the "Cannonball Special," crashes into another. This is the final verse of one version of the original song:

> *Casey Jones, he died at the throttle,*
> *Casey Jones, with the whistle in his hand.*
> *Casey Jones, he died at the throttle,*
> *But we'll all see Casey in the promised land.*

In Hill's song, Casey makes it to the promised land all right—but not for long. Hill's Casey ignores his fellow Southern Pacific workers' pleas that he support their walkout:

> *The workers on the S.P. Line to strike sent out a call;*
> *But Casey Jones, the engineer, he wouldn't strike at all;*
> *His boiler it was leaking, and its drivers on the bum,*
> *And his engine and its bearings, they were all out of plumb.*

Casey thinks he doesn't need the shopmen to keep "his junk pile running." He just keeps working "double time," and the company rewards him with a "wooden medal for being good and faithful on the S.P. Line."

The workers again appeal to Casey to "help us win this strike."

> But Casey said: "Let me alone, you'd better take a hike."
> Then someone put a bunch of railroad ties across the track,
> And Casey hit the river with an awful crack.

He breaks his spine, which earns him "a trip to heaven on the S.P. Line."

> "You're just the man," said Peter, "our musicians went on strike;
> You can get a job a-scabbing any time you like."

Casey takes St. Peter up on the offer.

> Casey Jones got a job in heaven;
> Casey Jones was doing mighty fine;
> Casey Jones went scabbing on the angels,
> Just like he did to workers on the S.P. Line.

But the angels' union complains that "it wasn't fair for Casey Jones to go around a-scabbing everywhere." And sure enough, Casey is booted "down the Golden Stair."

> Casey Jones went to Hell a-flying.
> "Casey Jones," the Devil said, "Oh fine;
> Casey Jones, get busy shoveling sulphur—
> That's what you get for scabbing on the S.P. Line."

Hill's song caught on quickly, first among Southern Pacific strikers in Los Angeles and San Pedro, where it was printed on small cards (roughly the size of a playing card) and sold in support of the strike fund. Workers passed the songcards around the country—and to union halls across the ocean. Not only was "Casey Jones—the Union Scab" on its way to becoming "the classic American song about the scab," as one scholar writes, but it was also taking hold in Europe. "'Casey Jones' made an awful [big] hit in London," Hill told his friend Sam Murray, "'and Casey Jones he was an Angelino' you know and I never expected him to leave L.A. at all."

That "Casey" did travel far beyond Los Angeles was a sign of Hill's growing importance to the IWW. And the song's popularity within the broader labor movement portended the widespread support Hill would receive while in prison from countless AF of L affiliates and unionists around the world.

AS HILL MADE HIS WAY back to San Pedro from the Imperial Valley after the Battle of Tijuana, many other Wobbly war veterans wound up in San Diego. Of those, about a hundred had been detained by the U.S. Army at nearby Fort Rosecrans after giving themselves up at the border. Before long, the army had released them, or as a colonel put it candidly, "We just turned them loose on San Diego, which was a dirty trick." The officer so characterized the situation because despite the rebel troops' calamitous final battle in neighboring Tijuana, the war in Baja California had confirmed for San Diegans just how dangerous Wobblies could be. No longer did it appear that they were content with the tactic of mixing nonviolent, passive resistance—soapboxing and goading the police to fill the jails until taxpayers cried uncle—with mere revolutionary *rhetoric*. That would explain why their mere presence in the city's working-class district, the Stingaree, so unhinged the ruling powers and their daily newspapers that by early 1912 the populace of San Diego would be whipped, as a magazine writer of the day described it, "into a hysterical frenzy, into an epidemic of unreasoning fear and blind rage, into a condition of lawlessness so pronounced that travelers feared to visit the city."

Hill initially stayed away from San Diego out of fear that the IWW would only squander its resources there. There were few industrial jobs in the small city (population: forty thousand), and he saw no reason to provoke a fight over free speech or anything else. He thought it wiser, as he told a friend, "to spend a little more money and energy in organizing the women workers especially in the big industrial centers in the East." To Hill, San Diego was one of those "'jerk water towns' of no industrial importance," a town where "the main 'industry' consists of 'catching suckers'"—tourists—and that was therefore "not worth a whoop in Hell from a rebel's point of view."

Nonetheless, many rebels stayed in town (if only for the splendid weather—San Diego justly claimed the title of "Most Equable Climate in America"). Attendance swelled at the existing IWW local's thrice-weekly street meetings in the Stingaree, a development that did not go unnoticed by the union's redoubtable adversary, Harrison Gray Otis. In

November of 1911, six months after the Mexican *federales* had chased the rebel army off his ranchland, Otis spoke in San Diego at a secret meeting of the city's power elite. Before a hundred or so merchants, manufacturers, law enforcers, and politicians assembled at the opulent U.S. Grant Hotel (newly built by the son of the former president), Otis inveighed against ignoring or mollycoddling the "I-Won't-Workers" and the "I-Want-Whiskeyites"; he shook the city's movers to repress IWW propaganda and defeat "labor terrorism" by enacting stringent anti-picketing and anti-street-speaking ordinances modeled on those in Los Angeles.*

The distempered old lion's roar of resistance and suppression roused his audience to action. Within a week or so, his *Los Angeles Times* published an "exclusive dispatch" from San Diego reporting that its city officials "are determined to rid the street corners of Socialists, IWWs and other agitators, who, each night, congregate and exhort to a curious throng." The article continued, "So rabid have been the utterances of this class of street speakers that the City Council decided to seek *extraordinary methods* of ridding the city of their presence." (Emphasis added.) The piece outlined only statutory means of accomplishing that goal: "such laws as will prohibit this class from using the streets to incite threats against peaceable citizens." The headline, RADICALS TO BE RESTRAINED, left no doubt—they *would* be restrained. But even those many Wobblies who had run the gauntlet of free speech fights in Spokane and Fresno, whose experience had taught that "extraordinary methods" of restraint meant harassment, beatings, false arrests, suspension of due process, even mob violence, could not have foreseen that in the year to come San Diego would broaden the definition to encompass kidnapping, torture, and murder.

UNTIL THE BEGINNING of 1912, the IWW was unfamiliar to most people who were not "students of the labor problem" or otherwise "on the spot when a fight was on," according to the first historian of the IWW, Paul Brissenden, who wrote in 1919. It was the impending free speech fight in San Diego, along with the landmark and virtually concurrent "Bread and Roses" strike across the country in the mill town of Lawrence,

---

* Although his audience awarded him "a hero's welcome," Otis was not known for his goodwill toward San Diego, which he considered a rival of Los Angeles for tourism. His *Times* went so far as to exclude San Diego from its published maps of Southern California.

Massachusetts, that "really introduced the Industrial Workers of the World to the American public," Brissenden writes.

Situated thirty miles north of Boston, Lawrence was a city of eighty-six thousand people. Fully half of its residents over the age of thirteen worked in one of the thirty mills that lined the banks of the Merrimack River. On their first payday of 1912, the thousands of women workers, as well as girls and boys under the age of eighteen, received distressing news in their pay envelopes: mill owners had cut their wages to correspond with a state-mandated reduction in hours (from fifty-six a week to fifty-four). Two hours less pay, which amounted to thirty-two cents, spelled three fewer loaves of bread a week, a significant loss to workers and their families who already lived on crumbs. The cry "Short pay, short pay!" cascaded from mill to mill, as if carried along by the rushing waters of the Merrimack. By day's end, nearly half of the town's thirty thousand millworkers, most of them European immigrants, had shut down their machines. "Better to starve fighting than to starve working," they reasoned.

Despite the fact that the IWW had no more than three hundred dues-paying members in Lawrence, Wobbly organizers took control of the walkout (which soon grew to almost twenty-three thousand strikers). That single, insufferable fact was enough for the head of the local affiliate of the American Federation of Labor, John Golden, to condemn the strike. To Golden, the president of the United Textile Workers of America, what mattered was not the economic shock wave that had jolted the wretched millworkers into the streets; the real issue was the IWW's lack of jurisdiction. The IWW was "an outlaw organization without the slightest standing in the world of labor," Golden told a congressional committee. What was happening in Lawrence was "a revolution, not a strike," he testified, and on another occasion he dismissed it as "a revolution led by men whose hold upon the wage workers lies in the fact that they stir up bitter class hatred."

Whether a labor strike or a harbinger of revolution, the reality was that more than twenty thousand workers were on the snowy streets of Lawrence marching and singing under the red flag of the IWW. Still, to the AF of L and its local craft-union affiliates, the IWW was officially nonexistent—a posture that seemed to defy the force of gravity. A reporter asked G. W. Ramsden, a spokesman for the Lawrence Central Labor Union, if the CLU was cooperating with the IWW. Of course not, Ramsden said; there was "nothing to cooperate with" because the AF of L did not "recognize the IWW as an organization."

The reporter followed up: "Is it not a fact that twenty-two thousand men and women are out on strike and organized?"

"I suppose they are," Ramsden replied. "But what of it?"

WRITERS FOR SOME of the leading publications of the day went to Lawrence to address that question and to document how working-class immigrants of divergent backgrounds—they reportedly came from fifty-one nations and spoke forty-four languages and dialects—maintained a united front against the mill companies, their hired guns (the ever-present Pinkertons and other accomplished strikebreakers), the police, and the state militia. For two months, the strikers and their families faced down hunger, arrests, and evictions (the mills owned the tenements they lived in), as well as clubbings, stabbings, bullets (police killed a young Syrian man with a bayonet and shot and killed a female Italian striker), and every other weapon in the employers' arsenal of intimidation. And then, in the middle of March, with the manufacturers' spring orders unfilled due to the work stoppage and the strikers showing no sign of remorse and no sign of breaking ranks, the employers laid down their bayonets; they were ready to settle. Their offer provided for virtually everything the workers had demanded at the outset: an average wage increase of 15 percent for hourly workers; a 5 percent increase for pieceworkers; time and a quarter for overtime work; and a pledge not to discriminate against anyone for strike activities. Bill Haywood hailed the Lawrence strike as "the most signal victory of any organized body of workers in the world."

Writing in the *American Magazine*, Ray Stannard Baker marveled, "This movement in Lawrence was strongly a singing movement. It is the first strike I ever saw which sang! . . . It is not short of amazing, the power of a great idea to weld men together . . . There was in it a peculiar, intense, vital spirit, a religious spirit if you will—that I never felt before in any strike." A *Harper's Weekly* reporter, Mary Heaton Vorse, recalled a similar feeling in her memoir: "It was the spirit of the workers that seemed dangerous," she wrote. "They were confident, gay, released, and they sang. They were always marching and singing. The gray tired crowds ebbing and flowing perpetually into the mills had waked and opened their mouths to sing, the different nationalities all speaking one language when they sang together."

They sang standards such as "The Internationale" ("Arise, ye prisoners of starvation! / Arise, ye wretched of the earth / For justice thunders condemnation / A better world's in birth"). They also sang a new song by Joe Hill, "John Golden and the Lawrence Strike." Hill aimed his jab squarely at the jaw of the AF of L and, as the muckraking journalist Lincoln Steffens put it, its "suspicious intimacy with capital." Writing in 1985, the historian Donald E. Winters Jr. called the song "one of the most devastating attacks on 'business unionism' ever written." As with "The Preacher and the Slave," Hill arranged "John Golden and the Lawrence Strike" to a familiar Sunday school hymn, "A Little Talk with Jesus."

> *In Lawrence, when the starving masses struck for more to eat,*
> *And wooden-headed Wood* he tried the strikers to defeat,*
> *To Sammy Gompers wrote and asked him what he thought,*
> *And this is just the answer that the mailman brought:*

> CHORUS
> *A little talk with Golden*
> *Makes it right, all right.*
> *He'll settle any strike,*
> *If there's a coin in sight*
> *Just take him up to dine*
> *And everything is fine—*
> *A little talk with Golden*
> *Makes it right, all right.*

> *The preachers, cops and money-kings were working hand in hand,*
> *The boys in blue, with stars and stripes were sent by Uncle Sam;*
> *Still things were looking blue 'cause every striker knew*
> *That weaving cloth with bayonets is hard to do.*

> *John Golden had with Mr. Wood a private interview,*
> *He told him how to bust up the "I double double U."*
> *He came out in a while and wore the Golden smile.*
> *He said: "I've got all labor leaders skinned a mile."*

> *John Golden pulled a bogus strike with all his "pinks† and stools."*
> *He thought the rest would follow like a bunch of crazy fools.*

---

* William M. Wood headed American Woolen Company, the largest employer in town, and directed the employers' antistrike coalition.
† Pinkerton Agency detectives.

But to his great surprise the "foreigners" were wise
In one big solid union they were organized.

FINAL CHORUS
That's one time Golden did not
Make it right all right.
In spite of all his schemes
The strikers won the fight.
When all the workers stand
United hand in hand,
The world with all its wealth
Shall be at their command.

Hill followed the strike closely from afar. He was either in San Pedro or in the Territory of Hawaii. A fellow Wobbly songwriter, Harry "Haywire Mac" McClintock, recollected long years later that during the winter of 1911–1912, he and Hill had been in Hilo, the port town on the eastern coast of the (big) island of Hawaii. McClintock said they had worked as longshoremen bucking sugar bags for the American-Hawaiian Steamship Company. (The company's freighters hauled sugar between the Hawaiian Islands and West Coast ports and had recently made San Pedro one of their ports of call.) "I worked with Joe on the job and ate and slept in the same 8 × 12 shack," McClintock wrote in a 1950 letter to Fred Thompson, then editor of the *Industrial Worker*. Though no corroborating evidence could be turned up, that of course does not preclude the veracity of McClintock's statement. Still, one might consider Thompson's remark that in McClintock's "later years"—he died in 1957—he supposedly took to "cadging drinks by telling about his alleged days with Joe Hill."

HILL EVIDENTLY FINISHED the song after the strike was won in mid-March. If he had been in Hawaii for all or part of the winter, by then he was back in Southern California. But it hardly matters where he was. The more interesting and important question, as one Wobbly asked, is "How did Joe Hill come to write such songs as that?" And:

How did he know how the workers . . . felt? How did he know how it felt to have your pay envelope short of the price of two loaves of bread so you went out on the streets with the workers from the textile mills of Lawrence . . . Wherever Joe Hill was he somehow felt like the workers and he wrote for them a song . . . How astonishing! People from all parts of the world, all speaking different dialects and all singing the same song.

On March 14, 1912, the day the pattern-setting American Woolen Company acceded to the strikers' demands, the IWW reached its high-water mark. It came in the wake of those decisive, if bloody, victories in Spokane and Fresno and the short-lived but exhilarating rebel conquest of Baja California, all in the previous two years. But that water level was about to recede. On that same day, March 14, the *Industrial Worker* published an open letter from a writer across the country in San Diego, where the most volcanic of all free speech fights had recently erupted. "To All Red Blooded IWW's," the letter began, "**ACT! DAMN YOU! ACT!**"

The battle in San Diego had been simmering since the city council had passed two ordinances at the beginning of 1912: one banned public speaking on "congested" downtown streets; the other granted the police the authority not only to "disperse any unusual and unnecessary assemblage" that was "obstructing or impeding," but also to disperse any gathering that an officer deemed "*likely* to obstruct or impede" traffic on downtown streets. (Emphasis added.) "We are going to rid the city of beggars and crooks and the idle who don't want to work," Chief of Police Keno Wilson asserted.

Wilson's hands—and jails—were full. By the time the *Industrial Worker* published the open letter from San Diego, the city had locked up some two hundred "Red Blooded IWW's" and charged them with vagrancy or with conspiracy to break one or both of the new ordinances (or an even more recent anti-picketing ordinance). Police had also shipped men to jails in nearby counties, and vigilantes had established armed, mounted patrols at the San Diego county line to capture, torture, and turn back all Wobblies. "They threaten to make an example of these men," reported J. Edward Morgan, the *Industrial Worker*'s correspondent. He continued,

They swear they will show Spokane [and] Fresno . . . how to handle the "Damn Tribe" that ought to be "wiped out of existence." Do you get it! Do you get it! Damn your red-blooded, rebellious livered souls, get on the job! Get on the Job! San Diego! San Diego! It is the only place on the map for you. Get busy men! Get busy locals! Money and Men! Men and Money!

As in Spokane and Fresno, the San Diego authorities learned that to treat free speech prisoners as caged beasts—to cram seventy-eight men into

San Diego police administer the "water cure" to IWW free speech demonstrators, 1912. (Labadie Collection, University of Michigan)

a bull pen intended for no more than twenty, or to deny them wash water for days on end, or to serve them rancid food—was to inspire greater resistance and a constant ruckus. "I do not know what to do," Chief Wilson confessed to an investigator. "I cannot punish them. Listen to them singing. They are singing all the time, and yelling and hollering, and telling the jailers to quit work and join the union. They are worse than animals."

Dispensing justice was proving to be as costly for San Diego's taxpayers as it was noisy for its jailers—too costly, in the opinion of the city's establishment. But rather than see his city relent—empty the jails, that is, and clear the court dockets of free speech prisoners as had Spokane and Fresno in the past two years—San Diego's most influential citizen and leading taxpayer, John D. Spreckels, urged a more expeditious solution to the rampant lawlessness. Spreckels, an heir to a sugar and shipping fortune, owned the city's two ultraconservative daily newspapers, the *San Diego Union* and the *Evening Tribune*, which he wielded, as Harrison Gray Otis did the *Los Angeles Times*, with the rough justice of an axe.* (And also like Otis, Spreckels held a significant financial stake in Baja

---

* E. W. Scripps owned the other daily, the *San Diego Sun*. While wealthy himself, Scripps styled himself a "left labor galoot." His paper, while in no way radical, was certainly more measured and less convulsive on labor issues.

California.) "Why are the taxpayers of San Diego compelled to endure this imposition?" Spreckels's *Evening Tribune* asked. "Simply because the law which these lawbreakers flout prevents the citizens of San Diego from taking the impudent outlaws away from the police and hanging them or shooting them. This method of dealing with the evil that has fastened itself on San Diego would end the trouble in half an hour."* In an editorial, RAISING VAGRANTS TO THE DIGNITY OF GREAT CRIMINALS, the *Tribune* offered a rationale for knotting a noose around the trouble. Of the IWW it wrote, "Hanging is none too good for them and they would be much better dead; for they are absolutely useless in the human economy; they are the waste material of creation and should be drained off into the sewer of oblivion there to rot in cold obstruction like any other excrement."

EMBOLDENED AND ABETTED by the police and Spreckels's newspapers, a vigilante organization called the Committee of 1000 undertook a campaign of terror against the IWW. One night some four hundred vigilantes waited for a San Diego–bound freight train at San Onofre, about fifty-five miles north of the city and the point of entry for the lone rail line that served San Diego County. The train carried ninety-three Wobblies. The liquored-up vigilance committee, each member with a gun in one hand and a club in the other, surrounded the boxcar. First they forced the IWW men off the train and searched them for weapons and loose change. Next they clubbed or kicked or otherwise roughed them up, then ordered them to put up their hands—and keep them up. The vigilant citizens then paraded their captives into a cattle pen and marched them in circles two by two, their hands still in the air. After ninety minutes, the detainees were allowed to collapse on manure piles and made to spend the night. They received neither blankets nor food nor medical attention. "Several men were carried out unconscious and I believe there were some killed, for afterwards there were a lot of our men unaccounted for and never have been heard from since," a Wobbly named Alfred R. Tucker wrote in a letter to Vincent St. John, the union's general secretary-treasurer. "In the morning," Tucker continued, "they took us out four or five at a time and marched us up the track

---

* There were certainly voices of moderation among the establishment. "I don't believe that guns and bloodshed are necessary," a former parks commissioner said. "Horsewhips are enough to deal with these fellows."

to the county line . . . where we were forced to kiss the flag and then run a gauntlet of 106 men, every one of which was striking at us hard as they could with their pick axe handles. They broke one man's leg, and every one was beaten black and blue, and was bleeding from a dozen wounds." Then Tucker and his fellow workers were told to hike up the track toward Los Angeles and that if they were caught again in San Diego they would be killed and dumped in the bay. As a correspondent for *Solidarity* named Stumpy wrote of the vigilance committee, "The jails are full, but they seem to think there is plenty of room in the cemetery."

Due to the extensive and graphic coverage in the radical press of the appalling conditions and abuses the agitators faced, thousands more—as many as five thousand, all told—responded to the IWW's call for reinforcements to pack the jails and gum up the judicial works by insisting upon individual trials by jury. As a summons in the *Industrial Worker* put it,

> *Come on the cushions*
> *Ride up on top;*
> *Stick to the brakebeams;*
> *Let nothing stop.*
> *Come in great numbers;*
> *This we beseech;*
> *Help San Diego*
> *To win* FREE SPEECH

Whatever Hill's gripes about draining the union's treasury in a "jerk water town" of "no industrial importance," in time he joined the protest. On March 20, he most probably was one of a party of twenty-eight Wobblies who took passage on a steamer from San Pedro to San Diego. A day later, the group took to the downtown streets to sell copies of the *Industrial Worker*. Police seized the newspapers, arrested the salesmen, and then released them. The following afternoon around two o'clock, thirteen of the San Pedro men started to hold a street meeting. As usual, they began with a song. On that day they chose "Casey Jones— the Union Scab." Plainclothed police and vigilantes immediately surrounded the choir, and all thirteen were arrested on a charge of "singing revolutionary songs." The men were marched to the police station, where they were separated and some "put through the third degree," Alfred Tucker wrote in his letter to Vincent St. John. "None of us had eaten for 24 hours," he went on, "but they kept us without food until about midnight." Tucker said they were then "ordered to march" out of town. The next night, most of the group caught a freight train back to Los Angeles—only to return two weeks later with fresh recruits.

There is no reliable record of who besides Tucker was arrested; as was customary, quite a few detainees used aliases. There was one Swede, according to police records. He admitted that he was an IWW member and that he had arrived from Los Angeles the previous night. Based on what is known—that Hill was in San Diego on or near that day, that he was beaten, jailed, and quickly released, and that eight days later he spoke at a public forum in San Francisco—it is plausible that Hill was the Swede in custody for singing his own song. The police recorded the Swede's name as "L. Jorgensan," which perhaps was an inverted play on his given name, Joel, or "Jo-EL," as he had signed the postcard written from San Pedro to his boyhood friend Karl Rudberg.

Hill was not one of those who returned to San Diego after being removed from the city. Instead, he headed up the coast. But unlike during his past travels, on this trip he was not merely drifting to the next town or job, or serving himself up as a warm body in another free speech fight. He had a destination, and an appointment. He was going to San Francisco, not as another anonymous hobo riding the rods in a "side-door Pullman" but as a representative of the newly formed California Free Speech League—a coalition of the IWW, the Socialist Party, and other organizations muted by the street-speaking ordinances. He had been invited to speak at a rally on behalf of the San Diego protesters. The invitation signaled his growing importance to the IWW—an acknowledgment of his talent and contributions. Already, workers all over were singing his songs—from mill hands in Massachusetts to striking railroad shopmen throughout the western United States to industrial unionists in the United Kingdom to jailed soldiers in the free speech wars. But until he took the stage before a large crowd at the Building Trades hall in San Francisco on March 31, 1912, never had he stepped out from behind the curtain of his writing paper. He spoke only briefly, yet his appearance marked a turning point. He began to see himself as less of a worker and more of an artist: the IWW's bard-in-residence.

Hill was the final speaker on that Sunday afternoon. (The gathering was one of several around the country held in response to the California Free Speech League's appeals to "Organized Labor and All Lovers of Liberty" for donations and support.) He followed the Socialist lawyer and orator Austin Lewis, who stressed that the right to speak on the streets was an "absolute necessity" for the IWW—the only way the union could reach migratory workers. Hill was in none too good shape. "He looked as though he had just risen from a sick bed," the San Francisco–based IWW organizer Caroline Nelson reported in the *Industrial Worker*. "His face was pale and pinched." Hill wryly explained that he "had just come from the hospitality of the M&M [Merchants and Manufacturers Association] in San Diego" and that "owing to that hospitality he was physically unable to make any lengthy speech." Nelson remarked on his clothing. He wore overalls, an outfit that "bespoke [a] low standard of living but not of intellect," she wrote. "Fellow Worker Hill," she went on, "spoke more intelligently and eloquently than many a widely heralded upper class jawsmith, who has had nothing to do all his life but to wag his tongue and to look up references." She added that Hill had "nailed the widely circulated lie that the upper class have bought out all the workers who have any intelligence, and that every intelligent man can get work."

Hill described jail conditions in San Diego. He cited the dreadful food, and how hungry prisoners "practiced sabotage" by banging on the iron doors of the cells and singing so loudly that the judge presiding in the second-floor courtroom, directly above the jail, demanded silence. The prisoners, in turn, demanded edible food, and sent word that until they were fed properly, they would keep up the awful racket. Hill ended his talk with a proposal that "brought down the house." He suggested that the "army of fifty thousand unemployed of San Francisco move on to San Diego." The San Diego jails were full, he said, and with the free speech fighters already "running up the expenses of the taxpayers fearfully," an enormous "army of invaders would scare them stiff."

Hill's proposal scared stiff the *Los Angeles Times*. Otis's paper covered the rally and an outdoor meeting the next day at which, it reported, plans were "being agitated" for a march down the coast. Under a headline that read like a telegraphed distress signal, REDS. TO INVADE SAN DIEGO. HUNDREDS OF LOAFERS COMING SOUTH, the *Times* fretted "that within a week an army of at least 10,000 will be organized and started out from San Francisco. This will be increased by a large contingent from Oakland and other large cities along the line of the march until it reaches Los Angeles, where it will be augmented by several thousand."

HILL HIMSELF WOULD NOT JOIN the army marching south. He was heading in the opposite direction: north toward Canada. Four days before his speech in San Francisco, IWW organizers in British Columbia, Canada's westernmost province, had ignited a wildfire of a strike that had jumped from one railroad construction camp to another over a stretch of nearly four hundred rugged and mountainous miles. Hill was not going to British Columbia to volunteer for jail duty or to look for work. (Only "scabs" would be on the job.) Nor was he moving in a new direction only geographically. He was going to British Columbia because the strike afforded him the opportunity to fuse work and art in a novel, immediate way. He was going as a new weapon in the class struggle. He would write topical songs on the spot, and as fast as he could write them, workers would sing them.

The little town of Yale, in the Fraser River Valley, was the center of strike activity. Half a century before, in the late 1850s, Yale had been a gold rush boomtown, its one street, writes a resident of the time, "crowded from morning till night with a surging mass of jostling humanity of all sorts and conditions. Miners, prospectors, traders, gamblers and painted ladies mingled in the throng." By the early twentieth century, the ore was long played out. The valley's latest lure was the potential of gainful work on the Canadian Northern Railway grade that would connect inland Canada with both coasts.

But there was nothing gainful about the work. By the time Hill arrived in Yale in early April, a week to ten days after the walkout had begun, eight thousand railroad stiffs had walked off their jobs along the winding and untamed Fraser River to protest low wages, long hours, "punk grub," and, most of all, unsanitary and dangerous conditions in the camps and on the job sites of contractors for the Canadian Northern. Wages ranged from a dollar and seventy-five cents to two dollars and twenty-five cents a day. That was gross pay: before the employers' myriad deductions. "One dollar per day is charged for board," a disenchanted worker recorded, "25¢ per month is charged for mail they never get, and one dollar per month for a doctor they never see.* The price of a pair of boots is $12 to $18, and other things in proportion."

The deductions added up to no money for anything, it was said, but "overalls and snuff"—work clothes and tobacco. Hill borrowed that saying for the title of one of at least three songs he wrote in Yale. (He had made himself at home in the office of the strike secretary, a young fellow Swede.) He set "Overalls and Snuff" to the tune of "The Wearing of the Green," a traditional Irish rebel song. (Hill found that tune

---

* The monthly hospitalization charge was especially galling. Not only was the lone "hospital" in a barn, but it was said that the resident doctor was so inept that "a horse would run if it saw him coming."

so conducive to parody that he used it for another song he wrote there, and he or another writer used it for a song that was soon to appear, un-credited, in the *Industrial Worker*: "We're Bound for San Diego."*)

"Overalls and Snuff," though never published, became "very popu-lar" in the far-flung strike camps. This is the only known stanza, as re-called by an IWW "camp delegate," Louis Moreau, in a letter he wrote half a century later:

> *We have got to stick together boys*
> *And fight with all our might*
> *It's a case of no surrender*
> *We have got to win this fight*
> *From the gunnysack contractors*
> *We will take no more bluff*
> *And we won't build no more railroads*
> *For our overalls and snuff*
> *For our overalls and snuff, for our overalls and snuff*
> *We won't build no more railroads*
> *For our overalls and snuff.*

It was not only the miserable wages that had prompted the strike. The men worked mainly for American firms under contract to the Canadian Northern, a railroad that was vying with two others for transcontinental supremacy in Canada. Speed was paramount to the contractors; as to the health and safety of the workers, the employers were, as one railroad stiff writes, "indifferent." He says that it was common to hear from someone who had lost an arm or a leg "that men were cheaper to the contractor than timber, and that it cost him less if a worker lost a limb than it would to provide timber that would have prevented the fall of rock that had caused the accident." After all, he adds bitterly, there were always more workers, "so why waste money or time in safeguarding the[ir] lives?"

As poorly as their jobs paid, and as dangerous as they were, the work-ers' chief grievance, the main reason for the walkout, was the atrocious living conditions. Contractors herded workers into overcrowded bunk-houses with three tiers of beds, dirt floors, no windows, and scant

---

* Though that song lacks the bite and polish of Joe Hill's finer work, the lyrics contain trace inflections of his style. A verse: "They're clubbing fellow workingmen who dare their thoughts express / And if old Otis has his way there'll be an awful mess. / So swell this army, working-men, and show them what we'll do / When all the sons of toil unite in One Big Union true."

ventilation. Not all camps had so much as an outdoor toilet. Some camps had bathhouses, but those facilities were "of the vilest sort," the *Industrial Worker* reported. At least one camp discharged its waste into the river immediately upstream from the site where water was drawn for cooking. "The worker under such conditions becomes more beast than man," observed the *British Columbia Federationist*, the Vancouver-based organ of the British Columbia Federation of Labor, adding, "Along the Fraser River human life was held in contempt by the contractors."

The workers struck to reclaim their humanity. They established clean, orderly, disciplined strike camps, each with its own commissary, sleeping

---

WHERE THE FRASER RIVER FLOWS
(Tune: "Where the River Shannon Flows")

Fellow workers pay attention to what I'm going to mention,
For it is the fixed intention of the Workers of the World.
And I hope you'll all be ready, true-hearted, brave and steady,
To gather 'round our standard when the Red Flag is unfurled.

CHORUS

Where the Fraser river flows, each fellow worker knows,
They have bullied and oppressed us, but still our Union grows.
And we're going to find a way, boys, for shorter hours and better pay, boys;
And we're going to win the day, boys; where the river Fraser flows.

For the gunny-sack contractors have all been dirty actors,
And they're not our benefactors, each fellow worker knows.
So we've got to sitck together in fine or dirty weather,
And we will show no white feather, where the Fraser river flows.

Now the boss the law is stretching, bulls and pimps he's fetching,
And they are a fine collection, as Jesus only knows.
But why their mothers reared them, and why the devil spared them,
Are questions we can't answer, where the Fraser river flows.

Why should any worker be without the necessities of life when ten men can produce enough for a hundred?

For every dollar the parasite has and didn't work for there's a slave who worked for a dollar he didn't get.

53

From *The Little Red Songbook*, Joe Hill Memorial Edition, 1916.

quarters, rules (no more than two drinks daily, for example), and self-governing court to adjudicate any supposed violations. One reporter described the Yale camp as "a miniature republic run on Socialist lines." In their spare time between picket duty, strikers read, studied, and listened to Wobbly soapboxers lecture on class division and, presumably, salvation through industrial unionism. They preached that even though the eight thousand striking workers represented sixteen different nationalities, in reality "there are only two nationalities, and . . . these nations are divided by class and not by geographical lines." And, as always, the workers united in song. They sang the favorites from *The Little Red Songbook*, and, with great relish, they sang Joe Hill's songs about their own strike as fast as he could write them. He wrote his first within days of his arrival in Yale. Setting it to "Where the River Shannon Flows," a sentimental Irish favorite, Hill titled his decidedly unsentimental song "Where the Fraser River Flows."

> *Fellow workers pay attention to what I'm going to mention,*
> *For it is the fixed intention of the Workers of the World.*
> *And I hope you'll all be ready, true-hearted, brave and steady,*
> *To gather 'round our standard when the red flag is unfurled.*

> CHORUS
> *Where the Fraser river flows, each fellow worker knows,*
> *They have bullied and oppressed us, but still our union grows.*
> *And we're going to find a way, boys, for shorter hours and better*
>   *pay, boys*
> *And we're going to win the day, boys, where the Fraser river flows.*

> *For these gunny-sack contractors have all been dirty actors,*
> *And they're not our benefactors, each fellow worker knows.*
> *So we've got to stick together in fine or dirty weather,*
> *And we will show no white feather, where the Fraser river flows.*

> *Now the boss the law is stretching, bulls and pimps he's fetching,*
> *And they are a fine collection, as Jesus only knows.*
> *But why their mothers reared them, and why the devil spared them,*
> *Are questions we can't answer, where the Fraser river flows.*

The main contractor for the Canadian Northern was an American firm, Foley, Welch and Stuart. (The "gunny-sack contractors" to which

Hill's song refers were the small subcontractors hired by Foley, Welch.) During the walkout, the firm tried desperately to recruit replacement workers. It tried first in Vancouver, British Columbia. But the strike was so well publicized there, according to the *Federationist*, that "all the endeavors of the contemptible reptiles to obtain scabs [came] to naught." Foley, Welch also sent recruiters to U.S. cities in the Pacific Northwest, to San Francisco, and as far east as Minneapolis. In each locale, the IWW and the American Federation of Labor, in an uncommon show of solidarity, established joint picket lines in front of the offices of the employment agencies. In Seattle, for instance, the secretary of the strike committee bragged that Martin Welch, a principal in the construction firm, "could carry all the scabs he could get . . . in his coat pocket and still have room for a large-size prayer book."

Reports of Welch's futile recruiting efforts trailed him all the way back to Yale. When he spotted the strike secretary, he lashed out: "Get up out of here, you red necktie son of a bitch, or I'll kick you in the mush." One day, Welch happened by the strike camp, and as he spoke with some Swedish workers sitting on the side of the road, the camp's "groaning brigade," a sextet of singers, broke into another of Hill's timely new compositions. Also written to the tune of "The Wearing of the Green," it began,

> *Martin Welch is mad as hell and don't know what to do*
> *And all his gunnysack contractors are feeling mighty blue*
> *For we have tied their railroad line and scabs refuse to come*
> *And we will keep on striking till we put them on the bum.*

"When [we] started to sing the song Joe had made for him," Louis Moreau remembered, "Martin tore his hair and swore he'd get us . . ." Welch made good on his vow. Along with other contractors for the Canadian Northern, he asked the premier of British Columbia (the ranking provincial officeholder) to send in strikebreaking troops. In conspiratorial language reminiscent of that employed by the politicos of Southern California, the contractors declared that the strike was part of the IWW's "stupendous scheme for tying up the leading industries of the Pacific Coast." And like its publishing brethren in Los Angeles and San Diego, the leading British Columbia newspaper tirelessly slapped the Wobblies with the back of its editorial hand. "The whole movement represents an invasion of the most despicable scum of humanity," the *Vancouver Sun* proclaimed, adding, "The government must show its strength and drive these people out of the country even if the use of force is required to do so."

The premier, however, nixed troop deployment. Instead he authorized the contractors to deputize and arm their own supervisors as "constables" and encouraged the firms to hire private detectives to protect strike-breakers. Ultimately the police ordered the men back to work. When none budged, the authorities razed the strike camps and made wholesale arrests. The strikers' alleged crimes ranged from vagrancy to unlawful assembly to "inciting to murder." By June, 250 men were in jail, and many others had been deported. Though the IWW never called an end to the walkout, by July most of the railroad stiffs had returned to work. The strike was broken.

HILL HAD SINCE RETURNED to San Pedro. The wharves were booming in 1912; no port in the world unloaded more board feet of lumber. Yet steady work for a Wobbly was hard to come by. The local IWW membership was up against a hiring system controlled by the American Federation of Labor, or "Labor Fakirs," as Hill called them. To join a "longshore gang" required the nod of a straw boss for the AF of L, Hill's friend Alexander MacKay later recalled. "Consequently, Joe had a hard time getting on a crew, unless an actual shortage of hands developed, which was seldom."

Nor was it only Wobblies whom the AF of L hiring bosses shut out. It was the foreign-born as well. Nationally, the labor federation had branded newly arrived, unskilled immigrants as "impossible to assimilate or unionize"; worse, they were seen as a detriment to the American worker for their willingness to settle for lower wages or serve as strike-breakers. And worst of all, as was demonstrated in Lawrence, the foreign-born were susceptible to the propaganda of "trouble-makers" and "radicals of all sorts." (On that last score, the AF of L was in lockstep with the National Association of Manufacturers, the big business lobby, which dismissed southern European immigrants—of whom there were many in Lawrence and San Pedro—as "nothing but seeds of socialism and anarchy with which to thistle our fertile land.")

This was not an academic issue in San Pedro in 1912. Local newspapers were reporting the impending arrival of European immigrants recruited by the stevedore companies to, in essence, depress the wages of existing dockworkers. With IWW members severely underemployed, it is easy to imagine that the local union might have expressed concern—might even have agreed with the AF of L's exclusionary immigrant policy. That was not the case. Due at least in part to Joe Hill, the local reacted differently. A Wobbly by the name of Frank Lefferts later remembered a street meeting at which Hill had spoken. The meeting had opened with the singing of Dick Brazier's "Good-Bye Dollars" ("Good-bye dollars; I must leave you / For a job with you I've got to buy. / Something tells me I will need you. / When I'm hungry and get dry"). Then Hill took the soapbox. "I shall never forget what Joe said," Lefferts wrote a friend near the end of his life. (Like many Wobblies, Lefferts spoke fluent gallows humor: "I am a dilapidated broken-down old cull, living on borrowed time; about ready for the bone yard, 80 years of age, (senile) just a few days ahead of the undertaker and only living to save funeral expenses.") "Now boys," Lefferts quoted Hill as saying, "the reactionary subsidized press is telling us that they will soon be bringing shiploads of four thousand [workers] at forty dollars a head from Europe. Now the question is, what are *you* going to do: are you going to the dock and sneer at them and say, 'here is another load of damn ignorant foreigners to take our jobs,' or are you going to try and make friends with them and invite them to our IWW hall?"

The local reached out to the new workers, and in July some of them walked off their jobs under the IWW banner. Hill served as secretary of the strike committee. On strike were about two hundred lumber handlers—most of them Italians. They walked after the stevedore companies scoffed at their demands: a raise to forty cents an hour from thirty cents; a ten-cent-hourly increase in overtime pay, to sixty cents; an hour-long lunch break; and an end to the monthly fee for hospitalization. The strikers won some early rounds: they shut down the loading of one steamer; forced another to unload its cargo fifteen miles distant; and delayed a few other ships. And the IWW took its usual beating in the local press. NO I WON'T WORKERS TO BOSS THIS WHARF, the *Los Angeles Times* reassured its faithful, a sentiment echoed in the *San Pedro Daily News*: IWW GRAFTERS ARE DOOMED IN SAN PEDRO.

Yet the press did not sink the strike; the AF of L did. Without the support of its craft unions, which, to be sure, instructed their members to cross the waterfront picket lines, the walkout ended quickly, within a week. An official of one struck company, Crescent Wharf and Warehouse, then announced new hiring restrictions. "We will employ Americans if we can get them," he said, "but not if they belong to the IWW."

On August 1, Local 245 conceded defeat. A statement signed "San Pedro Press Committee" was written inimitably by the strike secretary,

Hill. (He acknowledged as much in 1915, when he told a Salt Lake City newspaper that he had served in that capacity in San Pedro.) In the statement, Hill caustically tipped his hat to

> our old friend Otis of the *Los Angeles Crimes* [who] did all he could to advertise the strike and devoted about two columns of fiction and pictures every day to spread the news. We also wish to extend our thanks to the editor of the *San Pedro Daily Nuisance* for his valuable services. In our opinion said editor is only wasting his time printing a 2 by 4 sheet like the *Daily Nuisance*. A man with his imagination and utter disregard for the truth would surely make a hit as a lawyer or Diamond Dick novel writer.

Hill spent one more year in San Pedro. He seems not to have worked much, if at all. If jobs for Wobblies were scarce before the strike, employment afterward was virtually nonexistent. As for Hill, the waterfront "pie-card artists"—the AF of L's management-friendly officials—"practically black-balled" him, Alexander MacKay recalled.

MacKay had met Hill upon arriving in San Pedro, fresh from the free speech fight in San Diego. The fight had ended gradually; during the summer of 1912, violence against IWW members had tapered, as had the jail population. That was in part because of a report harshly critical of the city's conduct issued by the nominally Progressive governor of California, Hiram Johnson. The governor's appointed investigator, Colonel Harris Weinstock, made clear that he had no use for the IWW and its teachings. And yet Weinstock held up IWW members as veritable Eagle Scouts next to San Diego's "so-called vigilance committee," of which he wrote,

> Every blinded member . . . has, in the eyes of the law, made of himself a criminal—a far greater criminal than those whom he brands as 'anarchists,' 'revolutionists,' 'dynamiters' and 'the scum of the earth' . . . The question naturally arises, therefore, who are the greater criminals; who are the real anarchists; who are the real violators of the Constitution; who are the real undesirables—these so-called unfortunate members of 'the scum of the earth,' or these presumably respected members of society?

MacKay was one of the last Wobblies released from jail, apparently following his acquittal. (Of the sixteen the city eventually tried for conspiracy to violate the free speech ordinances, five were acquitted and eleven were convicted. Not one vigilante was prosecuted in connection with the free speech fight.) He got out in September and, along with another former jailbird, caught a "coaster," or steamer, for San Pedro. When they arrived, MacKay said, "we tackled the first guy we saw in overalls, and pulled out our red cards." The fellow they tackled also carried a red card. He introduced himself as Joe Hill and invited them to his home: a "tiny tar-paper shack" right on the pier in Happy Hollow, a derelict section of the waterfront that was home to many immigrant longshoremen, or dock wallopers. Hill fed MacKay and his friend from the pot of mulligan (a catch-as-catch-can stew) simmering outside on the dock and showed them where they could "flop and jungle up" as long as they wanted to.

LACKING WORK, Hill concentrated on his craft over the next year. From inside his little shack, he was emerging as the IWW's preeminent musical voice. Four of the seven songs in the 1912 edition of *The Little Red Songbook* were his: "Casey Jones—the Union Scab," "Where the Fraser River Flows," "Coffee An'," and "John Golden and the Lawrence Strike." (The book was published in early July, just prior to the dockworkers' strike.) And during the first five months of 1913 alone, the *Industrial Worker* published eight new songs of his, beginning with "Mr. Block" in the January 23 edition and continuing with "Scissor Bill" in the issue of February 16; "We Will Sing One Song," March 6; "What We Want," March 27; "Should I Ever Be A Soldier," April 3; "The White Slave," April 10; "The Tramp," May 22; and "Stung Right," May 29. Those and two more of his, "There Is Power in a Union" and "Everybody's Joining It," comprised ten of the twelve songs in the 1913 edition of the *Songbook*.

But the writing seldom came easy. "Every word of his songs [was] hammered out with a copious amount of sweat—if not blood and tears," MacKay remembered. Over the course of several letters written nearly four decades later, MacKay described Hill's songwriting process—his "tremendous struggles" in musical composition and how the act itself transformed him. He was "a most reticent cuss," MacKay said, "a real close-mouthed guy, but he did loosen up when he had a song on the griddle." MacKay described how Hill "actually knocked out" a song:

> A few of us would be sitting around the dock. We would be working over a mulligan and shooting the bull . . . Suddenly his face would light up and he'd dash into the shack. In a minute or so we'd

hear the plunk-plunk of a guitar. If the line or quatrain [four-line stanza] panned out to his satisfaction, he would dash out to us simply aglow at his latest rhyming achievement. His joy when he hit the jackpot of jingle was a joy to behold.

When inspiration eluded Hill on the dock, or when the mulligan ran thin, or when he needed a piano to audition his new songs, he could usually be found at the Sailors' Rest Mission, a nondenominational church (NO LAW BUT LOVE, NO CREED BUT CHRIST, ran the motto above the entrance) and relief organization that provided food, shelter, and gospel services for wayward maritime workers. Hill was no more interested in salvation than ever, no less disparaging of "long-haired preachers." But the superintendent of Sailors' Rest, John Makins, a kindly Canadian-born minister in his late forties, was not the sort, as Hill's lyric had it, to "tell you what's wrong and what's right." Makins "liked Joe and was very good to him," the Wobbly editor Ralph Chaplin later reported, and Hill "appreciated" and "reciprocated" Makins's friendship. "But it was the piano," Chaplin wrote, "that was the chief attraction" of the mission.

Makins himself seemed to say so. "He used our piano a great deal, for he was a musician," Makins noted in a Sailors' Rest annual report, "[but] he refused to be a Christian." Still, Makins made Hill welcome, and Hill occasionally furnished the music for the church's meetings. Perhaps the mission's cultural activities and diversions reminded him of the Workers' Federation in Gävle, where as a longshoreman a dozen years earlier he had studied painting, music, and English and attended the regular evening concerts. For in addition to Makins's warmth and the lure of the piano (on which, Chaplin reported, Hill wrote "Casey Jones—the Union Scab"), Sailors' Rest provided workers with a reading room, writing tables, and board games, and it hosted night-school classes on Tuesdays, "first-class" musical entertainment, usually choral or instrumental concerts, on Wednesdays, and on Sunday evenings, meetings of Swedish seamen.

THERE WERE THREE Swedish seamen in San Pedro to whom Hill grew closest. One was Otto Appelquist, who in the spring of 1913 shared Hill's dockside shack. At twenty-three, Appelquist was a decade younger than Hill. He, too, had grown up in an ancient port town, Helsingborg, just across the sound from Denmark on Sweden's southern coast. Before he came to San Pedro, he possibly worked on merchant ships in and out of

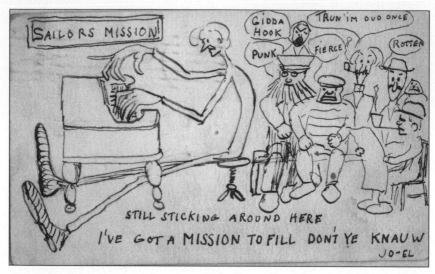

The Sailors' Rest Mission in San Pedro offered food, shelter, religion—and a piano. Above, Hill's self-portrait; below, the shelter side of the mission, circa 1914. (Above: Walter P. Reuther Library, Wayne State University; below: Special Collections Department, J. Willard Marriott Library, University of Utah)

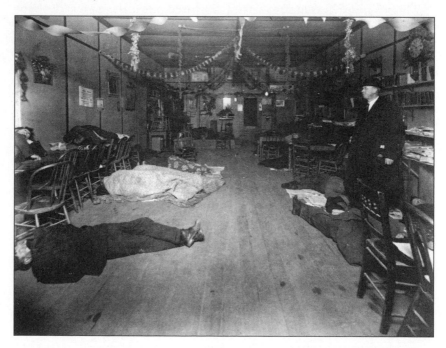

Sweden as well as Alaska and Seattle. Hill's other close Swedish-born friends in Happy Hollow were the brothers John and Ed Eselius. John Eselius was thirty; Ed, thirty-two. They had quit jobs in the noxious lead and copper smelters of their adopted hometown, Murray, Utah, to join the species of "common pacific coast wharfrat," as Hill called himself and his kind.

The Eseliuses, too, had trouble finding steady employment on the wharves, and sometime in the late spring of 1913, they gave up and went home to Murray, the working-class suburb south of Salt Lake City. The brothers invited Hill and Appelquist to follow them to Murray and stay at their family's cabin while they hunted for work. Appelquist went immediately, or nearly so; by late spring, he was employed as a structural ironworker on an office building in Ogden.

For Hill, the decision to follow his friends to Utah was likely more difficult. Despite the lack of work, San Pedro suited Hill. He had bonded with Reverend Makins, a father figure of sorts. He had liberal access to the mission's piano. He was a key member of Local 245. And he had never been more productive as a writer. Alexander MacKay, himself a literary sort, believed that Hill would have remained "more or less permanently" in San Pedro had he been able to make a bare living. "He seemed to like his little shack and the leisure to sweat great gobs of agony at the parturition of a new parody."

But Hill left his shack for good, probably toward the end of July and certainly no later than the second week of August. Besides his inability to earn a living, there was one other factor that pointed him toward Utah, or, at any rate, out of San Pedro: legal trouble. On June 4, he was arrested on suspicion of robbing a streetcar. There had been a wave of such robberies rippling across Greater Los Angeles—no fewer than twenty-three attempts in the first four months of the year. One such job was pulled in San Pedro on the night of April 27, when two armed and masked men relieved the passengers of Pacific Electric car no. 312 of about two hundred dollars. Five weeks later, San Pedro police commander J. A. Smith arrested Hill for that stickup. The evidence consisted of black clothing said to have been worn by one of the perpetrators and recovered near the scene of the robbery. No witness tied Hill (or anyone else) to the clothing. Neither did anyone place him at the scene. The charge was summarily dismissed in police court.

Within days, Commander Smith rearrested Hill. The offense was vagrancy; the sentence, thirty days in jail. Was the vagrancy charge a pretense to hold him pending additional evidence in the streetcar robbery?

Possibly, but none was forthcoming. Or, as Hill believed, was he targeted as a prominent Wobbly? "I was secretary of the strike committee," he theorized later, "and I suppose I was a little too active to suit the chief of the burg."

Whatever the reason, San Pedro authorities wanted Joe Hill removed from the waterfront. And if the local police could not muster the evidence to lock him away for committing a violent crime, the United States government could do one better: it could deport him for *advocating* violence; that is, for being an anarchist—a class of alien prohibited in the United States under federal immigration law. On June 18, 1913, nine days into his sentence, Hill was served in the Los Angeles city jail with a federal warrant for his arrest. Citing restrictive language in the Immigration Act of 1907 (and an amended law Congress had passed in 1910), the warrant charged that because Hill was both an alien and "an anarchist or person who believed in or advocated the overthrow by force or violence" of the U.S. government, "or of all forms of government, or of all the forms of law, or the assassination of public officials," he "belonged to a class of persons excluded from entry into this country." He was, in a word, deportable.

A government hearing a week later to determine Hill's immigration status centered on two questions: to what political philosophy did he subscribe, and had he illegally reentered the United States from Mexico in 1911 after his six-week stint in Baja California with the rebel army? Hill "stoutly denied" that he was an anarchist, according to Immigration Service notes of the hearing. The previously undisclosed notes shift awkwardly between first-person and third-person point of view. The first-person portions, though tendered between quotation marks, seem like a court reporter's clumsy, wooden summary of Hill's words: "I am a strong disciple of Karl Marx and believe in everything that he teaches. I am a socialist and a firm believer in Karl Marx's principles. I have read his books at different times and I think his ideas are the best."

Asked why he had reentered the United States from Mexico in 1911 "without being questioned by a United States Immigrant Inspector," a violation of federal law, he explained that he had been on the run "from Mexican federal troops pressing the command to which he was attached" and that he had been "three or four miles east of Tijuana" when he had crossed into the United States "as a refugee seeking asylum."

The regional supervising inspector for the Immigration Service, who served as the hearing officer, found Hill's claim to be a war refugee credible. The inspector ruled that because asylum cases were "ordinarily" exempted from inspection, it followed that Hill, too, should be spared from prosecution on that ground. As for the other core issue, the inspector found unpersuasive the arrest warrant's *"prima facie* case" that Hill was an anarchist. With "no additional evidence" presented to validate the charge, the inspector recommended that Hill be freed once he had paid his thirty-day debt to society for committing vagrancy. On July 9, he was released from custody in Los Angeles. Due to the hearing officer's humane reading of the punitive immigration law, Hill had survived a close brush with deportation. But he could not evade the far more punitive law of unintended consequences. After all, had the hearing officer recommended expulsion, Hill would not have set foot in Utah. Instead, able to go as he pleased, he fatefully chose to leave behind his troubles with the San Pedro police for a fresh start in Salt Lake City. On July 8, 1913, the federal government revoked Joe Hill's arrest warrant. A year to the day later, the state of Utah issued his death warrant.

III

A SONG ON HIS LIPS

If it had not been for these thing, I might have live out my life, talking at street corners to scorning men. I might have die, unmarked, unknown, a failure. Now we are not a failure. This is our career and our triumph. Never in our full life can we hope to do such work for tolerance, for joo-stice, for man's understanding of man, as now we do by an accident. Our words our lives our pains—nothing! The taking of our lives—lives of a good shoemaker and a poor fish-peddler—all! That last moment belongs to us—that agony is our triumph.

—BARTOLOMEO VANZETTI, EXECUTED,
ALONG WITH NICOLA SACCO, IN 1927

And if death is to be the reward for being true to the working class, we'll die with a song on our lips.

—*INDUSTRIAL WORKER*, JULY 25, 1912

10.

Bracing for War

He was imprisoned for twenty-two months, from the night of his arrest in mid-January of 1914 until the morning of his execution in mid-November of 1915. During that period, he appeared in court for a plea hearing, a preliminary hearing, the trial, a sentencing hearing, an appellate hearing, a resentencing hearing, a hearing before the Utah Board of Pardons (he declined to appear at a second hearing of the pardons board), and another resentencing hearing. Through the partial transcripts of those proceedings known to exist; through the extensive but thoroughly biased coverage in the Salt Lake City dailies and the equally biased coverage in the IWW weeklies and other radical organs; through accounts of his jailhouse meetings with reporters, supporters, lawyers, and lawmen; and not least through his own persistent writings—during this period, Joe Hill comes into focus more sharply than ever.

And yet, at a certain point during those long months in prison, Joe Hill the individual fades from view. The IWW had orchestrated a worldwide drumbeat to call attention to his plight—and, not incidentally, to the union. (As one member wrote, "This is hard on Joe Hill but it is excellent propaganda for the IWW.") The publicity campaign was so effective that it attracted for Hill the support of the king of Sweden and the president of the United States. Hill was thrust into the spotlight on the international stage, the foremost symbol of collateral damage in the war between capital and labor. He became a lightning rod for class tensions—a conductor of so much anger and idolatry that, as with anyone who survives a bolt from the blue, the experience changed him profoundly. All those powerful reactions he absorbed seemed also to absorb his sense of self; Joe Hill the metaphor was replacing Joe Hill the man. On both sides of the class divide, people spoke of him as representative of a movement; he had become larger than himself, and inseparable from the IWW. As one Salt Lake City newspaper framed the case on the eve of the execution date, it was not about Hill's guilt or innocence (he was "no longer a factor in the equation") but about whether the rule of "law or anarchy" would reign in Utah. Or conversely, as *Solidarity* put it a week before he was to be shot, the real crime was "about to be perpetrated by the capitalist class against the workers."

HILL WAS ARRESTED for first-degree murder on Wednesday, January 14, 1914. It will be recalled that he was suspected of being one of two masked intruders who had entered a grocery store near closing time on the previous Saturday, shouted, "We've got you now," and then shot to death the proprietor, John G. Morrison, and Morrison's seventeen-year-old son, Arling. (Hill's friend Otto Appelquist, also late of San Pedro, was his suspected accomplice.) Police believed that Arling had shot one of the gunmen moments before he had been killed; if so, the bullet was never recovered. Detectives took that to mean that whomever Arling had shot—if he had shot anyone—was walking around with a bullet lodged inside him.

Sometime between seventy-five minutes and two hours and fifteen minutes after the murders, Hill knocked on the door of Dr. Frank McHugh, whose home office in suburban Murray was near the Eselius family's house, where Hill was staying, and about five miles south of Morrison's grocery. Hill had been shot in the chest. His overcoat was "soaked with blood, which was still spurting from the wound," the doctor later said, an indication that the wound was fresh. McHugh said that the bullet had entered Hill through the bottom of the left lung and "came out just under the left shoulder." Hill told McHugh that he had been shot in a dispute over a woman. He named neither the shooter nor the woman. However, as discussed previously, I turned up a handwritten letter that the woman, Hilda Erickson, wrote in 1949 in which she stated that her former fiancé, Otto Appelquist, had shot Hill because he thought that Hill had caused her to break off the engagement.

IT WAS DR. MCHUGH who tipped police to Hill's gunshot wound—not immediately, but several days later, most probably after hearing that the governor of Utah had posted a five-hundred-dollar reward for information leading to the arrest and conviction of the Morrisons' killers. It was also almost certainly McHugh who first told police of Hill's affiliation with the Industrial Workers of the World. McHugh was a prominent Socialist—in 1916, he would run unsuccessfully for governor as the party's nominee—and as he later recalled, he had "seen Hill at a meeting or two" during the five months or so in which Hill had been in town. McHugh most probably passed along the incriminating bulletin that Hill was a Wobbly even before police arrested him. That information, coupled with corroboration from the police commander J. A. Smith in San Pedro that Hill and Appelquist were a "bad pair," that they had "held up a street car" in San Pedro the previous May, and that Hill was "somewhat of a musician" and "a writer of songs for the IWW song books," rigged the game against Hill from the outset. "YOU HAVE THE RIGHT MAN," Commander Smith confirmed in a congratulatory note to Brigham Grant, the Salt Lake City chief of police—a pat on the back that arrived just in time to make headlines such as this on the day of Hill's first court appearance, his plea hearing: SAN PEDRO POLICE COMMANDANT SAYS HILLSTROM AND APPELQUIST WERE THE MEN WHO ROBBED TRAIN; "YOU HAVE RIGHT MAN," HE WRITES.

But Commander Smith's map of Joe Hill's "trail of crime," in the words of the *Deseret Evening News*, was strewn with outright falsehood presented as fact and innuendo offered as evidence. As to the charge of streetcar robbery, a police court judge had promptly tossed it out for lack of evidence. In his letter to Chief Grant, Smith also declared of Hill, "He is certainly an undesirable citizen, and is in the United States unlawfully." But that charge, too, was unsupported by fact, and indeed had been refuted by the immigration officer who found no reason to deport him.

Still, the news coverage of the letter from San Pedro set the tone for much of what would follow. The *Herald-Republican* quoted Hill implausibly confessing to his jailer that he was guilty of the highway robbery charge in San Pedro. "I was mixed up with some street car holdups who certainly could operate with the best of them," Hill reputedly said. The self-incriminating quote complemented the San Pedro mug shots of Hill that the *Deseret Evening News* published the same day under the fevered headline HILLSTROM'S CRIME RECORD IN CALIFORNIA SENT HERE. The article, though, negated its title. The nearest it got to a "record" was that Hill was "accused of participation in the street car holdups." (Even that was a distortion: Commander Smith's letter claimed that Hill had perpetrated *one* holdup; now, suddenly, Hill was retroactively charged with plural holdups.)

Eventually, Hill's "record" as reported in the Salt Lake press swelled from mere streetcar banditry in San Pedro to *killing* a San Pedro police officer during the "labor troubles" there to a variety of other violent offenses. In short, to newspaper readers (and potential jurors) in Salt Lake City, Hill was a murderous, larcenous, bomb-throwing alien anarchist who in his spare time wrote inflammatory, revolutionary songs for the I-Won't-Workers.

Hillstrom's Crime Record In California Sent Here

JOE HILL ALIAS JOE HILLSTROM
From a Photograph by the Bureau of Identification by the Department of Police of Los Angeles.

Additional information tending to connect Joe Hillstrom, charged with the murder of John G. Morrison and Arling Morrison, with crimes in California was received this morning by Chief Grant in a letter from Chief Sebastian of the Los Angeles police force, in which it is stated that Hillstrom, under the name of J. Hill, was arrested in that city last June and accused of participation in the street car holdups.

Information to the same effect was received yesterday from Precinct Captain Smith of the San Pedro district of Los Angeles, telling of the record of Hillstrom in that city. Like Smith, Chief Sebastian suggests that Otto Applequist also has a record and was suspected of being one of the gang in the street car robberies.

Along with the letter from Chief Sebastian was received a Bertillon photograph and description of Hillstrom, which appears in the accompanying cut. This was made at the Los Angeles police headquarters immediately after the arrest of Hillstrom and his associates as the car robbery suspects. The Bertillon photograph tallies in every respect with the pictures made at the Salt Lake county jail following Hillstrom's arrest and shows clearly the lines of Hillstrom's face and the expression of the eyes, which were hidden to some extent by the rather unsatisfactory photographs obtained at the county jail while the man was suffering from his wounds and had a heavy growth of beard.

The *Deseret Evening News*, January 24, 1914. The misleading headline helped set the tone for coverage of Hill's case. From then on, Hill was generally portrayed in the Salt Lake press as a hardened criminal.

In reality, there was virtually no evidence to suggest that the police had the right man. The state's case was entirely circumstantial and leaned heavily on the theory that the younger Morrison, in the moment before he had died, had fired the shot that had torn through Hill's chest. But the prosecutor could not prove that Morrison's gun had been fired, let alone that Hill had been at the store. Nor could the state show a motive, or produce the murder weapon, or elicit testimony that positively identified the defendant. In short, the state failed to meet Utah's statutory standard for a case based on circumstantial evidence: that the chain of proof "be complete and unbroken and established beyond a reasonable doubt." (That, as will be seen, was where the rigged game came in.)

Notwithstanding the weak case against him, Hill did himself no favors in the courtroom. Perhaps out of some myopic strain of naïveté, he seemed to not recognize what was in plain sight: the severity of his predicament. That might explain why at certain critical times it was as if he were all but helping the state fit the rope around his neck. For instance, early in the trial, he lost his temper in front of the jury, fired his lawyers, and then argued heatedly with the judge about whether he had the right to represent himself. The day's news coverage—ACCUSED SLAYER OF J.G. MORRISON DRAMATICALLY DISCHARGES HIS COUNSEL DURING TRIAL; THRILLING SCENE IN MURDER TRIAL—centered on whether Hill was pursuing an insanity plea. (He was not.) And as terribly as that outburst hurt him, what sealed his conviction was his refusal to take the witness stand in his own defense: to tell who had shot him and where. Of course he had no legal obligation to prove his innocence; the burden of proof lay with the state. Just as obviously, however, the prosecutor would—and did—portray his silence as an admission of guilt.

Less certain is *why* Hill kept mum. I would cite three plausible reasons, all having to do, in one way or another, with idealistic notions of duty and honor. First, there was his immovable devotion to bedrock legal principles—such as the presumption of innocence, the constitutional right to silence, and procedural due process. Second, there was his apparent romantic devotion to Hilda Erickson and his desire to protect her privacy.* And third, there was his need to shoulder the burden of perceived expectations of an iconic hero of the labor movement.

_____

* He would not have wished on Hilda the sort of unwanted scrutiny that the women in his own family had had to put up with. Hill's mother, Catharina, it will be recalled, had been born out of wedlock, for which the omniscient Church of Sweden had branded her *oäkta*, or "whore's child," and his grandmother, Catharina's mother, *slampa*, or "slut."

The irony of Hill having taken on the role of good soldier in the class war was as inescapable as the penitentiary. For he was on trial for his life for a crime that had nothing to do with politics. Yet his prosecution, baseless as it was, in the end was about nothing *but* politics: about a partial judge, as we shall see, abetting an ambitious prosecutor to make the case that *State of Utah v. Joseph Hillstrom* was as much a class action against the IWW as it was a murder trial.

The establishment in Utah—the state's tightly interwoven political, industrial, and Mormon church leadership—had reason to wage class warfare. Twelve months before he would be tried in June of 1914, the IWW-led strike of some fifteen hundred shovel stiffs in Tucker had humiliated the state's most powerful corporation, Utah Construction Company. "You IWWs caught us with our pants down this time," a company official had admitted—before promising in the next breath that "before the end of a year every damn single IWW will be run out of the state of Utah." Though the company undertook to make good on its promise, most infamously in August 1913, when twenty of its gun- and club-wielding thugs turned a peaceful IWW street meeting in Salt Lake City into a bloody riot, the union's numbers in the state seemed to multiply in the months after the attack. "Every construction camp, stone quarry, mines and every other job within a radius of 100 miles had its little group of agitators," a Local 69 official named George Child (or Childs) recounted. "The girls in the factories sang our songs as they worked. Our street meetings attracted large crowds."

The tensions only heightened during the period leading to Hill's arrest and trial. In its first issue of 1914, *Solidarity* published a caustic year-end review of "recent events" in Utah, "this so-called Garden of Paradise." Written by Ed Rowan, who would soon help organize Hill's legal defense committee, and another member of Local 69, the article imparted lessons learned from the strike at Tucker, among them: "Profit is a serious proposition to tamper with" and a corollary of sorts, "The masters never forgive or forget any action tending to reduce their bank rolls." The authors went on to discuss the August 1913 riot in Salt Lake City, lamenting that almost five months later one Wobbly was still in legal limbo: in jail and unable to make bail or secure a trial. "Clear as crystal it can be seen that justice is precisely of the same brand in Utah as elsewhere," they wrote. "Concerted action is now going on all over the country, to imprison members of our organization on some pretext or other." That edition of *Solidarity* appeared on the streets of

Salt Lake City no more than a couple of days before Hill was jailed for murder. The stage that story set, the history and animosity it described, formed a key piece of the backdrop against which Hill's case is best seen.

There were, of course, other "recent events" that informed Hill's case. In the fall of 1913, Local 69 invited the fiery English socialist Tom Mann to Salt Lake City for a lecture. (Mann was in the midst of a barnstorming tour of North America.) As the news broke in late October of Mann's impending address, some capitalists of long memory and short fuse sought to block his appearance. Foremost among them were Axel Steele, a former deputy sheriff who had instigated the riot two months before on behalf of Utah Construction, and "Diamondfield" Jack Davis, a mine operator who had once feuded with the IWW in the goldfields of Nevada. In a telegram to immigration officials in Washington, D.C., Steele, Davis, and others urged that Mann be deported before he purveyed his revolutionary snake oil in Salt Lake City. Davis also claimed that the IWW had "marked" him for death. The secretary of Local 69, Sam Scarlett, replied that the union wanted nothing to do with Davis. "We are not looking for any trouble with this person who styles himself 'Diamondfield Jack' or others. All we want is not to be molested, and especially on the night that Tom Mann speaks . . . We do not anticipate any trouble, but warn Davis and the rest of them not to start anything." Mann came to Salt Lake without incident and, on a Sunday evening in November before a full house in the Garrick Theater, delivered what the *Deseret Evening News* reported as a two-hour "tirade against capitalism."

The *News* and the other local dailies, the *Tribune*, the *Herald-Republican*, and the *Evening Telegram*, were naturally attuned to IWW rumblings in Utah, but not only in Utah. To read the front page of a Salt Lake City newspaper in the five months of 1914 between Hill's arrest and his trial was to be exposed almost daily to lurid stories of migrating plagues of Wobblies decimating everything in their path from coast to coast. On the day of Hill's preliminary hearing, a wire service story ran about the trial of four IWW-linked hop pickers charged with killing the district attorney in Wheatland, California. The story described the moment when the DA and a sheriff's posse attempted to disperse a mass meeting of striking pickers on the hop ranch. The strikers, the article noted, were singing "'Mr. Block,' which contains an attack on the so-called 'capitalist classes.'" There was no mention of the songwriter, but the article added that the small book containing the song "was bound in red and bore the title: 'Industrial Workers of the World songs to fan the flame of discontent.'" And the widely available *Little Red Songbook* did credit the song to "J. Hill." Also out of Wheatland came a report of a California state investigator's finding that the "revolutionary doctrines" and "propaganda" that the IWW had spread among the hop pickers "without doubt" constituted "a criminal conspiracy." The investigator ominously added that "this propagandizing of the IWW" posed "a definite and increasing danger in California."

No more so than in New York, where a freak snowstorm during the first week of March 1914 paralyzed the city. The emergency meant work for the unemployed; there were immediate openings for fifteen thousand snow shovelers. The city's private contractors scoured lodging houses and charity missions for able bodies, handing a shovel and a dollar a day to any and all takers. For that wage, though, the IWW urged the unemployed to keep their hands warm in their pockets. "We want work, but we will not work for fifty cents or a dollar a day," a twenty-one-year-old Wobbly named Frank Tannenbaum announced. "We want three dollars a day for an eight-hour day. We want union wages and union conditions and we will not work unless we get them. We would rather go to jail."

They got their wish. INDUSTRIAL WORKERS RAISE PANDEMONIUM, the *Deseret Evening News* headlined a wire service report that several hundred Wobblies had invaded a Roman Catholic church in Manhattan during Lenten services. The "mob" sought food, lodging, and attention paid to the city's inadequate services and shelters for the unemployed. The churchwomen "screamed," the police rushed to the scene, the "wildest disorder" ensued for half an hour, and 190 men were jailed. A *News* editorial blamed the IWW not only for rioting for riot's sake—"to terrorize the peaceful citizens"—but also for promoting joblessness: "By agitation they induce men to leave their work and swell the ranks of the unemployed." The *Salt Lake Tribune* agreed: "Work is the last thing in the world that an Industrial Worker of the World desires. His principles are based on the 'general strike' and the 'social revolution.'" But rather than leave it at a critique of Wobblyism, as did the *News*, the *Tribune* employed Wobbly-like rhetoric and advocated Wobbly-like militancy. Of the IWW's refusal to accept "such a natural compromise as work and wages," the *Tribune* declared, "It is a challenge to society that can be met only with retaliation. The IWW makes war upon society . . . and society can only defend itself by warlike measures."*

SALT LAKE CITY was bracing for war: an incursion by Kelly's Army of the Unemployed, a roving band of Wobblies under the command of "General" Charles T. Kelly. In early March, the army set out for points east from San Francisco, a bellwether city for both staggering unemployment—at least forty thousand were jobless at the end of 1913—and what the IWW regarded as an indifference to widespread "want and misery." Some fifteen hundred recruits had traveled first to the state capital, Sacramento, where Governor Hiram Johnson, a Progressive Party leader, had sneered at their demand for relief and redress.

"Rained on and starved out," as one writer on the road with Kelly's desperate troops observed, the Army nonetheless decided to take its grievances all the way to Washington, D.C. It would follow the path of Jacob Coxey's Army of the Unemployed, which had hiked to Washington from all corners of the country during the depression of 1894. (General Kelly had been an officer in Coxey's Army.) For Kelly's Army, the road to Washington cut through Salt Lake City, where, as the *Deseret Evening News* assessed it, "not only the authorities but also the local laboring men" were "arrayed against them." There were at least eight thousand jobless in Salt Lake—the carpenters' union alone reported in March that fewer than 250 of its 600 members were working. Yet neither the carpenters' local nor any other affiliate of the American Federation of Labor intended to offer Kelly's men so much as a meal. "We have enough of unemployed right here in our own ranks and men who have their homes here to take care of without borrowing trouble in the care of shiftless outsiders," an ironworker said.

And that was before the *Evening Telegram* broke the sensational story of the supposed real intentions of Kelly's Army. Its cross-country expedition was not aimed merely at forcing society to "look facts in the face"—to take notice of the "starving amid plenty," as an IWW publication put it.

---

* The *Tribune* sometimes went as far as employing the rhetoric of annihilation against the IWW. In response to Bill Haywood's call for a general strike and his statement that "it is better to be a traitor to your country than a traitor to your class," the *Tribune* advised that were Haywood and "the other agitators" to attempt to "put into practice" such a plan, it would "probably result in their removal from the scene of all earthly activities in short order."

Rather, Kelly was preparing to carry out a plan reminiscent of, and as shockingly audacious as, John Brown's famous antislavery raid on the federal arsenal at Harpers Ferry, Virginia, in 1859. As the Army approached Salt Lake, the *Telegram*, citing the findings of the California National Guard, reported that Kelly's men were on their way east to seize the federal arsenal at Rock Island, Illinois, "in order to equip an army of *five hundred thousand* men with arms and ammunition for a revolution against the government." (Emphasis added.) The unemployed but dauntingly armed force would then commandeer the railroads out of Chicago and rush toward Washington, "where it would have the Federal Government at its mercy."

THOSE HYSTERIA-INDUCING STORIES of IWW thuggery and terror and violence culled from around the nation and bannered in the Salt Lake City press in early 1914 effectively shackled the ankle of Joe Hill's case to the cast-iron ball and chain of the IWW. At first, though, Hill underestimated the full weight of the restraint. He still saw and understood himself as an individual, someone separable from the IWW. But that's not how the oligarchy in Utah portrayed him. From the outset, the legal, political, and journalistic powers in Utah depicted Hill as organic to the IWW—a malignant growth of a spreading cancer—and they determined, in essence, to put the IWW on trial alongside him.

Still, Hill thought he could represent himself at his preliminary hearing. And so when Ed Rowan, the newly elected secretary of Local 69 and coauthor of that prescient *Solidarity* piece published days before Hill's arrest—it had lamented the "concerted action" to imprison Wobblies "on some pretext or other"—first visited Hill in the county lockup in January, Hill declined Rowan's offer of IWW assistance. Hill said he wanted no financial aid, arguing (as he had during the run-up to San Diego) that the union's limited resources be dedicated to organizing. Besides, he explained, there was no need for a lawyer. "Thinking that there was nothing to my case," he wrote later, "and always being willing to try anything once, I decided to 'go it' alone and be my own attorney."

The preliminary hearing was held before a justice of the peace on January 28, 1914. For a high-profile defendant both prized and vilified by the authorities and the press for his ties to the IWW, Hill was naïve, curiously so, to think that there "could be nothing against me," as he put it. His misjudgment could probably be ascribed to his innocence; if he had not committed murder, what did he have to worry about?

He apparently had not yet glimpsed in the eyes of his adversaries his symbolic value. In addition to his naïveté, he was ignorant of courtroom and criminal procedure, a well-nigh-fatal combination for a murder suspect—let alone a notoriously radical murder suspect—without competent counsel. That mix of confidence and cluelessness would explain why, when asked if he objected to the state's witnesses remaining in the courtroom during the hearing, Hill replied that it was "immaterial." As he recounted, "All the witnesses then remained inside, and I noted that there was a steady stream of 'messengers' going back and forth between the witnesses and the county attorney . . . delivering their messages in a whisper."

Hill called no witnesses of his own. He did glancingly cross-examine three of the state's sixteen witnesses, employing, one reporter noted, "keenness and cunning"—a sure sign, it was implied, of prior brushes with the law. (The hearing transcript vanished almost immediately, making hazardous an attempt to accurately depict the tribunal or to gauge Hill's legal acumen. The fragmentary picture here is drawn from sketchy press coverage and Hill's own recollections.)

Hill first questioned Merlin Morrison, the thirteen-year-old who had been inside or near the rear storage room of the grocery when his father and brother had been shot to death eighteen days before. As has been noted, within hours of Hill's arrest, the *Herald-Republican* dispatched a car and driver to the Morrisons' home to take Merlin to jail for a pre-dawn look at the suspect.* Hill later recalled the brief encounter: "Being only a little boy, [Merlin] spoke his mind right out in my presence, and this is what he said: 'No, that is not the man at all. The ones I saw were shorter and heavier set.'" Predictably enough, the sponsoring newspaper plucked a contradictory assessment from the boy's mouth. Yet even Merlin's published statement, equivocal as it was, seemed to fall short of a positive identification: "I *believe* that is the man my brother shot." (Emphasis added.)

This is the *Herald-Republican*'s account of their exchange at the preliminary hearing:

> Hill: Is it not a fact that you told a jailer close to my cell during the early morning of January 14 when you came to the jail that you didn't think I was the man who shot your father?

---

* What role, if any, the police played in this venture is unknown. But it is certain that neither Merlin nor any other witness was asked to identify the suspect through a police lineup.

Morrison: That is not true. I never said anything like that.

Hill: But didn't you tell someone that I know that you did not identify me when you were taken to the county jail during the early
   morning after my arrest?

Morrison: I did not.

Hill asked Vera Hanson, who lived kitty-corner to Morrison's store, about her direct testimony that at nine-thirty P.M. she had seen a man bent double outside the store and heard him exclaim, "Bob," or "O, Bob," or "Bob, I'm shot." (Press accounts varied.) "Bob" supposedly referred to Bob Erickson, a nephew of the Eselius brothers (and Hilda's brother) who police believed had been a "lookout" that night for Hill and Otto Appelquist, the alleged accomplice who remained at large. But there was a problem with that theory: Erickson had proved that he had been at the Utah Theatre at the time with two of his uncles and a brother and that after the show they had stopped at a saloon and had not departed until after midnight—nearly three hours after the murders.

On direct examination, the state's attorney asked Hanson, "Would you recognize that voice if you heard it again?"

"I think I would . . . I heard a voice that sounded very much like it *the next day*." (Emphasis added.)

"Where was that?"

"At the county jail."

"Whose voice did you hear at the county jail?"

"This man's," Hanson replied, pointing at Hill.

Even if Vera Hanson could have later recognized a man's voice from the three syllables or fewer that she swore she had heard him utter from inside her house (it was not likely that her door or windows had been open on that subfreezing night), it was definitively not Hill's voice she had heard at the county jail "the next day." All that Sunday, he had been laid up on the folding iron cot in the front room of the Eselius family's home in Murray, recuperating from his gunshot wound. He would not be jailed until early on the Wednesday morning after the Saturday-night murders. Yet Hill, strangely, did not challenge Hanson's claim. Instead he asked her, "Do you think you could identify me as the man running out of the store merely by the sound of a human voice calling, 'Bob, I'm shot'?"

"No, I could not; I could not," Hanson admitted.

Upon which Hill dismissed the witness with a curt "That is all" and a slow wave of his hand, "much after the fashion of a veteran criminal lawyer."

There was another bit of Hanson's testimony that might have troubled a veteran criminal lawyer. According to the *Tribune*, she said she had seen and heard the commotion at nine-thirty. Her recollection matched that of a streetcar passenger named John E. Thompson. He testified that at nine-thirty he was gazing out the window of the car at Eighth South and West Temple when he saw two men with red handkerchiefs around their necks, one of them "resembling Hillstrom," running south. Yet according to the Utah Supreme Court record, the murders were committed between nine-forty-five and ten P.M., an hour that tallies with the testimony of the state's principal witness, Merlin Morrison, who said that his father and brother were shot at "a quarter to ten or ten minutes to ten, right around there."

Fortunately for the prosecution, the next witness injected a bit of useful ambiguity into the proceeding. Nellie Mahan, another neighbor to Morrison's store, had also told detectives canvassing the neighborhood after the murders that she had heard a fleeing man exclaim, "Hold on Bob, I'm shot." By the day of the preliminary hearing two weeks later, however, the police had cleared Bob Erickson, and Mahan either was no longer sure of what she had heard or altered her story to fit the lone outstanding suspect, Appelquist. She testified, according to the *Herald-Republican*, that "she did not hear the name 'Bob' distinctly, but thought it more resembled Otto."

Hill also sought to deflate the testimony of a lesser witness, a streetcar passenger who said that he had seen a man resembling Hill on a southbound car headed to Murray, and that the man had exited the car in the vicinity of Dr. Frank McHugh's house. Apparently Hill succeeded; the witness was not heard from again during further court proceedings.

However, Hill failed to question one crucial witness, Phoebe Seeley. As has been described, she and her husband, Frank, were walking home from a night on the town when they crossed paths with two men near Morrison's store about ten minutes before the murders. Both men wore red handkerchiefs around their necks, cowboy-style, Phoebe Seeley testified. That was all the newspapers reported of her testimony. But there was more, according to excerpts of the hearing transcript that were cited during the trial and referred to in the account Hill later gave. Seeley also said that one of the men had "small features and light bushy hair." Hill wrote that Seeley's description "did not suit the county attorney, so he helped her along a little by saying, 'You mean medium colored hair like Mr. Hillstrom's, don't you?'" Hill added that after the prosecutor had led her along for a while in that fashion, he asked her, "Is the general appearance of Mr. Hillstrom anything like the man you saw?"

"No, I won't, I can't say that," Seeley answered, according to Hill. (He cited the exchange in his open letter to the Utah Board of Pardons, "A Few Reasons Why I Demand a New Trial," which the *Deseret Evening News* published six weeks before his execution.)

But when she was sworn in as a witness five months later at the trial, Phoebe Seeley said she had no doubt that the man looked like Hill.

TO THE *DESERET EVENING NEWS*, Hill's tactic of spare questioning and a closing statement of fewer than fifty mostly extraneous words was attributable to "shrewdness, rather than owing to a lack of knowledge." And yet whatever courtroom skill he exhibited proved without reward: the justice of the peace ruled that there was probable cause to try him for the murder of John Morrison. (The missing Appelquist was charged with Arling Morrison's murder.) The justice ordered Hill held in the county jail without bail.

In hindsight, Hill must have figured that his decision to "'go it' alone" without an attorney had been a mistake. For when he returned to court on March 7 for arraignment, he brought one along: Ernest D. MacDougall, who had appeared, unsolicited, at Hill's jail cell seemingly out of nowhere a few days after the preliminary hearing. "He said he was a stranger in town and had heard about my case and would be willing to take the case for nothing," Hill later wrote. "Seeing that that proposition was in perfect harmony with my bankroll, I accepted his offer." MacDougall (who in fact came from neighboring Wyoming) in turn brought on as co-counsel Frank B. Scott, an established local attorney and a Socialist of electoral ambition. (That November, he ran unsuccessfully for a seat on the Utah Supreme Court.)

As Hill stewed in jail over the next couple of months, it had to have dawned on him that he and his case had transcended the horrific events of January 10; also, that it was not possible to keep his union out of a situation that it had been dragged into almost immediately after his arrest—from the afternoon of his plea hearing, when the newspapers had hog-tied him as "a writer of songs for the IWW song books." In late March or early April, he authorized Ed Rowan of Local 69 to establish an IWW defense committee. The April 18 edition of *Solidarity* carried the news: MAN WHO WROTE "MR. BLOCK" AND "CASEY JONES" CAUGHT AND HELD ON TRUMPED-UP CHARGES.

> The master class have again shown their hand, in a dastardly attempt to railroad to the gallows . . . one of the best known men in the movement. They have picked for their victim a man who is beloved by all who know him; one who at all times has worked untiringly for the cause of industrial freedom . . . Now there is not one in this organization who can say that he does not know this man. For wherever rebels meet, the name of Fellow Worker JOE HILL is known. Though we may not know him personally, what one among us can say he is not on speaking terms with "Scissor Bill," "Mr. Block" or . . . "Casey Jones" . . . and many others in the little red song book.

The story concludes with a request for donations: "Fellow workers, it is up to us to get busy; form choruses to sing Hill's songs on the streets and take up collections, give away song books and send 50 per cent to the defense of Joe Hill." (A month later, Rowan could report that the appeal had yielded about two hundred dollars.)

HERE, IT SEEMS, is where Hill found himself in a strangely impersonal place. For months, he had been on exhibit in the Salt Lake press, implicitly and explicitly, as the captive embodiment of the IWW "troubles." And now, with his trial approaching, the IWW had begun a worldwide campaign to display him as an icon of capitalist oppression. The campaign caught on, and as it did, as activists held protest meetings and rallies in countless cities, as tens of thousands of letters and petitions and telegrams on Hill's behalf poured into the governor's office, he became so well known that it was as if his jail cell had become a stage, replete with a spotlight that would grow ever brighter and hotter over the next eighteen months or so. It would profoundly affect how he saw himself and the decisions he made surrounding his trial and his future.

At the arraignment, Hill had pleaded not guilty to murder, but what defense could there be for what his attorneys considered the prosecution's most damning evidence? "The main thing the state has against Hill is that he is an IWW and *therefore sure to be guilty*," MacDougall and

Scott wrote a few weeks before the trial began. "Hill tried to keep the IWW out of it . . . but the papers fastened it on him. For this reason he is entitled to be helped and [should] not [be] allowed to hang for being an IWW . . . It should not be necessary for him to prove his innocence and it would not if he was not an IWW."

But Joe Hill *was* an IWW. And so he was something other than a murder defendant about to go on trial for his life. He was a prisoner of war.

11.

The Majesty of the Law

It was billed as the world's longest circus parade: two miles of clowns and cowboys and Indians and soldiers on horseback, riders and ropers and ranch girls, "ferocious animals of field and forest," a "blood-sweating behemoth," and, in the lead, saluting from the saddle of his white stallion as it galloped round his performers, the old scout himself, Buffalo Bill Cody. It was Thursday, June 11, 1914, and Buffalo Bill's Wild West Show—"half circus and half history lesson," as one historian put it—had set up camp in Salt Lake City for two shows later that day. At sixty-eight, Cody was "a handsome man for his age and still looked wonderful on a horse," a colleague wrote, but in the late spring of 1914, Cody was nearing the end of his ride.

He had founded his touring circus and Wild West Show in 1883, seven years before the U.S. Census had officially declared the frontier closed, and would keep it going nearly until his death in 1917. As much as anyone, Buffalo Bill embodied and defined that century-straddling moment in American history, when the frontier had yielded to urbanization and early modern industrial capitalism had overtaken the agrarian economy. His Wild West Show molded and buffed and obscured that transitional epoch through a series of dramatic "reenactments." It did so in the service of commerce and entertainment and, in no small proportion, to create and perpetuate the living legend of Buffalo Bill.

The centerpiece of the show depicted a battle between Cody and his cowboys and a band of Indians who had attacked a white settler's cabin. (Cody hired actual Indians to portray their vanquished selves.) It was not a fair fight; every spectator in the horseshoe-shaped arena knew before Buffalo Bill swept in on horseback that he and his sharpshooters would save the day for "progress" and "civilization"—that is, it was understood, for Caucasians, capitalism, and Christianity. Entertainment though it was, Cody's twice-daily conquest (at two-fifteen and eight-fifteen P.M.) of the "dark forces of barbarism and savagery" surely resonated with his audience members in Salt Lake who believed that Utah still needed saving—no longer from the frontier menace of Indians, but from the red peril of the modern West: the anticapitalist, anti-Christian, multiethnic Industrial Workers of the World.

SALT LAKE WAS A CITY of 110,000 people in 1914, small and insular enough that its elites—political, religious, and business—straddled conjoined circles. As has been seen, copper kings owned newspapers; Mormon church president Joseph F. Smith operated countless secular enterprises; Governor William Spry, a Mormon, concurrently presided over a bank and, along with U.S. senator Reed Smoot, the Mormon apostle and political kingmaker, owned a share of the *Herald-Republican*. The Third Judicial District judge Morris L. Ritchie, who would preside over Joe Hill's trial, and the district attorney, Elmer O. Leatherwood, who would prosecute the case, also bestrode those circles. Both Ritchie and Leatherwood belonged to the Alta Club, the city's elite private association, and to the Elks Lodge and Utah Commandery No. 1 (a Masonic organization). And they shared some similarities in their backgrounds. Both were Midwesterners, both had practiced law in Kansas (where Ritchie had also been elected to the state legislature), and both were ardent Republicans and, in the eyes of Mormons, gentiles. (Ritchie was an Episcopalian; Leatherwood, a Methodist.)

On the morning of June 11, as the Wild West Show parade made its way along South State Street past the Salt Lake City & County Building, upstairs, in a fourth-floor courtroom, jury selection in *State of Utah v. Joseph Hillstrom* was just getting under way. And though not scripted or rehearsed, as such, like Cody's climactic gun battle, in reality the trial was no fairer or more authentic a fight. It starred a prosecutor, Elmer Leatherwood, whose indifference to facts and embellishment of the historical record were as admirable as Cody's and who, with all his grandstanding, might as well have been riding a white horse of his own around the courtroom.

But Leatherwood could not have staged a fight without collusion any more than Cody could have; the prosecutor needed a judge who would bend or suspend the rules of criminal procedure when necessary, and in

Hill was tried in the courtroom of Judge Morris L. Ritchie, above, on the fourth floor of the Salt Lake City & County Building, below. (Above: Special Collections Department, J. Willard Marriott Library, University of Utah; below: used by permission, Utah State Historical Society, all rights reserved)

his fraternal-organization brother Morris Ritchie he had one. As will be seen, Judge Ritchie's partiality toward the prosecution was manifest at every step of the trial, from jury selection on that morning of June 11 through his final act two weeks later of issuing the all-important jury instructions. Certainly it would stand to reason that the prosecutor and judge were friends as well as social and professional acquaintances. But friendship is not at issue. Rather, the concern is whether the interlocking power relationships in Salt Lake City that concentrated economic and political strength in the hands of the few diluted the institutional possibility of a Joe Hill securing his constitutional right to equal and impartial justice under the law. Or, put another way, did a prized, latter-day red menace stand any better chance of getting a fair trial than did Buffalo Bill's show Indians of retaining their scalps?

JURY SELECTION in *Utah v. Hillstrom* had actually commenced a day earlier, but that session had failed to yield a single honest man and true—let alone twelve. This morning's voir dire was no more fruitful: an entire pool of twenty-five potential jurors was dismissed. At one point, the judge scolded the defense for wasting time: taking two and a half hours to question veniremen, as opposed to the mere eighteen minutes spent by the prosecutor, whom he praised, in front of the jury pool, as having "not consumed very much time." Ernest MacDougall answered the criticism: "The matter is of great weight and I think counsel who are conscientious are under bounden obligation to their client to see that the prejudice which is very apt to occur in a community such as Salt Lake City, and in a case such as this, where the newspapers have given so much publicity to the matter . . . we have had to be careful and to exercise great pains in the selection of a jury."

By noon, the fifty-six-year-old judge's patience had worn skeletal: if the defense would not expedite matters, he would do it for them. Prior to the afternoon's examination of another panel of prospects, Ritchie had received word from a jury deliberating another trial that it had reached a verdict. He admitted that jury and the relevant parties to the courtroom, and after hearing the verdict, he released the jurors—all but three, that is, whom he called back to the jury box. The men seemed "very surprised," as Hill later remarked, that the judge was retaining them to serve in another trial. As Hill said, the three jurors "were never subpoenaed for the case but were just simply appointed by the court." None of the newspapers delved into the legitimacy of the court's seizure of jury selection. The *Evening Telegram* noted only that the three jurors had been "chosen between panels." It made no mention of *who* had chosen them or of the fact that neither side had been invited to solicit their views. Hill complained to his lawyers, MacDougall and Frank Scott, that already it seemed like the fix was in. "Object to this manner of examining a jury," he instructed them. "I want the jury that shall try me, I want them drawn from the box. I don't want a hand-picked jury." The lawyers, though, did not object.

District Attorney Elmer O. Leatherwood. (Used by permission, Utah State Historical Society, all rights reserved)

One of the jurors the judge handpicked, Joseph Kimball, would be selected as jury foreman. Kimball, whom Hill referred to as "a very old man" (he was sixty-two), was a prominent Mormon, a son (if perhaps a distant one: he was one of sixty-five children) of Heber C. Kimball, who had been first counselor to President Brigham Young (and husband to forty-five wives). Joseph Kimball was also a director of the Utah Society of the Sons of the American Revolution, a "patriotic" fraternal organization. Among his fellow board members was Judge Morris Ritchie.*

It took five and a half days to pick the jury. At two o'clock on the afternoon of Wednesday, June 17, 1914, District Attorney Leatherwood opened the state's case. Like most officeholders in Utah, Leatherwood was a cog in Senator Reed Smoot's Republican political machine, the "Federal Bunch." The DA, who was forty-three, owed his political career to Smoot. Leatherwood had been in private practice until six years before, when the senator had "induced" the state legislature to appoint him to the newly created position of assistant district attorney. In 1911, he ran a losing campaign for mayor. Even so, Smoot eyed potential in his

---

* A month after Hill's execution, the Utah Society of the Sons of the American Revolution would "unanimously endorse" the action of the Utah Board of Pardons in the case. Not only were Ritchie and Kimball officers of the Utah Sons, but its president was state attorney general Albert R. Barnes—himself a member of the Board of Pardons.

Ohio-born protégé. In 1912, he saw to it that Leatherwood ascended to the office of district attorney when the incumbent joined Ritchie on the bench of the Third Judicial District. And now, two years later, Smoot was once again promoting Elmer Leatherwood for higher office: as the Republican nominee for the U.S. House of Representatives from Utah's Second Congressional District. The election was to be held in November, some five months down the line. And that is why, when Leatherwood made his opening statement in the murder trial of Joe Hill, he fixed one eye on the jury and the other on the political horizon.*

Leatherwood opened by saying he would prove that two men, one tall, one short, had been seen near John Morrison's grocery store a few minutes before Morrison and his son Arling were murdered, and that the taller of the two had been Joe Hill. The district attorney said he would show that a few minutes after the killings a man staggered near the store and cried, "Oh, Bob, I'm shot," and that the man's "general build" was similar to that of the defendant. He said the state would prove that in the moment before he was shot to death, Arling Morrison fired a shot at the intruders, and added that two doctors would testify that within a few hours after the murders they treated Hill for a gunshot wound in the chest, and that Hill refused to tell them how he had received it. Also, the district attorney said the doctors would testify that at the time that they were dressing Hill's wound, he carried a revolver that he later disposed of.

Speaking for the defense, Ernest MacDougall told the jury the evidence would show that Hill had no revolver of the caliber with which the Morrisons had been killed. He also said the prosecutor had erred in stating that Hill did not tell how he had been shot; in addition, MacDougall said, the defense would prove the circumstances of his shooting. "There is just one thing in this trial," MacDougall added, "and that is did Hillstrom kill Morrison? We expect to show that he did not."

TO SHOW THAT Hill did kill Morrison, Leatherwood first had to place the defendant in the grocery store, a task complicated by the lack of direct evidence and a traumatized thirteen-year-old with a mutable story. Merlin Morrison was sworn in on the morning of Thursday, June 18, the second day of testimony. As the *Tribune* surmised in its next edition, if Hill was to be convicted, "it undoubtedly will be due in a large measure

---

* Leatherwood would narrowly lose the House election. He ran successfully the next time around, in 1916, and served continuously in Congress until his death in 1929.

to the story told on the witness stand yesterday by Merlin Morrison, aged 13 years, who was the only survivor of the murderous fire of the highwaymen in the little grocery store." But Merlin's tearful story was shaky and imprecise and at times diverged significantly from those he had told to the press and police in the immediate aftermath of the murders and at the January 28 preliminary hearing. (In January, for example, after his predawn visit to see the suspect in his jail cell, Merlin told the *Tribune* that Hill "appears to be very much the same build as the man who entered the store first and whom I *saw* fire at my father." (Emphasis added.) He said much the same thing at the preliminary hearing, adding the detail that the first shot fired by the taller man struck his father. In his trial testimony, however, Merlin said that as soon as he heard the two intruders enter and yell, "We've got you now!" he ducked into the rear storeroom. From there, he said, he heard the first shot, but did not see who had fired it and was uncertain whether it had struck his father.)

Merlin's replies to a series of Leatherwood's leading questions were as near as he came to identifying the defendant.

Q: How is his height as compared with that of the taller of the men who entered the store on the night of the shooting?
A: It is about the same as that of the man who fired the shot at my father.
Q: Does the general appearance of Hillstrom resemble that of the tall man?
A: He looks the same.
Q: How does the shape of the defendant's head compare with that of the taller man?
A: It is about the same.
Q: Does this man's general appearance correspond with that of the man who shot your father?
A: Yes, sir.

MacDougall fussed about the district attorney's leading questions. The judge overruled the defense's objection and ordered the lawyers to stop "squabbling."

On cross-examination, MacDougall misplaced his nerve. Rather than pin Merlin down on the crucial inconsistencies in successive iterations of his narrative, the defense counsel limited himself to "gently" reviewing with the boy his direct testimony. Hill was furious. He "wanted him gone at like a bull—torn to pieces," MacDougall's co-counsel, Frank Scott, later recalled. But as Scott explained, he and MacDougall were "afraid" that browbeating Merlin "would make the little boy cry and we well knew what effect that would have on the jury."

Their client, however, was afraid of the effect of his counsel's timidity on his chances for survival. Hill contended that an artful, meticulous cross-examination of Merlin Morrison, of tender age or no, was more important than whether tears streaming down the boy's face might turn the jury against the defendant. He argued that the defense needed to obtain from Merlin a precise accounting of his movements in the store immediately prior to and during the murders, what he saw and did not see, heard and did not hear. And he insisted that his counsel needed to place in the record the discrepancies between Merlin's previous sworn statements and his present testimony. To fail to seek answers to those questions, Hill believed, was to forfeit a critical opportunity to impeach the state's key witness. MacDougall and Scott disagreed. Hill later wrote of his lawyers that "they blandly informed me that the preliminary hearing had nothing to do with the district court hearing and that under the law they had no right to use said records."

After a night's reflection, and fearing another session of listless cross-examination, Hill returned to court the following morning with a plan as astonishingly brash as it was reckless. He had determined to "get rid of these attorneys and either conduct the case myself or else get some other attorney." The prosecution's first witness on Friday was Herman Harms, a state chemist who testified about the origins of a blood sample he had analyzed that had been scraped off a sidewalk on Jefferson Street, south of the Morrison store. He said he could tell only that it was mammalian blood; as to the species he was unsure.

As Scott stood to cross-examine the chemist, but before he could speak, Hill leaped to his feet. He was dressed impeccably in a neat blue suit with a white collar and a flowing black bow tie. After six months in jail, however, his face was gaunt and pallid, "more hatchetlike than ever," the *Evening Telegram* reported.

Hill beckoned Judge Ritchie. "May I say a few words, your Honor?"

Spectators and court officials alike gasped. The gallery leaned forward, straining to hear what the defendant had to say—and whether the judge would let him say it. "You have the right to be heard in your own behalf ordinarily," the judge replied. MacDougall was now on his feet, too. "Everyone realized that something unusual was about to take place," the *Telegram* reported. Everyone, that is, but the judge, who failed to excuse the jury.

"I have three prosecuting attorneys here," Hill said. "I intend to get rid of two of them, Mr. Scott and Mr. MacDougall." The judge was speechless. "See that door?" Hill said, pointing with one hand at his attorneys, with the other at the exit. "Get out. You're fired."

Finally the judge spoke. "Mr. Hillstrom, you need not carry out in detail any difference you may have had with your counsel if there is any—"

The defendant cut him off. "I wish to announce that I have discharged my counsel, my two lawyers."

Said Scott, "If you have discharged us, that is all there is to it." It was probably then that MacDougall started to gather his files from the defense table. Hill grabbed them from the lawyer's hands.

"You are fired," he repeated. "Those belong to the defense and they have been paid for. I will keep them."

Hill turned back to the judge. "If the court will permit, I will act as my own attorney, and cross-examine all the witnesses, and I think I will make a good job of it . . . Bring buckets of blood for all I care, I intend to prove a whole lot of things here; I will prove these records here of the preliminary hearing are the rankest kind of fake . . . And I will prove a whole lot of other things. I will prove I was not at that store."

MacDougall, whether humiliated, enraged, or both, hurried from the courtroom. Scott remained at the defense table. He was moved to say that his sudden dismissal was "entirely unexpected." He added, "Before I retire, I merely want to state . . . that Mr. Hillstrom and I have had no difference whatever in any respect."

"Get out," Hill begged to differ. "You're fired!"

As per usual, however, the court overruled the defense. "I think until further order counsel [for] the defendant may proceed," Ritchie said.

Hill: "Haven't I a right to discharge my counsel?"

Ritchie: "The court will make due inquiry into that, Mr. Hillstrom, and if the court is convinced that you really mean what you say, the court will accord you that right."

"Yes, sir," the defendant replied, "I mean what I say."

Nevertheless, the judge instructed Hill's erstwhile attorney, Scott, to proceed with cross-examining the state chemist, Harms. And he motioned to MacDougall, who had poked his head in the door, to return to the defense table. The judge told Scott that he and MacDougall were to consider themselves amici curiae—friends of the court—for the duration of the trial. The status afforded them the right to examine and cross-examine witnesses for the defense and otherwise "protect the defendant's interests." The ruling to effectively reinstate his dismissed attorneys bewildered and further inflamed the defendant.

"Without my permission?" Hill demanded.

Ritchie's limited reservoir of patience was depleted. "We will see that the orders of court are carried out," he said.

"I am the defendant in this court," Hill cried. He remained standing, "pale and defiant," as the *Telegram* put it.

"The court directs you to sit down now," Ritchie responded. At which point a bailiff showed Hill, forcefully, to his chair. "The court will give you an opportunity . . . to cross-examine this witness, after counsel who have been representing you have completed."

Scott started to question the witness. But his unrepentant client—former client—again interrupted.

"Mr. Scott, there's the door. Why don't you go?"

"I am acting under the Court's instruction," Scott replied, adding a patronizing but likely accurate assessment of Hill's mental state. "I think you are a little beside yourself at present."

Hill asked the judge for clarification. "Who is counsel for the defense?"

Ritchie: "You have the right to act in your own behalf; the court has asked these gentlemen as friends of the court—"

Hill cut him off. "My counsel is dismissed."

Ritchie picked up in midsentence: ". . . to sit here and give the court such advice as may be necessary to see that you are properly defended."

Hill: "They can't bluff me."

Scott managed a further question of the chemist, and then Hill had his turn. He asked a single, redundant question (Harms had answered it on direct), found the reply satisfactory, and told the court he had nothing further.

"May Mr. Harms be permitted to return to his laboratory?" the prosecutor asked.

"Yes," the defendant said.

THE STATE NEXT CALLED Phoebe Seeley. She testified about her and her husband's encounter with the two surly men on a sidewalk near the Morrison store a few minutes before the murders. "We had to step out," she said. "They made us give the entire sidewalk to them while they came shoulder to shoulder and we stepped to the side and let them pass."

She said that she turned and looked at them after that awkward dance, and that the taller of the two men turned and looked at her.

Five months had passed since Seeley testified at Hill's preliminary hearing that she did not know if the defendant and her sidewalk tormentor were one and the same. ("No, I won't, I can't say that," she had reportedly said.) Now it was June 19, the eve of the summer solstice, and the doubt Phoebe Seeley had expressed in January had melted away with the winter snows. Here is a portion of her exchange with Elmer Leatherwood on direct examination:

Q: Did this man that turned, the taller of the two, did he look directly at you?

A: Yes.

Q: And did you look directly at him?

A: Yes.

Q: Did you notice anything peculiar about the [facial] features of the man that turned . . . and looked at you?

A: Yes.

Q: I wish you would just tell in your own way, Mrs. Seeley, what there was about the face of that man that attracted you.

A: Well, his face was real thin; he had a sharp nose, and rather large nostrils. He had a defection on the side of his face or neck.

Q: On the side of the face or neck?

A: Right here on his face.

Q: What do you mean by that—apparently a scar?

A: Yes, it looked as though it might be a scar.

Q: And you observed that?

A: Yes, sir.

Q: Did the nose appear to be particularly sharp?

A: Yes.

Q: And the nostrils were peculiar?

A: Yes, the gentleman that I met was a sharp-faced man with a real sharp nose, and his nostrils were rather large.

Despite Leatherwood's patently leading questions, the defendant, sitting without counsel, never once objected. And the judge, for his part, never obstructed or rebuked the prosecutor for feeding Seeley her lines. That exchange, though, was too much for Ernest MacDougall, now a "friend of the court," to suffer through in silence. "As *amicus curiae*," he said, he wished to advise that "the nature of these questions . . . are unfair in that they are all leading and have been during all this examination." He went on to suggest, "If the witness knows anything, let the witness tell without receiving the answer from counsel."

Hill again jumped to his feet. "The counsel seems to be very insistent on holding the job. Have I not the right to fire my counsel? I will conduct this case myself."

After Ritchie again sought to clarify the function of the dismissed attorneys, Leatherwood resumed his inquiry of Mrs. Seeley. She went on to say that the defendant's height, build, and nose were "very much the same" as that of the taller man on the street, and that their respective scars, too, "look a great deal alike." She did allow that their hair was "entirely different." And that point *was* consistent with her testimony at the preliminary hearing, when she had sketched the taller man as having "light bushy hair"—a description the county attorney had found unsatisfactory. "You mean," he had asked her, "medium-colored hair like Mr. Hillstrom's, don't you?"

Now, at trial, the hair question again tripped her up. "He had light hair, yes, the man I saw," she told Leatherwood.

"Light hair?" he asked, as if to say "Are you *sure*?" With the prompt she regained her footing.

"Yes," she answered, "medium-complexioned like this man."

Seeley's unsteadiness disturbed Judge Ritchie enough that he directed Leatherwood to pass *him* the witness. Ritchie seemed concerned that Seeley's testimony about the men's dissimilar hair could color the jury's perception of her credibility. The judge's questions, no less leading than Leatherwood's, highlighted the defendant's similarities with the man on the street at the expense of his marked differences.

Q: How does Mr. Hillstrom, as he sits here, compare in regard to his thinness with the man you saw that day?
A: His thinness is about the same, but his hair—
Q: Just about as thin, had you finished your answer?
A: But his hair is entirely different.
Q: How does he compare in thinness of the body with the man you saw that day?
A: I never paid any particular attention.
Q: You did not pay any attention to the thinness of his body, but the thinness of his face is just the same as the man you saw?
A: Just the same.

That last exchange particularly, in which the judge inserted in the witness's mouth a comparison unmade and then elicited an answer—the injurious "Just the same"—to a question unasked, was exemplary of what Hill's appellate attorneys would later complain was examination by "suggestion and invitation of comparison and a searching of the witness's memory to invite her to say that Hillstrom was the man 'who turned and looked at her.'"

At one point, Frank Scott noted aloud, without quite objecting, that the witness had been made to say the word "scar"—a word not of her choosing. The defendant in turn registered his disapproval of Scott's intervention.

"My counsel seem to be very insistent upon holding the job," Hill repeated. The judge said he would further investigate the proper role of a friend of the court "in a moment or two."

"I wish you would," Hill said.

Only then did Judge Ritchie finally call a thirty-minute recess and excuse the members of the jury. He was never called to account for allowing the fireworks at the defense bar to detonate in the jury's presence—the entire "sensation after sensation," as the *Tribune* had it—or, for that matter, for allowing the trial to continue while the defendant was deprived of counsel "in whom he had confidence," as his appellate lawyers would later argue. But one might reasonably ask how the judge reconciled his rulings and actions in these proceedings with his understanding of the defendant's constitutional right of due process under the law.

During the recess, the district attorney broached the theory that Hill's conduct that morning was a ruse that he and his counsel had scripted—"a wholesale grandstand play of insanity." Hill assured the court it was not: "There will not be any insanity pleas . . . no brainstorm either."*

MacDougall stood up for his former client. "I do not believe the defendant insane," he said, and added, "The evidence we have prepared will abundantly establish the defendant's innocence." MacDougall also offered a rationale for Hill's behavior. Referring to himself and Scott in the third person, he said that the defendant "feels they are in collusion with the state and I think that is . . . the only explanation."

"The defendant," Hill chimed in, "has a very good reason for doing so."

---

* The "brainstorm," or temporary insanity, defense had famously been used by the millionaire Harry K. Thaw, who in 1906 had murdered the architect Stanford White. Thaw's novel defense won him a few years in an asylum and then his freedom.

The judge implored Hill, Scott, and MacDougall to reach an understanding of their respective roles for the duration of the trial. He sent them off to his chambers to confer privately. Additionally, Hill was granted time to meet alone with friends: two fellow Wobblies, unidentified in the newspapers but presumably Ed Rowan and George Child of Local 69, who were coordinating his legal defense fund and covering the story for the IWW press; and then, for fifteen minutes, the "fair-haired and blue-eyed" Hilda Erickson, who, one newspaper reported accurately enough, was "said to be the sweetheart of Hillstrom and who, it was also rumored, might prove to be the mysterious woman who has figured in the story told by Hillstrom of how he was wounded." Hill and Hilda "greeted each other warmly," the *Herald-Republican* reported, "and for some time were in close conference." (Asked by a reporter about the "mystery woman," Scott said, "I do not know who she is. Hillstrom will not tell us and he shuts up like a clam when we ask him questions concerning this woman . . . I do not know whether she is the woman whom Hillstrom says he was with the night of the murder, and over whom he says he became involved in a quarrel and was shot in the breast.")

Back in the courtroom, the bickering defense parties indicated they had reached an uneasy truce. MacDougall and Scott would stay on as amici curiae, they told the judge, and one or the other, along with the defendant if he wished, would question each witness. The jury filed back in, and then Phoebe Seeley retook the stand for her cross-examination.

Her inquisitor, Scott, was engaged and invigorated, as though during the interlude he had come around to the defendant's view that solicitude was no substitute for vigorous cross-examination. Scott confronted Seeley with her own words: her testimony at the preliminary hearing in January. He asked her to verify that she had answered affirmatively to this question that the justice of the peace had posed: "You want the court to understand you have an honest doubt as to the identity of this man [Hill] and the one [on the sidewalk] on Eighth South?"

Scott: "Now, is that a fact, Mrs. Seeley? Had you any doubt?"

Seeley: "I never made any statement at the preliminary hearing that I had any doubt as to this man's identity. No, there is a mistake. I never said that."

Scott asked her how it was that she was able to so vividly recall the facial features of the man on the sidewalk during direct examination on this morning in June, but had said nothing of those features at the preliminary hearing less than three weeks after the murders. Had her memory sharpened? "No, sir," she said, "they didn't ask me."

Again Scott bored in on her earlier identification crisis, quoting from an exchange at the preliminary hearing. "Mrs. Seeley, was this question asked you: 'Are you able to state positively whether the defendant is the man or one of the men you saw there that night?'"

Scott recited for her the answer she had given as recorded in the hearing transcript: "No, I wouldn't do that."

"Yes," Seeley now had to admit, "I said that."

THIS WAS THE SECOND DAY of testimony, and the deficiencies of the prosecution's case were becoming obvious: the state had put forward no motive for the crime, and its key "identification" witnesses had wavered as to whether on the night of the murders it had been the defendant they had seen or someone of similar height and build who *could* have been the defendant. (Even the *Herald-Republican* granted that the defense had scored "some important points.") Just as obvious, however, was the judge's unwavering sympathy for the prosecution. It seemed the case hinged on how the jury reconciled that dynamic: the weak evidence against the intensely politicized setting—both inside and out of the courtroom.

Outside, the press was hammering as hard as ever on the IWW. On the afternoon of June 19, for example, the lead story in the *Deseret Evening News* beheld the spectacle of Hill's outburst: HILLSTROM CAUSES STIR IN COURT THIS MORNING. Although the article did not cite Hill's IWW affiliation, it was accompanied by a lengthy editorial, FANNING THE FLAMES, that could have served as a primer for any jurors who needed a refresher course in IWW history and ideology: "The aggregation known as the IWW . . . is a peculiar product of the labor agitation of our day," the column began. "A few years ago it was not known. All of a sudden it came into prominence, as mushrooms that grow over night." It continued,

They are revolutionaries. They believe in a violent overturning of the established institutions . . . They hold that millions of workers are without a voice in the government. They count among them women and children employed by factories, the black men of the South, and the aliens who cannot become citizens until they have lived in the Country for a number of years . . .

The IWWs are agitating for higher wages, shorter hours, more safety appliances in dangerous occupations, but they also hope that the workers will acquire the necessary economic power to "take possession of the machinery of production" . . . and they propose that "the giant Labor shall stop the arteries that convey the golden stream of toil to coffers of the exploiting class. In a word the general strike is the measure by which the capitalist system will be overthrown." . . .

This is the doctrine of the IWWs . . . It is no wonder that wherever such influence is strong, there are disturbances, war and bloodshed.

And just so there would be no mistaking that the defendant was a prime purveyor of that doctrine, the next day's *Tribune* pointed it out. Hill, it said,

is the author of a score or more of poems and songs, many of which have been adopted by the IWW organization and the Socialist party and have been sung all over the country, according to his friends . . .

The song book of the IWW under the caption "Songs to Fan the Flames of Discontent," contains a total of thirteen songs by Hillstrom. All are parodies on either popular or sacred music and all are of an inflammatory nature and in keeping with the caption of the book quoted above.

The bashing that Hill and the IWW absorbed from the press also attracted the attention of some influential supporters, including, improbably enough, a daughter of a former president of the Mormon church. Virginia Snow Stephen was the daughter of the late Lorenzo Snow, the fifth president of the Mormon church. (He served from 1898 until 1901, when he died in office.) She was a fifty-year-old instructor of art at the University of Utah and "prominent in educational, social and art circles," the *Tribune* noted. Despite her pedigree (or maybe because of it), Virginia Stephen had a passion for social and economic justice. She belonged to the local Unitarian Society and the Socialist Party,* where she had come under the sway of William Thurston Brown, a Yale-educated minister who had traveled the country "denouncing the evils of capitalism and upholding the rights of labor, free speech and free sex." (Brown was the pastor of the First Unitarian Church in Salt Lake from 1907 until 1910.)

Stephen was moved to help Hill for two reasons. One was her "violent" opposition to the death penalty. The other was his musical compositions, two of which she had read and found incongruous with the

---

* Stephen was not alone as a Mormon Socialist; some 42 percent of Utah party members were Mormons.

mind of a murderer. The two songs she was much taken with had been found by police with Hill's possessions at the Eselius family's house in Murray. Neither tune was characteristic of the body of Hill's work. They might have been written to fan the flames, all right, but not those of discontent—these were love songs, unabashed and syrupy. One was titled "Come and Take a Joy-ride in My Aeroplane"; the other, "Oh, Please Let Me Dance This Waltz With You."

A writer of such songs, Virginia Stephen told Frank Scott, "simply could not be guilty of so brutal a murder as the killing of the Morrisons." Hill had written the pair of songs during his stay with the Eselius brothers, when both he and Otto Appelquist had been smitten with the brothers' niece, Hilda Erickson. (Hill finished both songs "just before his arrest," according to the *Tribune*, which suggests he was moved to write them in the days immediately after Hilda broke off her engagement to Appelquist.)

As to the death penalty, Stephen was an abolitionist. "Even if a man kill another, does that give a community of men the cold-blooded right, or privilege rather, to go and deliberately commit a worse murder?" she wrote a friend. "If it is an evil to kill in the heat of passion, is it not a double evil to kill by a supine community consent called law?"

"From what I hear of Hillstrom," Stephen went on, "I do not believe he could possibly commit murder under such circumstances. Anyway, do you believe there is absolute justice for the poor man in this country—particularly one charged with crime? . . . If you knew and have seen right here in Salt Lake what I have seen with my own eyes you might change your view."

A year earlier, Stephen had seen her friend Alfred Sorensen, a jeweler and a well-known Socialist in Salt Lake, acquitted of first-degree murder. His lawyer had been Orrin Hilton of Denver, a nationally eminent criminal-defense and labor lawyer. As Hill's trial got under way, Stephen was preparing to depart for New York City, where she was enrolled in a summer art class. At the behest of Ed Rowan, she stopped over in Denver to see "Judge" Hilton about joining Hill's defense team. Hilton told her that he was tied up with a Western Federation of Miners case in Michigan—for twenty-five years he served as the union's chief counsel—but that he would be available for an appeal, if necessary. He referred her to his associate in Salt Lake, Soren X. Christensen, whom he had Stephen wire: "Sit in Hillstrom case now on trial in Ritchie's court, saving all exceptions possible with view to taking to supreme court."

On Saturday, June 20, the story broke that Christensen was joining the defense, that the IWW was footing the legal fees, and that the widely respected and respectable Virginia Stephen was mixed up in all of it. The banner headline in the *Herald-Republican*: SALT LAKE WOMAN REPRESENTING THE DEFENSE COMMITTEE OF THE IWW ENTERS INTO THE HILLSTROM CASE. By Sunday morning, the papers were reporting that a "perfectly reliable" source had informed the sheriff that should Hill be convicted, "IWW sympathizers" were planning to "rescue" him from the courtroom—that "the officers will never be permitted to return him to jail." The sheriff thereafter assigned "every available deputy" either to guard the defendant inside and out of the courtroom or to swarm the corridors "watching for the slightest evidence of any . . . trouble."

IF THE PROSECUTOR HAD FAILED to sculpt the eyewitness testimony of Merlin Morrison and Phoebe Seeley into a monument of positive identification, the state had one other hope of placing the defendant at the scene. It would show that Arling Morrison shot Joe Hill with the Colt .38 army revolver found on the floor of the grocery near Arling's outstretched arm. And to prove that, the state would have to show that the gun was actually fired that night. That task fell to George Cleveland, a police detective of unsavory reputation.* Cleveland testified that upon arriving at the grocery at about ten-fifteen or ten-thirty P.M.—he was imprecise, perhaps deliberately so—he determined that the revolver had been fired "within an hour." He said that five of the weapon's six chambers were loaded when he examined it. "The gun smelled fresh with powder," Cleveland assured the jury, "and that smell leaves it in a short time." (An expert witness for the defense later testified that it was impossible to determine when a gun such as John Morrison's, which used smokeless or semismokeless powder, as opposed to black powder, had been discharged.)

If one accepted Detective Cleveland's testimony, it followed that Arling must have fired the gun. If he did, that would explain why one of the pistol's six cylinders was empty and the others loaded—the condition in which Cleveland said he found the weapon. But there was another plausible explanation for the missing bullet. A police officer who

---

* Three summers past, Cleveland had shot and killed an elderly Chinese man. The unarmed man had operated an opium den and allegedly had refused to "pay tribute" to the police in exchange for protection. "There seems to be no justification for the killing," the *Deseret Evening News* editorialized, even as it acknowledged that "to many the doing away with a Chinaman is but a trifling incident." Following the coroner's inquest, a reporter tipped Cleveland that some Chinese "hatchet men" planned to retaliate. "Well then, in that case," he replied, "the next Chinaman I shoot I'll scalp."

later testified for the defense said that officers in Salt Lake customarily loaded only five of the six chambers of their revolver, letting the hammer of the pistol rest on the empty chamber. So if John Morrison, who had served as a police officer in 1906 and 1907, had formed a habit then of loading his gun according to police custom, it stood to reason that he continued the practice in his return to civilian life.

Maybe, though, Morrison was the exception to that custom; maybe he kept his six-shooter fully loaded. If that were so, and if Arling fired his dying father's gun in a heroic last act, there remained the vexing question: what happened to the bullet?

According to Detective Cleveland, who led the search for evidence inside the store on the night of the shootings, again the following morning, and later in the week, the bullet left no trace. The only spent bullets accounted for were from the six shots fired at the Morrisons: four near the cash register on the south side of the store, where Arling Morrison was struck, and two near the showcase on the north side, where John Morrison fell. (All six were .38 caliber and steel jacketed; Morrison's revolver shot only lead bullets.) "Have you ever been able to discover any more than these six bullet marks anywhere in the store?" defense attorney MacDougall asked Cleveland. "I have not," he replied.

That left two possibilities: either Arling did not shoot, or he did and the bullet lodged inside whomever it struck. (Assuming an exhaustive search of the store.) If Arling did not squeeze off a shot, then obviously Hill's wound did not result from a gunfight at the Morrison store. And if Arling did shoot, the bullet struck someone other than Hill; the bullet he took tore through his left breast and kept going: it exited below his left shoulder blade. In all probability, Arling shot no one. There was no lead bullet, no blood in the store besides that in the vicinity of the murder victims, and no testimony by the only living witness, Merlin Morrison, that he saw his brother fire the gun, or that he saw the defendant recoil or heard the defendant (or anyone else) yelp or scream or otherwise react as one would were one shot with a high-caliber bullet.

Late on Monday afternoon, June 22, the state rested. The defense moved for a directed verdict: dismissal of the case on the basis that the state had presented no credible evidence. Judge Ritchie denied the motion.

ON TUESDAY MORNING, Frank Scott opened for the defense. Before an unfriendly judge and no fewer than "several" jury members who (as they later confessed to Scott) believed that Hill's "uncalled for outbreak" had "all the earmarks of guilt," Scott laid out the case. Speaking directly to the jury, he said that the defense would "meet circumstance with circumstance, suspicion with suspicion." The first issue he addressed, that of other suspects "answering the general description" of Hill, not only raised the question of false identification but also spoke to *the* fundamental question of any criminal prosecution built on circumstantial evidence: motive. The state had rested without explaining *why* Joe Hill had killed John Morrison; he just *had*. But "in terms of logic," as a law-review article of the time put it, "an action without a motive would be an effect without a cause."

At the time that Morrison was killed, the police and press seemed certain of the motive: Under the headline HOLDUPS KILL FATHER AND SON FOR REVENGE, the *Tribune* declared that the murder was linked to Morrison's past gunfights—one just four months before his death, the other in 1903—with assailants unknown. Following his most recent shoot-out, on the night of September 20, 1913, Morrison had told a reporter for the *Evening Telegram* that he was acquainted with one of the gunmen, and that, as noted earlier, he was convinced that the man "did not want my money, he wanted my life."

Why? Why did someone want John Morrison's life? Was the motive as the murder victim himself had feared and implied? Morrison told not only the *Telegram* reporter, Hardy Downing, but also others—his wife; his close friend John Hempel, with whom he had served on the police force; a neighbor named Herbert Steele—that he believed his life was in jeopardy. ("This fellow knows I suspect him and he will get me the next time," Morrison told Steele after the September 1913 attack, as was recounted earlier.) If one agrees with the early press and police theories that revenge was the motive, then the question becomes: did Hill and Morrison know one another? If they did, what about their relationship pushed Hill to the point that he would commit premeditated murder? And if they did not know one another—and the state never intimated that they did—why was Joe Hill on trial in the first place?

To the questions of who Morrison believed wanted him dead and why, the defense sought answers from Downing of the *Telegram*. Clearly Downing's testimony could have implicated a man other than the defendant—a prospect intolerable to the state and, apparently, to the judge: other than swearing to tell the truth, Downing was not permitted to speak a single word from the witness chair. Frank Scott began his aborted examination by asking Downing about his conversation with Morrison in the aftermath of the gunfight on September 20, 1913.

Scott: "Didn't Mr. Morrison state to you at the time that the purpose of the hold-up was not to rob him but to kill him?"

The district attorney objected to the question "as incompetent, immaterial and irrelevant."

Judge Ritchie sustained the alliteration. "I have heard no intimation so far of the particular line of defense that would make, under any circumstances, such evidence competent."

Soren Christensen stood up for the defense:

This is the theory . . . that this apparently was not a hold-up; this was just simply a shooting, not for the purpose of getting money; that on a previous occasion at a time when this defendant couldn't possibly have done it, others did the same thing, and that Mr. Morrison so told this man, that it was not for the purpose of hold-up; it was apparently an attempt to kill him; that is the conversation he had with the reporter; that is the thing we are trying to get before the jury.

The judge agreed with the district attorney that Hardy Downing's words on this subject were unfit for jurors' ears. Ritchie said that under the rules of evidence such testimony was permitted only if the defendant was pleading self-defense; that is, the judge explained, "the presumption of a possible attack [by] the deceased . . . or belief of danger of attack." A plea of self-defense was, of course, inapplicable: Hill and Morrison were unknown to one another. But the reproach did not deter the defense from trying again to insert Downing's testimony into the record.

Christensen: "Mr. Downing, isn't it a fact in your conversation with Mr. Morrison that Mr. Morrison stated to you that he knew who it was that desired to take his life?"

The district attorney pounced. "Leading and suggestive," Leatherwood cried, "simply an attempt [by] counsel to state something here which is improper."

Ritchie sustained the objection with a flash of morbid, tasteless wit: "One sufficient reason is the conversation was with a man alleged to be dead, known to be dead by all the evidence in the case so far."

Beyond the lingering uncertainty of who Morrison believed wanted him dead, the premature dismissal of Downing as a witness raises a more troubling question: was Judge Ritchie more interested in guilt than innocence? Might that explain why the court seemed determined to smother evidence that one or more former suspects (in addition to

Otto Appelquist, Hill's alleged co-conspirator) remained at large or were confined elsewhere on a lesser charge, as was true of the initial prime suspect, Frank Z. Wilson?

The defense knew about Wilson and had developed a theory and a strategy to essentially try Wilson in absentia, or, at any rate, slip into the record as much evidence of Wilson's guilt as possible. However, as determined as Christensen was to get evidence of Wilson's guilt in front of the jury, the judge was equally determined to suppress it. That tension would inform the entirety of the defense's case.

It will be recalled that Wilson (or Magnus Olson, as on his Norwegian birth certificate and his juvenile criminal dossier*) had been in Salt Lake City police custody on January 28, 1914, the day of Hill's preliminary hearing. On that day, police released him to the sheriff of Elko, Nevada, to stand trial on the lesser charge of boxcar burglary to which he had confessed. Wilson pleaded guilty (under yet another name, James Morton) to that offense and was sentenced to between ten and eleven years in the Nevada State Prison.

As best as can be determined, Wilson was never asked to account for his whereabouts on the night of September 20, 1913, the night Morrison foiled a pair of unidentified robbers by returning gunfire. What has been learned is that Wilson was a career criminal who was riding a crime wave at the time. He was wanted for questioning (under two other aliases) for crimes in Elko and Ogden, Utah, railroad towns that bookended Salt Lake. As described earlier, the Elko crime was especially heinous: authorities suspected that on September 18 he had torched a brothel after a botched diamond heist. A local paper reported that the unnamed arsonist had intended to "burn it down and roast [the madam] to death in revenge for the jailing of his pal." Though it must be emphasized that Wilson was not prosecuted (nor was anyone, from what I could tell), it bears repeating that the crime bore several of his trademarks: preternatural amorality; unrestrained rage and aggression; and murderous vengeance in the wake of failure.

It also must be said that there is no evidence to suggest that Wilson shot it out on the street with Morrison on the night of September 20, 1913. It is fair to say that after the arson early on the morning of September 18, Wilson almost certainly left Elko by eastbound train and went to Ogden. There he attracted the attention of a Southern Pacific agent. On September 20, the agent asked a prison official for Wilson's mug shot

---

* Although earlier I principally referred to him as Olson, here I'll call him Wilson, the name that was used for him during the trial.

FROM SALT LAKE COUNTY JAIL "MUG BOOK" LEDGER

Hill admitted January 14, 1914	Wilson admitted August 10, 1911
Joe Hill (aka Joseph Hillstrom; born Joel Hägglund)	**Frank Z. Wilson** (aka at least nineteen other aliases; born Magnus Olson)
Age: thirty-four	Age: thirty in August 1911 (thirty-two in January 1914)
Height: six feet	Height: six feet and one-half inch
Weight: 143	Weight: 152
Complexion: good	Complexion: good
Hair: light	Hair: light brown
Eyes: blue	Eyes: blue
Teeth: good	Teeth: good
Beard: no	Beard: no
Nativity: Danish (actual: Swedish)	Nativity: American (actual: Norwegian)

Note: *author's addenda in parentheses.*

and description. Because he was wanted in Ogden and Elko, did Wilson seek refuge in between, in Salt Lake City?

He was somewhat familiar with Salt Lake, although more so with the state prison, where he had spent sixteen months on a burglary charge. In the nine months between his release at the end of 1912 and the September night when Morrison returned fire on his assailants, Wilson had left and returned, probably more than once. The police were unsure how long Wilson had been back in town prior to January 10, 1914, the night the Morrisons were killed. According to newspaper accounts, he was spotted a few days before and then again by a prison guard that afternoon—hours before the murders.

Four days afterward, a police sergeant who took a look at the freshly jailed "right man" declared that the suspect was lying about his name. He was not "Joe Hill," the officer told the *Tribune*, but "Frank Z. Wilson." To compare facts and figures from the jail's admittance log, the "mug book," is to forgive the officer his confusion.

OF THE ELEVEN WITNESSES the defense called, the last four were all questioned about Wilson's movements over the course of the first three hours or so after the murders. Soren Christensen asked Peter Rhengreen, the railroad machinist who was walking to his overnight shift at the roundhouse, about encountering the man later identified as Wilson. It was eleven-twenty-five P.M., barely ninety minutes after the shootings. Rhengreen was approaching the corner of Eighth South and Eighth West streets, a mile west of John Morrison's store. He said he first noticed the man huddled with a slightly shorter fellow from a distance of a block and a half. (He could see that far owing to the brightness of a full moon and the snowy ground, he said.) The two men separated as the fifty-six-year-old Rhengreen neared. He suspected that the taller one—"Wilson"—was about to stick him up. But then the fellow "either fell down or lay down" on the snow-crusted sidewalk, Rhengreen said. "He was resting on one elbow, his left elbow when I come up to him, and the other hand I didn't see." The witness said that as he stood directly over him, the man's eyes were shut and he was moaning in pain: "I stopped and looked at him . . . I didn't know what to do." Neither spoke, and after a minute Rhengreen went on his way, crossing the street. As he did, Wilson arose and started tailing him. It was almost eleven-thirty. At eleven-twenty-six, an inbound South Eighth West streetcar had left its origination point two blocks south of where the distressed stranger had collapsed. The car reached the corner of Eighth West and Seventh South just as Wilson "came right behind me and was about catching up to me there," Rhengreen said. The conductor opened the doors. Wilson boarded. Rhengreen exhaled and went on to work his graveyard shift.

The conductor thought his passenger drunk. "A man got on my car that acted suspiciously," James Usher testified. "He got on the left hand side," or exit side, and "should have got on the right hand side." Wilson walked up front to pay his fare, standing within a foot of Usher. The close encounter changed Usher's mind. "Well, I couldn't smell any booze on him," Usher recalled. He described the passenger as tall, about six feet one, and "rawboned," the adjective that Rhengreen had also chosen. In an interview with police on the Monday morning following the murders (about thirty-six hours before Hill's arrest), Usher had identified Wilson from a gallery of mug shots. (When Usher testified at the trial five months later, he erroneously referred to Wilson as "W.Z. Williams," which, save for one initial, was the name Wilson had used when police had arrested him soon after he had departed Usher's car.) Usher had told police that Wilson "evidently was not familiar with the district," and that he had inquired of a passenger "which car to take to reach the uptown district."

Usher also had said that Wilson had "sat hunched over in his seat all the way to town." And now that Usher sat in the witness chair and took a close look at the defendant both sitting and standing, he could plainly see that the defendant was not the man he had seen that January night. Frank Scott for the defense:

Q: Does he resemble him in any way?
A: No, he does not resemble him, more than he is tall.
Q: Only he is tall and rawboned?
A: Yes.

It was nearing midnight on Saturday, January 10, when Wilson stepped off the car near the end of the line at Second South and Main. He stood six blocks north of Morrison's store. Although the temperature was in the twenties, Wilson ditched the black overcoat that Usher would describe to a newspaper as "rather worse from wear." At that hour, a dragnet of some forty police officers was spread across the city. At one A.M., as officers continued to sift for clues in the vicinity of the crime scene, a speeding taxicab screeched to a stop in front of the store. "Are you the one who ordered this car?" the driver asked a police captain, who had not. The driver said that whoever had telephoned him had spoken gruffly and told him to "use all speed."

As the frustrated cab driver roared off into the night, police inspector Carl Carlson noticed a man "walking leisurely" on West Temple Street, heading south from the store. The inspector and several other officers followed as the man strolled around the block. When he returned to the corner near the store, they moved in on him.

He gave his name as W. J. Williams and said he was twenty-eight years old. "Thinly clad and with no overcoat he was shivering," the *Evening Telegram* reported. Yet he claimed he was "merely taking a walk before going to bed." He had not called for a cab, he said, and he knew nothing of the murders. He told the police that he was staying at the Salvation Army and that he worked in the restaurant at the Hotel Utah, but neither story checked out, according to the newspapers. He said he had been in town for about three months and earlier that night had gone to a movie. A hasty search of his person turned up no weapon or anything else of interest. Still, Carlson testified, police jailed him pending further information. Later that Sunday, Detective George Cleveland searched "Williams" again. This time he found something: a bloody handkerchief in the suspect's pocket.

Detective Cleveland was the final defense witness. Twice Ernest Mac-Dougall asked him about that handkerchief, twice the district attorney objected to the question as immaterial and without proper foundation, and twice the judge sustained the objection. MacDougall persisted:

Q: You had in custody . . . as under suspicion for this murder, one by the name of Frank Z. Wilson?

A: . . . I know we were looking for Frank Z. Wilson; I don't know whether he was apprehended or not.

Q: Do you know the general appearance of this Wilson?

A: Yes, sir.

Q: He is an ex-convict, isn't he?

A: Yes, sir.

Q: And of the same general appearance as the defendant?

A: No, sir.

Q: In what respect does his appearance differ from that of the defendant?

As if on cue, Leatherwood interrupted: "Immaterial and irrelevant." But was it? Or was it that MacDougall was delving toward bone? Why, he wanted to know, if the police had in custody a logical suspect—an ex-con with a bloody handkerchief who ninety minutes past the murders was prostrate and moaning in pain on a sidewalk one mile from the scene, and then acting "suspiciously" on a streetcar, and who apparently and transparently lied to police about where he was staying, where he was working, and why at one o'clock on that subfreezing morning, three and a quarter hours after the murders, he was walking, coatless and shivering, on the block surrounding Morrison's store—why, MacDougall wanted to know, did the police clear Frank Z. Wilson, by whatever alias, of the crime?

Judge Ritchie agreed with the district attorney that MacDougall's line of questioning was materially lacking: "The court is not called upon to investigate the conduct of the officers, what they did, why they arrested this man or arrested another, unless it can be shown there is something beyond that."

Again MacDougall pleaded: Because the state is relying "upon indirect and circumstantial evidence," and because that evidence befits "other defendants against whom suspicion points with equal force and clearness," why, he asked, were those men "held and turned loose"?

Ritchie would not allow the detective to answer: "The question here is whether *this* man is guilty, not what suspicions may have been directed against others, whether rightfully or wrongfully."

"I take it, if the court please," MacDougall replied, "that if suspicion is rightfully directed at others, it is a complete defense, a perfect defense of this present defendant."

Ritchie ended the colloquy: "The objection is sustained."

BUT THE DEFENSE had managed to elicit testimony that tended to implicate Wilson and therefore, one would suppose, to throw a shadow of reasonable doubt over Hill's guilt. The testimony of one other defense witness in particular seemed to impeach the state's central premise, which, peeled to its core, amounted to this:

Arling Morrison shot someone on the night of January 10, 1914. Joe Hill was shot that night. Arling Morrison therefore shot Joe Hill.

According to Dr. M. F. Beer, a Salt Lake City surgeon who had examined Hill on the eve of the trial, Hill's exit wound—only slightly larger than his chest scar—was inconsistent with a lead bullet. Lead typically flattened out, or "mushroomed," and left a jagged, irregular exit wound two or three times as large as the entrance wound, Beer testified. He said the bullet that had penetrated Hill's chest had not mushroomed; rather, it had ricocheted off Hill's eighth rib and "keyholed," by which he meant that it had turned slightly sideways upon impact with the rib and left an elongated exit wound only slightly larger than the rounded entrance wound. If the doctor was correct—and the prosecutor did not cross-examine him on that point—Joe Hill had been shot with a steel bullet, ammunition not manufactured for Morrison's Colt .38 army revolver.

Dr. Beer pointed to other gaping holes—literal ones—in the state's case: those in the overcoat Hill was wearing when he was shot. Beer testified that when he visited Hill in jail to examine Hill's entrance and exit wounds, he also compared the position of the wounds relative to the bullet holes in the front and back of his coat. Beer found that the two holes in the coat were four inches lower than the scars both on Hill's chest and just under his left shoulder blade, where the bullet had exited. Then Beer asked Hill to raise his arms above his head as high as he could, he told Hill's lawyer Frank Scott, who asked him a series of questions:

Q: If I raise my arms, Doctor, and stand in an erect position, would the hole in the coat then come to where the hole was in the body?

A: It would be on the same elevation.

Q: Did you make the test . . . with the defendant?

A: Yes, sir.

Q: And did you find that when his hands were raised at extreme length over his head, and he was in an erect position, whether then the hole in the coat exactly corresponded with the wound in the body?

A: It does.

Then came Scott's climactic question for Dr. Beer, the answer to which the defense intended to demonstrate that Hill and whoever had shot him had been face-to-face and that Hill had had his hands up—positions and movements inconsistent with those in the store, as Merlin Morrison had described them.

Scott: "Would you then say, Doctor, that it was possible for the bullet to have struck him with his arms in any other position than directly over his head, and himself in a perpendicular position?"

The obvious answer was not one the prosecutor wanted the jury to hear. Leatherwood objected to the question on the ground that it was beyond the scope of expert testimony. Judge Ritchie, as was his habit, sustained the state's objection. Still, the defense had made its point. The *Herald-Republican* reported that Dr. Beer believed "the defendant must have been shot when standing erect with his hands elevated above his head."

IT WAS TWO O'CLOCK on the afternoon of Wednesday, June 24. The defense had taken only a day and a half to make its case. The brevity was due in no small part to the judge's rulings to muzzle key witnesses or otherwise severely restrict the scope of their testimony. But all the same, the defense had actually landed some solid punches. Still, given the hostile climate in the courtroom and beyond, unless Hill testified about the circumstances of his bullet wound—unless he named names—he had virtually no chance of saving himself.

After six months of self-imposed silence and two weeks in court during which he had been betrayed, by turns, not only by his counsel but also by his pride and naïveté, would he now endeavor to help himself? Would he tell the story of Hilda and Otto and how his shooting had been a crime of passion? Or would he hold fast to his constitutional right to silence, even though he had to know that the prosecutor would damn him loudly for it and the jury would hear the damnation as a virtual admission of guilt?

His lawyers were reportedly split on whether he should testify. For reasons unclear, Christensen supposedly advised him to stay mum.* Scott and MacDougall were said to have urged him to take the stand. MacDougall, for one, believed that Hill could convince the jury that his pistol was not a Colt .38 automatic, as had been used to kill John Morrison, but a Luger .30. (Hill no longer had the gun; he apparently threw it away the night he was shot.)

Hill himself had been so eager to prove that his gun was not the murder weapon that on the Saturday before the trial started, he asked his attorneys to arrange a trip to the downtown pawnshop where he had bought the gun. The sheriff granted the prisoner's request, and Hill, accompanied by three deputy sheriffs and his lawyers, was driven to the store and permitted to examine the ledger book. Sure enough, the record showed that he had purchased a gun on December 15, 1913, for which he had paid sixteen dollars and fifty cents, the date and price he had given the authorities. Unfortunately for Hill, though, there was no record of the gun's caliber or make, and his sales clerk was in Chicago at the time. He was "crestfallen," the *Herald-Republican* reported, yet adamant: he had his attorneys send the clerk a telegram. Came the reply from Chicago: "Remember selling Luger gun at that time. What's the trouble?"

With no other defense witnesses to call, the time had come for the defendant to take the stand, or not. His counsel asked for and were granted a fifteen-minute recess to meet privately in chambers with their client. Little is known about the meeting but the outcome. When they returned to the courtroom and the jury was reseated, it was Christensen who spoke up: "The defendant rests."

NO TRANSCRIPT WAS MADE of the closing arguments, but a crowded and captivated press gallery preserved the essence of the district attorney's ninety-minute statement. Leatherwood called the crime "one of the most dastardly in the history of Salt Lake County" and its perpetrator "some brutal monster." And although he dutifully reminded the jury, "You are concerned about the killing of J.G. Morrison; Hillstrom is not

---

* One student of the case, Joseph A. Curtis, suggests that Christensen dissuaded Hill because, like Hill, he did not trust Scott and worried that Scott was plotting to introduce through Hill's testimony some unspecified damaging evidence.

on trial for the killing of Arling Morrison," he went on to attribute *both* murders to the defendant: "It is clear from the evidence that some brute—I repeat some brute—not satisfied with shooting down that child Arling Morrison, went to the counter, reached over it and shot that child once, twice, perhaps three times, until he shot out every spark of life." He continued,

> If I should be asked to picture in my mind the fiend who could do that deed, I would not conjure up some monstrous Cyclops, but rather some cold thing, some bloodless thing, some thing in which the springs of humanity had been stopped up, some thing through the veins of which runs the acid of hate. That is the kind of thing that could kill that boy.

Leatherwood's play here was to justify the state's inability to offer a motive for the crime. If the defendant was so unfeeling and unthinking as to not be human, but rather "some cold thing, some bloodless thing," then it followed that, devoid of human impulses, Hill could and did kill Morrison "in cold blood, without cause or reason." The prosecutor was telling the jury that the state had not introduced a motive because there *was* no motive; in this case, the effect needed no cause.

Leatherwood then apologized to jurors for their having to sit through the tedious and useless ballistics testimony that the defense had put on. "I don't care much about bullets and cartridges in this matter," he said, slamming the door in the face of unwelcome but legitimate scientific and legal inquiry. "I care not about the expert testimony of someone about the angles at which a bullet must have been fired or probably was fired," he told the jury, implying, of course, that neither should they.

What was material and relevant, Leatherwood declared, was the mystical "hand of fate." He explained: "It seems that fate directed that shot of Arling's, for it placed the indelible mark on the murderer of his father." As Leatherwood spoke, he wheeled and pointed his finger at the defendant. "That man was Hillstrom, and the bullet fired by that boy just before he, too, fell under the fire of the cowardly brute, penetrated the breast of the murderer and by that token the law has sought him out. Murder will out and I tell you it speaks louder than a voice from the mountain top."

Leatherwood was undoubtedly a more accomplished orator and performer than litigator. (The *Tribune* applauded his closing act as "rich in dramatic values" and a "veritable sledge hammer of eloquence and logic.") But that was not necessarily a drawback: trying a case was *at least* as much

about presentation—performance, charisma, charm—as about prepara-
tion and mastery of the technical facts in evidence. And if Leatherwood's
strength was not the "bullets and cartridges" of a case, he excelled at playing to an audience: the twelve gentlemen of the jury. Still, given the remarkably underwhelming evidence, *Utah v. Hillstrom* required a bravura
performance. After all, what had the state really proved except that a father and son had been shot and killed the same night that the accused
himself had been shot through the chest?

THE DEFENSE, of course, argued that the state had not proved that Arling Morrison had shot the defendant. As Soren Christensen asked jurors to consider during his closing argument, if Arling had shot Hill,
what had happened to the bullet, and why was there no trace of a mark
where the bullet had struck in the store after passing through Hill? "If a
man was shot he must have carried the bullet away in his body," Christensen said. "Hillstrom could not have been that man."

Or had the bullet "dropped to the floor and then disappeared," as Hill
later characterized the prosecutor's argument? In a letter written more
than a year after the trial, Hill made sport of Elmer Leatherwood's
ballistic flight of fancy:

> It left no mark anywhere that an ordinary bullet would. It just
> disappeared, that's all . . . I don't know a thing about this bullet,
> but I will say this, that if I should sit down and write a novel, I
> certainly would have to think up something more realistic than
> that, otherwise I would never be able to sell it. The story of a bul-
> let that first makes an upshoot of four inches and a half at an angle
> of 90 degrees, then cuts around another corner and penetrates a
> bandit and finally makes a drop like a spit ball and disappears for-
> ever, would not be very well received in the twentieth century.

Christensen aimed most of his closing argument at the prosecution's
abject failure to show intent. "Men do not kill without a motive," he
told the jury. "What was the motive in this crime? . . . There has been
absolutely nothing to show that [Hill] even knew the man or that their
paths had ever crossed in any way." Further, he said, "no attempt was
made to rob the store, no word of robbery was spoken. No one was
made to throw up his hands. The murderers merely exclaimed to Morrison, 'We've got you now,' and then began shooting . . . Remember

that, gentlemen, when you retire to the jury room. Unless you find a motive, and you cannot since none was shown by the state, you must acquit this man."

Ernest MacDougall's closing argument for the defense could hardly have been more argumentative. He called the state's key identification witness, Phoebe Seeley, a liar. Referring to the most recent of her inconsistent accounts about how close a look she had gotten at the face of the man she had bumped into near Morrison's store a few minutes before the murders—a face, she said, that had looked a lot like Hill's—MacDougall said, "I don't believe Mrs. Seeley's testimony that she ever saw the scar, the defection on his face, the nose and the nostrils of Hillstrom before she looked at him in this courtroom . . . I believe she lied, gentlemen, and . . . I believe her testimony was a frame-up."

MacDougall then gamely took on the procedural elephant in the room: Hill's refusal to testify. "The defendant may sit back in his dignity and demand that the state produce proof of his guilt," MacDougall told the jury. "He is not bound to open his mouth or speak one word and the fact that he does not is no concern of yours and you cannot consider it as evidence against him."

"It is true," MacDougall acknowledged, "that if you or I were wounded and were accused as this man is, we would take the stand and tell how it happened, but Hillstrom won't. He won't tell me how it happened . . . What his reason is I don't know, but it is none of my business and none of yours.

"This I do know: he was not shot in Morrison's store. Where he was shot does not matter so long as it has been proven, as it has been, that he was not shot in Morrison's store."

MacDougall took four hours (over two days) to make his argument. When he was not blasting away at the weak links in the state's chain of evidence, he was firing potshots at the prosecutor himself. "The presumption of innocence is but a theory with . . . Mr. Leatherwood," McDougall told the jury. He charged the prosecutor with several attempts to "prejudice your minds against the defendant." The counts included implying Hill's guilt for his refusal to testify; embellishing the narrative of Arling's final moments with details unwitnessed; and suggesting that the defendant belonged to a class of men who, as the *Evening Telegram* paraphrased it, "would rather kill than work"—an unsubtle reference to the defendant's membership in the Industrial Workers of the World.

Lastly, in an accusation that he perhaps later wished he could recant and that certainly did his putative client no good, MacDougall flailed at Utah's "machinery" of criminal procedure, of which the very group he needed to win over constituted one component. "I have seen," he said, "where the court, judge, prosecutor *and jury* were but machines of the government to convict defendants—machines to make records for the prosecuting attorney and to do his bidding." (Emphasis added.) MacDougall was understandably frustrated. He had endured Hill's self-destructive behavior as well as two weeks of judicial rulings and prosecutorial grand-standing, if not misconduct, that had blocked the defense at every turn. Still, all that might explain but cannot excuse a defense counsel's strata-gem of insulting the twelve men in whose hands rested the life of the defendant.

THE LAW GAVE THE PROSECUTOR the last word—the state's response to the defense's closing arguments. Leatherwood tore into MacDougall's injudicious charge of systemic corruption like an expectant child unwrap-ping a Christmas present. For Leatherwood, this *was* a gift—a shimmer-ing package of stupidity and arrogance to be held aloft for the disrespected judge and jurors to behold:

> When a man charges that the courts are tools, that juries are cor-rupt, and public officers are false to their trusts and intimates that Utah is a state where a man cannot procure a fair trial, when he strikes at the very root of our American institutions of justice and freedom, I resent it. I care not whether such criticism comes from pulpit or soapbox. I resent it.

MacDougall's attack fit snugly into Leatherwood's narrative that *Utah v. Hillstrom* might just as well have been styled *Us v. Them*, wherein the plaintiff was "civil society" and the defendant was, in the prosecutor's word, a "parasite" on same. Leatherwood never identified the parasite, but there was no need to. No one in the jury box could have missed his many signals, as we shall see, to yoke Hill's alleged high crime to those of the Industrial Workers of the World. Leatherwood, with Judge Ritchie riding shotgun, had hijacked this murder case, left the facts in evidence for dead, and turned it into a referendum on the IWW. The pros-ecutor's final argument to the jury was not a rebuttal to the defense but a morality play with a simple message: to convict Joe Hill would be to set a blaze of liberty against the dark sky of anarchy. Leatherwood:

> My blood boils with keen resentment, gentlemen, when I hear such unwarranted attacks [as MacDougall's] on American institutions— institutions which are the foundation stones of our glorious concepts of liberty, equality and justice, and I tell you that when any considerable number of our fellow beings subscribe to the doctrines you heard enunciated here this morning, then liberty flees the confines of our fair land and anarchy begins its sway.

As for the defendant's invoking his right to silence, Utah law was unequivocal that it not be taken as evidence of guilt. The statute read, "[A defendant's] neglect or refusal to be a witness shall not in any manner prejudice him, nor be used against him on the trial or proceeding." But the prosecutor was having none of it. "Joseph Hillstrom," Leatherwood shouted, again thrusting a malicious finger in his direction,

> if you were an innocent man, you would have told how you received that wound. Why in God's name did you not tell so that your name could have been cleared from the stain upon it? Because you did not dare, Joe Hillstrom! Because you were a guilty man and you could not tell a story that could be corroborated. That is why.*

The prosecutor ended his discourse with a raw appeal to jurors' prejudices and fears. He suggested that their fact-finding jurisdiction extended beyond sealing the fate of one foot soldier in an unnamed but not disguised army of idlers, thieves, and killers. A guilty verdict and the penalty of death for Joe Hill, the district attorney assured, would advance "civilization" a step toward exterminating "those parasites on society." Leatherwood closed with the wish that he could "restore the lives of J.G. Morrison and his little son Arling. But I cannot, and you jurors cannot."

"But this," he urged, "you can do and must do":

> enforce the majesty of the law as framed by the people of this great state; enforce it so that anarchy and murder and crime shall be pushed back another step beyond the pale of civilization; enforce it

---

* The question of whether Leatherwood's prejudicial rant met the standard of prosecutorial misconduct was raised on appeal, but due to the lack of a transcript was never adjudicated.

so that you and your wives and your daughters and your sons and all upright men shall walk the earth free from the danger of those parasites on society who murder and rob rather than make an honest living.*

Leatherwood dispensed to the jurors precious few tools with which to implement the law's majesty. He provided them with no motive, no murder weapon, no positive identification, no bullet recovered from the deceased's gun—no direct evidence at all. Rather, he steered them into a dense thicket of conjecture and suspicion and improbability, and left them to grope their way out along a chain of circumstantial evidence so fraught with missing and broken links as to be rendered useless for finding the guilty verdict Leatherwood so badly wanted.

The battered chain was useless because Utah statute prescribed that for cases built upon circumstantial evidence, the chain of proof "must be complete and unbroken and established beyond a reasonable doubt." Moreover, if the state failed to meet that standard, the law required the trial judge to direct a verdict of acquittal. Could the prosecutor reconcile his flimsy chain of evidence in *Utah v. Hillstrom* with the state's strict standard of proof?

He could not. But with the mercifully tender Judge Morris Ritchie presiding, nor would he need to.

In his charge to jurors, the judge circumnavigated Utah case law (and the defense's similarly worded request) in his all-important instruction regarding consideration of circumstantial evidence. Rather than employing the doomed metaphor of a chain of interdependent links that was no stronger than its weakest one, Ritchie instructed the jury to equate circumstantial evidence with a cable woven of independent strands. If one strand were to fray or break, it could well weaken the state's case, he implied, but it would not definitively follow that the entire cable was helpless to support a conviction. Circumstantial evidence, he explained, "is the proof of such facts and circumstances connected with or surrounding the . . . crime, . . . and if these facts and circumstances, *when considered*

---

* Though Leatherwood never identified the "parasites" by name, his closing statement borrowed liberally from a *Tribune* editorial that most certainly did. "The anarchistic spirit of that class of idlers who style themselves the Industrial Workers of the World was shown when a mob composed of 1000 members of this 'working' organization attempted to break up a . . . peaceable and law-abiding assemblage" in New York City, the editorialist wrote, adding, "These parasites just now seem bent upon creating all the trouble they can in various parts of the country."

all together, are sufficient to satisfy the . . . jury of the guilt of the defendant beyond a reasonable doubt, then such evidence is sufficient to authorize a conviction." (Emphasis added.)

The ruling, sandwiched amid Ritchie's twenty-two numbered instructions for the jury, was likely the greatest among the many gifts the judge bestowed on the prosecution. As one scholar of the case concludes, if Ritchie's evidentiary instruction had adhered to Utah precedent, "there is no question . . . the jury would have been morally and logically bound to return a verdict of not guilty."

THE JURORS MADE hasty work of their deliberations. They were excused from the courtroom at four-forty-five on Friday afternoon, June 26. They elected as foreman Joseph Kimball, the fraternal-organization brother of Ritchie's whom the judge had personally drafted from another jury panel. After a review of the instructions and the exhibits, followed by a dinner break, the jurors began deliberations at seven o'clock. By nine o'clock, they had informally agreed on a verdict, apparently without dissent, and just before eleven, when the judge ordered bailiffs to sequester the jurors for the night, a unanimous first ballot confirmed the result.

In the meantime, a crowd of Wobblies that had gathered for the final hours of the trial stayed on inside the City & County Building. They were made to leave when the jury retired for the night but were back early in the morning, milling and pacing about the hallways, waiting for word of the verdict. A contingent of wary deputies was there, too. SHERIFF IS WATCHFUL, the *Tribune* reported, REMAINS ON GUARD LEST IWW FRIENDS OF ACCUSED MAKE DEMONSTRATION.

The jurors reconvened at nine o'clock on Saturday morning. Apparently none had changed his mind overnight; a second ballot yielded the identical outcome. Shortly before ten, the jury notified the judge that it had reached a verdict. The judge summoned the parties to court.

At exactly ten, the jury filed into a courtroom that overflowed with spectators and law enforcers. Eight deputies and the sheriff himself ringed the room; several more were on duty in the corridors.

"Gentlemen of the jury, have you agreed upon a verdict?" the judge asked.

"We have," foreman Kimball said.

Kimball passed a slip of paper to the bailiff, who handed it to the judge. Ritchie glanced at it, then passed it to the clerk of court. The clerk stood somewhat behind the defendant. Hill swiveled halfway in his chair and stared at the clerk as he pronounced the verdict:

"We, the jurors, find the defendant Joseph Hillstrom guilty of the crime of murder in the first degree as charged in the information."

Though first-degree murder was a capital crime, the jury could have recommended "mercy" for the defendant, which would have commuted the sentence from death to life in prison. The jury made no such recommendation.

As the words came, Joe Hill looked as vacant as a corpse. He listened "without even the flutter of an eye nor a change of color in his cheeks," the *Deseret Evening News* reported.

ELEVEN DAYS LATER, on Wednesday, July 8, 1914, Hill returned to court for sentencing. The majesty of Utah law offered the condemned a choice: death by firing squad or hanging. "Mr. Hillstrom," Judge Ritchie asked, "which method do you elect?"

"I'll take shooting," Hill replied. "I'm used to that. I have been shot a few times in the past and I guess I can stand it again."

12.

"New Trial or Bust"

At first they trickled in to the office of the governor of Utah: telegrams, postcards, petitions, and letters—some neatly or haphazardly typed, some on letterhead, others carefully composed and painstakingly handwritten on lined notepaper, and others scrawled indecipherably. They arrived, as would be expected, from IWW locals and members around the country. They came, too, from other radical organizations and affiliates of the American Federation of Labor, from individual wageworkers, from merchants, educators, publishers, doctors. Most were signed; others, anonymous. Some appealed to the humanity of Governor William Spry, pleading that he grant Hill a new trial or pardon him or commute the death sentence to life in prison. Others sought to shame the governor. A fellow from Massachusetts wrote that Hill's execution "will be a blot upon the name of your state . . . which can never be effaced." Some made implicit or explicit threats. From Minnesota, a not-quite-bilingual countryman of Hill's wrote, "If Joe Hillstrom are going to be mördad we will write your name in his Blodd."*

From the day the jury sentenced him to death, Hill would spend almost seventeen months in prison. Estimates vary as to how much protest correspondence the governor received during that period. Spry himself later wrote that "some forty thousand letters or more" had poured in.

Tens of thousands of people were in the streets, too. In major American cities—from Seattle to New York to Minneapolis to San Francisco to Boston, to name a handful—and not just in cities but in far-flung miners'

---

* Unless otherwise indicated, the correspondence to Spry is unedited.

camps in northern Nevada, in obscure logging towns in Washington, and among threshing crews in the Dakotas, and not only in America but on isolated railroad branches in British Columbia (where Hill wrote "Where the Fraser River Flows") and on English docks and in Australian goldfields (where representatives of thirty thousand unionists announced that until Hill was released, "we have instituted a strict boycott of all American goods"), workers rallied in support of Joe Hill, sang his songs, signed petitions, generated publicity, and raised money for his defense. In short, the IWW and its allies had transformed what had begun as a murder case of strictly local concern, in a remote city of the intermountain American West, into an international cause célèbre.

IN THE PROCESS, Hill was transformed, too. He became an icon of courage and resistance: not so much a person as an idealized *representation* of a person; a "Tin-Jesus," he jokingly called himself. The idolatry surely strengthened his resolve and amplified his voice; the jail cell became his pulpit. He wrote constantly, at times feverishly: songs, sometimes by request; poems and essays that opined on any number of issues and opportunities facing labor; and many, probably hundreds of, letters.

But with adulation and fame came pressure—pressure to live up to his iconic status and conform to the movement's hopes and expectations. Wittingly or not, he had been thrust into the spotlight as the leading player in the class struggle. He seemed to embrace the role, even as it came to define and narrow his options. Surely, for example, it affected his decision to uphold his principled refusal to testify about the circumstances of his shooting, a choice that left him for dead, albeit a hero for the cause.

It had been Bill Haywood's front-page story in *Solidarity*, SHALL JOE HILL BE MURDERED? that had elicited the first wave of protest correspondence to the governor. Haywood's urgent appeal for money for Hill's defense fund and for letters to Governor Spry did not come too soon: the story ran on July 25, 1914, and Judge Ritchie had scheduled Hill's death for September 4.*

---

* Ritchie probably would have set the date sooner—he seemed impatient to be done with it—but he had had to delay the sentencing hearing for lack of a trial transcript. The court reporter, E. M. "Ned" Garnett, who was also the state tennis champion, was busy defending his title.

On September 1, fewer than seventy-two hours before what Hill told a friend was "supposed to be my last day on earth," Ritchie heard oral arguments on the defendant's motion for a new trial. Soren Christensen rehashed the points that he and co-counsel had made at the close of the trial: that the state had failed to identify Hill as John Morrison's murderer and that it had failed to prove that Hill had received his gunshot wound in Morrison's store. Christensen also argued that the dispute in open court between Hill and his attorneys, Ernest MacDougall and Frank Scott, and the judge's refusal to allow the defendant to fire the attorneys, and his retaining them as "friends of the court," had ensured the jury's prejudice against Hill. District Attorney Elmer Leatherwood asserted that Hill had been fairly tried and convicted and that, as the *Herald-Republican* put it, "he should pay the penalty without any further ceremony."

The judge ruled promptly: motion denied for a new trial. Christensen immediately filed notice of appeal to the Utah Supreme Court, thus triggering a stay of execution and, to the state's dismay, "further ceremony" aplenty.

Hill seemed pleasantly surprised to have survived his execution date. "This is Sept. 4," he wrote a friend and fellow worker, E. W. Vanderleith, who had recently left Salt Lake for San Francisco, ". . . but I am still wriggling my old lead pencil and I might live a long time yet—if I don't die from 'Beanasitis' (that's a brand new disease)." Yet his humor was tinged with melancholy. He had already been jailed for nine months, and he knew he was looking at no less than another six months in lockup before the state supreme court even heard his appeal, let alone issued its ruling.* For the first time, but not for the last, he told a friend to stop thinking about him.

> Well, Van, all joking aside, I guess I have a long wait ahead of me and I think the best you . . . boys can do is to forget me and use your energies and your financial resources for the One Big Union.
>
> I think some of you are making too much fuss about me anyway. I wish you would tell those who are writing poems about me

---

* Utah law allowed criminal defendants six months between giving notice of appeal and filing the appellant's brief. This and other "delays" afforded the defendant galled Hill's prosecutor, who recommended to the state legislature that it reduce the time to file the appeal from six months to forty days. "A man can prepare his appeal to the supreme court just as well in forty days as he can in forty years," Elmer Leatherwood said.

that there is no poetry about my personality. I am just one of the rank and file—just a common pacific coast wharfrat—that's all.

The poetry to which he referred had appeared in the latest *Solidarity*. Titled simply "Joe Hill," it was written by Ralph Chaplin, the paper's editor and the leading propagator of Hill as the beloved "laureate of labor"—the singing, fearless rebel who lived only for the cause and who, if need be, would die for it. Here are the final three stanzas:

> *Now boys, we've known this rebel long—*
> *In every land we've sung his song—*
> *Let's get him free and he may see*
> *The day of our great victory!*
>
> *He made them hate him high and low,*
> *They feared his tuneful message so;*
> *He'd fight for us while he had breath—*
> *We'll save him from the jaws of death.*
>
> *No harm to him can we allow,*
> *He needs our help and needs it now;*
> *He's in their dungeon, dark and grim—*
> *He fought for us; we'll stand by him.*

Hill appreciated the heartfelt if maudlin tributes Chaplin and others offered in published verse, but as he confided to Vanderleith in another letter, "I know they mean well, and the poems are swell, but it kind of gets my goat to be mushed up that way. . . . Here I am a martyr, a Tin-Jesus. Well, honestly, wouldn't that jar ye?"

He used the solitary time to advantage. With nothing to read except for missionary-delivered books "full of moral uplift and angel food," as he grumbled to a friend by the name of Gus, he taught himself to "keep still and sit still"—"I'd make a first class toadstool," he observed. Jail freed him to write, gave him time, space, tranquillity. "A fellow like myself," he told a friend, "can do just as well in jail. I can dope out my music and 'poems' in here and slip them out through the bars and the world will never know the difference." He wrote nonstop, or so it seemed: music and poetry, of course, as well as philosophical essays and, especially, letters. "Write me when you can," he told Gus. "One thing this jail has made out of me is a good correspondent."

In September, *Solidarity* published the lyrics to his anthemic "Workers of the World, Awaken," the first song he slipped "out through the bars." As others have pointed out, a portion of the song is derivative of "The Internationale." Hill otherwise composed the music and words:

> *Workers of the world, Awaken,*
> *Break your chains, Demand your rights.*
> *All the wealth you make is taken*
> *By exploiting parasites.*
> *Shall you kneel in deep submission*
> *From your cradles to your graves?*
> *Is the height of your ambition*
> *To be good and willing slaves?*
>
> *If the workers take a notion,*
> *They can stop all speeding trains.*
> *Every ship upon the ocean*
> *They can tie with mighty chains.*
> *Every wheel in the creation,*
> *Every mine and every mill,*
> *Fleets and armies of the nation,*
> *Will at their command stand still.*
>
> *Join the Union, Fellow Workers,*
> *Men and women side by side.*
> *We will crush the greedy shirkers*
> *Like a sweeping, surging tide;*
> *For united we are standing*
> *But divided we will fall,*
> *Let this be our understanding:*
> *"All for One and One for All."*
>
> *Workers of the World, Awaken,*
> *Rise in all your splendid might,*
> *Take the wealth which you are making,*
> *It belongs to you by right.*
> *No one will for bread be crying,*
> *We'll have freedom, love and health,*
> *When the grand Red Flag is flying*
> *In the Workers' Commonwealth.*

Though the seventh edition of *The Little Red Songbook* was already in press when Hill sent out that song, the issue of *Solidarity* in which it was printed, September 19, carried the announcement that from then on all orders for the *Songbook* (ten cents each; five dollars per hundred) would be filled and include an insert (designed to fold into the pocket-size books) that described Hill's case and advised "the necessary action to prevent his being shot by the authorities of Salt Lake City." In this way, the editors explained, "the songs of which he has contributed so many, will be a medium of arousing the workers in his behalf."

IN DECEMBER, Hill published a timely piece in the *International Socialist Review*. "How to Make Work for the Unemployed" appeared during an economic downturn so severe that the Socialist leader Eugene V. Debs, speaking in Salt Lake City, claimed "there were more unemployed and hungry men in the United States now than at any other time." Certainly there were more Wobblies out of work than ever before. The membership had fallen from a peak in 1912 of more than eighteen thousand members (following the successful Lawrence strike) to eleven thousand as Hill wrote at the end of 1914. The union attributed the declining membership to the "industrial depression" then gripping the entire country and particularly the Pacific coast, where Kelly's Army of the Unemployed had been on the march that spring and where 75 percent of the membership was jobless and unable to pay dues.

At the IWW's annual convention in Chicago in the fall of 1914, delegates unanimously resolved to recommend to the workers the "necessity" of slowing their output—that is, engaging in a form of sabotage. "Wherever I go, I inaugurate sabotage among the workers," said Frank Little, the bullet-ridden survivor of virtually all of the union's Western free speech fights (who would be lynched three years later). "Eventually the bosses will learn why it is that their machinery is spoiled and their workers slowing down."

In his magazine article, Hill expanded on that theme, and not for the first time. On the very day he had been convicted of murder, June 27, 1914, *Solidarity* had published "The Rebel's Toast," his ode to sabotage:

> *If Freedom's road seems rough and hard,*
> *And strewn with rocks and thorns,*

Then put your wooden shoes on, pard,
* And you won't hurt your corns.*
To organize and teach, no doubt,
* Is very good—that's true,*
But still we can't succeed without
* The Good Old Wooden Shoe.**

He also devoted a new song, "Ta-Ra-Ra Boom De-Ay," to the efficacy of sabotage. (The antihero of his 1911 hit "Casey Jones—the Union Scab," it will be recalled, is a victim of sabotage—he meets an untimely death when his train hits "a bunch of railroad ties" someone has left on the tracks.) Hill set "Ta-Ra-Ra Boom De-Ay" to the silly and popular 1891 tune of the same name. The song tells of a wheat stiff, a thresher, whose boss (the "rube") makes him work all night under a bright moon after already putting in a full day. The worker "'accidentally' slipped and fell," which causes his pitchfork to lodge in the cogs of the threshing machine:

CHORUS
Ta-ra-ra boom-de-ay!
It made a noise that way,
And wheels and bolts and hay,
Went flying every way.
That stingy rube said, "Well!
A thousand gone to hell."
But I did sleep that night,
I needed it all right.

Next day that stingy rube did say, "I'll bring my
* eggs to town today;*
You grease my wagon up, you mutt, and don't
* forget to screw the nut."*
I greased his wagon all right, but, I plumb forgot
* to screw the nut,*
And when he started on that trip, the wheel slipped off
* and broke his hip.*

---

* This was a symbol and a tactic the Wobblies had derived from French revolutionaries, who, legend had it, had thrown their wooden shoes—*sabots*—into the machine cogs.

SECOND CHORUS
Ta-ra-ra boom-de-ay!
It made a noise that way.
That rube was sure a sight,
And mad enough to fight;
His whiskers and his legs
Were full of scrambled eggs:
I told him, "That's too bad—
I'm feeling very sad."

And so on for another verse, another chorus, until the "rube" finally catches on: "He said 'There must be something wrong; I think I work my men too long.'" And with that, happily, "He cut the hours and raised the pay, / Gave ham and eggs for every day, / Now gets his men from union hall, / and has no 'accidents' at all."*

In his essay in the *International Socialist Review*, Hill harked back to when he had worked on docks and in lumberyards on the West Coast, where, he said, nearly all the jobs were "temporary." Employers hired men to unload the boats and laid them off when the work was done. Naturally, Hill wrote, the workers wanted to "'make the job last' as long as possible." Without mentioning the word "sabotage," he told of the time when he and three others had been ordered to load about three thousand bundles of shingles into five boxcars. "When we commenced the work we found, to our surprise, that every shingle bundle had been cut open"—somehow the little band of sheet metal used to tightly bundle the shingles had been sheared. "When the boss came around we notified him about the accident and, after exhausting his supply of profanity, he ordered us to get the shingle press and re-bundle the whole batch. It took the four of us ten whole days to put that shingle pile into shape again."

His lesson was that every worker, skilled or unskilled, could and should avail himself of this method of "striking on the job." What's more, he said, it was "*without expense* to the *working class* and if intelligently and systematically used, it *will* not only *reduce* the *profits* of the *exploiters*, but also *create more work for the wage earners*." He called striking on the

---

* In some of the state and federal conspiracy trials of IWW members to come several years later, prosecutors pointed to the song as evidence, writes the historian Joyce Kornbluh, "of IWW intent to commit acts of sabotage if the workers' requests for better working conditions were not granted."

job "the only known antidote for the infamous 'Taylor System'"—the clipboard-and-stopwatch technique of "time management"—the aim of which, he wrote, "seems to be to work one-half the workers to death and starve the other half to death."

STARVATION WAS ON Hill's mind when he composed "It's a Long Long Way Down to the Soupline." Sam Murray, a confidant and fellow veteran of the Wobbly brigade in Baja California during the Mexican Revolution, had written him from San Francisco on the eve of the opening of the city's 1915 Panama-Pacific Exposition, a world's fair to celebrate the completion of the Panama Canal. Murray's idea was that with the eyes of the world on San Francisco, a song that spoke to and of the hungry and unemployed masses there could have a powerful impact. He suggested to Hill that he parody the British army's marching song "It's a Long Long Way to Tipperary." Hill replied that he did not know the tune but said that if Murray would send along the sheet music, "I might try to dope something out." He also asked Murray to provide him with some details about the "actual conditions of Frisco at present," because, he explained, "when I make a song I always try to picture things as they really are. Of course a little pepper and salt is allowed in order to bring out the facts more clearly."

The IWW in San Francisco printed Hill's "Soupline" song on cards, charged a nickel per, and donated the profits—nearly fifty dollars—to Hill's defense fund. The first verse and chorus follow:

> Bill Brown came a thousand miles to work on
>   Frisco Fair
> All the papers said a million men were wanted
>   there
> Bill Brown hung around and asked for work three
>   times a day,
> 'Til finally he went busted flat, then he did sadly
>   say,
>
> CHORUS
> It's a long way down to the soupline.
>   It's a long way to go.
> It's a long way down to the soupline
>   And the soup is weak I know.

Good-bye, good old pork chops.
  Farewell beefsteak rare,
It's a long way down to the soupline,
  But my soup is there.

By the middle of February, the tune had bounced back to Salt Lake, where a *Deseret Evening News* reporter watched some 250 unemployed marchers (*Solidarity* maintained there were 700) en route to the state capitol unite "in shouts and songs, a parody on 'Tipperary' being most conspicuous among the musical numbers." And by late March, Hill could report to Murray that he heard the song was "spreading like the smallpox": "The unemployed all over the country have adopted it as a marching song in their parades, and in New York City they changed it to some extent, so as to fit the brand of soup dished out in N.Y." In fact, Hill was able to track the song's progress across the continent more closely than he could the progress of his own case. "The Sup Court will 'sit on it' sometimes in the sweet by & by & that's all I know about it," he had told Murray in mid-February. A month later, he knew that the court had postponed oral arguments. His frustration was palpable. "They [his lawyers] are trying to make me believe that is for my benefit," he wrote Murray, "but I'll tell you that it is damn hard for me to see where the benefit comes in at. Damn hard."

When he was not philosophizing in prose or verse for publication, he was trying, at times vainly, to keep up with the steady flow of correspondence. "I have about a dozen letters to answer," he apologized in one tardy reply. He received more requests for new songs; thanked supporters for their moral and financial uplift (including, to his surprise and delight, a company of soldiers stationed "near the Mexican line" that donated ten dollars); encouraged a young girl to study violin ("I would rather play the fiddle than eat," he wrote to her); and even enjoyed a taste of epistolary flirtation with Elizabeth Gurley Flynn, a twenty-five-year-old traveling IWW jawsmith and far and away the best-known of the few female Wobblies.

Flynn would become a pivotal figure in the fight to save Hill's life, eventually using her connections to wangle a meeting at the White House with President Woodrow Wilson to plead Hill's case. Flynn (or "Girlie," as her fellow workers called her) grew up in the Bronx and climbed atop her first Wobbly soapbox in 1906, at the age of fifteen, to speak on "What Socialism Will Do for Women." By 1915, she had organized (and gone to jail) practically everywhere for the IWW—from Western logging and mining

Elizabeth Gurley Flynn speaking to striking workers during the 1913 silk strike in Paterson, New Jersey. (Courtesy Barrie Stavis)

camps to the big textile strikes in Lawrence in 1912 and Paterson, New Jersey, in 1913. She was a petite but leather-lunged "hellion that breathed reddish flame"—one of the "She-Dogs of Anarchy," the *Los Angeles Times* dubbed her. The spectacle of a young female soapboxer who combined a "quick brain and a facile oratory," in the words of the *New York World*, with a thundering voice and effusive hand gestures—"pothooks, curves, dots and dashes written in the air," as a Philadelphia reporter saw it—was so mesmerizing that by the time Flynn stepped down from the box, it was said, "the perpetual inebriate forgot about the swinging doors" and "the corner loungers stood straight."

Hill wrote to Flynn for the first time on January 18, 1915, and regularly thereafter. Before long he was admiring her productivity. (Not only was she a full-time organizer, but she was also the single, divorced mother of a six-year-old boy.) "Have been trying to figure out how you can have the time to write me such nice, fat letters and hold big meetings every night besides," he wrote her in March, "but I guess you are like Tommy Edison, you don't sleep more than four hours a day & work twenty." (In another letter, he joked about seeing her "boil spuds, iron clothes, and sling the ink all at the same time.")

A month before he first wrote to her, Hill had referred to her in a published letter to the editor of *Solidarity*. He suggested that the union needed to attract more women workers, who, he said, "are more exploited than the men." "Especially on the West Coast," he said, the IWW had "sadly neglected" women, "and consequently we have created a kind of one-legged, freakish animal of a union." He recommended that the union redeploy its female organizers, "Gurley Flynn, for instance," to work "<u>exclusively</u>" on recruiting women.

By early February, he was working on a song for her, one that, he told Sam Murray, he hoped would "help to line up the women workers in the OBU [One Big Union.]" Hill later told Flynn that when he composed it, "you was right there and helped me all the time." Decades later, she borrowed Hill's song title for that of her autobiography, *The Rebel Girl*.

There are women of many descriptions
In this queer world, as everyone knows.
Some are living in beautiful mansions,
And are wearing the finest of clothes.
There are blue blood queens and princesses,
Who have charms made of diamonds and pearl;
But the only and thoroughbred lady
Is the Rebel Girl.

CHORUS
That's the Rebel Girl, the Rebel Girl!
To the working class she's a precious pearl.
She brings courage, pride and joy
To the fighting Rebel Boy.
We've had girls before, but we need some more
In the Industrial Workers of the World.
For it's great to fight for freedom
With a Rebel Girl.

Yes, her hands may be hardened from labor,
And her dress may not be very fine;
But a heart in her bosom is beating
That is true to her class and her kind.
And the grafters in terror are trembling
When her spite and defiance she'll hurl;
For the only and thoroughbred lady
Is the Rebel Girl.

The Rebel Girl herself stopped in Salt Lake City in early May of 1915 for a lecture on her cross-country speaking tour (forty-seven cities in nineteen states) and to see her faithful correspondent. The sheriff granted her a one-hour visit. It was the only time she and Hill met. "He is tall, good looking, but naturally thin after sixteen months in a dark, narrow cell, with a corridor and another row of cells between him and daylight, and 'nourished' by the soup and bean diet of a prison," Flynn reported for *Solidarity*. (Hence the "Beanasitis" that Hill had kidded about dying from.) She called him a "free spirit" and "the inimitable songster and poet of the IWW." "Let others," she continued,

> write their stately, Whitmanesque verse and lengthy, rhythmic narrative. Joe writes songs that sing, that lilt and laugh and sparkle, that kindle the fires of revolt in the most crushed spirit and quicken the desire for fuller life in the most humble slave. He has put into words the inarticulate craving of 'the sailor, and the tailor and the lumberjack' for freedom, nor does he forget 'the pretty girl that's making curls.' . . . He has crystallized the organization's spirit into imperishable form, songs of the people—folk songs.

Flynn reported that they spoke not at all about his case, in part because they had no privacy—they met in the sheriff's office with others present—and also because the prisoner was more interested in hearing about the IWW's progress than in talking about himself. "And so the hour was spent in giving him the news of the movement, and a few words of encouragement," Flynn wrote. "I've seen men more worried about a six months' sentence than Joe Hill apparently worries about his life. He only said: 'I'm not afraid of death, but I'd like to be in the fight a little longer.'"

When they were made to part, Hill could see that Flynn was shaken. Indeed, she was thinking, Am I leaving a tomb? And how long *will* he stay in the fight? As they said their good-byes at the barred door, he pointed outside toward a bearded old man cutting the grass. "He's a Mormon," Hill joked, "and he's had two wives and I haven't even had one yet!"

ON MAY 28, 1915, the Utah Supreme Court heard Hill's appellate argument. From Denver came the esteemed defense attorney the IWW had recruited, "Judge" Orrin Hilton. He and Soren Christensen made the case for reversal of the trial court verdict. Hilton spoke before what the *Tribune* cited as "an unusually large attendance of those who had watched the proceedings from their inception"—a roomful of Wobblies. He argued mainly to two points: the inadequacy of the state's evidence and the trial judge's error-ridden response to the defendant's sudden and dramatic dismissal of his attorneys. In summary of the former, Hilton said that there had been "insufficient" identification and a failure to show motive, and that the proof of guilt had in no way exceeded a reasonable doubt. To the latter argument, he maintained that it had been Judge Ritchie's "duty" to stop the trial and appoint new defense counsel rather than merely naming Hill's former attorneys, MacDougall and Scott, as "friends of the court." Most important, Hilton argued, the judge's maneuver had left Hill without counsel and the court in violation of the defendant's right to due process. The Utah Constitution and criminal code, Hilton told the justices, "intended clearly [to ensure] that at every step [counsel] should be present . . . so that any excess or advantage sought to be taken by a diligent prosecutor might be properly objected to."

In his closing statement, Hilton cast aside the constitutional law arguments in favor of an appeal to the three justices' sense of morality and integrity:

> I now ask your honors frankly if you or anyone that is dear to you was condemned upon these inconclusive, disjointed fragments of suspicion misnomered by the state as evidence against this defendant, *would you* say that you or they were justly condemned and

Hill's appellate lawyer Orrin N. Hilton. (Courtesy Barrie Stavis)

that the crime charged had been proved against you beyond a reasonable doubt? Would you go or would you permit anyone dear to you to go to his death under this flimsy testimony and then say that you or he had been tried fairly or impartially . . . ?

Unless you can answer these questions fairly by "yes," you must reverse this case, so far as the law is concerned. You must each stand in Hillstrom's place, and standing in that place, you must be able to say upon your conscience, that you have been proven guilty beyond a reasonable doubt after a full opportunity to present and prove your defense both in person and by counsel, and that you are condemned because you are the guilty agent of the crime that the state here tries to punish.

Representing the state, an assistant attorney general by the name of Higgins countered that Hill, in the words of the *Tribune*, "was in no way prejudiced by the action of the court"—Ritchie's reinstatement of Hill's dismissed attorneys—"and that the court only performed its duty in the matter." Higgins concluded by saying that the testimony of the state's "identification" witnesses excluded all reasonable doubt that "the man who committed the homicide and the defendant were the same."

Hilton walked out of the Supreme Court chambers satisfied that his client would be granted "speedy relief." From the judges' "comments upon the evidence as we went along," Hilton later said, "there seemed to be no doubt but that the case would be reversed and a new trial granted." Hilton's confidence rubbed off on Hill. As Hill wrote Sam Murray a week after the hearing, "[Hilton] is sure of getting a reversal, and if so, there hardly will be another trial for the simple reason that there won't be anything to try if I can get an attorney that will DEFEND me." Ed Rowan, the secretary of Local 69 in Salt Lake City, reported on June 12 for *Solidarity* that Hilton had made a "splendid plea" and that he hoped "to be able to wire . . . good news before long."

ON JULY 3, the Utah Supreme Court unanimously affirmed the lower court verdict, crisply concluding that Joe Hill had "had a fair and impartial trial in which he was granted every right and privilege vouchsafed by the law." The papers carried the story on Independence Day: SUPREME COURT SAYS HILLSTROM MUST DIE.

The opinion, authored by Chief Justice Daniel N. Straup, is a model of judicial demagoguery. Many of the facts as presented were not facts at all, but misstated or modified or misrepresented or fabricated facts that the court regarded as stepping stones to arrive at otherwise unreachable conclusions. *State of Utah v. Joseph Hillstrom* did not so much affirm the lower court verdict as provide it cover; it rationalized an unreasonable ruling.

The decision spun certitude out of uncertainty. For example, to link Joe Hill's gunshot wound to the murder of John Morrison—a connection that prosecutor Leatherwood had failed to make—the Supreme Court simply conflated the trial testimony of the two doctors, Frank McHugh and Arthur Bird, who had attended Hill at McHugh's office some ninety minutes after the homicide. McHugh had testified that he was unable to determine the caliber of the gun used to shoot Hill, other than to say that judging from the size of the wound it was of a caliber "larger than .32 and somewhere from .38 to .40, or .41." Bird, for his part, had seemed more confident at trial, stating that the bullet that had wounded Hill "I should judge of .38 caliber." (Although Bird's statement was inconsistent with his testimony at the preliminary hearing, when both he and McHugh had declined to "hazard an opinion as to the caliber of the bullet," according to the *Tribune*.) Yet the high court stated as a matter of fact that the doctors "gave it as their opinion that the gun was a .38 caliber automatic gun, and that the handle was similar to a Colt's automatic .38 gun."

Chief Justice Straup's opinion also took liberties with Merlin Morrison's testimony concerning the six-shooter that his brother Arling was said to have fired in the seconds before he died. Although Merlin had said nothing at trial about having examined the gun prior to the murders and having noticed that it was fully loaded, Straup's opinion stated otherwise: "Merlin testified that he saw the revolver in the ice chest earlier that evening, and that then *all six chambers* were loaded." (Emphasis added.) Straup's assertion in turn licensed his deduction about Hill's "unexplained" bullet wound. Straup wrote that insofar as Hill's description "answered" that of one of the perpetrators of the crime, his wound should be deemed "a relevant mark of identification" and "quite as much a distinguishing mark as though one of the assailants . . . had one of his ears chopped off." Straup then alluded to what Hill had told Dr. McHugh on the night of the murders regarding the circumstances of his wounding:

> The only explanation the defendant gave of his wound was that he received it at some undisclosed place in a quarrel with some undescribed man over some undescribed woman, in which he "was to blame as much as the other fellow." With other evidence in the case, that unexplained or unsatisfactorily explained wound might,

to the triers of facts, point with as much certainty to the defendant as one of the perpetrators of the offense as though that night at eleven-thirty or twelve o'clock some stolen and identified article from the store had been found in his unexplained or unsatisfactorily explained possession.

The chief justice's reasoning could not support the weight of its hypocrisy. In one paragraph he inveighed against the defendant's silence, declaring that Hill's failure to testify about how he had been shot was evidence—nay, proof—of guilt every bit as damning as if he had turned up at the doctor's office minus an ear found at the crime scene. And yet the justice immediately thereafter invoked the defendant's constitutional protection against self-incrimination—and then added a caveat. "He had a right to remain silent," Straup wrote, adding, "Nor can his neglect or refusal to be a witness in any manner prejudice him or be used against him." *But*, Straup went on,

the defendant, without some proof tending to rebut them, may not avoid the natural and reasonable inferences deducible from proven facts by merely declining to take the stand or remaining silent.

Absolutely, the state carried the burden of proof, the court acknowledged, but its insistence that Hill shoulder a bit of the load underscored the consequences of his refusal to testify. For even as the court solemnly muttered that the defendant's silence could not be held against him, the court unquestionably *did* hold it against him. "The defendant was not a witness in the case," Straup wrote, "and at no time explained or offered to explain the place where, nor the circumstances under which, he received his wound, except as stated by him to the doctors, that he received it in a quarrel over a woman; nor did he offer any evidence whatever to show his whereabouts or movements on the night of the homicide."

Lastly, the court found irrelevant the defense's argument that the state's failure to show motive was a ground for reversal. "Since the evidence is sufficient to show that the defendant was one of the perpetrators," Straup wrote, "it is immaterial . . . whether the motive was assassination or robbery." Besides, he added, "nothing but a wicked motive emanating from a depraved and malignant heart is attributable to the commission of such a crime as is here indisputably shown."

*   *   *

HILL'S SHELF of options was nearly bare. He could appeal to the Supreme Court of the United States to vacate the conviction, and failing that, he could apply to the Utah Board of Pardons for a commutation. As to the Supreme Court, Orrin Hilton advised that it was unlikely that the court would see a federal question in the case; it would leave the lower court verdict to stand without review. But even if there was a slim chance that the Supreme Court would hear the case, Hill had decided that the cost to the IWW was prohibitive. As he told Elizabeth Gurley Flynn, "We can not afford to drain the resources of the whole organization and weaken its fighting strength just on account of one individual." He notified her, as he did Hilton, Bill Haywood, and Ed Rowan, "that the case is dropped."

Hill told Hilton the same thing he had told Flynn: "I am afraid we'll have to let it go as it is—because I cannot expect my friends to starve themselves in order to save my life." Hill was writing on July 14, eleven days after the Utah Supreme Court had denied his appeal. And for the first time, he hinted that the idea of martyrdom had begun to take hold.

"Well, Mr. Hilton," he added,

if circumstances are such that nothing can be done, I want to thank you for what you have already done for me. And you can just bet your bottom dollar that I will show this gang of highbinders, that are operating here in the name of Justice, how a MAN should die.

Hilton replied in penciled longhand: "The irony of the whole miserable matter is intensified when we know that it could all have been avoided if you had even a decent defense in the Court below." He closed the note with a compliment that could have unintentionally added to the pressure Hill felt to live up to others' expectations. "I am greatly distressed as I read your letter, yet admire the manly, courageous stand you take—*for good game people are scarce.*"

On August 2, Hill was returned under heavy guard to Judge Ritchie's court for resentencing. The judge dutifully asked the condemned man if he wished to make any remarks prior to his sentencing. "Nothing except this," Hill answered. "I want to know if the court has any right to pick out any man he chooses and put him in the jury box to try me for my life?"

"I am not here to answer questions," Ritchie said. "Have you anything to say why sentence should not be pronounced?"

"Only that I want to know if the court has any right to pick out any one he chooses for the jury."

"Your remarks are irrelevant," the judge answered.

Hill told the judge that if he were allowed to question the jury foreman, he would "prove he was never subpoenaed, and that many others were never subpoenaed."

"Your statements are untrue," Ritchie declared, and went on to the procedural task at hand: to reprise the question he had asked eleven months earlier. "Have you any choice as to the method in which death shall be inflicted upon you?"

Hill dropped his head in silence for a few moments, as if lost in thought. His attorney Christensen leaned over and whispered to him.

"I want to get shot," Hill told Ritchie.

The judge pronounced sentence: Hill was to be executed by firing squad within the exterior walls of the state penitentiary, and between sunup and sundown on the first of October, 1915. He had sixty days to live.

THE UTAH BOARD OF PARDONS was his last hope. His lawyers had persuaded him to apply for a hearing before the board. "Nothing else is left," Hilton despaired in a letter to Hill, ". . . and even this may be futile." Hilton knew it was futile—unless Hill could also be persuaded to testify about his gunshot wound. The lawyer's pessimism was born of the incontrovertible reality that the Utah Board of Pardons had effectively already passed judgment on Hill's case. For the board consisted of the holders of the following five offices: the governor, the attorney general, and the three justices of the Utah Supreme Court. In other words, Hill would have to ask mercy of Governor William Spry, who in addition to his contempt for the IWW was on record as having endorsed the state supreme court decision.* And Hill would have to ask the attorney general, whose office had just successfully argued before the state supreme court that Hill should die. Finally, and most farcically, a plea for mercy would require the three state supreme court justices to review *their own ruling* that Hill was unfit to live—he, as their unanimous opinion stated, of the "depraved and malignant heart."

Even with the action of the pardons board a fait accompli, however,

---

* Spry had been mailing copies of the opinion to many hundreds, if not thousands, who wrote the governor in protest. He did so, as the cover letter explained, "in order that you may be correctly informed as to the facts."

key members of Hill's defense committee—Flynn in New York, Haywood in Chicago, Rowan in Salt Lake City—agreed with Hilton that Hill should apply for a commutation. "You will be worth more to the organization alive than dead," Haywood wired Hill. "We will work for your vindication."

Hill's terse reply: "Received telegram. Will not ask favors. New trial or bust."

He would not be moved—not by his lawyers or friends, and certainly not by Utah officials. "I suppose that they are going to give me life if I beg for it real nice," he explained in a note to Flynn. "Now I'll tell you Gurley, I never did like the ring of the word 'pardon' and I think I'd rather be buried dead, than buried alive."

He was too proud and principled and stubborn to beg the board's pardon for a heinous crime he had not committed. As he told Flynn, "I never 'licked the hand that holds the whip' yet and I don't see why I should have to start it now." Yet he agreed to file the papers for a hearing, if only to make his case in person for a new trial by jury. "My life is a drop in the bucket," he told Ed Rowan, "but there is a principle"—the presumption of innocence—"involved back of this case!" In any event, Rowan and the others were not about to abandon the fight for Hill's life—or let him do so. Without legal recourse, save the pardons board, the defense committee ratcheted up the publicity and the pressure campaign on the governor.

Each weekly issue of *Solidarity* bubbled with exhortation and information about the case. "AROUSE, YE SLAVES! . . . Our song bird is about to be executed, . . ." Emma B. Little of Fresno wrote. (Emma was the sister of Frank Little, the IWW agitator.) "All together we say he shall not go. We need him in our business. The singing of songs and the writing of books is an important work in civilizing the world. This is Joe's work and we say he shall do this work and no damnable capitalist court shall railroad him to the other side."

Little urged *Solidarity* readers to "HOLD MASS MEETINGS [TO] SHOW UP THIS CAPITALIST CONSPIRACY TO MURDER A COMMON WORKING MAN LIKE YOURSELVES"; "SING JOE'S SONGS" ("in your union hall, on the streets everywhere where two or three are gathered together"); and "CIRCULATE THE PETITIONS." She recommended to signature collectors that they "point out the fact that the accused is a common working man, that he is unusually intelligent—a poet, a song writer . . . Just ask everyone you meet, that's a good way to get acquainted, and you can do some propaganda work for the IWW at the same time," adding, "This is hard on Joe Hill but it is excellent propaganda for the IWW."

Indeed, the theme of the campaign—that Hill was victim and symbol of an anti-IWW "capitalist conspiracy"—naturally and intentionally raised the profile of the union. The dual focus joined Hill with the IWW in the mind of the general public, and, it seems, in his own mind as well (another example of the partly self-imposed pressure Hill must have felt to do right by the union). Nearly every letter of protest to the governor mentioned the IWW, although many writers emphasized that they neither belonged to nor sympathized with the IWW, that they were appealing to the governor only as justice-loving persons who believed an injustice had occurred and wished it remedied before it was too late.

The protest correspondence that had trickled into William Spry's former office in the City & County Building (where Hill had been tried) the previous summer in the aftermath of Hill's conviction now deluged the governor in his new office in the nearly completed state capitol building. Letters, wires, and petitions arrived from all forty-eight states. The tone of the correspondents spanned from tactful and conciliatory to tactless and ominous, like that of some who had written a year earlier vowing, as a Detroiter put it, to "exact 'measure for measure' from your class." Many warned that the execution would "intensify the class hatred," as a Seattle physician wrote, and thus speed "the approaching economic revolution"—a revolution that, a writer from St. Paul, Minnesota, forecasted, "approaches like a tornado." The proprietor of a printing company in Coshocton, Ohio, was especially worked up about that prospect. He pointed out to Spry the futility of killing Hill, for "you will never kill the winning power that is coming soon, Socialism, Socialism, doesent that have a Meaning it is thrilling, it Makes the Blood in me run Hot."

Virtually every letter of protest began with the fundamental point that Hill had been denied a fair trial—"railroaded" was the verb of choice. A New York court reporter expressed a typical sentiment: "I cannot believe that the evidence presented . . . would justify the conviction of a yellow dog for the larceny of a bone." From Massachusetts, the renowned Helen Keller told Spry, "Thousands of intelligent people believe that Hillstrom is innocent. I shall feel doubly deaf and blind if I hear that this young singer has been taken from us. You alone can save him." (Keller, of course, was famous as an inspirational author and lecturer. Less well known was her radical bent: she was a Socialist who displayed a large IWW banner on the wall above her desk.)

A great majority of the letters crackled with the tensions of class division: the belief that Hill had ended up in the death house because he was poor and poorly represented, and because the constitutional guarantee of equal justice for all did not extend to the working class, and most definitely not to those red-card-carrying radicals whom the employing class perceived, rightly or wrongly, as like dynamite to the bedrock of capitalism.

Some wrote to ridicule Utah's provincial judiciary. Had the lower court verdict been reviewed by "an appellate court in this state," a New Yorker harrumphed, it "would have resulted in an instant reversal of the judgment." Even Utahns were openly critical of their courts. A. M. Hodge of Salt Lake City, a daughter of a Mormon pioneer, told Spry that she had not much followed the case, but that upon reading the Supreme Court decision, she had become convinced that the jury had based its guilty verdict "not on the evidence but rather to the fact that the defendant was a member of a despised and militant organization." Hodge called on Spry to grant Hill a new trial.

From the "gentile" wing of the state's religious establishment, the Episcopal bishop of Utah, Paul Jones, registered his disapproval—an act that was said "to have shaken considerably" one of the most prominent members of the church, Judge Morris Ritchie, and that seemed to lead to the bishop's dismissal.* Jones asked the governor to commute Hill's sentence on the ground that there remained "so many possible doubts" as to Hill's guilt and out of a concern that the "infliction of the death penalty . . . may . . . later . . . prove the State of Utah to have been murderer of this man rather than the administrator of justice."

ON THE THIRD SATURDAY of September and with thirteen days to live, Joe Hill appeared before the Utah Board of Pardons. With a fresh shave and a "modish" pompadour, he looked "immaculate," the *Tribune* observed, or as near as one could in a prison uniform that seemed to hang off his gaunt body like billowing drapes over a narrow window frame. (The *Tribune* reporter deemed him in good health, "with no suggestion of prison pallor in his cheeks," but noted that "the skin appeared tightly drawn over the bones.")

---

* Two years later, when the United States entered World War I, the pacifist Jones preached that war was irreconcilable with Jesus's teachings. The diocesan Council of Advice, the six-member governing board, on which Judge Ritchie sat, passed a resolution "condemning the peace attitude" of the bishop, and a national church commission found him guilty of "promulgating unpatriotic doctrines." He was forced to resign. When the war ended, there was talk of Jones returning to his bishopric duties in Utah; Ritchie led the opposition. "There is no objection to his character," Ritchie told a newspaper, "and Episcopalians of Utah would be perfectly satisfied to have him take a diocese elsewhere if any would care to accept him."

Again Orrin Hilton came over from Denver to make the appeal. He opened by invoking several cases in Utah of men who had been convicted of murder solely on circumstantial evidence and who had ultimately been exonerated. He also cited the infamous recent case in Georgia of Leo Frank, who had been condemned to die for the murder of a factory girl. Frank's trial had been a travesty, Hilton said, and though the Georgia Supreme Court had affirmed the verdict, the governor had in June of 1915—three months past—commuted Frank's sentence to life.* Hilton suggested that the Utah Board of Pardons do for Hill as the governor of Georgia had intended to do for Frank: commute the sentence pending further investigation.

Hilton had impugned the board's integrity by suggesting that it might allow an innocent to die. Then he did it again during a discussion about whether the district attorney, Elmer Leatherwood, had poisoned the trial by infusing the proceedings with the specter of IWW bogeymen. (Leatherwood had urged the jury to push back against "those parasites on society who murder and rob rather than make an honest living," it will be recalled.) At which point Associate Justice J. E. Frick felt called to defend himself and his colleagues: "I believe that everyone in the state of Utah knows that every member of the Supreme Court, every member of this pardon board, would much rather cut off his own right arm than to condemn a man either because he was or because he was not a member of any labor organization."

TOWARD THE END of the long afternoon—the hearing had begun at two o'clock, and it was nearing six—the board finally acknowledged the condemned man's presence.

"Say Hilton," Governor Spry said, "can't you make that fellow talk over there?"

"Well, what do you want him to say?"

"Well, I want him to give an explanation of where he received the wound."

Hilton: "See? Still trying to make him prove himself innocent. He doesn't have to do it; that isn't the law. The people should prove him guilty, and I stand by that principle of law. I don't care, Joe can talk if he wants to, but I am not going to ask him to, because he is right and you

---

* In August, just a month and a day before Hill's hearing, Governor John Slaton's heroism had been rendered moot: a mob had kidnapped Frank from a prison hospital and hanged him.

are wrong, and you know . . . there is not a text book that was ever written but what contains that elemental doctrine."

Hilton turned to his client and asked if he had something to say. "I would just as soon say a word or two," Hill told him.

"Now Mr. Hillstrom," the governor said, "the board would be glad to hear from you . . . Understand, you are not required to say anything or to make any statement whatever. We would be pleased to hear you, but it will not count either for or against you if you decide to remain silent."

Hill stood. "Gentlemen, I have a little proposition to make to you. If you grant me a new trial, I will guarantee to prove absolutely my innocence and to send four or five perjurers to the penitentiary, where they belong."

Spry: "But why did you not bring forward this proof at your trial?"

"I didn't think it was necessary to prove my innocence," Hill replied. "I thought the state would have to prove a man guilty . . . Anyway, I never thought I was going to be convicted on such ridiculous evidence. The district attorney furnished the evidence. He asked it in all the questions. All the witnesses did was to say, 'Yes, sir.'"

Chief Justice Straup: "You understand, do you not, that this body cannot grant you a new trial. It has no power to do so."

"You had the power to deny a new trial," Hill said. "Why can't you grant me one now?"

"This is not the Supreme Court," the governor explained. "This is the state pardon board, of which the three Supreme Court justices are members, but they are sitting not as a Supreme Court but as members of the pardon board."

"Then I have nothing to say," Hill said. "If I can't have a new trial, I don't want anything."

APART FROM THE SIX INTRANSIGENT MEN in that hearing room—Joe Hill and the five-member pardons board, none of whom was going to budge on the matter of a new trial—there were two persons not in the room who could most probably have saved Hill's life: the man who had shot him and the woman over whom he had been shot. Why, then, did neither Otto Appelquist nor Hilda Erickson come forward with an alibi?

Of Appelquist, next to nothing is known. He was asleep inside the Eselius family's house in Murray around one A.M. on January 11, 1914, when Hill arrived there after treatment for the gunshot wound. He and Hill were said to have spoken privately, and around two o'clock on that cold Sunday morning, Appelquist announced to his incredulous hosts

Hill faces the five members of the Utah Board of Pardons. *Solidarity*, November 27, 1915.

that he was going out to look for work and that he needed to catch the last streetcar to Salt Lake City. Then he vanished. Had he fled because he feared that Hill would die and he'd be facing a murder charge? Hilda thought so, but because she never saw or heard from Appelquist again, she was left to guess. It seems more likely that he disappeared for good to dodge prosecution as Hill's accomplice in the Morrison killings. As to where he went after leaving Murray, or where he was during Hill's criminal proceedings, I have no idea. There was a tantalizing clue or two, as we shall see, of his presence in Buffalo, New York, in the fall of 1915, but nothing that anyone at the time, or I, could pin down. I have learned that he was not dead, as some, Hilda among them, surmised. According to Swedish emigration records, he was working as a marine fireman on transatlantic freighters during 1917 and 1918, and I know that in September of 1917 he registered for the World War I draft in New Orleans.

More is known about Hilda Erickson, yet her silence is more puzzling than Appelquist's. She was right there with Hill along every step of his long legal ordeal—and after: she stood vigil outside the prison when he was shot and served as one of his six pallbearers. She visited him in the county jail every Sunday for eighteen months—until he was transferred to the state penitentiary, which barred visitors. Thereafter they exchanged weekly letters. Hill wrote two love songs for Hilda in the week or so between when she broke her engagement with Appelquist and the night that he, Hill, was shot. Or presumably he wrote them for Hilda; the timing strongly suggests so, as do his sweetheart's "loving eyes of blue" in one song and "dreamy eyes of blue" in the other. (As the *Tribune* noted, Hilda was "fair-haired and blue-eyed.")

Some excerpts from both songs:

Come and Take a Joy-ride in My Aeroplane

If you will be my sweetheart, I'll take you for a ride
Among the silv'ry clouds up in the sky.
Then, far away from sorrows like eagle we will glide,
And no one will be there but you and I.
Say, darling, if you'll be my little honey dove,
We'll fly above and coo and love.

CHORUS
Come and take a joy-ride in my aeroplane tonight,
Way beyond the clouds, where all the stars are shining bright.
Then I'd like to look into your loving eyes of blue,
And if I should fall, then I know I'd fall in love with you.

Oh, Please Let Me Dance This Waltz With You

CHORUS
Oh, please let me dance this waltz with you,
And look in your dreamy eyes of blue.
Sweet imagination,
Smooth, gliding sensation,
Oh! love, I would die just for dancing
This waltz with you.

During the trial, Hilda was a constant presence in the courtroom, and she generated quite a buzz herself on the morning that Hill fired his attorneys. It will be recalled that after the initial ruckus, Judge Ritchie called a forty-five-minute recess. He directed Hill and the attorneys to his chambers to privately work out their differences. The conference did not last long—Hill wanted nothing from them but their swift departure. Afterward, Hill was permitted to talk with two IWW members and then, for fifteen minutes, with Hilda. "Considerable importance was attached to the conference with the [Erickson] woman," the *Deseret Evening News* reported, "in view of the fact that Hillstrom has declared that he received a gun shot wound in a quarrel over a woman and that he would not bring her name into the case unless she was willing to come forward and tell her story."

THIRTY-FIVE YEARS LATER, she came forward. But the story she told in her 1949 letter to a scholar was lost to history, unpublished and moldering in the attic of a house in Michigan. She told it to a professor of education by the name of Aubrey Haan, then at the University of Hawaii and formerly at the University of Utah. Haan had won a fellowship to write a novel about Joe Hill.* He was a dogged and skilled researcher, particularly so for a writer of fiction. Unfortunately, however, the book never found a publisher, a situation that could well have reflected the collision of its radical subject matter against the Red Scare politics of the era, as much as any lack of literary merit. (The federal government investigated Haan for possible subversive leanings.) In any event, Haan ended up shelving the manuscript and notes.

During my own archival wanderings some sixty years later, I ran across some correspondence among Haan, archivists, and a couple of IWW oldtimers. Since I could find no trace of his novel, and since he had clearly done a great deal of research, I started looking for his papers. I found them in Ann Arbor, Michigan, in his daughter's attic. (Or rather, I found his daughter, and she discovered the papers and made them available to me.) Among the documents was an exchange of letters between Haan and Hilda Erickson in the spring and summer of 1949.

When Haan located Hilda, she was living in Aberdeen, Washington, a lumber town that had once been a center of IWW activity.

On June 22, 1949, Hilda sent Haan a six-page letter handwritten on

---

* He had a lot of company: Wallace Stegner was at work on his novel of Hill, Barrie Stavis was writing a play about him, and a writer in Salt Lake City, Joseph A. Curtis, was in the formative stages of his decades-long project on Hill, a nonfiction book that also was never published.

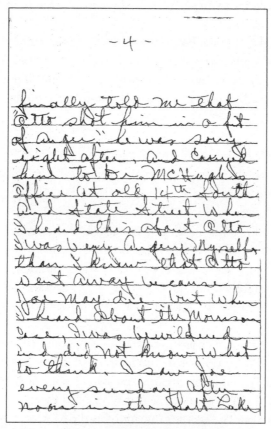

A fragment of Hilda Erickson's 1949 letter to Aubrey Haan. Below, Hilda at middle age, around the time she wrote the letter. (Letter: courtesy Haan family; portrait: courtesy Susan Tuttle)

lined notebook paper. It recounted her conversation with Hill the day after he was shot.

"Dear Mr. Haan," she began, first thanking him for having sent her the address of Virginia Stephen (the art instructor whom the University of Utah had gone on to fire for her vocal support of Hill during his trial). Then Hilda took up Haan's questions about the night of Saturday, January 10, 1914:

> I do not know anything about the Morrison case because that evening Miss Christine Larson and I were seeing a play in a Salt Lake theater.* She and I lived next door to each other. I at 229 East South Temple in Salt Lake, but I will tell you about Otto Applequist [sic], Joe Hill, and myself. I was engaged to marry Otto. All the neighbors knew that, because my little brother August had told them that. A week before Joe was wounded, I told Otto that I had changed my mind, that I was not marrying anybody. He got very angry and asked me "if I liked Joe better than him." I said no.
>
> I heard Joe tease Otto once, that he was going to take me away from him. Please do not misunderstand me. Otto and Joe were perfect gentlemen. They treated me with the utmost respect, because they thought so much of our whole family.
>
> Joe was wounded on the same night as the Morrison case. I came home from Salt Lake the following Sunday afternoon.† I saw Joe in my grandmother's parlor. He was lying on her old fashioned iron cot, that folds up at each side for a bed. I asked him what was the matter, he said "Nothing much." But I was not satisfied with the answer, so he finally told me that "Otto shot him in a fit of anger." He was sorry right after, and carried him to Dr. McHugh's office at old 14th South and State Street.
>
> When I heard this about Otto I was very angry myself, then I knew that Otto went away because Joe may die. But when I heard about the Morrison case, I was bewildered and did not know what to think. I saw Joe every Sunday afternoon in the Salt Lake Jail.

---

* In a letter written eight days later and prompted by a follow-up question from Haan, Hilda recalled that Appelquist had joined her and Larson that night at the Empress Theater, and that "we found Joe in a back seat when we were going out of the show."

† Her home was the Eselius family's cabin in Murray, where three generations of the family lived in quarters so tight that she had moved to a boardinghouse in Salt Lake.

I would speak English to him, but he would talk Swedish to me in a low voice and tell me not to say a word because he was innocent of the Morrison case. Therefore the state of Utah could not prove him guilty . . .

Dear Mr. Haan I hope that my letter will help you with your novel.

Yours for the O.B.U. [One Big Union]

Mrs. Hilda Erickson

The letter surely helped the novelist tease out Hill's personality, but it also raises some obvious and troubling questions to which, I'm sorry to say, I don't have answers: Why did Hilda wait sixty years to tell her story? Why not tell it during the trial, when it counted? Why did the defense not insist on questioning her? Or if Hill's lawyers did wish to put her on the stand, why did Hill overrule them? Was it, as she implied to Haan, that Hill was intent on upholding the principle of presumed innocence at any cost? Or that he saw no need to expose her because, as he would tell the pardons board, he never expected to be convicted, and once he was, he assumed that the Supreme Court would reverse the verdict? Or, as Virginia Stephen and her second husband (a former IWW organizer) considered the question many years later, was it that one should not discount "the power exerted by police, deputies and detectives to frighten Hilda and family into silence"?

UPON HEARING FROM HILL that he wanted nothing from the Utah Board of Pardons but the promise of a new trial, Supreme Court associate justice William M. McCarty offered a counterproposal: "If you can show us any proof of circumstance that proves your innocence, we will grant you an immediate and unconditional pardon, and you will walk out of the door a free man."

"I don't want a pardon or commutation; that is humiliating," Hill said. "I want an acquittal by a jury. I want a new trial so that I can show up the things that are going on in Judge Ritchie's courtroom. I want the people to know the dirty deal I got in that court."

Attorney General Albert R. Barnes had heard enough. "Now look here, Hillstrom, if there is . . . any reason on earth why you should not pay the penalty for the crime, this is the time to show it to us. I am deadly in earnest, old man, and I want to do everything on earth to save you if you are innocent. Won't you think it over and produce any proof you have here before us?"

"I *have* thought it over," Hill said. "I know what I'm doing."

"Wouldn't a pardon be as good or better than a new trial?" McCarty asked.

Justice Frick: "An unconditional pardon would be an absolute acquittal."

"I've stated my position," Hill replied. "I want a new trial."

There ensued more to and fro, and then a five-minute recess during which Hill resisted his lawyers' urgent entreaties to cooperate with the board. When the hearing reconvened, Soren Christensen could only report, "It seems that he wants to be considered a martyr." As Hilton told it the next day, Hill delivered a one-sentence valedictory: "Gentlemen, the cause I stand for, that of a fair and honest trial, is worth more than human life—much more than mine."

The pardons board hardly dithered; it met in executive session for fifteen minutes before announcing its unanimous vote. HILLSTROM IS DENIED REPRIEVE BY BOARD, the Sunday *Tribune* reported. Short of

Solidarity, September 25, 1915. (Courtesy of the Tamiment Library, New York University)

the governor granting executive clemency, Hill was to be shot a week from the following Friday.

A NEW WAVE of urgent and angry correspondence washed over the governor. "Look out for your own head," advised an anonymous writer from Winfield, Kansas. That and other unsigned threats prompted the *Tribune* to decry the "thousands [who] have allowed themselves to be duped . . . and lent themselves to a campaign of intimidation as dastardly as anything recorded in the history of the country." The press fixated on one particularly sensational note: a warning from an operative of the mysterious "order of K.O.D." Handwritten in block letters and bearing a Salt Lake postmark of September 20, the letter warned Governor Spry, on penalty of his life, that he "must, on or before the (30th) day of Sept. A.D. 1915, commute the sentence of one Joseph Hillstrom, from DEATH TO LIFE IMPRISONMENT . . .

> Please consider this well, for we mean no ill will to you or yours if you act as we direct . . .
>   Upon the receipt of correspondence from us containing the Jack of Spades you are to consider yourself condemned to death. We work silently but when the time comes for a reckoning . . . the vengeance of the K.O.D. is silent, swift, sure and terrible. We never fail.
>   Yours with regards or regrets,
>   No. 7, K.O.D.

Publicly, Spry was unfazed. "I am going about my business as I have always gone about it," he told a reporter. "I do not want any police officers to guard me, for I am afraid of none of those who have made threats." But behind the governor's façade of nonchalance was a set of stringent security measures erected for him and his family by local law enforcement agencies in cooperation with private detective firms. (William A. Pinkerton, a principal of the nation's most famous detective agency, was on the job along with thirty Pinkerton operatives.)

Meanwhile, Hill's supporters reached out to anyone who might have the political muscle to lean on the governor. Foremost among them was the Swedish minister to the United States, Wilhelm A. F. Ekengren. Ekengren requested and read the legal record and concluded, as he told the acting U.S. secretary of state, Frank L. Polk, that the execution "would entail a miscarriage of justice."

The State Department agreed, "as a courtesy to the Swedish minister," to forward his request for diplomatic relief to Governor Spry. The governor convened the pardons board in emergency session. It released a lengthy manifesto that was part paean to the board's wisdom and even-handedness, part thrashing of what it termed the IWW's campaign of "misinformation." It is "almost inconceivable," the release stated, "how any impartial and unbiased mind reading the record in its entirety can reach any reasonable conclusion other than that of the applicant's guilt."

Minister Ekengren and Governor Spry went back and forth, the minister urging a stay of execution, the governor adamant that without new information "tending to justify commutation," there would be no reprieve. On Tuesday, September 28, fewer than seventy-two hours before Hill was to be shot, Ekengren's wire to Spry dispensed with diplomatic pretense. "As I understand it," he wrote,

> it is a state's duty to prove beyond doubt the guilt of an accused. In this instance it looks as if the burden of proof were on the accused, as if he must prove where he received his wound etc. His refusal to take the stand in his own behalf seems to have actually while not expressly operated against him with both court and jury . . .
>
> What motive could Hillstrom have had? It appears that he had been in Salt Lake but a short time and could hardly have made such enemies that he would shoot and kill them out of pure malice. From the information that I have on hand about the man, I draw the conclusion that while he might be radical and haughty, he has led a comparatively honest life previously and robbery as motive for the crime would therefore not seem any more reasonable than pure malice.
>
> Today I have been telegraphically instructed by my Government to endeavor to secure a new investigation in the case and on their behalf and in my own I ask you again very earnestly to consider at least a postponement of the execution.

Pressed hard by Ekengren, Spry pushed back. "You have furnished us nothing except arguments from the briefs of Hillstrom's counsel," the governor replied.

ON WEDNESDAY MORNING, with fewer than forty-eight hours to go, Elizabeth Gurley Flynn and Edith Cram, a friend from New York of high social standing and with Democratic political connections—her husband was a fixer for the boss of the Tammany Hall machine—walked into the White House for a meeting with Joseph P. Tumulty, Woodrow Wilson's private secretary. Tumulty suggested that they encourage the Swedish minister to make a protocol-leaping appeal directly to the president, a plan that Ekengren welcomed. Later that day, the women met with acting secretary of state Polk. He promised to contact Governor Spry, if only to forward Ekengren's forthcoming appeal to the president.

Even as Flynn and Cram conferred with Polk on Wednesday evening, the warden of the Utah State Penitentiary placed Joe Hill under a death-watch and announced that he and the sheriff had completed preparations for the execution. Near midnight, Ekengren wired the president, asking him to intercede and describing the evidence, "which is only circumstantial, [as] insufficient to warrant capital punishment." Ekengren was satisfied that he had done his "utmost" to help his countryman. But he knew that unless Hill broke his silence, it would not be enough. As he told Hill on Thursday in a final plea for information, "I am doing all I can to head off the execution. Without your cooperation I fear the result will not be good. Please wire me collect."

Hill did not reply. Hilda said nothing. Appelquist was nowhere to be found.

As one newspaper reported on Thursday, "Barring a miracle, for only a miracle can save him now, Hillstrom will be shot some time Friday morning."

13.

Law v. Anarchy

Around eleven on the morning of Thursday, September 30, a little more than twenty hours before he was to be shot, Hill and his deathwatch guard were chortling over a story the guard was telling about Frank Scott, Hill's reviled former attorney. It seemed that at a murder trial a few years back, the guard had witnessed Scott tripping and falling over a courtroom cuspidor—an image Hill found deeply amusing. He was in stitches when Soren Christensen arrived at his cell. The lawyer asked Hill whom he wished to invite as witnesses to the execution—a "privilege" the state extended to its condemned. "Some of the boys want to be with you to the end," Christensen said. Hill told him he would provide the warden with the names of four IWW members to be invited. (The sheriff had already approved Hill's only other request: "I want to be shot in my good clothes.")

And then Christensen dropped a bombshell: the Associated Press was reporting that the president of the United States had just asked Governor Spry for a stay of execution. The telegram was a single sentence:

> Respectfully ask if it would not be possible to postpone execution of Joseph Hillstrom, who I understand is a Swedish subject, until the Swedish Minister has an opportunity to present his view of the case fully to your Excellency.
> WOODROW WILSON

"That's nice," a curiously unaffected Hill said, according to the *Salt Lake Evening Telegram*. "I'm glad to hear it."

Nevertheless, Christensen advised his client, "you would better not

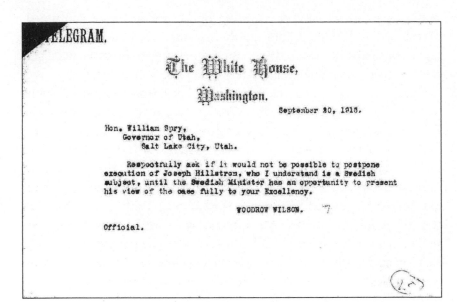

The White House,

Washington.

September 30, 1915.

Hon. William Spry,
    Governor of Utah,
        Salt Lake City, Utah.

        Respectfully ask if it would not be possible to postpone
execution of Joseph Hillstrom, who I understand is a Swedish
subject, until the Swedish Minister has an opportunity to present
his view of the case fully to your Excellency.

                        WOODROW WILSON.

Official.

(National Archives)

rely too much on the report from Washington, . . . for there might be some slip and you might face the firing squad tomorrow, after all."

"Oh, I'm prepared to go any minute they're ready," Hill replied.

THE AIRY CALMNESS, the casual banter with his minder and his lawyer, was wholly at odds with the clamor and chaos swirling about Hill's case beyond the high stone walls of the prison. Even as Hill handed Christensen a passel of farewell letters for mailing late on Thursday morning, the Utah Board of Pardons was meeting in an emergency session, trying to formulate a reply to the president's wire. Around noon, Governor Spry advised the press of his decision: "I have told the president that it is on his request, and that alone, that I have granted this respite." Spry hastened to add that he was not happy about it. "This is the only case on record, that I know of, where the President of the United States has interfered in any murder case under the laws of a state."

In his telegraphed reply to the president, Spry was a bit more politic: "The undisputed records of the Hillstrom case show he was convicted of a most revolting murder, that the evidence shows his guilt and that he had a fair trial." And in what critics of criminal procedure in Utah might have termed faint or damning praise, the governor continued, "His case has been more thoroughly investigated by the board of pardons, consisting of the three Supreme Judges, the Attorney General and the Governor, than any similar case in the history of the State."

Such was the power of the presidency: Spry, who like other Republican governors kicked and brayed reflexively at the first whiff of the Democratic administration's encroachment on states' rights, was left with no political option but to back down. As the pardons board member and state supreme court associate justice J. E. Frick explained, "President Wilson is the president of 100,000,000 people and his request must be granted." Governor Spry advised President Wilson that the stay would be in effect for sixteen days—until Saturday, October 16, the date of the next scheduled meeting of the pardons board. (At that meeting, the board would either commute the sentence from death to life or remand Hill to the district court for resentencing to death.)

In a column titled LAW OR ANARCHY published the day the respite was issued, the *Herald-Republican* dismissed Hill as "no longer a factor in the equation." The issue now, it said, "is whether law shall continue to be law or whether a hue and cry may suspend, even destroy, it." The

Governor William Spry, hat in hand, at the state capitol ground-breaking ceremony, circa 1910. (Used by permission, Utah State Historical Society, all rights reserved)

paper instructed the state not to "yield to bullying or bulldozing" and not to allow "an organization whose apparent aim is existence without working and without the sobering restraint of law" to appropriate a case of "ordinary, prosaic murder" as a platform for "a few radicals . . . to vent their extreme views."

If Spry and the *Herald-Republican* were unhappy about having to accede to the president, a fellow member of the pardons board, Associate Justice William McCarty, was fairly foaming at the mouth: "There is no doubt in my mind but that the lawless element with which Hillstrom is associated, the Industrial Workers of the World, will construe the president's action as tacit approval of their course and methods." He warned of the probability that "hundreds of [IWWs] will swarm to this state and using Hillstrom as an excuse, will undoubtedly attempt to create a reign of terror . . . If this course occurs, only President Wilson is to be held responsible."

And yet: As Utah's leaders were publicly pillorying President Wilson for trespassing on their state's rights, privately Spry was pleading for the administration's help in launching an IWW-eradication drive. On October 5, five days after the state told Wilson to mind his own business, Spry and his gubernatorial counterparts in California, Oregon, and Washington secretly wired Secretary of the Interior Franklin K. Lane. Their respective states, they wrote,

> are experiencing abnormal disorder and incendiarism. These experiences are coincident with threats made by IWW leaders in their talks and publications, and are in harmony with doctrines preached in their publications. Local or state apprehension of ring leaders impracticable, as their field of activity is interstate . . . Through federal machinery covering the whole territory involved, the national government might get at the bottom of this movement . . . Exigencies of the situation demand absolute secrecy.*

Inside prison, Hill busied himself, as usual, with correspondence. He sent one of his farewells in the form of an open letter to *Solidarity*:

---

* Wilson endorsed the recommendation of Secretary Lane and Attorney General Thomas W. Gregory to appoint a special agent to investigate the IWW. But a two-year search turned up no evidence of an interstate conspiracy. Rather, the underwhelmed agent reported, IWW membership consisted "chiefly of panhandlers, without homes, mostly foreigners, the discontented and unemployed who are not anxious to work."

Dear Friends and F.W.'s [Fellow Workers]:

"John Law" has given me his last and final order to get off the earth and stay off. He has told me that lots of times before, but this time it seems as if he is meaning business. I have said time and again that I was going to get a new trial or die trying. I have told it to my friends. It has been printed in the newspapers, and I don't see why I should "eat my own crow" just because I happen to be up against a firing squad. I have stated my position plainly to everybody, and I won't budge an inch, because I know I am in the right. Tomorrow I expect to take a trip to the planet Mars, and if so, will immediately commence to organize the Mars canal workers into the IWW, and we will sing the good old songs so loud that the learned star gazers on earth will once and for all get positive proofs that the planet Mars really is inhabited. In the meantime I hope you'll keep the ball a-rolling here. You are on the right track and you are bound to get there. I have nothing to say about myself, only that I have always tried to do what little I could to make this earth a little better for the great producing class, and I can pass off into the great unknown with the pleasure of knowing that I have never in my life, double crossed a man woman or child.

With a last fond farewell to all true rebels and hearty thanks for the noble support you have given me in this unequal fight, I remain,

Yours for International Solidarity,
Joe Hill

To Elizabeth Gurley Flynn he wrote, "Well Gurley I guess I am off for the great unknown to-morrow morning . . . They can kill me I know, but they can never make me 'eat my own crow' . . . I would like to kiss you Good-bye Gurley, not because you are a girl but because you are the original Rebel Girl."

To Sam Murray: "Well Sam old boy, you shouldn't feel quite so senti-mental . . . This dying business is not quite so bad as it is cracked up to be." He said he knew the end was at hand because he was "given a 'swell feed' for the first time in God knows how long, and that is one of the surest signs."* And after alluding to the "little pleasure" they had shared as

---

* Indeed, the warden allowed him to choose his last meals. Breakfast: three soft-boiled eggs, two apples, fried potatoes, coffee. Dinner: mutton chops, fried potatoes, apple pie, coffee. Supper: two bananas, ten English walnuts, grape juice.

rebels fighting under the red flag in Mexico, he bade his friend to move on. "Now, just forget me," he wrote, "and say goodbye to the bunch."

He wrote those letters on the morning of September 30 before he learned of the reprieve; as far as he knew, it was to be the last full day of his life. In the first letter, written for publication, he was playing his public role, class jester and class warrior of "unswerving courage under fire," as the editor of *Solidarity* wrote, and he would play it until literally his final breath. Perhaps that was to be expected. Even more revealing are the personal notes to Flynn and Murray. The humor is present, as is the bravado and fighting spirit. But there is also his generosity of spirit, his *humanity*.

That spirit was repeatedly in evidence over his last weeks of life. Two days before the pardons board would almost certainly terminate the respite, Hill mentioned nothing of it in another letter to Flynn. Instead, he thanked her for the photograph she'd sent of her six-year-old son, Buster, on a pony. "You certainly have a right to be proud of your boy," Hill wrote. "He's got a forehead like old Shakespeare himself." With the brief

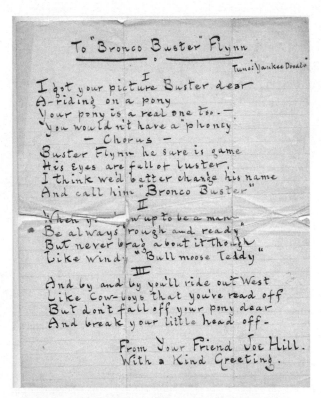

(Courtesy of the Tamiment Library, New York University)

note to Flynn, he enclosed a song inscribed "To 'Bronco Buster' Flynn" and written to the tune of "Yankee Doodle."

> *I got your picture Buster dear*
> *A-riding on a pony*
> *Your pony is a real one too.*
> *You wouldn't have a "phony."*
>
> CHORUS
> *Buster Flynn he sure is game*
> *His eyes are full of luster,*
> *I think we'd better change his name*
> *And call him "Bronco Buster."*
>
> *When you grow up to be a man*
> *Be always "rough and ready"*
> *But never brag about it though*
> *Like windy "Bull Moose Teddy."**
>
> *And by and by you'll ride out West*
> *Like Cow-boys that you've read off*
> *But don't fall off your pony dear*
> *And break your little head off.*
>
> From Your Friend Joe Hill
With a Kind Greeting

THE PARDONS BOARD convened at ten o'clock on the morning of Saturday, October 16. Hill's case would not be called until three P.M., which left plenty of time for readers of that morning's *Tribune* to absorb the startling revelations leaked atop its front page:

DECLARES HILLSTROM SHOT MAN AT LAYTON OFFICER IDENTIFIES MURDERER AS HAVING BEEN ARRESTED THREE YEARS AGO FOR SHOOTING A DEPUTY SHERIFF . . .

---

* Theodore Roosevelt, having lost the 1912 Republican presidential nomination to Taft, ran in the general election as a Progressive, or "Bull Mooser," a name derived from his answer to a reporter's question about the state of his health: "I'm feeling like a bull moose!"

CRIMINAL TRAIL LEADS TO MEXICO

WAS AN OFFICER IN THE ARMY OF INVASION OF I.W.W.; MAY HAVE
BEEN CONNECTED WITH CALIFORNIA DYNAMITING OUTRAGES.

The malicious and deceitful article stated that the pardons board had
"uncovered" a map of Hill's tawdry criminal wanderings across the West.
The first of the story's many lurid falsehoods occurred in Layton, Utah, in
north suburban Salt Lake, where in 1911 Hill had purportedly shot a deputy during an attempted safe blowing and robbery at a hardware store. He
had been apprehended and jailed for six weeks, the story went, under the
alias James Corbett, then released for lack of evidence. "There is no doubt
in my mind but that Hillstrom is the Corbett we held here four years ago,"
a Layton deputy sheriff told the *Tribune*. The doubtless deputy, though,
was mistaken, for the shooting had occurred on May 4, 1911—when Hill
had been in northern Mexico fighting under the red flag with the rebel
army. (The deputy admitted his error the day *after* the board hearing.)

The article then traced other milestones along Hill's supposed criminal
trail: he had helped transport dynamite from San Francisco to Los Angeles; in 1910, he had assisted the "unionists" who allegedly blew up the *Los
Angeles Times* building.* Further, in 1911 he had been a "lieutenant" in the
"gang of several hundred IWW members . . . [that] attempted to *loot*
the Mexican town of Tia Juana"; in 1913, he had been arrested in San
Pedro for streetcar robbery (he did thirty days for vagrancy, as earlier
described); and he had supposedly spent "several months" in the Butte,
Montana, jail for an unspecified and undated offense. (Emphasis added.)

That afternoon's *Evening Telegram* advanced or, more accurately, em-
bellished the story. Its lead, so pungently malevolent, seemed intended
to soothe the conscience of any Utahn who was still uncertain about the
condemned man's character and capacity for terrible evil.

> That Joseph Hillstrom . . . has a criminal record extending back for
> many years and which embraces murder, highway robbery, dyna-
> miting and the invasion of a neighboring country with the intent to
> loot and kill, has been satisfactorily established in the minds of Gov.

---

* The next day's *Tribune* quoted Soren Christensen and Hill discussing the allegations.
"Where is Layton?" Hill asked. "Just north of Farmington," the lawyer replied. "Never
heard of either of those places," Hill said. As to the dynamiters, said Hill, "If I was
connected with them in any way, why was I not arrested?"

William Spry, members of the state board of pardons and the warden of the state penitentiary.

The *Telegram* sourced the story to an unidentified prisoner serving time for robbery, who, as that paper alone reported, "will be pardoned in return for the information covering Hillstrom's career that he has given the authorities." The prisoner claimed to be a former Wobbly and an accomplice of Hill's in at least one dastardly plot. He said that Hill had personally transported dynamite by automobile from San Pedro to San Diego and that during the free speech fight of 1912, Hill had planted enough explosives under the then-soon-to-open Spreckels Theatre—named for and commissioned by the local publishing magnate and ardent foe of the IWW—"to blow it and adjoining buildings into the ocean." (The informant said the plot had failed only because he himself had notified the police at the last minute.) The fellow also told Utah authorities that John Morrison was not the first man Joe Hill had murdered; Hill, he said, had gotten away with shooting to death a police officer in Long Beach, California.

As to the convict's name and whether in fact he had been promised a reduced sentence, Governor Spry would only say, "It would not do to give this out." (The governor later denied he had cut a deal.) Justice Frick assured the *Telegram* that, in its words, the information had been "corroborated by responsible people and officers."

Was it providence or coincidence that the pardons board revealed Hill's supposed thieving and homicidal tendencies on the very day that the board was to reconsider his case? And if not, why was it done? One plausible explanation was suggested by a question asked and answered in the *Herald-Republican* by Virginia Stephen, who had recruited attorney Orrin Hilton to handle Hill's appeal. Said Stephen, "Why is the board not satisfied with what it already has? It seems to me that the governor and the board of pardons are not entirely satisfied in their minds of this man's guilt."*

The board's unanimous resolution betrayed no misgivings. Excepting

---

* Nine days earlier, Stephen's employer, the Board of Regents of the University of Utah, had decided it was entirely satisfied that it had heard quite enough of her "utterances in connection with the Joe Hillstrom case." The board fired her as instructor of art, effective at year's end, but chose not to tell her until "the IWW agitation incident to the Hillstrom case had subsided." Stephen later explained that the board had also charged her with "attending an anarchistic meeting" in New York and researching "the condition of working girls in Utah."

the fourteen armed guards on duty in and around the conference room at the prison, the public hearing was perfunctory. The board heard only from Soren Christensen, who stated that he had nothing further for the record, and that his client declined to appear before the board because "he had nothing to say" about the circumstances of his gunshot wound. "It's none of their business," Hill had reiterated to Christensen that morning.

The board's business that Saturday afternoon was to terminate the reprieve and affirm the denial of commutation. This it did on the ground that during the sixteen-day respite neither the Swedish minister nor Hill's counsel had presented "any matter of fact or thing, new or additional" that threw "any further light on the case," as Chief Justice Daniel N. Straup said.

On the following Monday, a shackled and heavily guarded Hill, wearing a baggy prison-issued gray uniform under a long black overcoat, was returned to the courtroom of Judge Morris Ritchie for resentencing. The statute mandated that the execution date be set for no sooner than thirty days and no later than sixty days. Ritchie settled on thirty-one days.

As the judge pronounced the date, November 19, 1915, Hill sat between Christensen and the deputy warden, his eyes riveted on the floor, the eyes of eleven guards—four surrounding him, the rest scattered among the gallery—riveted on him. As he stood to leave and await reshackling, Hill abruptly pointed toward Ritchie and snapped his fingers for attention.

"I am here and I want to make a statement," he said.

The warden spoke up. "Judge, do you wish to hear him?"

"No," Ritchie replied, "the case is disposed of."

ORRIN HILTON HAD KEPT quiet in the month since the pardons board had rejected his argument for clemency. Now, though, that the case was "disposed of," he accused the board of smearing Hill with a fantastical coating of evil to justify its denial of clemency. From Denver, Hilton penned an "Open Letter" to the board, offering to publicly debate "the facts at any time [prior to November 19] in any City in the United States with any member of your Board, or all of them." He issued the invitation, he wrote, "to refute . . . the false, wicked and cowardly aspersion on [Hill's] character—that Hillstrom has heretofore committed any crime or that he has now, or ever has had, any criminal record—now for the first time so bravely urged as a sufficient justification for taking his life." Hilton continued,

This matter, as you all must realize, is one now of national, if not international importance, and has excited intense interest from New York to San Francisco; and I would be, as the attorney for this condemned man, of "meaner stuff than men are made of" if I did not in the brief time of life now allotted him, challenge you and each of you to the proofs.

I am only anxious and determined that if Hillstrom is judicially murdered, the people of this country—the great jury to whom we must all go at last—shall fully understand just where rests the full measure of responsibility for "the deep damnation of his taking off."

The pardons board refused the lawyer's bait. "Hilton apparently is seeking as much notoriety as his client" is all Governor Spry had to say. The editorial boards, though, eagerly bit on Hilton's lure. "Why," the *Tribune* asked, "does he accuse the most reputable men in Utah of trying to deceive the public and never raise his voice in protest against the nation-wide propaganda of the IWW and others to deceive the public?" To the *Herald-Republican*, Hilton's "shamefully unprofessional" voice should "never again be raised in a Utah court except as a defendant." The paper expounded, "As a citizen, Mr. Hilton may enjoy the legal right to foment class hatred, to inflame the prejudices of the vicious and the criminal, to appeal from justice to mawkishness, to seek to render the law and the courts a hissing and a byword. As a lawyer, clothed with the borrowed dignity of an officer of the court, he carries obligations he cannot so lightly ignore."

But what, Hilton might have asked, if the law and the courts were anathema to justice? What if publicity before, during, and after the trial was manifestly and intensely prejudicial to the accused? What if the presumption of innocence was disregarded, and what if, from jury selection forward, there was virtually nothing fair and impartial about the trial itself? What if the appellate court compounded the trial court's partiality and introduced its own misstatements, misrepresentations, and distortions of fact? What if the state pardons board, the final arbiter of whether a condemned person should live or die, was composed of a majority who had already passed judgment on the accused? What if, on the eve of the board's final consideration of the matter of life or death, the board itself released false and inflammatory information—supposedly based on the word of an unidentified convict to whom the board had promised leniency—that purported to reveal the accused's long record of violent crime? Could—should—these means justify the end?

And what, then, were the accused's lawyer's obligations to the law and the courts? Was he bound to abide and dignify a system that excepted for some—the poor, the immigrant, the minority, the radical—the constitutional guarantee of equal justice for all? Or was the lawyer morally and ethically obliged to rebuke and expose such a system?

Hill congratulated Hilton for challenging the board to a debate, but recognized it for the piece of theatrical propaganda it was. "Well Judge," he wrote Hilton on October 27, "I guess the legal part of the case is done now, and I am glad of it. I've had a lawful trial, they say, and as I don't think there is much danger of anybody accepting your challenge, we might as well consider the case closed."

But Hilton was not ready to close the file. A week or so prior to his receiving Hill's letter, Elizabeth Gurley Flynn had forwarded him a sensational, unsigned letter mailed to her from Buffalo, New York. The writer intimated firsthand knowledge of how Hill had come to be shot on the night twenty-one months earlier that John and Arling Morrison had been murdered.

> January 10, 1914—ten o'clock P.M. at the home of the Eseliuses, Joe Hillstrom remembered having an appointment with a women acuantience in Murray, there upon Joe Hillstrom left the house alone and went to the house of said aquaintience and upon arrival he come in contac with a man how was in a great state of exitement and before they recognized each other the other drew a gun and fired the fatal shot through Joe's body and in the struggle that followed, Joe Hillstrom rested the gun from the man whereupon Joe remarked that it would be a suvenier if He, Joe lived through it, and from there he went to Dr. Mo Hugh's office. This is all I can say at present.

Had the long-lost Otto Appelquist—he who had vanished from the Eselius brothers' house on the night of the murders, who was wanted by the police as Hill's accomplice, and who, as Hill had confided to Hilda Erickson, had shot Hill in a dispute over her affections—at last been heard from? Hilton was so hopeful that this was so that he all but guaranteed Hill that the letter could save his life. "This letter gives me for the first time knowledge of the real facts in your case," Hilton wrote on October 30. ". . . If the details are shown to be true, the Governor assured me personally that he would issue a respite up to the last moment if he was assured a mistake had been made, and your story was substantiated."

But Hilton promised Hill he would not publicly release the letter without his consent. And then, as if making a closing argument to a jury, the lawyer implored Hill to allow him to publicize it "and so save you from your impending fate."

"Now Joe," Hilton pleaded,

> if I have ever deserved the full confidence of a client, it is in your case. I most earnestly beseech you to tell me truly. I will take such action as will result in your vindication. I am fully persuaded without this you will be executed and while you say your life is of no importance, nevertheless no one wishes wantonly to shed your blood . . . These, my last words to you, express the hope that you may be guided and helped in your decision by a realization of the awful responsibility that rests on all and that in this supreme moment I may hear from you that I am at liberty to make the facts public if they are true.

It is not certain that Hill received Hilton's letter; in any case, he did not reply. By then, the interests of the client and his lawyer were probably irreconcilable. Already enshrined by labor as an icon of courage and resistance, Hill had reached that extraordinary place that martyrs come to: the belief that he was worth infinitely more to the cause as a symbol than as an individual, and that by dying a dramatic death, the symbol would live in perpetuity. Just the same, Hilton wished to save Hill's life, and with the letter from Buffalo, he thought he held the "trump card." To play the card, though, required Hill's acquiescence—meaning he would have to demonstrate his innocence. But Hill was resolute: he would face the firing squad before he would "budge an inch" off his position on where the burden of proof lay. "I'm going to get a new trial or die trying," he often said, and he was out to show the world—on both sides of the class divide—that he meant it, that his convictions ran deeper than the grave Utah was digging for him.

THE STATE OF UTAH was in a public relations quandary. As much as its officials wanted to be seen as unyielding defenders of law and order and state sovereignty, the state was also fixated on altering its provincial image: its Mormon otherness. Not long before, the *Herald-Republican* had noted the passing of the "dark days" when "Utah was considered the scarlet sister among the states," and in a recent speech the governor had proclaimed, "Old prejudices [toward Utah] are gone. We have prestige that we never had before . . . American ideals are as great here as anywhere else." But to many residents of other states who were somewhat familiar with the Hill case, Utah must have seemed less the paragon of modern secular virtue that it purported to be and more the bastion of frontier justice. That notion was doubtlessly helped along by the "quaint provision" of Utah law, as one Eastern newspaper put it and as many commented on, that gave the condemned the choice of "being shot or being hanged."

To remediate its public image, a reporter for the *Boston Globe* counseled Governor Spry in a personal letter, Utah "should insist upon the fullest investigation, followed by the fullest publicity," if only to signal to the country "that it is safe for any man to enter her borders, assured of the constitutional guarantees." He was writing on November 7, the day the IWW local in Salt Lake buried its president, Ray (or Roy) J. Horton, himself a victim of Utah-style frontier justice.

Shortly after midnight on October 31, Horton, who was twenty-five, had been talking politics with a few friends outside a downtown bar. The talk turned to law enforcement.

"Any man who would pack a star is a dirty ——," Horton said, according to a witness. (A newspaper account omitted the offending noun.)

The slur rankled an onlooker, "Major" Howell P. Myton, an old gunfighter and lawman who had worn a badge for most of his adult life. (He had once been a deputy under Sheriff W. B. (Bat) Masterson in Dodge City, Kansas, a town synonymous with frontier justice.) Myton approached Horton: "What do you mean by those insinuations?"

"That is meant for you or any other —— who will wear a star," Horton was said to reply.

"I'll kill you for that," Myton said.

He shot the unarmed Horton three times, the last two while Horton staggered away, his back turned. He died on the sidewalk. Myton was arrested for first-degree murder and jailed. A day later he was let out for lunch at the Elks Club, where he enjoyed a hero's welcome. "Two score of Major Myton's friends met him at the club," the *Salt Lake Evening Telegram* reported. "Each one shook his hand and told him of their support." Eventually the charge against him was reduced to involuntary manslaughter. In an editorial show of support for Myton, the *Herald-Republican* explained the leniency shown him by invoking a guiding principle of frontier justice: the IWW president had had it coming to him. "Deeds of blood in the street are but the natural, logical sequence

316 / A SONG ON HIS LIPS

of the doctrines of hate that have been preached by agitators in this community."

A jury of Myton's peers evidently agreed. It deliberated for less than four hours before returning a verdict of not guilty.

The *Boston Globe* reporter who recommended to Spry that Utah fully investigate Hill's case wrote to him after covering a rally of a thousand Joe Hill supporters on Boston Common. The principal speaker was Joe Ettor, a well-known Wobbly who had helped organize the great textile strike of 1912 in nearby Lawrence. "There is only one hope for him," Ettor said of Hill, "and that is to turn the searchlight of criticism toward Utah."

That was on Sunday, November 7. On November 9, Ettor spoke in New York before another audience of a thousand. He stood at a podium at the Manhattan Lyceum beneath a canvas banner that read, "On November 19 Joseph Hillstrom will be shot through the heart by six hired gunmen of the State of Utah. Shall we let him die?"

Ettor, who chaired the mass meeting, spoke only briefly. He was followed by Elizabeth Gurley Flynn, the radical journalist Jack Reed, and then one of the greatest of all labor orators, Big Jim Larkin, the Irishman known as the "Dublin Giant." Larkin clearly foresaw Hill's value as a martyr even as he stressed that class solidarity could still save him.

"If Joe Hill dies," Larkin said, "spare your tears.

Erect no monument to his memory, as the man by his example has builded himself a monument that shall endure for all time. At the moment of this man's death you will have erected a monument, not to the man but in commemoration of the weakness of class union and the failure of solidarity. But let the monument of failure and of shame be not erected. Let the case of Joseph Hillstrom go to the greatest jury of all—the jury of the workers. Let the working class pass judgment and liberate Joe Hill. If we but say the word nothing can stop us. So let us speak and act that Joe Hill may again be with us and sing for us as we march on toward industrial emancipation.

Of course, there was nothing the audience at the Lyceum could do to keep Hill alive and singing beyond the next ten days—not least because Hill was ready to die. And also because despite a publicity and propaganda campaign that *Solidarity* hailed as "the biggest protest ever uttered in behalf of a rebel prisoner," this time around Governor William Spry could not be moved. Indeed, in all likelihood the campaign forced Spry into as unbending a position as Hill found himself in. The pressure was such that neither man could or would "budge an inch." Were Spry to buckle, as he had six weeks earlier in the intense heat and glare of the national exposure generated by the president's wire, he would appear politically weak-kneed as opposed to pragmatic. And, too, the governor would be seen as having submitted to the ever more desperate and doomful letters threatening death, most along the lines that if Hill was "judicially murdered," Spry or members of his family or other state officials would also be class-war casualties. (Though there was good reason to believe—as the Salt Lake County sheriff did—that some of the most hair-raising threats came from a local private detective: a provocateur intent on drumming up business for his protection racket.)

BECAUSE APPEALING DIRECTLY to the governor seemed futile—even the Swedish minister, Wilhelm Ekengren, concluded that "it would be perfectly useless" for him to trek to Salt Lake City to plead in person for another reprieve—Ekengren and the IWW once more shifted their focus to Washington. Ekengren went first to Utah's most powerful politician, U.S. senator Reed Smoot. He asked the senator for "anything you can do" to effect a commutation. Smoot's reply to the minister, if any, is unrecorded, but a diary entry the senator made on September 30, the day Spry issued the reprieve, leaves no question as to his disposition toward the case. "The President . . . offered an insult to our state by requesting the Governor to grant a respite to Joseph Hillstrom, the cold-blooded murderer who has had a fair and impartial trial," Smoot wrote. "There is no doubt of his guilt."*

Short of indisputably exculpatory evidence, which, as Orrin Hilton assured Ekengren, would not be forthcoming because Hill "is quite resigned [to die]," only Woodrow Wilson could possibly rescue Hill. As Joe Ettor telegraphed the president, "Utah governor apparently deaf to appeals of humanity, only nation's first citizen can save him." On Thursday, November 11, Elizabeth Gurley Flynn and Edith Cram, her socially and politically well-connected friend, took that message straight to the Oval Office. (Two days prior to Hill's earlier execution date, it will be recalled, the pair had met with the president's personal secretary. This

---

* Yet in a letter to a man who had written to ask him to intercede, Smoot pleaded ignorance of the facts. "I have taken no interest in the case, have not read the evidence, and it would be foolish of me to interfere with the . . . courts of our State, with the little information I have at my command."

time, Cram's husband, John Sergeant Cram, the Tammany Hall lawyer, and her brother-in-law Gifford Pinchot, the former chief of the U.S. Forest Service, arranged their private audience with the president.)

The president "greeted us cordially, in fact he held Mrs. Cram's hand," Flynn recalled in her memoir, *The Rebel Girl*. He listened "attentively" and recounted his earlier intervention at the request of the Swedish minister. Wilson wondered, though, "if further insistence might do more harm than good."

"But he's sentenced to death," Flynn interjected. "You can't make it worse, Mr. President."

"Well, that's true," Wilson said, smiling. The women left with his promise of further consideration.

The women's meeting with the president made national news and triggered what Secretary of State Robert Lansing described to Wilson as a "deluge" of correspondence on Hill's behalf. Leaders of the United Hebrew Trades, representing 250,000 Jewish workers in New York City, called on the White House to stop the execution. The Central Labor Council of Alameda County, California, asked the president to direct a justice of the Supreme Court of the United States to order the chief justice of Utah "to sign a writ of error . . . , which will give the defendant a new trial, all that he has asked for." Fifteen thousand members of the Cloak and Suit Tailors Union, No. 9, begged Wilson to "give the man a chance to prove his innocence." (Never mind that Hill stood for and was willing to die for the right *not* to have to prove his innocence.)

Other correspondents appealed to the president to intervene for the good of the country. A former U.S. commissioner of Indian Affairs, Robert G. Valentine, advised that it would be "an act of great social wisdom" to postpone the execution until "the clearer headed of all the parties to social and industrial questions . . . could reasonably feel that Hillstrom had had every kind of fair judicial consideration." Helen Keller asked Wilson "to use your great power and influence to save one of the nation's helpless sons." She added that a new trial would "give the man justice to which the laws of the land entitle him." Wilson replied to Keller that he was "very much touched" by her telegram and "deeply interested in the case." "Unhappily," though, he told her, because the "matter lies entirely beyond my jurisdiction and power . . . I . . . am balked of all opportunity."

Even so, as the president had promised Flynn and Cram, he did reconsider the matter. And surely their visit to the Oval Office, the pleas from the Swedish minister, and the worldwide uproar contributed to Wilson's decision to rethink his position. But it was the strangest of

IWW bedfellows, the American Federation of Labor and its powerful president, Samuel Gompers, that likely made the biggest impact on the president's thinking. (Gompers and Wilson needed one another. The AF of L had endorsed Wilson in 1912 and would again in 1916, and the president generally supported the unions' legislative agenda.)

It happened that the AF of L was holding its thirty-fifth annual convention, in San Francisco, during the week leading to Hill's execution date. Gompers and his party, traveling from Washington, D.C., to California by private Pullman coach, had stopped over in Salt Lake City. Asked by a local reporter about Hill's case, Gompers had allowed that he hoped Governor Spry, "in the bigness of his heart, will extend clemency . . . until . . . his case can be further investigated." It was a magnanimous gesture given the hostilities and ideological differences between the IWW and the AF of L. (In his autobiography written a decade later, Gompers memorably described the IWW as "a radical fungus on the labor movement.")

At the convention, Gompers permitted an IWW ally and acquaintance of Hill's, Tom Mooney, to address delegates on Hill's behalf. (Like almost all of Hill's supporters, Mooney was far better acquainted with Hill's songs than with Hill; they had met just once, in San Pedro.) He spoke as a representative of the militant International Workers' Defense League, an organization dedicated to the liberation of "class-war labor prisoners."*

Mooney asked the AF of L to approve a resolution that urged Governor Spry to stop the execution, requested that Hill "be given a new and fair trial," and, further, directed Gompers to personally forward the resolution to Spry, the Utah Board of Pardons, Minister Ekengren, and President Wilson. The resolution passed unanimously on Tuesday, November 16, and that day Gompers complied with the directive. The next morning, with Hill set to die in less than forty-eight hours, Woodrow Wilson, for the second time in six weeks, telegraphed a one-sentence appeal to the governor:

With unaffected hesitation but with a very earnest conviction of the importance of the case, I again venture to urge upon your

---

* The following year, Mooney himself was convicted of first-degree murder for the bombing deaths of ten people during the Preparedness Day parade in San Francisco. Though testimony against him and a co-defendant was later found to be perjured, Mooney served twenty-three years in prison, before the governor of California pardoned and released him.

Excellency the justice and advisability, if it be possible, of a thorough reconsideration of the case of Joseph Hillstrom.

Upon receipt of the president's telegram late Wednesday morning, Spry convened a series of closed-door meetings with the pardons board. Over the course of Wednesday and into Thursday morning, the board worked through three drafts of a reply to the president. The first draft was brief, a single paragraph, and deferential: "We are not wanting in respect for the high office which you hold," it said in part. "Indeed, we have the greatest respect for it."

From the polite posture of that draft, the pardons board stiffened its spine and sharpened its prose. Writing in the first person singular, the governor accused the president of pandering to Gompers for votes: "I most emphatically resent the imputation carried not only in your message to me but also in your message to the president of the American Federation of Labor that this convict has not had justice in the courts of this state." (Wilson had advised Gompers, "I have telegraphed Governor Spry of Utah urging justice and a thorough reconsideration of the case of Joseph Hillstrom.")

In the final revision, which Spry wired to the White House at two o'clock on Thursday afternoon, the governor was somewhat more tactful. Still, he derided the president as a know-nothing meddler who based his "unwarranted interference" on "a misconception of the facts or some mysterious "reason of an international nature that you have not disclosed."

After reviewing for Wilson the chronology of events in the case, from Hill's conviction in June of 1914 to the reprieve granted on September 30, 1915, Spry further chided the president:

Forty six days after the granting of the respite and at the eleventh hour you, as the President, without stating any reasons therefore, again wire urging a thorough reconsideration of the case because of its importance and the justice and advisability of such a course. Your interference in the case may have elevated it to an undue importance and the receipt of thousands of threatening letters* demanding the release of Hillstrom regardless of his guilt or innocence may attach a peculiar importance to it, but the case is important in Utah only as

---

* The previous draft cited only "hundreds" of such letters.

establishing after a fair and impartial trial the guilt of one of the perpetrators of one of the most atrocious murders ever committed in this State.

Spry's telegram was mild compared with the vitriolic editorials the local papers published that day. The *Herald-Republican* declared Wilson's duly respectful appeal for reconsideration "an attack upon a sovereign state" and went on to all but convict the president of the United States of treason; it indicted Wilson for "giving aid and comfort to the champions of lawlessness, of sedition and of disorder." To the *Tribune*, the president had "stooped from the dignity of his high office to pander to the class consciousness that takes no account of facts but only of prejudice." And the *Deseret Evening News* was plain befuddled, finding it "most difficult to understand" what drove Woodrow Wilson to join the "hysterical effort to save the brute's life."

As to the president's motive, the bombastic William McCarty, associate justice of the Utah Supreme Court, agreed with the governor that Wilson hoped to reap a great electoral bounty for venturing again "to liberate a proven guilty murderer." Wilson's "unwarranted and indefensible attempted interference" would, the judge predicted, "undoubtedly insure him not only the vote but the active support of practically every thug, yeggman [criminal] and ex-convict in the land as well as those of that class who are now doing time in the different state and federal prisons but whose sentences will expire in time for them to exercise their franchises at the next general election, and there are many thousands of them."

McCarty added that if said "lawless and criminal" elements were to carry out one or more of their threats to kill state officials or destroy public property, President Wilson would, "in a moral, though not in a legal sense, be an accessory before the fact."

ON THURSDAY EVENING at eight o'clock, about six hours after the governor notified the president that he would not obstruct "the course of justice" and that Joe Hill would die in the morning as scheduled (absent the introduction of new and "tangible facts"), members of the IWW, the Verdandi Society (a social and cultural organization of Swedish workers), and hundreds of other individuals gathered for a protest meeting at the corner of East Second South and Commercial streets. The corner was where Wobbly soapboxers had held forth since the founding of Local 69 five summers past. And it was where, two summers before, the hired guns of Utah Construction Company had turned a lawful, peaceable IWW street meeting into a bloody riot. Now, on Hill's last night, his fellow workers gathered there to sing his songs, pay tribute to his life, and denounce his imminent death.

Wobblies hawked the current edition of *Solidarity*, its "Joe Hill Special." Atop the front page was a schematic cartoon of the state prison yard. Titled STAGING THE MURDER OF JOE HILL AT SALT LAKE, the drawing diagrammed the layout of relevant prison facilities—the warden's office, the deathwatch cell, the spectators' waiting room, the blacksmith shop (from which protruded, through five narrow rectangular slits in a canvas covering the door, the tips of five rifles aimed at the condemned man), and the prison hospital, where the autopsy would be performed.

As the gathering crowd passed around the copies of *Solidarity* and awaited the speakers, a singing soapboxer warmed them up with rounds of Hill's songs. Periodically he ended a tune with the cry *"And Joe will be shot in the morning,"* to which many in unison shouted back, *"Not if we can help it."* But there was no helping Joe Hill. As Orrin Hilton had been quoted as saying a day earlier, "The powers that be in Utah have ordained that he shall die and die he will." Still, as the night wore on, some among the throng held out hope for a miracle: that before the sun rose, "something is going to happen. Joe Hillstrom will never die," as one speaker cried. "Do you hear it everybody? Joe Hillstrom will never die."

14.

To Be Found Dead in Utah

his is my busy day," Hill joked to his deathwatch earlier on Thursday, November 18. At eleven A.M., Sheriff John S. Corless came by
the cell to review the procedures of the execution plan and to ask whether
he wanted a "spiritual adviser" present. No, Hill replied, "I have worked
out my own religion, and I have peace from it. That is all I need, and
I couldn't be helped any by seeing a minister." At one P.M., his lawyer
Soren Christensen dropped by to relay the news that the governor was
expected to reject the president's request for a stay. (Spry would wire Wilson of his intention within the hour.) Shortly after Christensen said
good-bye, just before two o'clock, there appeared outside Hill's cell reporters from the four dailies for which the warden had arranged a press
conference.

Hill seemed eager to chat. Seated on his cot near the cell door and
separated by two sets of bars from his visitors, he wore a coarse, dark blue
prison shirt and matching pants, white canvas shoes, and a white silk
handkerchief knotted neatly around his neck. He also wore a green cellu-
loid eyeshade that, he explained, helped him accommodate to the difference between the darkly lit cell and the glare of the natural light from the
corridor window. He had reached his thirty-sixth birthday on October
7—a milestone due only to the reprieve Governor Spry had granted eight
days earlier. His six-foot frame had been rendered "all bones," he said,
during his twenty-two-month confinement, and though he still weighed
about 140 pounds—the same as when he had been arrested—he lamented
that the lack of exercise "took the edge off my appetite and my muscles
got flabby." Other than that and an unshakable chest cold, he was holding
up remarkably well. He "showed no physical signs of breakdown" and

"an absolute lack of nervousness," an admiring reporter wrote, adding that Hill had impressed him as being "a mentally clear, self-assured personality, raised above the pall of the doom he knew was approaching."

The looming question on the reporters' minds was whether Hill would discuss at last the circumstances of his gunshot wound or name the woman over whom he had purportedly been shot. "Why should I at this time go into a statement concerning my whereabouts that night?" he said, cutting off that line of inquiry. "Why should I now drag in a woman's name? . . . It is only public curiosity that wants to know that. I am not here to satisfy public curiosity."

Asked if he begrudged his fate, Hill replied, "I am not vindictive. I nurse no hard feelings, but I do sense a very real feeling of being the victim of an unfair trial and injustice." He reiterated his stance on a pardon. "I wanted a new trial . . . , but I am not going down on my knees and beg for my life." What could he have accomplished with a new trial? "This, which is everything: my innocence. How? I would go on the stand myself. Why didn't I go on the stand before? Because this case was so badly mishandled and mismanaged and confused that I was disgusted. I felt certain that sufficient error had crept in to assure a new trial when I could make my defense properly and advantageously."

Lastly, he was asked, what did he expect his death to accomplish? Behind his glib answer may lie as good a summary explanation as he ever gave for his self-sacrifice. "Well," he said, "it won't do the IWW any harm, and it won't do the State of Utah any good." Though that remark nicely distills the blend of inscrutability, pride, and wit he displayed so often during his legal ordeal (albeit not always profitably), about the benefits and costs of his imminent martyrdom he was not necessarily correct, as we shall see.

AFTER THE PRESS CONFERENCE, around five o'clock, Hill summoned Sheriff Corless to ask for an unusual dispensation, one that would burnish his reputation for fearlessness: that he be allowed to die without the customary blindfold. "I want to look in the eyes of the men who are to commit willful murder," he explained.

That would be fine, Corless said. With that, Hill handed the sheriff a letter and said, "Well, good bye, I'll see you in the morning, sheriff." Corless went straight to the warden's office, where he read the strange but endearing note. It read like nothing so much as a glowing—if macabre—letter of reference.

"To whom it may concern," it was addressed,

I understand that the sheriff of Salt Lake county has been assigned to the duty of having charge of my execution. During my stay in the county jail I had the opportunity to come in personal contact with Mr. Corless and wish to state that he, in my opinion, is an officer worthy of the respect of any man or citizen. It gives me a feeling of immense satisfaction to know that my execution, at least is being superintended by an upright officer and a real man.

Hill had made a few other requests. In his last letter to Orrin Hilton, dated October 27, 1915, he closed by asking a favor that suggests he was aware of his place in history. He wanted Hilton to ship to IWW headquarters in Chicago the entire record of his case—transcripts of the preliminary hearing and district court trial ("the two to be kept for comparison"); appellate briefs and the state supreme court decision; pardons board records; and the original of his comprehensive statement to the board ("A Few Reasons Why I Demand a New Trial"). "In case someone, in the future," he explained, "should want to learn the details of my case, from beginning to end, I would like to have it all together."*

In a telegram, he appealed to members of the "Frisco Local" of the IWW: "Forget me and march right on to emancipation." To Bill Haywood at IWW headquarters, he famously sent two requests, or instructions, really, in separate wires. The first contained his immortal exhortation:

Good-by, Bill. I will die like a true-blue rebel. Don't waste any time in mourning—organize.

Later truncated to "Don't Mourn, Organize," his dying words became a rallying cry for future generations of activists, from civil rights workers to antiwar protesters to unionists "in every mine and mill." (As the tribute song "Joe Hill" puts it, "From San Diego up to Maine / In every mine and mill / Where workers strike and organize / It's there you'll find Joe Hill.")

In his last message to Haywood, he asked a favor he would also ask of Ed Rowan. It was a sobering request, but like virtually everything he

---

* Unfortunately, as deplored earlier, a good chunk of the record, most critically the transcript of the preliminary hearing and the first volume of the two-volume trial transcript, vanished no later than the late 1940s from the office of the Third District clerk of court in Salt Lake County, and decades earlier from IWW headquarters, many papers of which were seized during federal raids in September of 1917 or burned in a subsequent fire.

wrote, Hill spiked it with humor. When Haywood received the wire, Frank Little and some other fellow workers were with him at headquarters. Haywood read it silently, then stared out the window. Finally he "shoved it across the desk" to Little, who read it aloud, "rather stumblingly," to the others.

> It is a hundred miles from here to Wyoming. Could you arrange to have my body hauled to the state line to be buried? Don't want to be found dead in Utah.

"Goodbye, Joe," Haywood wired back. "You will live long in the hearts of the working class. Your songs will be sung wherever the workers toil, urging them to organize."

ED ROWAN AND TWO FELLOW MEMBERS of Local 69 arrived at the prison around five-thirty P.M. "He was overjoyed to get to see us," Rowan recalled in a letter to Elizabeth Gurley Flynn, "and gave me a silk handkerchief he had around his throat for a parting token . . . Also . . . thanked us for standing by him so well, and was very anxious that we did not bury him here. Which I assured him that we would certainly attend to . . . We couldn't shake hands from the outer cage, so he clasped his two hands [and] shook them saying 'Good bye boys.'"

Hill spent the remaining hours of the night telegraphing his goodbyes to distant friends and fellow workers. He had received a message that day from the Reverend John Makins, the founder and superintendent of the Sailors' Rest Mission in San Pedro. Despite that Hill had "refused to be a Christian" during the entirety of his stay in San Pedro, Makins had welcomed him at the mission any time he had liked—which, due especially to the piano there for the playing, had been nearly all the time. Makins's telegram urged Hill to pray the publican's prayer ("God, be merciful to me a sinner").

"Why should I be afraid to die?" Hill wired back. "You will find me the same Joe as in days of yore, in disposition and in ideas. When you get to heaven you will find me on a front seat."

He sent best wishes to all in the Minneapolis local, which had wired him, "We the members of Local 400 IWW decide you shall die of old age. Four thousand of us stand back of you to fare you well."

He telegraphed Elizabeth Gurley Flynn: "Composed new song last week, with music, dedicated to the 'Dove of Peace.'* It's coming. And now, good-by, Gurley dear. I have lived like a rebel and I shall die like a rebel."

In hindsight, it seems he decided that the terseness of a telegram was inadequate for what he wished to say to Flynn. At ten P.M., just before he fell into a deep sleep, he wrote her a letter, his last.

> Dear Friend Gurley,
> I have been saying Good Bye so much now that it is becoming mo-
> notonous but I just cannot help to send you a few more lines be-
> cause you have been more to me than a Fellow *Worker*. You have
> been an inspiration and when I composed The Rebel Girl you was
> right there and helped me all the time . . . be sure to locate a few
> more Rebel Girls like yourself, because they are needed and needed
> badly. I gave Buster's picture [to] Hilda and she will watch so his
> pony doesn't run away. With a warm handshake across the conti-
> nent and a last fond Good-Bye to all I remain Yours as Ever.

Apart from the prized photograph of Flynn's son that he bequeathed to Hilda Erickson and the silk handkerchief that he gave to Ed Rowan, he had "nothing to dispose of," he told the *Herald-Republican*. "As for trinkets, keepsakes and jewelry, I never believed in them nor kept them about me. But I have a will to make, and I'll scribble it. I'll send it to the world in care of Ed Rowan and my IWW friends."

While he slept, telephone and telegraph lines jangled all night long, rat-tling the nerves of sleepless officials from Salt Lake to Washington. The messages were a blur of sadness, rage, desperation, and renewed vows of retaliation. The most fantastic message, and the one that caused the great-est consternation, was an affidavit of alibi signed by one William Busky of Seattle, a twenty-one-year-old German émigré. Busky swore that he knew Hill was innocent because he and Hill had been together in Murray at the time that the Morrisons had been murdered in Salt Lake. He attested,

> I, William Busky, do solemnly swear that on the 10th day of January,
> 1914, I was in the company of one Joseph Hillstrom continuously

---

* This was Hill's final song, an antiwar ballad called "Don't Take My Papa Away from Me."
He wrote it from the perspective of a little girl whose mother is dead and whose father,
drafted into the "great war," will "never kiss her good night again / For he fell 'mid the
cannons' roar."

from the hours of 2 P.M. until 10 P.M. at Murray, Utah, and that we also received rustling cards* from a foreman named Hines at the Murray smelter.

When Hillstrom left me at 10 P.M. on the night of January 10, he had received no bullet wounds.

Were these the "tangible facts" the governor had demanded of Hill's defenders to effect another reprieve? Did the affidavit herald the very predawn miracle of which the previous night's IWW soapboxer had foretold? *"Do you hear it everybody?"* he had declared. *"Joe Hillstrom will never die."* Or had the IWW local in Seattle dreamed up a literary variation on the "Good Old Wooden Shoe"—that is, as Hill himself had written about the utility of industrial sabotage, a means to "'make the job last' as long as possible."

Between two and three A.M. mountain time, the secretary of the IWW local in Seattle wired the text of the affidavit to Governor Spry, President Wilson, and Orrin Hilton. Wilson referred it to Secretary of State Robert Lansing, who forwarded the message to Spry for "your information and consideration." Hilton at once telegraphed Spry and the other members of the Utah Board of Pardons. He wired the president and the Swedish minister and Sheriff Corless and prison warden Arthur Pratt; to all he pleaded for a ten-day reprieve to investigate the claim.

Spry turned to his colleagues on the pardons board. Polled by telephone, they agreed to direct the warden to ask the condemned man if he knew a fellow named Busky. Hill knew no Busky, he was said to tell the warden, and Busky's claim, as fleshed out in an interview he gave to a Seattle reporter, was not investigated further. Was it plausible? Not likely. For one, Busky said he had been a witness for the defense at Hill's trial; he had not. For another, his chronology—that he and Hill had been together in Murray from two to ten P.M. on the day of the murders—seems at variance with that of two other sources. Members of the Eselius family, with whom Hill had been boarding, said that Hill and Otto Appelquist had been together at their house all that day trying to repair a motorcycle. (The Eseliuses said nothing about Busky or anyone else having been there.) And as noted earlier, Hilda Erickson, the Eselius brothers' niece, recollected that she, another woman, and Appelquist had attended the vaudeville show at the Empress that evening, and that when the show

---

* A rustling card was required to obtain work.

had let out around nine P.M., they had "found Joe in a back seat" of the theater.

SENATOR REED SMOOT was in New York City attending to a few days of politics and pleasure, but he was no less restless in the predawn hours of Friday, November 19, than the telegraph wires in his home state. At two A.M. eastern time, the telephone rang in Smoot's hotel room. On the line was Elizabeth Gurley Flynn's friend Edith Cram, the well-born socialite turned agitator for social justice.

"She demanded that I telephone Governor Spry requesting a stay of Hillstrom's execution," Smoot recalled in his diary. "I told her that I could not and would not do so."

Even if it *was* two o'clock in the morning, *especially* because it was two in the morning and Joe Hill had fewer than eight hours left, Cram—who had fought as vigorously and effectively as anyone for Hill; who had sent countless telegrams to persons of influence in Utah and Washington; who twice in the past six weeks had strong-armed her way into the White House to plead Hill's case—was not about to let the senator ring off easily.

"She wanted to come to the hotel with another woman"—without doubt Flynn, her fellow New Yorker and traveling companion—"to see me, but I refused." Cram kept him on the telephone for as long as possible, pleading that he alone could save Hill. Only after twenty-five minutes, Smoot recalled, was he able to "shut her off."

HILL AWOKE or was awakened at five-twenty. Press accounts later claimed that he spent the next two and a quarter hours—all but the last five minutes of his life—in a state of frenzied breakdown. As the papers told it, he barricaded himself inside his cell with all available tools. He tore his blankets into long strips, then looped them through the bars of the door, knotting them as tightly as he could. Then he ripped the laces from his canvas shoes and tied them, too, around the bars. Next he was said to prop his mattress against the inward-opening door and grab a broom left overnight in his cell. He snapped the broom handle in two across his knee. He wedged one part of the handle in the door for further fortification, and with the jagged end of the other piece he began, like a mad fencer, thrusting and "shrieking" at his lone guard.

One can appreciate the eleventh-hour emotional and mental collapse of a condemned man, and one can believe that Hill barricaded himself as an act of rebellion—to "die like a rebel," as he had promised Flynn. But the tale fed to the press by his jailers does not seem credible. Tearing blankets takes time; it is not an easy job. And then to knot the blankets. And haul the mattress. And snap the broom handle. Why wasn't Hill stopped? Where was the deathwatch guard? What was he doing?

The newspapers said the guard eventually sounded the alarm. The deputy warden and a bevy of other deputies rushed to the scene. Two grabbed broomsticks of their own, and there ensued through the cell bars an awkward jousting match. It seems doubtful that such a fight—a shrieking prisoner equipped with half a broom handle against a squadron of presumably armed guards—occurred at all, let alone lasted the good two hours it was said to. It also seems unlikely that Hill would have attempted to wound guards with whom he had become friendly and who he knew were only doing their jobs.

Sheriff Corless arrived at seven-thirty-five, there to read Hill the death warrant and lead the procession to the prison yard.

"Joe, this is all nonsense," Corless reportedly said when informed of the fracas. "What do you mean? You promised to die like a man."

"Well, I'm through," Hill conceded, throwing his hands over his head in mock surrender. "But you can't blame a man for fighting for his life."

Perhaps Corless did not blame him. Perhaps the skirmish was a fiction, fabricated out of the thin Utah air like the account of Hill's alleged long and vicious criminal record ("murder, highway robbery, dynamiting and the invasion of a neighboring country with the intent to loot and kill"). The newspapers had printed that sensational story on the day of his final hearing before the pardons board—his last chance for a reprieve. Were both these stories—each illustrative of Hill's purported violent nature—intended to help justify railroading a man to his death for his politics? And was the latter story invented also to justify denying Hill his dignity and his last requests? If so, it succeeded: the sheriff, for whom Hill had professed such high regard, revoked the agreement that he be allowed to die in his good clothes and without a blindfold—to face his executioners and his friends "like a rebel."

The death warrant dutifully read, Corless directed his deputies to restrain Hill and tie a white cloth over his eyes. Next, according to one account (or maybe earlier; the chronology is foggy), the chief prison doctor, H. Z. Lund, injected Hill with "strong stimulants" to prepare him for the "march to the death chair." Another report, though, had Hill rebuffing Lund's offer of morphine for what the doctor advised was the "pretty stiff ordeal ahead of you."

"If they won't give me a new trial, they don't need to give me any-thing," Hill reportedly replied.

"Well, then, what about a slug of whiskey?"

"No, I have never used it, and I don't intend to start taking the stuff now."

"Perhaps you're right, Hillstrom," the doctor supposedly quipped, "it might be habit-forming."

At seven-twenty, the anonymous sharpshooters of the firing squad had furtively entered the prison grounds. They arrived via closed tour-ing car, their faces hidden behind whitewashed windows. Immediately, the gunmen entered their improvised shooting gallery, the rear of the blacksmith shop, its long, east-facing window shrouded by a blue cur-tain through which there were five slits—one for each man's rifle.

At around seven-thirty-five, as Sheriff Corless was escorting Hill out of his cell and the sun peeked over the Wasatch Range to the east, the prison gates opened for thirty-three invited guests. Deputies ushered them along the south driveway to the designated viewing area: an open space southeast of the blacksmith shop.

Besides four newspaper reporters (whom the sheriff deputized for the occasion), the witnesses were all law enforcement officers, some wearing out-of-town badges, including the sheriff of Utah County, whom Ed Rowan recognized as "the guy that pinched me in the Tucker strike." Rowan was aghast at the high spirits of the witnesses, "all laughing, jok-ing and gloating over the prospect of seeing a 'damned IWW' shot." But Rowan could watch only from outside the prison gates; he and Hilda Erickson and the others whom Hill had invited as witnesses were denied entry. The deputy warden had just informed them, certainly fictitiously, that Hill had changed his mind: he "did not want any of his friends to see his death."

Those who did see it saw Sheriff Corless lead the death march into the prison yard at seven-thirty-seven. Following the sheriff, and guided on either side by two deputies, walked Joe Hill, his neck craning this way and that as if to defeat his blindfold. (Apparently, though, he could see nothing: he "stepped with uncertainty," one witness noted, "as one walking in darkness.") Next in line were two doctors, trailed by the war-den and his assistant. Awaiting the procession's arrival was Dr. Lund, who, having just inspected the death chair and its straps, stood beside it: an "ordinary arm chair" bolted at the legs to a small platform and from behind to a makeshift, upright bunker of boards and sand built to block any stray bullets from glancing off the high wall that surrounded the

Utah State Prison, 1903. Hill was shot in the high-walled yard at left. (Used by permission, Utah State Historical Society, all rights reserved)

yard. The chair was placed, depending on the account, some twenty-five to thirty-five feet from the rear window of the blacksmith shop.

As the walking dead man and his escorts approached the chair, someone in the party, presumably the sheriff or the deputy who would call the commands, signaled the firing squad, and from inside the blacksmith shop, the snouts of five rifle barrels poked through the small portholes in the canvas window covering.

The deputies guided Hill to the chair, and he was said to take his seat "easily and naturally." As his ankles, legs, arms, and shoulders were being strapped, Hill started talking.

"Gentlemen, I have a clear conscience. I have never done anything wrong in my life. I will die fighting, and not like a coward."

After the last strap was adjusted, a doctor placed his stethoscope on Hill's chest to precisely locate his heart. The sheriff then handed the doctor a four-inch-wide square of white paper with a three-quarter-inch black bull's-eye drawn in the center. ("Aim so death will be instantaneous," the sheriff had instructed the squad during a practice session.) The doctor pinned the paper target to Hill's blue convict shirt.

"Ouch!" cried Hill, victim of a pinprick.

Sheriff Corless issued a stand-back order. Hill squirmed and tilted his head back as far as possible, evidently again trying to best the blindfold.

"I am going now, boys," he shouted. "Goodbye."

He swiveled his head, plainly expecting a reply from his invited witnesses. Silence.

Again: "Well, goodbye, boys. Let 'er go. Fire away. I'm going now." He lowered his voice. "I am going."

Deputy Sheriff C. L. Schettler, who oversaw the squad, was positioned midway and out of firing range between the executioners and the paper heart that was their target.

Schettler raised his right hand. It was seven-forty on the cold, clear morning of Friday, November 19, 1915.

"*Ready* . . ." he commanded.

A beat.

"*Aim* . . ."

A beat.

"*Yes, aim,*" Hill cried, "*let it go! Fire!*"

Joe Hill, ever the rebel, threw back his head and smiled.

The last laugh was his.

ED ROWAN and his fellow workers who were denied entry into the prison yard were left to stand at the gate. Although they were unable to hear Hill's farewells, they knew when the firing squad had completed its barbarous task. The "shots rang out like musketry in battle," Rowan wrote Flynn a month later. "I could hear the report ringing in my head night and day for two weeks."

After the spectators and the firing squad had departed, Rowan walked into the warden's office. He asked first for Hill's photograph of Flynn's son, Buster. "Yes, yes, yes," the warden said, handing over the picture, "it's for Miss Hilda, by all means." Rowan then said he was there to claim the body. The warden said he would have to check first with the governor. He told Rowan to wait outside. Five minutes later, the deputy warden ran out excitedly. "Rowan," he said, "you can send for Joe any time you like."

As soon as he could, Rowan telegraphed Flynn in New York: JOE HILL SHOT AT SUNRISE. DIED GAME. He wrote similarly to *Solidarity*, adding, FUNERAL SERVICES SUNDAY, AND HIS REMAINS WILL BE SHIPPED TO CHICAGO FOR FINAL INTERMENT BY ORGANIZATION.

By Friday evening, E. G. O'Donnell's little mortuary at 225 South

West Temple Street was overrun with hundreds upon hundreds of mourners and, to the *Evening Telegram*'s eye, the "morbidly curious." Demand to see Joe Hill was so heavy that the undertaker moved the body from the "slumber room," where viewings usually occurred, to the funeral chapel. Still, the line was so long, and so many lingered once they reached the stretcher, that at times impatience got the best of decorum. After some fifteen hundred or two thousand people had passed through the chapel, O'Donnell locked the doors, advising those many whom he denied admittance to try again the following afternoon. "They are of all stations in life, of all ages, and are variously affected," the mortician observed. Indeed, the *Telegram* reported that the "majority" of the throng were "not members of the IWW or persons in the lowly walks of life" but "well-known people of high positions and standing" who waited until dark to visit, "probably," the newspaper speculated, "so that as few of their friends and associates as possible would see them."

O'Donnell reopened the chapel on Saturday afternoon, shortly after one o'clock. All day and late into the evening, until ten-thirty, they came: thousands upon thousands, as many as seven thousand by one estimate. By then the body had been embalmed and clothed in a black broadcloth robe for the next day's funeral. It reposed in an open, oak (or

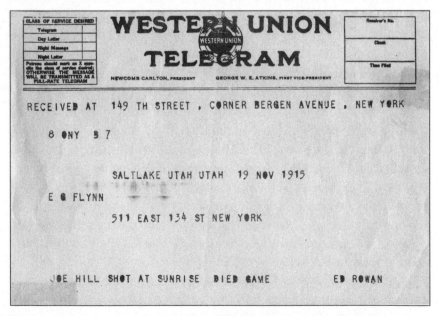

(Courtesy Barrie Stavis)

imitation oak, or pine, per other accounts) casket draped in yards of IWW-red velvet. In Hill's right hand were placed two roses, one red, one white. Pinned to his lapel was an IWW button.

The mortuary chapel's capacity for a funeral service was about two hundred—a figure magnitudes less than the thousands who could be expected to turn out for what the IWW said was sure to be "the best rebel funeral ever held." But over Hill's dead body, IWW officials could find no suitable space to rent. And so, long hours before three o'clock on Sunday afternoon, the appointed time of the funeral, enough people milled about the premises to fill O'Donnell's chapel twice or three times over. "No hall could be secured," the IWW's George Child apologized to the several thousand disappointed mourners left to stand outside, "and we have to do with this."

Child, the chairman of Local 69, presided over the services. No minister was present, and as appalled reporters had noted at the rebel funeral of Ray Horton two weeks earlier, "not once . . . was the name of God mentioned." But Child did invoke Horton's name, as well as that of his killer, "Major" Howell Myton. Child pointed out that although Hill and Myton had both been charged with first-degree murder, police had escorted Myton from jail to a hero's reception at the Elks Club two days after his arrest, and later a judge had granted him bail, while Hill had been incarcerated for twenty-two months without relief and had not even been allowed to shake hands with his friends the afternoon before he had died. "Is it any wonder we are indignant when we see such inequality?" Child said.

"Poor Joe understood all those things," he continued. "He had been in the lumber and construction camps; had traveled in box cars and knew the suffering of the workers. He wrote with feeling because he knew conditions. Joe's memory will live when the memory of his murderers has long been dead."

As Child finished, the Verdandi Society choir led the gathering in singing "The Red Flag," the socialist anthem written by the Irish agitator Jim Connell and set to the tune of "O Tannenbaum." The first verse and chorus:

> *The people's flag is deepest red,*
> *It shrouded oft our martyred dead,*
> *And ere their limbs grew stiff and cold,*
> *Their life-blood dyed its every fold.*

CHORUS
Then raise the scarlet standard high.
Within its shade we live and die,
Though cowards flinch and traitors sneer,
We'll keep the red flag flying here.

Hilda Erickson was one of the six pallbearers, all women, who crowded around the casket as the mourners sang. Each wore a white dress and a red sash over her shoulder. Their eyes fixed on Hill's face, they held aloft the sheath of flaming-red velvet covering the casket and, as the chorus commanded, raised "the scarlet standard high."

A visiting Wobbly from Denver, George Falconer (or Faulkner), read aloud the lyrics to Hill's "The Preacher and the Slave," newly published in *The Cry for Justice*, an anthology of protest literature edited by Upton Sinclair. Falconer attacked the press coverage of Hill's case, describing the "modern newspaperman" as a harlot of the master class, an "intelligent prostitute who is permitted to pass as a desirable citizen while industrial workers are under threat of being run out of town." And he professed surprise that of all states, Utah should have executed a dissident: "I am amazed that a great commonwealth, boasting of its religious foundation, a people who came here to get away from persecution, [has] acted in such a way in the Hillstrom case."

There were other songs, other speakers from local radical circles. M. Brennan of the Socialist Party said that to adequately describe the cowardice of the Utah Board of Pardons would require a trip back in time "with Darwin to the worm he found that had neither backbone nor guts." Brennan also took up Hill's admonition not to mourn but to organize. "It is not a time for tears nor for fears," he said. "I am glad he behaved the man all through; glad he told them to go to hell; glad he lived; glad he died. Let us so live that there may be a little more justice for the poor."

Ed Rowan said that Hill had "gone to a higher tribunal to be judged. That higher tribunal is composed of the great working class of the whole world. They will answer and their reply will ring from pole to pole. They are the judges and their verdict will be heard . . . Hillstrom will be remembered when the authorities of the state are forgotten . . . Time will tell, and time will show the sterling qualities of the man." Rowan told of the silk handkerchief that Hill had given him and the treasured picture of Buster Flynn that Hill had wanted given to Hilda. And then Rowan reached into his pocket for the slip of paper on which

Hill had written what *Solidarity* would later call his "valedictory to the world," but what Hill himself, scribbling on the edge of his cot on the last night of his life, had titled simply "My Last Will."

Fittingly written in verse, it is a wonder of economy and whimsy and beauty, redolent of the natural world, and fragrant with hope for better yet to come. Rowan read it aloud:

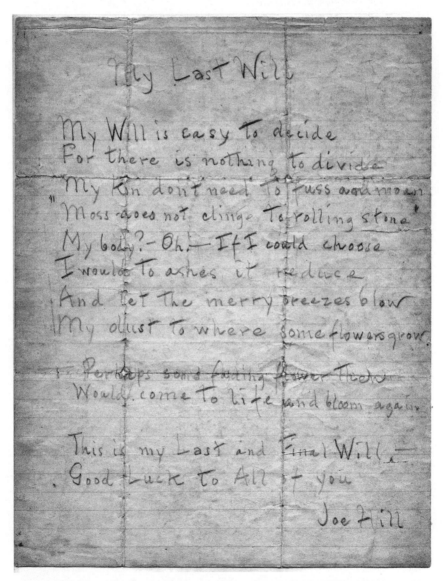

Hill "scribbled" his will on the eve of his execution. (Courtesy of the Tamiment Library, New York University)

My Will is easy to decide,
For there is nothing to divide.
My kin don't need to fuss and moan—
"Moss does not cling to a rolling stone."

My body? Oh! if I could choose,
I would to ashes it reduce,
And let the merry breezes blow
My dust to where some flowers grow.

Perhaps some fading flowers then
Would come to life and bloom again.
This is my Last and Final Will,
Good Luck to All of you,

> Joe Hill

DUSK WAS SETTLING OVER Salt Lake City by the time the two hundred mourners exited the chapel. They were met by no fewer than a couple hundred of those who had been unable to squeeze inside two hours earlier and who had lingered on the street. In accordance with Hill's desire that he not "be found dead in Utah," there was no time to dally: there was a train to make, the five-fifteen to Chicago, where Bill Haywood and the IWW general executive board were planning a funeral for him like no other the great metropolis had ever witnessed.

The crowd formed a singing cortege to accompany the automotive hearse the half mile to the Oregon Short Line depot. Ed Rowan and Hill's countryman and friend Oscar Larson, the Verdandi secretary, stepped off the lively procession. Behind them marched the six pallbearers, three on either side of the slow-rolling hearse, followed by the mass of people walking four abreast and singing Hill's marching song "There Is Power in a Union":

There is pow'r, there is pow'r
In a band of workingmen,
When they stand hand in hand,
That's a pow'r, that's a pow'r
That must rule in every land—
One Industrial Union Grand.

At the station, the pallbearers, their "tear-stained faces" evident to a reporter, helped slip the coffin into a gray shipping box, adorning it with bouquets of roses. A letter to Bill Haywood from the Salt Lake local was placed atop the coffin, and the shipping box was screwed shut. As an inspired afterthought, one and then all of the pallbearers pulled off their red sashes and looped them through the fasteners of the container, giving it a kind of festive appeal. Then they watched until the box, labeled "Joseph Hillstrom, Chicago, Ill.," disappeared inside the baggage car. "We can do no more," a pallbearer said. "Let's go."

A lone Wobbly, Bert Lorton, accompanied the body to Chicago. Not quite forty-eight hours later, on Tuesday, November 23, the train pulled into the North Western depot, where Haywood and thirty-five or forty fellow workers were waiting in the fog and rain. All that day and the next, Hill's body lay in state in a small candlelit room inside the Florence Undertaking Chapel. From throughout the city came a constant stream of workers, untold thousands of "strong weather-beaten men who were not ashamed of anything," Ralph Chaplin wrote, "and who were ashamed of their own swimming eyes when they found themselves once more in the hard glare of the street."

ON THANKSGIVING MORNING, the fog lifted for a spell and the mercury soared; by Thursday afternoon, the temperature in Chicago would reach sixty-three, just shy of the record high for November 25. Inside the West Side Auditorium, at the corner of Taylor Street and South Racine Avenue, it was even warmer: five thousand persons had somehow packed into a room meant to hold no more than three thousand (proportionately, it was no bigger than O'Donnell's) to sing and listen to Joe Hill's songs and to hear the principal speaker, Orrin Hilton, deliver an impassioned funeral oration. For what he called the "brutal murder" of his client, "a martyr to the cause of revolution," Hilton boiled over with indignation, a rhetorical temperature he sustained for the entirety of his two-hour address.

As Hill's songs and Hilton's words rang out of the open windows of the second-story auditorium, as many as thirty thousand people jammed the streets around the building "solidly for three blocks," the *Chicago Daily Tribune* reported. The funeral let out around twelve-thirty, and the mile-long procession, led by the Rockford, Illinois, IWW local's forty-piece band, paraded to the elevated railway stop at Harrison and Halsted streets, where the casket was loaded onto a reserved train for delivery to Graceland Cemetery.

The Graceland funeral chapel was no better a match for the enormous audience that turned out to pay its last respects to Hill than had been O'Donnell's or the West Side Auditorium. Cemetery administrators, though, had allowed the IWW funeral committee to improvise a chapel: the grassy slope of an evergreen-lined hill. There, in the light mist under a pearl gray sky and over Joe Hill's body, a dozen Wobblies made "short but stirring addresses" in English and eleven other languages. Songs were sung, and the body was removed to the chapel again and for the last time to lie in state. As visitors shuffled in and out of the small, oak-beamed room to glance or gape at Hill's placid, faintly smiling face, the massive crowd outside sang his songs repeatedly. And when the bearers of the great scarlet banner of the Rockford local (that which had hung over the auditorium stage) appeared, the mighty chorus broke into "The Red Flag." Then it was three cheers for the revolution and the IWW, followed by more songs. Needless to say, the rousing wake, the ceaseless singing and cheering, was not something the cemetery officials saw every day. They were "stricken with undisguised amazement at the audacity of it all," Chaplin wrote. Still the singing continued, through the gloaming and deep into the night, until darkness swallowed nearly everything, he added, "but a few lights twinkling from out the shadows, and even then it continued."

At noon the next day, in compliance with his Last Will, Hill's body was cremated. (The crematorium was closed on Thanksgiving.) One year later, on the morning of November 19, 1916, the anniversary of the execution, fifteen hundred members of the IWW returned to the West Side Auditorium to attend the union's tenth annual convention. Bill Haywood gaveled the meeting to order and then distributed six hundred packets of Hill's ashes to 150 delegates from North America, South America, Europe, Asia, and Australia. He instructed them to scatter the ashes as they wished and to let him know how and where they did so. In time the merry breezes would blow the dust of Joe Hill over five continents and forty-seven of the lower forty-eight states—all except Utah.

HILL'S BODY had yet to be cremated, in fact his pulse was barely gone, when Governor Spry formally and unambiguously declared class war on the Industrial Workers of the World. "The fight has just begun," Spry pronounced on the morning of November 19, 1915. "The rights of decent citizens and taxpayers are going to be protected. If undesirables think they are going to run this state, threaten lives and public property and defy law and order, they are badly mistaken. We are not going to stop until the state is entirely rid of this lawless element that now infests it."

He continued, "They may shout about the throttling of 'free speech' . . . but I am going to see that inflammatory street speaking is stopped at once. Firebrand street speeches against law and decency and all other demonstrations of lawlessness, rebellion and revolution must be stopped."

"War against the lawless, undesirable element will begin at once," he added, and if Salt Lake City "peace officers" could not fulfill "their duty to drive them out," he would summon the state militia. Spry professed confidence that other states would emulate Utah, until eventually this "apparent wave of lawlessness, defiance of justice and right, and outspoken anarchy is suppressed."

It would take two more years and, ironically enough, the intervention of Spry's bête noire, the Wilson White House, but by the end of 1917 a coordinated nationwide campaign had effectively suppressed the IWW. In the spring of that year, as America prepared to enter World War I, states began passing "criminal syndicalism" legislation—laws that made it a crime to carry a red card. At the time, membership in the militantly antiwar ("CAPITALISTS OF AMERICA, WE WILL FIGHT AGAINST YOU, NOT FOR YOU!") IWW was surging: from an estimated forty thousand in 1916 to a peak in 1917 of no fewer than one hundred thousand.

The union was growing especially fast among Western and Midwestern workers in key war-production commodities—copper, timber, oil, iron, wheat. But a series of IWW-led strikes and slowdowns provoked vicious retribution, most infamously in the copper-company towns of Bisbee, Arizona, and Butte, Montana.

The United States was at war in the summer of 1917, and not only with Germany. To the allied enemies of the IWW who ran the courtrooms, newsrooms, boardrooms, and political back rooms of the West, the union posed—or so they said—as dire a peril to American civilization as did Kaiser Wilhelm; indeed, Wobblies were portrayed as "giving aid and comfort" to Germany in return for financial backing. "Perhaps there is no greater menace to the internal peace and domestic tranquility of our country than this diabolical association," the junior U.S. senator from Utah, William H. King, told the *New York Times*. King, a newly elected Democrat, continued, "I say that it is a treasonable organization . . . Their plan is to . . . sow the seeds of internal revolution; to spread sedition; to inflame the passions of the ignorant, and to demoralize and disorganize all of the forces that make for law and order."

Senator King prescribed "vigorous repressive measures," one of which was his pending Senate bill that sought "to punish them [the IWW] for their efforts to paralyze the arm of the Government and prevent it from prosecuting the war." King's bill was one of a series of congressional blasts aimed at the heart of the union and intended to fortify the states' scattershot anti-IWW laws.

Even so, by late July business interests were demanding that the federal government do more—*faster*—to suppress the IWW. "Why wait?" the *Wall Street Journal* asked. "The nation is at war, and treason must be met with preventive as well as punitive measures . . . Instead of waiting to see if their bite is poisonous, the heel of the Government should stamp them out at once." In Oklahoma, where the IWW had recently organized an Oil Workers Union local, the Tulsa *World* drafted a battle plan that disdained legal niceties: "The first step in the whipping of Germany is to strangle the IWW's. Kill them, just as you would kill any other kind of snake. Don't scotch 'em, kill 'em dead. It is no time to waste money on trials and continuance and things like that. All that is necessary is the evidence and a firing squad."

Senator King claimed to have the evidence, and his home state notoriously had a firing squad. "The evidence seems to be very strong," he told the *New York Times*, "though more or less circumstantial, that members of the [IWW] organization are in the employ of Germany. Certain it is that many of them are supplied with an abundance of gold, and denounce this country and speak approvingly of Germany."

Though neither King nor anyone else produced evidence that IWW members were on the kaiser's payroll, the allegation was repeated so frequently and with such hysterical certitude that Wobblies might as well have been caught on newsreel buying dynamite with German marks. By conflating patriotism with submission to capitalism and by equating dissent with treason, the American political and economic establishment used the pretext of war preparedness to suppress the IWW in a most un-American way: by criminalizing its ideas and principles. The union's successful wartime recruitment drive, its challenge to the legitimacy of war, and its agitation for higher wages and better working conditions were codified in the federal statutes and branded in the popular imagination as "acts committed with seditious or disloyal intent."

Throughout the spring and summer, Western politicians and industrialists had pleaded for federal relief; in July, Spry and seven other governors petitioned the Wilson administration to round up IWW "ring leaders" and confine them to internment camps for the duration of the war. Though the president rejected the constitutionally offensive internment plan, he agreed that *something* had to be done. IWWs "certainly are worthy of being suppressed," Wilson told his attorney general. And to a friend in Washington the president described the IWW as "a menace to organized society and the right conduct of industry." Wilson ultimately authorized the War Department to use federal troops as strikebreakers and the Justice Department to initiate prosecutions against the IWW as quickly as possible so that, as he told a foreign minister, "we will have done what is necessary in time."

Wilson signed off on a Justice Department plan that gave license to act under what the labor historian Melvyn Dubofsky calls "perhaps the broadest search warrants ever issued by the American judiciary." On September 5, 1917, federal agents, in cooperation with local law enforcement agencies, served those warrants on every IWW outpost in America—from the union's headquarters in Chicago to branch offices and halls in big cities and small towns to the homes of officers and other key members (those who *had* homes).

What evidential gold they struck is unknown; at any rate, the campaign's strategy, in the words of one government lawyer, was "to prove that the organization itself was essentially a criminal conspiracy," and its purpose, as another put it, echoing the president, was "very largely to put the IWW out of business."*

The government largely achieved its goal. The "dragnet" snared about a thousand Wobblies, of whom five hundred were indicted for "treasonable conspiracy" under the Espionage and Selective Service acts. In April of 1918, the first and largest of a handful of group trials began in the Chicago courtroom of U.S. district judge Kenesaw Mountain Landis. The government tried one hundred defendants, each charged with four separate counts of criminal conspiracy: two related to wartime strikes and sabotage; one for obstructing the Selective Service Act by advocating draft resistance and desertion; and one for violating the Espionage Act by uttering "disloyal, profane, scurrilous, or abusive language" about America's government, its Constitution, or its flag.†

---

* In achieving that goal, the government had help from another avowed foe of the IWW: the American Federation of Labor. The Justice Department passed along confiscated IWW membership rolls to the AF of L, which enabled the federation to purge Wobblies who had infiltrated its ranks.

† Before the government moved against the IWW, the *Industrial Worker* published one Wobbly poet's mordant reply to mandatory draft registration: "I love my flag, I do, I do, / Which floats upon the breeze, / I also love my arms and legs, / And neck, and nose and knees. / One little shell might spoil them all / Or give them such a twist, / They would be of no use to me; / I guess I won't enlist."

Testimony lasted nearly four months; it took less than an hour to return the verdict: all one hundred defendants were guilty on all counts.
Landis sentenced them to prison terms of up to twenty years. Said one
gallows-humored defendant, "Judge Landis is using poor English today. His sentences are too long."*

LIKE ALL RENOWNED MARTYRS, Joe Hill understood, as was said of
Gandhi, how to "make one's death count for life." Hill did so by maintaining his silence. Before his death, he was the good soldier in the class
war; afterward, he became one of the most decorated there ever was.
But the story of his death and his metamorphosis from individual to
icon, compelling as it is, obscures the details of his life, here recapitu-
lated briefly, that make his consequent ascent to labor heaven, as it were,
all the more astounding.†

Tuberculosis nearly killed him two decades before Utah did. He contracted the often fatal disease as a teenager in his hometown of Gävle, on
the Baltic coast of Sweden. By 1902, both his parents were dead, and he
and Paul, one of his five siblings, used their share of the proceeds from the
sale of the family house for steamship passage to New York City. At first,
the brothers clung to one another. As Paul wrote to their sisters in Sweden,
they lived "a dog's life" that first year in America, each having to with-
stand the staggering shock of initiation endured by all working-class
newcomers. As with hundreds of thousands of other unskilled immigrants, their constant companions were hardship, anonymity, and the in-
security inherent in the everlasting search for work, food, housing, and an
identity in the New World.

From New York, where it is said he cleaned the spittoons and swept
the floors of Bowery bars, Hill headed west, bobbing along in the
migrant stream toward the raw, extractive industries of the Pacific coast.
After a brush with death in San Francisco during the great earthquake
of 1906, he hoboed up the coast to Portland, where he joined the

---

* Landis would soon leave the bench to become the first commissioner of baseball. Club
owners hired him to restore integrity to the game after the Chicago Black Sox scandal of
1919. Although all eight players suspected of conspiring to throw the World Series were
acquitted, Landis nevertheless employed poor "grammar" again: he banned the ballplayers
from the game for life.
† Figuratively speaking, of course: IWW doctrine disclaimed the existence of the ethereal.

Industrial Workers of the World. Within the fellowship of the union, he found a home, shed his anonymity, and discovered his voice as a songwriter: a gifted satirist and parodist who helped pioneer—and became the leading practitioner of—the use of music as a political weapon and organizing tool. In time, his prominence as a writer of popular revolutionary songs for an organization profoundly feared and hated by the establishment led to his prosecution and, ultimately, to his martyrdom.

His transforming himself from an invisible and exploited itinerant worker into a powerful and influential player on the world stage—and his doing it while incarcerated in a small, remote city in the interior West—was a remarkable feat. It also may be what did him in. Over the course of his twenty-two months in prison, his self-identity seems to have become inseparable from his identity as a global icon of courage and resistance. It is that tension, between who he was and who he became, between the private individual and the public symbol, that helps answer the nagging, messy question at the core of this book: why did he choose to die rather than clear his name and live? (This, of course, assumes Hill's innocence.) My sense is that he reached his end through a mix of naïveté and highly principled stubbornness combined at some point with the realization, conscious or unconscious, that he needed to die to protect his iconic name, and that by dying he could make as powerful a moral and political argument for his cause as could be made.

His martyrdom, however, also left unresolved the question of actual guilt: who did kill the Morrisons? Hill's attorneys tried, mostly in vain, to argue that the state had the wrong man on trial, that it should have been prosecuting "Frank Z. Wilson," the multi-pseudonymous ex-convict toward whom the stronger circumstantial evidence pointed. Had Hill chosen to live, in the fullness of time perhaps Wilson (or another suspect) could have been brought to justice.

Hill suggested that he saw his death not as an end but as a *means* to an end: the liberation of the working class. But I doubt he would be pleased with his place in the American pantheon, and not only because the industrial democracy did not come to pass, or because equal justice remains illusory, or because the limits of dissent are as narrow as ever, or because unions continue to be blamed for the country's economic ills, or because America's concentration of wealth and inequality of income are even more pronounced than in his time. He would be at least as disappointed that the meaning of his death has been obscured in a gauzy haze of hagiography. "Americans don't take their folk heroes seriously," the historian William Preston Jr. observed in considering Hill's legend. He meant that few contemporary admirers—he was writing in 1971—bothered to understand the political and economic "realities" Hill had been up against, and the very real and very radical challenges to those realities posed by Hill's music and martyrdom. In legend, Hill had become "an anesthetic rather than a threat," Preston lamented, and a victim of what E. P. Thompson calls the "enormous condescension of posterity."

Perhaps another reason history has mistreated Hill is that his historical moment was over in a flash. Not only was Hill's time cut short, but the heyday of the IWW itself lasted only a dozen years: from its founding in 1905 through the government crackdown of 1917. The union eventually revived and survives to this day.* But it never regained the influence of those formative years when "socialism with its working clothes on," in Bill Haywood's phrase, offered a legitimate egalitarian alternative to unfettered industrial capitalism.

Though that world has vanished, however, the seeds of so many struggles for civil and economic rights in full flower today were planted or cultivated by Hill and his fellow Wobblies a century ago. To name but a few of those rights: the right to due process of law; the right to dissent and to freedom of expression and assembly; the right to a living wage, a safe workplace, affordable health care and housing. The IWW, and Hill's case directly or indirectly, also spoke to other fundamental issues of contemporary society that remain pressing today: the meaning of patriotism during wartime; the use of concentrated corporate power to leverage political power; the morality of capital punishment; the right to freely organize unions; resurgent nativism and immigration reform; the danger of Darwinian free markets to ordinary people; finding dignity and security in a new economic order. (Not to mention the economic wrecking balls unknown in Hill's time but swinging straight at today's workforce: globalization, capital flight, and deindustrialization.)

Despite the fact that the early IWW was crushed, it left a distinct cultural, philosophical, and tactical legacy. Its novel use of music and art for

---

* Twenty-first-century Wobblies continue to educate and agitate and organize, most notably among service- and food-industry workers. The IWW still publishes the *Industrial Worker* (monthly), and it maintains a vibrant Web site (http://www.iww.org) that, to paraphrase the war cry of one founding Wobbly, Mother Jones, remembers its past and exhorts its members to fight like hell for the living.

political and organizing purposes has been adopted widely by unions and community organizations. The IWW invented many forms of direct action, including civil disobedience campaigns to win free speech and civil rights; it popularized point-of-production agitation such as the sit-down strikes most famously used by the United Auto Workers in Flint, Michigan, in the mid-1930s. Above all, the IWW preached solidarity, that "an injury to one is an injury to all," a motto and a principle adopted by countless unions and progressive and civil rights organizations.

Union power peaked in 1954, when 28 percent of U.S. workers carried a union card. In 2010, 11.9 percent of workers belonged to unions, the lowest rate in over seventy years. Even so, organized labor remains the largest and most viable progressive movement in the country. It expends a great deal of resources on electoral politics, with decidedly mixed results. Many believe that if the labor movement is to remain relevant, it must do more to organize the unorganized—including reaching those unskilled and anonymous workers of whom Haywood a century ago said that it would require "going down in the gutter . . . to bring them up to a decent plane of living."

Were Hill writing songs for today's labor movement, there would be no shortage of material. Most of his songs would be topical, written in the moment "to fan the flames of discontent." But because the songs that he did write were not written for posterity but ripped, as his friend Alexander MacKay put it, "right out of the guts of the working class," Hill's work is little known today. Nonetheless, his songs are a cornerstone of protest music and have been an inspiration for those who have come since. As Bob Dylan said, Hill was "the forerunner of Woody Guthrie. That's all I needed to know."

ON OCTOBER 8, 1917, a month after the federal raids on the IWW, someone in Chicago, presumably from IWW headquarters, mailed a three-by-five-inch white envelope to a man on the south side of the city named Charles Gepford. Gepford never received the envelope; the U.S. Post Office intercepted it. Five days later, a postal inspector forwarded the envelope to the U.S. Bureau of Investigation with a cover letter that explained that the envelope was "accidentally mutilated" and "the contents were expelled and their nature unavoidably disclosed."

That may have been so, but under the provisions of the Espionage Act, virtually everything mailed from or to IWW offices and known members was subject to seizure and censorship: anything that advocated "treason, insurrection, or forcible resistance to any law of the United States," or, if the mailed matter did not rise to the level of illegality, anything that postal inspectors considered "intensely 'IWW' in tone."*

Such matter included Joe Hill's ashes. After the raid on IWW headquarters, someone had sent fellow worker Gepford the small envelope of ashes—about a tablespoon's worth—for safekeeping. Instead, Hill's intercepted remains were stashed in a file drawer at the Bureau of Investigation (the precursor to the FBI). There the ashes were kept until 1944, when the government transferred Post Office records concerning the Espionage Act to the National Archives in Washington. There, too, the packet would have stayed, had not the Archives publicized it in its calendar of events for May 1986. An item titled "Oddities in the Archives" listed some newly discovered arcana: penguin bones, a ventriloquist's dummy, the typewriter used by President Richard Nixon's secretary during the Watergate era, and a packet of Joe Hill's ashes.

News of the discovery made its way to the IWW, and in 1988 the union formally asked the government to return the ashes it had confiscated seventy-one years earlier. The request raised a novel issue: should human remains be classified as reference material? Once government lawyers had determined that the ashes (as opposed to the *envelope*) did not constitute a federal record, the Archives granted the IWW's request. On the eve of the seventy-third anniversary of the execution, in November 1988, an archivist presented two IWW representatives with a partially filled white plastic jar about the size of a cold cream container: Joe Hill's last earthly remains.

THE FOLLOWING JUNE, several hundred people gathered at the town cemetery in Lafayette, Colorado. They were there to dedicate a memorial to six coal miners whom Colorado state police had shot dead during an IWW strike at the nearby Columbine Mine in 1927. If the Wobblies among the crowd were there to mourn, they were also there to sing: "To bring to birth a new world from the ashes of the old," they sang from "Solidarity Forever." Other songs were sung, and then crimson roses were placed on each grave. After the unveiling of the new stone marker

---

* The IWW took to disguising certain mailings to evade censorship. One parcel, intercepted anyway, was sent under the return address of "The Christian Singing Society."

(LEST WE FORGET, it reads, above the names of the dead), a Wobbly poet and artist from Chicago, Carlos Cortez, dug from his coat pocket the small jar that the IWW had reclaimed from the government. "It's high time that you get back among your own people again," Cortez said. Then he sprinkled the last of Joe Hill's ashes over the miners' graves.

ACKNOWLEDGMENTS

My son had just turned a year old when I decided to write this book. As I type these words, he is six, or as he would tell you, six and a *half.* He of course cannot remember a time I was not at work on Joe Hill. And I can barely recall a week in which he didn't ask, in a tone that registered somewhere between exhortation and frustration, "Are you done with your book, daddy?"

"Soon, buddy," I'd say. "Very soon."

My wife knew better than to ask, not so much to spare both of us my artless evasions, but because she knew it was like asking when the world is going to end. Instead, she asked only what she could do to help. Sure, it's a cliché, but in no way is it hyperbole to say that I could not have written this book without her. For their abiding patience, encouragement, and unshakable belief that I would indeed complete the book before the world's end, and for so much else, I lovingly dedicate this book to Robin and Zeke.

I dedicate it, too, to Peter R. Decker, dear friend, careful reader of these pages, historian, novelist, and former professor who abandoned the academy for a cattle ranch when he realized, as he says, that he would rather look up the hind end of a thousand heifers every day than attend one more faculty meeting.

My deepest thanks to my editor Anton Mueller. When I delivered the manuscript, he did what any writer would hope for: he praised it unstintingly – and then tore it down to the studs. This is our second book together, and sixteen years after the other was published, I am ever appreciative and admiring of his demolition and reconstruction skills both. Thanks also to Anton's talented colleagues at Bloomsbury who shepherded this project: assistant editor Rachel Mannheimer, managing editor Mike O'Connor, and copyeditor Lynn Rapoport.

For her wisdom and warmth, thank you as always to Geri Thoma, my literary agent for more years than either of us would wish to count.

For financial support, I owe a great debt of gratitude to the Alicia Patterson Foundation, without doubt a freelance writer's best friend. In

2008, the foundation awarded me a generous and essential fellowship, along with its endorsement of Joe Hill as a biographical subject worthy of sustained study. Thank you also to another significant benefactor, the Charles Redd Center for Western Studies at Brigham Young University, which in 2007 granted me an Independent Scholar and Creative Work Award to fund an extended research stint in Salt Lake City.

Also in Utah, I thank Polly Stern and her late husband, Edgar, who along with Gil Williams and Jeanne Wood arranged for splendid housing in Park City for my family and me during one lengthy stay, as well as Cori and David Connors for making us feel at home in Salt Lake during another trip there. Thanks, too, to John Sillito, for his guidance and continuing friendship. John and his frequent collaborator John S. McCormick are the foremost chroniclers of Utah's rich and fascinating radical history. I also want to thank these Utahns (or former Utahns) for their assistance: Kirk Baddley, Steve Diamond, Gregory Lunt, and Ron Yengich. And Janet Holahan and Susan Tuttle were most helpful in my search for clues about Hilda Erickson.

A special thanks to John Arling Morrison and Marilyn Morrison-Ryan, grandchildren of John G. Morrison and nephew and niece of Arling Morrison. The Morrisons were gracious and helpful during the day we spent together. I do not expect that my verdict on the case will do anything to salve their family's wounds. I have tried to honor their forebears' memory by digging as deeply as I could for the truth; I only hope the Morrisons will feel that their decision to share their family history with me was well-founded.

I owe unpayable debts to reference librarians and archivists all over North America as well as Sweden. Let me begin in Salt Lake, where several institutions were fundamental to my research. Thank you to the staffs of the Salt Lake City Public Library, the Utah History Research Center, and the Government Documents and Special Collections departments of the University of Utah's J. Willard Marriott Library. (My appreciation also to the humans behind the terrific online resource, Utah Digital Newspapers (http://digitalnewspapers.org/).

I relied on public librarians in the following cities: Albion, Penn.; Burlington, Vermont; El Centro, Calif.; Evanston, Ill.; Fresno; Los Angeles (city and county libraries); Red Bluff (Tehama County), Calif.; San Francisco; Santa Rosa, Calif.; Seattle; and Spokane. I want to offer a special word of thanks to the unseen but greatly appreciated interlibrary loan officers at my hometown Denver Public Library, and to

Peggy and the staff at the Ross-Broadway branch for facilitating my steady and sometimes torrential stream of requests.

I had help from the following academic institutions: Franklin Trask Library, Andover Newton Theological School, Mass.; Bancroft Library at the University of California, Berkeley; the Tamiment at New York University; Norlin Library at the University of Colorado, Boulder (Western Federation of Miners/International Union of Mine, Mill & Smelter Workers Archive); the Music Library of the University of North Carolina, Chapel Hill; University of Vermont Special Collections; and the Kheel Center for Labor-Management Documentation & Archives in the School of Industrial and Labor Relations at Cornell University.

I must single out two university archives: first, the Labadie Collection at the University of Michigan, Ann Arbor, a goldmine of materials related to the history of anarchism and of radical protest movements of the nineteenth and twentieth centuries. Thanks especially to its curator, Julie Herrada, for her interest and assistance. The second invaluable collection is just down the road from Ann Arbor: the Walter P. Reuther Library of Labor and Urban Affairs at Wayne State University in Detroit. The Reuther is the official repository for the papers of the Industrial Workers of the World (and eleven other national unions). For anyone interested in studying IWW history, this is the first and only place to begin. Thank you especially to reference archivist William LeFevre, who went the extra mile for me so often I owe him at least one pair of new shoes.

Thanks, too, to historical societies or museums in these locales: Elko, Nev.; Garden City, Kan.; Fresno; Oceanside, Calif.; Park City, Utah; and San Pedro. I had help from state archives or libraries in California, Illinois, Missouri, and Washington. A deep bow to the Nevada State Library and Archives in Carson City, where archivist Susan Searcy was enormously helpful in piecing together the criminal life of "Frank Z. Wilson."

My gratitude also to the Huntington Library, San Marino, Calif., and the American Folklife Center at the Library of Congress.

In Sweden I would have been lost without Randy Nelson. A Hill scholar from Seattle of Swedish descent, Randy served as minder, translator, and companion. His understanding of Swedish culture, politics, history, and religion, and his willingness to impart what he could to me, were of incalculable help. Also indispensable was Rolf Hägglund, Joe's grandnephew, whose formidable research and translation skills and apparently genetic musicianship and good humor were deeply appreciated. (When Rolf and I met for the first time in the Stockholm central station, he was wearing a fake mustache—a reference to an earlier query of mine about whether Hill and his brothers were sporting faux whiskers in a group portrait I'd seen.)

In Hill's hometown of Gävle, the archivists and local historians could not have been friendlier or more helpful. *Stort tack till er alla för ert oumbärliga arbete*: Anna Forsberg of the Länsmuseet Gävleborg (the county museum archive); Sofia Hedén and Katarina Nordin, then of Arkiv Gävleborg (the county archive); Iréne Wretemo at Gävle Stadsarkivet (the city archive); Robert Herpai of the Swedish Railway Museum; Barbro Sollbe, independent journalist; Ulf Ivar Nilsson, a scholar of nineteenth century Gävle; and Christer Forsberg, singer/songwriter and curator of the Joe Hill Museum. Thanks, too, to the Järnvägshotellet (Railroad Hotel) for leaving the light on and for being conveniently located across from the train station and above a pub. And in Stockholm, I thank the National Archives of Sweden at both Marieberg and Arninge, as well as the Swedish Labour Movement Archives and Library.

Many good books have been written about the IWW, but none finer, I think, than Melvyn Dubofsky's *We Shall Be All*. I am grateful to him and the other historians whose works on the IWW inspired and educated me. Among them: Joyce L. Kornbluh, Paul E. Brissenden, and Philip S. Foner. And I'm grateful to those authors, published and unpublished, who devoted years to researching Joe Hill and whose works I turned to often. In rough chronological order: James O. Morris, Barrie Stavis, Ture Nerman (Swedish language), Gibbs M. Smith, and Ingvar Söderström (also Swedish). (I'm aware of but have not read Franklin Rosemont's 2003 book.)

I owe a special thanks to two deceased scholars whose works on Hill are unpublished yet vitally important. Aubrey Haan tracked down and interviewed Hilda Erickson in 1949 regarding the events on the night the Morrisons were murdered. His research notes and correspondence with Hilda and other principals were immensely helpful, and I thank Haan's daughter, Mary Haan, and his son, Peter Haan, for making available their father's materials. I leaned heavily on the work of Joseph A. Curtis, who left behind an 815-page typescript, his life's work.

Dianne Carlson Cook deserves more than a paragraph. An accomplished writer, editor, and teacher, Dianne read every word of the first draft, always offering useful stylistic suggestions and substantive comments. She also spent countless hours online helping me track down descendants of certain characters in these pages. I'm profoundly grateful to Dianne for her generosity, her editing, and her genealogical forensics.

Let me also again acknowledge Barrie Stavis for loaning me both his photo archive and the title of this book, which comes from his 1951 play. When we met in December 2006, just five weeks before his death, I congratulated him on having reached the age of one hundred. He looked at me like that was old news. "I'm a hundred and a *half*," he informed me.

Finally, I am grateful to family and friends for kindnesses great and small. Thanks to Lani, Tim, Rumby, and Sherri; and to Rosamond, Jim, Nan, Peter, Chris, and Jane, Hobarts and peaches all. And thanks to Len Ackland, Eric Bates, Cynthia Biggers, Doug Cosper, Deedee Decker, John Dugan, Gary Ferrini, Moe Fitzsimons, Brett Gary, Sam Guyton, Teri Havens, Nook Hedgepeth, Rebecca Huntington, Jody Jenkins, Charlotte Katzin, Michael King, Brad Koslin, Mark Kyle, Rick Levy, Rich Lee, Jim Magnuson, Lowell May, Carole McCabe, Dylan McCabe, Richard Myers, Syd Nathans, Peggy Plass, Dave Riddle, John Scibal, Carol Stutzman, Elisa Wolper, and Heidi Zwicker.

THE NIGHT I FINISHED the manuscript, I ducked into my son's room. It was way past his bedtime. I thought he was asleep. But he raised his head and propped himself on his elbow.

"Is Joe done yet, daddy?"

"Yes, honey, all done."

"Good, good," he said, cracking a sly, preemptive smile. "Now go to bed," he added, "it's a school night."

SOURCES AND NOTES

Abbreviations

ALUA: Archives of Labor and Urban Affairs, Walter P. Reuther Library, Wayne State University, Detroit.
BCF: British Columbia Federationist
BG: Boston Globe
CDT: Chicago Daily Tribune
DA: Defense abstract
DEN: Deseret Evening News
EDFP: Elko Daily Free Press
EI: Elko Independent
FMR: Fresno Morning Republican
HD: "Hillstrom Documents"
IUB: Industrial Union Bulletin
IW: Industrial Worker
LAT: Los Angeles Times
NYT: New York Times
OE: Ogden Examiner
OS: Ogden Standard
SDU: San Diego Union
SEP: Saturday Evening Post
SLH-R: Salt Lake Herald-Republican
SLT: Salt Lake Tribune
SLTele: Salt Lake Evening Telegram
SOL: Solidarity
SP: Gov. William Spry Papers
SPDN: San Pedro Daily News
SS-R: Spokane Spokesman-Review
TT: Trial transcript

Introduction: "Don't Waste Any Time Mourning"

Sources

Books

Asch, Moses, ed., *American Folksong; Woody Guthrie*; Bird, Stewart, Dan Georgakas, and Deborah Shaffer, *Solidarity Forever*; Brawley, Edward Allan, *Speaking Out for the*

Poor; Brissenden, Paul Frederick, *The I.W.W.: A Study in American Syndicalism*; Brody, David, *Workers in Industrial America*; Buhle, Paul, and Nicole Schulman, eds., *Wobblies!*; Carlson, Peter, *Roughneck*; Chaplin, Ralph, *Wobbly*; Dubofsky, Melvyn, *We Shall Be All*; Dylan, Bob, *Chronicles, Volume One*; Faulkner, Harold Underwood, *The Quest for Social Justice, 1898–1914*; Flynn, Elizabeth Gurley, *The Rebel Girl*; Foner, Philip S., *History of the Labor Movement in the United States*, vol. 4; Foner, Philip S., *The Case of Joe Hill*; Foner, Philip S., ed., *The Letters of Joe Hill*; Graham, John, ed., *"Yours for the Revolution"*; Green, Archie, et al., eds., *The Big Red Songbook*; Hampton, Wayne, *Guerrilla Minstrels*; Haywood, William D., *The Autobiography of Big Bill Haywood*; Hunter, Robert, *Poverty*; Kornbluh, Joyce L., ed., *Rebel Voices*; Limerick, Patricia Nelson, *The Legacy of Conquest*; Lukas, J. Anthony, *Big Trouble*; Milner, Clyde II, Carol A. O'Connor, and Martha A. Sandweiss, eds., *The Oxford History of the American West*; Preston, William Jr., *Aliens and Dissenters*; Robinson, Earl, *Ballad of an American*; Smith, Gibbs M., *Joe Hill*; Stavis, Barrie, *The Man Who Never Died*; Stegner, Wallace, *Joe Hill*; Townsend, John Clendenin, *Running the Gauntlet*.

Documents

Hilda Erickson to Aubrey Haan, June 22, 1949. In the author's possession.

Gov. William Spry Papers, series 2941, Joseph Hillstrom Correspondence, 1914–1916 (microfilm), Utah History Research Center, Salt Lake City (correspondence filed alphabetically by sender's surname, and then by date). Hereafter abbreviated as "SP."

U.S. Commission on Industrial Relations, *Final Report and Testimony*, vol. 5 (Washington, D.C.: Government Printing Office, 1916).

Journal and Magazine Articles

Chaplin, Ralph, "Joe Hill's Funeral," *International Socialist Review* 16, no. 7 (1916): 400–405.

——, "Why I Wrote 'Solidarity Forever,'" *American West* 5, no. 1 (1968): 18–27, 73.

Larkin, Jim, "Murder Most Foul," *International Socialist Review* 16, no. 6 (1915): 330–31.

Mitchell, John, "Burden of Industrial Accidents," *Annals of the American Academy of Political and Social Science* 38, no. 1 (1911): 76–82.

Reed, John, and Art Young, "The Social Revolution in Court," *Liberator*, September, 22. (Available online at Marxists Internet Archive, http://www.marxists.org/history/usa/culture/pubs/liberator/1918/09/09.pdf.)

Rosemont, Franklin, "The Legacy of the Hoboes," *WorkingUSA* 8 (September 2005): 593–610. Most of the issue is devoted to an assessment of the IWW on its centenary.

Stegner, Wallace, "Joe Hill: The Wobblies' Troubadour," *New Republic*, Jan. 5, 1948, 20–24, 38.

Recordings

Don't Mourn, Organize! Songs of Labor Songwriter Joe Hill, Smithsonian/Folkways SF 40026, 1990. (Liner notes by Lori Ann Taylor)

"Street-Corner Rhetoric of Arthur Boose, the Last of the Wobblies," tape-recorded by Benjamin A. Botkin, Portland, OR, Aug. 1–3, 1950, call number AFS 14,219A, Oregon Collections of the Archive of Folk Culture, American Folklife Center, Washington, D.C. (transcript in the author's possession).

Unpublished Typescripts

Hilton, O. N., "Funeral Oration in Memoriam of Joe Hill," West Side Auditorium, Chicago, Nov. 25, 1915. In the author's possession.

MacKay, Alexander, "The Preacher and the Slave: A Critical Review," n.d. (circa 1950). In the author's possession.

Web Sites

Dave Leip's Atlas of U.S. Presidential Elections, http://uselectionatlas.org; U.S. Steel, http://www.uss.com.

Notes

1 **"districts are buzzing"**: *CDT*, Nov. 25, 1915. **"'bums' and hoboes"**: *NYT*, Nov. 26, 1915.

2 **thirty thousand people**: Stegner, "Joe Hill: The Wobblies' Troubadour," 23. **"curb to curb"**: Chaplin, *Wobbly*, 189, 191. **oft-cited theory** (footnote): For a discussion of that and other possible derivations, see Buhle and Schulman, 4–5. **"plain folk running"**: Ibid., 2. **"working clothes on"**: Haywood quoted in *DEN*, May 4, 1915.

3 **"most damnable enemy"**: A Seattle Presbyterian minister quoted in Dubofsky, 378. **"America's cancer sore"**: *LAT*, Dec. 9, 1917.

3 **"instinct of the burdened"**: Bird, Georgakas, and Shaffer, 21. **"a singing movement"**: Kornbluh, 127.

3–4 **huge red banner**: *SLTele*, Nov. 26, 1915.

4 **"I never thought"**: *SLT*, Sept. 19, 1915.

4–5 **"fighting faith"**: Stegner, *Joe Hill*, 12–13. **"true and one"**: Boose, transcript no. 1. **"Your interest is"**: Ibid., transcript no. 2.

5 **"every-day experience"**: May 4, 1918, cited in Foner, *History*, 129. **"obscure Bill Jones"**: *IW*, May 18, 1913, cited in Dubofsky, 170. **"marks of capital"**: Lukas, 233.

5–6 **15 percent**: Carlos A. Schwantes, "Wage Earners and Wealth Makers," in Milner, O'Connor, and Sandweiss, 437. And see 432–39 for references to the "colonial relationship" between East and West. **"get in, get rich"**: Limerick, 100.

6 **"treasonable conspiracy"**: For a discussion of the government's campaign against the IWW, see chap. 14.

6 **"a raw struggle"**: Dubofsky, 42–43. **"entire working class"**: Haywood, 174. **"Continental Congress"**: Ibid., 181.

6–7 **"cooperative commonwealth"**: Graham, 1. *Appeal to Reason*: At its peak, in 1913, the paper circulated more than 760,000 copies. Ibid. **outpolling the Republican**: "1912 Presidential General Election Results," Dave Leip's Atlas of U.S. Presidential Elections, http://uselectionatlas.org/RESULTS/national.php?year=1912. The seven states were Arizona, California, Florida, Louisiana, Mississippi, Nevada, and Oklahoma.

7 **people perished annually**: Mitchell, 76. Mitchell was president of the United Mine Workers. **"mere tinkering"**: Preston, 38.

7 **an interesting case**: See Brawley's biography of Hunter. **Hunter estimated that**: Hunter, *Poverty*, 61. **"absolute yearly minimum"**: Faulkner, 22. **sink lower still**:

Ibid., 23. **wages "rapidly falling"**: Ibid., 24–25. **Henry Ford's unrelenting**: In 1914, Ford's new Highland Park, Michigan, plant could produce 250,000 Model Ts annually—a twenty-five-fold increase from the company's maximum output five years earlier. Brody, 7. **"nearly as desperate"**: Faulkner, 26.

7–8   **"near-starvation level"**: Preston, 36–37, citing U.S. Commission on Industrial Relations, 8–16, 23–76.

8   **"very large proportion"**: Hunter, *Poverty*, 61–62.

8   **"pork-chop unionism"** and **"talk of Utopia"**: Preston, 41. See also Kornbluh, 2.

8   **"worthless things"**: Rosemont, 594. **"in the gutter"**: Preston, 41.

10   **"fair day's wage"**: Faulkner, 69.

10–11   **to be capitalized**: See the corporate Web site, http://www.uss.com/corp/company/profile/history.asp. **vertical integration**: *SOL*, Sept. 13, 1913. **"baffling and intangible"**: Brody, 8–9. **"determines everything"**: *SOL*, July 31, 1915.

12   **"learned by heart"**: *SOL*, Dec. 29, 1914.

13   **a big man**: Lukas, 221, cites Haywood's height (five feet eleven and one-quarter inches) and weight (236 pounds) as recorded in a 1906 prison-admittance record. **"scarred mountain"**: Reed and Young, 22. **"sledge-hammer blow"**: Flynn, 120. **"tremendous magnetism"**: Art Shields, quoted in Carlson, 147.

13   **"strangely husky"**: *SOL*, Dec. 4, 1915.

13   **"dreamer of dreams"**: All quotes from the eulogy are from Hilton.

14   **Chopin's Funeral March**: Chaplin, "Joe Hill's Funeral," 401. On Sept. 28, 1915, three days before Hill's first execution date, von Liebich, in his capacity as a board member of the Anti Capital Punishment Society, wrote to Governor Spry of Utah to ask for mercy for Hill. Von Liebich to Spry, SP, reel 3.

14–16   **impromptu parade**: Chaplin, *Wobbly*, 191. **led the procession**: *CDT*, Nov. 26, 1915. **on their sleeves, "seemed to move," "song died down,"** and **"brightly colored floral"**: Chaplin, *Wobbly*, 191.

16   **to "highball" it**: Ibid.

16   **"working-class emancipation"**: Larkin, 330–31.

17   **"earned his mythology"**: MacKay, 1.

17–18   **five hundred men**: The figure is from "Testimony of Mr. George H. Speed," Aug. 27, 1914, U.S. Commission on Industrial Relations, 4937. Asked by a commission member to describe conditions in the lumber camps, Speed replied, "Well, I have been in camps where there has been four to five hundred men packed together in a camp in tiers, four tiers high, with only an alleyway of about 2 feet between them, and then boards put on the rafters for the men to sleep on there."

18   **"at all times"**: Chaplin, "Why I Wrote," 27.

18   **"Joe Hill"**: Lyrics reprinted in Lori Elaine Taylor, liner notes, *Don't Mourn, Organize!*.

18   **leftist summer camp** (footnote): Robinson, 52.

19   **Guthrie's Joe explains**: Asch, *American Folksong*, 23.

19   **"chain of political"**: Lori Elaine Taylor, liner notes, *Don't Mourn, Organize!* **"Ghost of Tom Joad"**: Lyrics, brucespringsteen.net/songs/TheGhostOfTomJoad.html.

20–21   **"real and important"**: Dylan, 52. **"guerilla minstrels"** (footnote): Hampton, *Guerrilla Minstrels*.

21 "much more dangerous": *NYT*, Nov. 20, 1915.

21 "probably guilty": Stegner, "Joe Hill: The Wobblies' Troubadour," 24. "as ever lived": Ibid., 20.

21–22 a 1951 play: Stavis, *The Man Who Never Died*. "worst travesties": Foner, *Case of*, 108.

22 "no more certain": Smith, 113.

22 Erickson unequivocally recollects: Erickson to Haan.

22–23 more compelling case: See chap. 3.

23 "cannot possibly understand": *BG*, Nov. 18, 1915.

23–24 "alive than dead": *SLTele*, Sept. 30, 1915. "or die trying": *SOL*, Oct. 9, 1915.

24 "good correspondent": Foner, *Letters*, 19. "can dope out": Ibid., 30.

24 "eat my own": *SOL*, Oct. 9, 1915.

24 "I have lived": *SLTele*, Aug. 22, 1915.

1. Fanning the Flames

Sources

Books

Alexander, Thomas G., *Grace & Grandeur*; Alexander, Thomas G., *Mormonism in Transition*; Alexander, Thomas G., *Utah: The Right Place*; Arrington, Leonard J., *Brigham Young: American Moses*; Brissenden, Paul Frederick, *The I.W.W.: A Study of American Syndicalism*; Dubofsky, Melvyn, *We Shall Be All*; Flynn, Elizabeth Gurley, *The Rebel Girl*; Foner, Philip S., *The Case of Joe Hill*; Green, Archie, et al., eds., *The Big Red Songbook*; McCormick, John S., *The Gathering Place*; McCormick, John S., and John R. Sillito, eds., *A World We Thought We Knew*; Smith, Gibbs M., *Joe Hill*; Stegner, Wallace, *Mormon Country*.

Documents

Gov. Lilburn W. Boggs to Gen. John B. Clark, 1st Div. of Missouri Militia, Oct. 20, 1838, box 1, folders 48–52, Mormon War Papers, 1837–1841, Missouri State Archives, Jefferson City.

General Services Administration, National Archives and Records Service, *Records Concerning Joseph Hillstrom, Alias Joe Hill, Etc.*, reference service report, Sept. 5, 1957, box 4, folder 6, Joseph A. Curtis Papers, Accn 1229, Special Collections, Marriott Library, University of Utah, Salt Lake City.

Joe Hill to E. W. Vanderleith, Sept. 4, 1914 (typescript "From Joe Hill's Letters"), General Correspondence, box 2, Frank P. Walsh Papers, Special Collections, Manuscripts and Archives Division, New York Public Library, New York City.

Frances E. Horn to Philip P. Mason, Jan. 29, 1980, box 13, folder 14, Fred Thompson Collection, ALUA.

Alexander MacKay to Aubrey Haan, Jan. 26, 1950. In the author's possession.

Journal and Magazine Articles

Davies, J. Kenneth, "Mormonism and the Closed Shop," *Labor History* 3 (Spring 1962): 173–74.

Fitzpatrick, Laura, "A Brief History of the Minimum Wage," *Time*, July 24, 2009.

Henry, W. G., "Bingham Canyon," *International Socialist Review* 13, no. 4 (1912): 341–43.

Papanikolas, Helen Zeese, "Life and Labor Among the Immigrants of Bingham Canyon," *Utah Historical Quarterly* 33, no. 4 (Fall 1965): 288–307.

Schirer, David L., "Murray, Utah, Families in Transition, 1890–1920," *Utah Historical Quarterly* 61, no. 4 (Fall 1993): 339-54.

Unpublished typescript

Tonnesen, M. Diane Dozzi, "Joseph Hillstrom (Joe Hill)," research report, University of Utah, circa 1959, Utah History Research Center, Salt Lake City.

Web Site

http://www.asarco.com.

Notes

27 **middle of August**: Hill and Appelquist roomed together at the Eseliuses for two weeks in August, according to *SLT*, Jan. 15, 1914. **tar paper shack**: MacKay to Haan. **had been secretary**: *SLTele*, Aug. 22, 1915. **sentenced to thirty days** and **Out of jail**: General Services Administration, *Records Concerning Joseph Hillstrom*.

27 **befriended two brothers**: *SLTele*, Jan. 14, 1914.

28 **As the smokestacks** (footnote): For more on the hazards of smelters in Murray, see Schirer, 347–54. **majority of Murray's population**: Fifty-four percent "were new immigrants, mainly Greeks," according to McCormick, 72. **world's largest**: Ibid. **ASARCO was a subsidiary**: American Smelting and Refining Co. merged with M. Guggenheim's Sons in 1901. By 1910, the firm owned mines or smelters in five American states and at least three Mexican states. For more on the history of ASARCO, see http://www.asarco.com/about-us/company-history/. **Nearly half of Murray's**: McCormick, 72. **Most others worked**: Schirer, 346.

28 **on a "skyscraper"**: *SLH-R*, Jan. 15, 1914.

28–29 **"made of lumber"**: The song was first published in the *IW*, Jan. 23, 1913. For lyrics, see Green et al., 60–61. **"greatest favorite now"**: *Marysville Democrat*, Jan. 30, 1914, cited in Foner, 15.

29 **born Joel Hägglund**: For sources regarding his Swedish years, and for a fuller discussion, see chap. 5.

30 **San Francisco earthquake**: The article was published May 16, 1906, and is reprinted in English in Smith, 49–50. **together they hoboed**: Horn to Mason; author telephone interview with Shirley Rudberg, the daughter-in-law of Hill's friend Karl Rudberg.

30 **anywhere for long**: See chap. 6. **fought with rebel**: See chap. 8.

30–31 *Little Red Songbook*: For a list of songs published in all known IWW songbooks, see Green et al., 477–88. **"Fan the Flames"**: This became the subtitle to *The Little Red Songbook*.

31 **Hill had immigrated**: See chap. 6. **worker-protection legislation**: Fitzpatrick, "A Brief History of the Minimum Wage."

31–32 **Western Federation**: Brissenden, 40–44. For a discussion of the role of the WFM in creating the IWW, and the subsequent split, see Dubofsky, 110–25.

32–33 **trailed only Denver**: Alexander, *Grace & Grandeur*, 32. **crisscrossed the city**: McCormick, 60–61. **"large mining camp"**: Ibid., 70.

33 **well-chronicled exodus**: "Of books on Mormonism as a belief innumerable have been the issues," wrote a *New York Times* critic on May 27, 1888. **"detestable customs"**: Arrington, 169.

33 **"vermin, rats"**: Alexander, *Utah*, 99. **ordered the "extermination"**: "The Mormons must be treated as enemies and must be exterminated or driven from the State if necessary." Boggs to Clark.

33–34 **"bankers, lawyers, and businessmen"**: McCormick, 15. **"theocratic in a democratic"**: Ibid., 14–15. **"family of heaven"**: Ibid., 5.

34 **disincorporated the church**: Alexander, *Mormonism in Transition*, 3–15.

34 **"bunch of fanatics"**: Stegner, 156. **"patriotic, progressive"**: *DEN*, Oct. 25, 1915.

34–36 **"critical of unionism"**: Davies, 174. **"annihilate union labor"**: Allan Kent Powell examines the strike in "The 'Foreign Element' and the 1903–1904 Carbon County Coal Miners' Strike," McCormick and Sillito, 130–53. The quote is on 145. **"olives and dirt"**: Ibid., 141. **Bingham Canyon**: For more on the latter strike, see Henry, 341–43; Papanikolas, 288–307.

36–37 **"saintly Salt Lake"**: *IW*, Sept. 24, 1910. **Declaration of Independence**: Flynn, 105. **"obstructing the street"**: *IW*, Sept. 24, 1910.

37–38 **twenty-five-cent daily**: *DEN*, June 11, 1913. **"something approaching human"**: *IW*, June 19, 1913; *SOL*, July 5, 1913. **"Tucker Contractors Concede"**: *IW*, July 10, 1913. **"final abolition"**: *SOL*, July 5, 1913. **"our pants down"**: *IW*, July 7, 1945, cited in Foner, 17.

38 **"fanatic IWW screacher"**: *OE*, Sept. 21, 1913. **armed posse**: For contrasting accounts of the melee, see the Salt Lake dailies for Aug. 13–14, 1913, as well as the IWW press: *SOL*, Aug. 30, 1913; *IW*, Sept. 4, 1913. **"sound was sickening"**: *SOL*, Aug. 30, 1913. **inciting a riot**: *SLH-R*, Aug. 13, 1913. **intent to commit**: *SLH-R*, Aug. 14, 1913.

38–39 **"no more street meetings"**: *SLTele*, Aug. 13, 1913. **"uphold the Constitution"**: Ibid. **"Any damn thing"**: *SLTele*, Aug. 14, 1913.

39 **in the "trouble"**: *DEN*, Aug. 13, 1913. **Silver King mine**: Chronology from *DEN*, Jan. 15, 1914; *SLT*, Jan. 15, 1914. And Hill writes in a letter to the editor, "Shortly before my arrest, I came down from Park City, where I was working in the mines." *SLTele*, Aug. 22, 1915. **Hill got sick**: Hill interview with *SLH-R*, Nov. 18, 1915. **Swedish folk songs**: Tonnesen, 20–21, describes four close-knit families whose members worked in the smelters and mines, including the Eseliuses and the Lindegrens. The families gathered regularly to drink and sing Swedish songs. In a telephone interview, Tonnesen told the author that during the course of her research in the 1950s, she had learned from her husband's mother and uncles that Hill had played at some of those gatherings.

39 **four-room cabin**: *SLT*, Jan. 15, 1914. The story also mentions an attic accessed from a pull-down ladder and an outhouse.

40 **"common pacific coast"**: Hill to Vanderleith.

2. The Man Who Wouldn't Be Held Up

Sources

Books

Alexander, Thomas G., *Mormonism in Transition*; Alexander, Thomas G., *Utah: the Right Place*; Alexander, Thomas G., and James B. Allen, *Mormons & Gentiles*; Andrews, Thomas G., *Killing for Coal*; Kazin, Michael, *The Populist Persuasion*; McCormick, John S., *The Gathering Place*; Stringham, Nathaniel G., and Bryant S. Hinckley, *Briant Stringham and His People*.

Documents

William Lasering, photograph 1721, Aug. 11, 1913, Salt Lake City Police "mug book," Police Museum, Salt Lake City. Courtesy of Police Lt. Steve Diamond (ret.), curator.

State of Utah v. Joseph Hillstrom, no. 3532, vol. 2, transcript of evidence introduced on behalf of the defendant (note: vol. 1 missing), Utah Third District Court. Hereafter abbreviated as "TT."

State of Utah v. Joseph Hillstrom, appellant's brief, appeal from the Utah Third District Court, Utah Supreme Court, n.d.

U.S. Bureau of the Census, Thirteenth Census of the United States, 1910 (Washington, D.C.: National Archives and Records Administration).

Interview

John Arling Morrison and Marilyn Morrison-Ryan, Salt Lake City and Provo, Utah, September 2007.

Journal and Magazine Articles

Lasch, Christopher, "Burned Over Utopia," *New York Review of Books*, Jan. 26, 1967 (online: http://www.nybooks.com/articles/12210 [subscription required]).

Miller, Douglas K., "The Quest to Become Chief of Police: The Illustrious Career of George Augustus Sheets," *Utah Historical Quarterly* 74, no. 1 (Winter 2006): 24–46.

Unpublished Typescripts

Curtis, Joseph A., *Right Man? The Tragic Saga of Joe Hill*, Joseph A. Curtis Papers, Accn 1229, Special Collections, Marriott Library, University of Utah, Salt Lake City.

Gleason, Herbert Lester, "The Salt Lake City Police Department: 1851–1949, a Social History," master's thesis, University of Utah, 1950.

Notes

41 **"ideal winter's day"**: *DEN*, Jan. 10, 1914. **"thrills, chills"**: theater notice, *DEN*, Jan. 7, 1914.

41–42 **"apparently cured"**: *NYT*, Jan. 9, 1914. **"fool-proof"**: *NYT*, Jan. 5, 1914.

42 **"means a struggle"**: *SLH-R*, Jan. 4, 1914.

42 **deported the octogenarian**: *SLH-R*, Jan. 5, 1914. For an illuminating study of the Ludlow massacre, see Andrews.

43 **Frank worked nights**: Frank Seeley obituary, *SLH-R*, July 5, 1915.

43 **"angered me slightly"**: *SLH-R*, Jan. 16, 1914.

43–44 **"old-time gambler"**: Gleason, 103. **"race horse touting"**: *SLT*, Jan. 9, 1914. For more on the anti-Mormon movement, see, for instance, Alexander and Allen, 163–65. **"criminals and other"**: *SLT*, Jan. 10, 1914.

44 **"name blotted out"**: *DEN*, Jan. 12, 1914.

44–45 **"real roughneck farmer"**: John Arling Morrison interview, Sept. 18, 2007.

45 **weed-borne pestilence**: Ibid. **ten thousand insolvent farmers**: For a thorough discussion of the People's Party, see Kazin, chap. 2.

45–46 **forty thousand people**: *DEN*, Apr. 8, 1893.

46 **whose maternal grandfather**: Briant Stringham was in the Third 10 of Young's original company of pioneers that left Winter Quarters, Nebraska, in April 1847. *SLT*, Apr. 16, 1997. **"chasing rainbows"**: For this quote and additional details on Marie's family, see Stringham and Hinckley, 183–85.

46–47 **"tobacco is not"**: Doctrine & Covenants of the Church of Jesus Christ of Latter-day Saints, 89:8. **a sin in the Book of Mormon**: *Book of Mormon*, Alma 39:5.

47 **"Where's my shotgun?"**: *SLTele*, Feb. 3, 1903.

47 **"O my God!"**. Ibid.

47–48 **"pumping lead" and "Brave Grocer"**: *SLT*, Feb. 3, 1903.

48 **regain his job**: Miller, 24–46. **promptly firing**: *DEN*, Jan. 23, 1906.

48 **"fiery steeds"**: *SLH-R*, May 13, 1906. **"Copper Who Cops"**: *SLT*, Aug. 1, 1906. **raving, suicidal mother**: *OS*, July 13, 1906. **day Morrison resigned**: Salt Lake City Council meeting minutes book 1907, 139. **charge of conspiracy**: *SLT*, Apr. 10, 1907; *SLTele*, Apr. 12, 1907.

48–49 **Master Workman**: A meeting announcement in the *SLH-R*, Nov. 11, 1904, identifies Morrison as the M.W.

49 **grocery-delivery run**: *OS*, Sept. 30, 1908.

49 **"sensational holdup"**: *DEN*, Jan. 12, 1914.

50 **"unaccommodating disposition" and "merry fusillade"**: *DEN*, Sept. 22, 1913.

50 **broad-banded fedora**: See William Lasering, photograph 1721. *including Morrison's*: *SLT*, Aug. 11, 1913.

50 **not only confessed**: *SLTele*, Oct. 22, 1913; *SLH-R*, Oct. 23, 1913. **convicted burglar**: Their father, Thomas Samuelson, pleaded guilty to burglary of the Wheelwright Store in Ogden, Utah. *OS*, Feb. 10, 1899. **themselves on probation**: *Davis County Clipper*, Oct. 31, 1913.

50–51 **"knows my habits"**: *SLTele*, Jan. 12, 1914.

51 **"badly mistaken"**: *SLH-R*, Jan. 12, 1914. **"the next time"**: *SLH-R*, Jan. 11, 1914.

51 **munching an apple**: *SLH-R*, Jan. 11, 1914. **building contractor**: Thirteenth Census of the United States. **lurking and watching**: *SLH-R*, Jan. 12, 1914.

51 **gleaming glass showcase**: For a photograph of the store, see *SLT*, Jan. 12, 1914.

52 **clutching his chest**: *SLH-R*, Jan. 11, 1914.

52 **"lying on his face"**: Quoted in *Curtis*, 196, from DA 22, citing TT, 88–89. **"hysterical, high-pitched"**: *DEN*, Jan. 12, 1914. **"both of them"**: *SLH-R*, Jan. 11, 1914.

52–53 **Westside home**: TT, 539.

53 **"stopped and looked"**: Ibid., 541. **passing streetcar**: Ibid., 542. **"Was Strange Man"**: *SLH-R*, Jan. 13, 1914.

53 **"premeditated murder"**: *SLH-R*, Jan. 12, 1914. **dispatched his entire**: *SLTele*, Jan. 12, 1914. **Merlin's initial description**: *SLT*, Jan. 11, 1914. **"not only incomplete"**: *SLH-R*, Jan. 12, 1914.

54 **"opened the intervening"**: *SLH-R*, Jan. 11, 1914. **"behind some shelves"**: *SLT*, Jan. 12, 1914.

54 **Seeleys' initial account**: *DEN*, Jan. 14, 1914; *SLH-R*, Jan. 16, 1914.

54–55 **he *thought* so**: As quoted in *SLT*, Jan. 12, 1914: "As father fell my brother turned around to the shelf by the icebox . . . There was a revolver there, and he picked it up. He certainly was brave, for he ran to where the scales are and shot. I think the bullet hit one man." **"Hold on Bob"**: *SLT*, Jan. 15, 1914. **"Oh, Bob"**: *SLT*, Jan. 29, 1914.

3. A Prime Suspect

Sources

Book
Nichols, Jeffrey, *Prostitution, Polygamy, and Power*.

Documents
Illinois v. Magnus Osburg, term no. 2414, case no. CR 86429 A, Jan. 10, 1908, Archives Room, Clerk of the Circuit Court of Cook County, Chicago.

Nevada v. J. R. Harris, J. D. Higgins and George Lightner, deposition of T. A. Gibson, Jan. 12, 1914, Justice's Court of Carlin Township, Elko County, Nevada.

Nevada State Prison Inmate Case Files, Nevada State Library and Archives, Carson City.

Prison Commitment Registers, series 80388, Utah History Research Center, Salt Lake City.

Records of the Illinois Boys' State Reformatory at Pontiac, intake ledger for Magnus Olson, no. 4317, May 3, 1900, Illinois State Archives, Springfield.

State of Utah v. Joseph Hillstrom, case no. 3532, vol. 2, transcript of evidence introduced on behalf of the defendant (note: vol. 1 missing), Utah Third District Court. Hereafter abbreviated as "TT."

State of Utah v. Joseph Hillstrom, 46 Utah 341, 150 P. 935, appellant's brief, appeal from the Utah Third District Court, Utah Supreme Court, 1915.

Magazine articles
Morton, James, with David G. Wittels, "I Was King of the Thieves," *SEP*, Aug. 5, 1950 (part 1); Aug. 12, 1950 (part 2); Aug. 19, 1950 (part 3).

Web Site
Ancestry.com, http://www.ancestry.com (subscription required).

Notes

56 **sensational headlines**: *SLH-R*, Jan. 11, 1914; *SLT*, Jan. 11, 1914; *DEN*, Jan. 12, 1914.

56–57 **"wanted my life"**: *SLTele*, Jan. 12, 1914.

57 **"Almost immediately"**: *DEN*, Jan. 12, 1914. **Wilson had been seen**: *SLT*, Jan. 11 and 12, 1914; *SLTele*, Jan. 12, 1914.

57–58 **"convinced" the department**: *SLTele*, Feb. 5, 1914.

58 **"sails under that"**: *EI*, Feb. 6, 1914. **used at trial**: *EDFP*, Feb. 9, 1914.

59 **completely fabricated**: "Farmer" wrote the appeal to the Nevada Board of Pardons in December 1909. See Nevada State Prison Inmate Case Files, Farmer, James, no. 1182. **another inventive memoir**: Morton, *SEP*.

59–60 **lengthy criminal career**: At least several states attempted to compile his criminal dossier. See, for example, the Michigan State Police report of Nov. 29, 1937, which lists sixteen aliases and fourteen criminal charges dating from 1900 through 1937. The report, in the author's files, was turned up in a search of Folsom State Prison records for "James Franklin," no. 5950, at the California State Archives, Sacramento. **rob "post offices"**: Morton, *SEP*, Aug. 5, 1950, 18. **"cops still haven't"**: Ibid., 19. **Al Capone**: *CDT*, Feb. 23, 1929, and May 19, 1933. For the various jobs he says he held for Capone, see Morton, *SEP*, Aug. 19, 1950, 130. **on Capone's payroll**: *SEP*, Aug. 19, 1950, 128.

61 **provided this description**: Nevada State Police, Office of the Superintendent, Carson City, Nevada, memo, Sept. 20, 1913, Nevada State Prison Inmate Case Files, Farmer, James, no. 1182.

62 **any of the variations**: The aliases are compiled in various states' investigative reports of Olson's criminal activities. For the most comprehensive lists, see California State Bureau of Criminal Identification and Investigation, Sacramento, to Mr. Edw. H. Fox, chief of detectives, Detroit, MI, memo, Aug. 12, 1925, Nevada State Prison Inmate Case Files, Morton, James, no. 1650; Michigan State Police report, Nov. 29, 1937.

62 **April of 1881**: Illinois Boys' State Reformatory. **city of Tromsø**: Moore/Eickhoff Family Tree, Ancestry.com. Note: The name is listed as Magnus "Jim" Olsen (with an *e*). Date of birth is given as May 16, 1884, a date sourced to his U.S. World War II draft registration card of 1942. From other data in the author's possession, it seems highly likely that the Draft Board was misinformed and that his correct birth year was 1881, as recorded by the Illinois Boys' State Reformatory in 1900. The date and place of death listed for Magnus Olsen in the Moore/Eickhoff tree correspond to that of James "Big Jim" Morton, which would become a favored alias. **immigrated to Evanston**: The family arrived in New York on June 30, 1884. New York Passenger Lists, 1820–1957, Ancestry.com. **parents were dead**: Morton, *SEP*, Aug. 5, 1950, 78. **steam laundry**: Corroborating information regarding his parents' deaths and his living and working relationship with his uncle C. G. Magnuson's family is derived from Illinois Boys' State Reformatory; City Directory, Evanston, IL (University Press Company, 1890, 1900). **"play hooky"**: Morton, *SEP*, Aug. 5, 1950, 78.

62 **"band of thieves"**: *CDT*, Feb. 16, 1900. **"burglary, larceny"**: *CDT*, Apr. 17, 1900.

62–63 **filched brass journals**: Ibid.

63 **"bad company"**: Morton, *SEP*, Aug. 5, 1950, 80. **"small burglaries"**: *CDT*, Mar. 22, 1902. **"pack my clothes"**: Morton, *SEP*, Aug. 5, 1950, 81. **adversary notified**: Illinois Boys' State Reformatory; Morton, *SEP*, Aug. 5, 1950, 81.

63 **"rambled down"**: Morton, *SEP*, Aug. 5, 1950, 81. **pilfering staples**: *Daily Red Bluff News*, Dec. 27, 1904. **Folsom State Prison**: *Daily Red Bluff News*, Jan. 4, 1905.

63–64 **"stealing trade"**: Morton, *SEP*, Aug. 5, 1950, 81.

64 **no apparent reason**: *CDT*, Oct. 17, 1907. **"answer[ed] closely"**: *CDT*, Nov. 6, 1907. Before the victim died, he reportedly told a relative that his assailant was scarred above one eye. Olson, as many of his prison admittance forms recorded, had a "vertical line scar" above his left eyebrow. See, for instance, as Frank Z. Wilson, no. 2261, Prison Commitment Registers, Aug. 26, 1911, and as James Morton, no. 1650, Nevada State Prison Inmate Case Files, Feb. 11, 1914.

64 **burglary and "incendiarism"**: *CDT*, Dec. 11, 1907. **"receiving stolen property"**: *Illinois v. Osburg*.

64–65 **Frisco Mickey**: For Cronin's criminal history, see Nevada State Prison Inmate Case Files, Cronin, William, no. 1183. **use "soup"**: Morton, *SEP*, Aug. 12, 1950, 96. **looting Southern Pacific**: *Reno Evening Gazette*, Aug. 12, 1908; *Nevada State Journal*, Aug. 13, 1908.

65–66 **fell into the arms**: *SLT*, Aug. 11, 1911. For "Wilson's" booking photograph and description, dated Aug. 30, 1911, see Prison Commitment Registers, no. 2661.

66 **red-light districts**: For a scholarly treatment of prostitution and its complex ties to government and business, see Nichols, especially 45–49.

66 **torn window screen**: *EI*, Sept. 5, 1913, and Sept. 19, 1913.

66–67 **"burn it down"**: *EI*, Sept. 19, 1913.

67 **"Will you please"**: Both requests (and the superintendent's reply) are included in Nevada State Prison Inmate Case Files, Farmer, James, no. 1182.

67 **"professional" burglars broke**: *EI*, Sept. 26, 1913. **"The usual description"**: *OE*, Dec. 12, 1913; *OS*, Dec. 12, 1913.

67–68 **Western Pacific pumpman**: *Nevada v. J. R. Harris, et al.* Also see *EDFP*, Dec. 17, 1913, and Jan. 12, 1914. **"final discharge allowance"**: In a note on Cullen Hotel letterhead dated Dec. 11, 1914, Higgins wrote, "Please pay remending [*sic*] Ten Dollars to James Morton and oblige." Nevada State Prison Inmate Case Files, Higgins, J. D., no. 1638. Incidentally, Higgins was arrested in Salt Lake City for grand larceny of an automobile on Nov. 19, 1915, the day Joe Hill was executed there.

68 **"shove his hands"**: *EDFP*, Dec. 22, 1913. **"dark suit much-worn"**: *Elko Weekly Independent*, Dec. 26, 1913. **substantial arsenal**: *OS*, Dec. 24, 1913. **"an organized gang"**: *EI*, Sept. 26, 1913.

68 **looking for "Wilson"**: *SLT*, Jan. 11, 1914.

68–69 **"suspicious-acting"**: TT, 553. **"smell any booze"**: Ibid., 554. **"rather worse from wear"**: *SLH-R*, Jan. 13, 1914. **end of the line**: TT, 555.

69 **alighted on one**: Ibid., 555–56.

4. A Deadly Certainty

Sources

Books

McCormick, John S., *The Gathering Place*; Miller, Jessie C., et al., eds., *Lawrence County Missouri History*; Mulder, William, *Homeward to Zion*.

Documents

Hilda Erickson to Aubrey Haan, June 22, 1949, and June 30, 1949. In the author's possession.

"F. Z. Wilson Criminal Record," Aug. 10, 1911, Salt Lake City Police "mug book," 496, Police Museum, Salt Lake City. Courtesy of Police Lt. Steve Diamond (ret.), curator.

Gov. William Spry Papers, series 2941, Joseph Hillstrom Correspondence, 1914–1916 (microfilm), Utah History Research Center, Salt Lake City (correspondence filed alphabetically by sender's surname, and then by date). Hereafter abbreviated as "SP."

W. R. Groom to J. P. Donnelley, Superintendent, Nevada State Police, Jan. 16, 1914, Nevada State Prison Inmate Case Files, Farmer, James, no. 1182, Nevada State Library and Archives, Carson City.

Aubrey Haan to Fred Thompson, Jan. 18, 1948, box 102, Correspondence, Jan. 1948, IWW Collection, ALUA.

Joe Hill to Utah Board of Pardons, "A Few Reasons Why I Demand a New Trial," Oct. 3, 1915, published in *DEN*, Oct. 4, 1915; Foner, *Letters*, 64–74.

"Joe Hillstrom Criminal Record," Jan. 14, 1914, Salt Lake City Police "mug book," n.p., Police Museum, Salt Lake City. Courtesy of Police Lt. Steve Diamond (ret.), curator.

Alexander MacKay to Aubrey Haan, Jan. 26, 1950. In the author's possession.

Frank M. McHugh correspondence with Vernon Jensen: Jensen to McHugh, Oct. 16, 1947; McHugh to Jensen, Nov. 26, 1947; Jensen to McHugh, Dec. 15, 1947; McHugh to Jensen, Jan. 26, 1948, Vernon Jensen Additional Research and Office Files, no. 4096, box 1, folder "Joe Hill," Kheel Center Archives, School of Industrial and Labor Relations, Cornell University, Ithaca, NY.

Nevada State Prison Inmate Case Files, Nevada State Library and Archives, Carson City.

State of Nevada v. James Morton, District Court of the Fourth Judicial District of the State of Nevada, Feb. 10, 1914 (microfilm), Fourth Judicial District Court, Elko, NV.

State of Utah v. Joseph Hillstrom, no. 3532, vol. 2, transcript of evidence introduced on behalf of the defendant (note: vol. 1 missing), Utah Third District Court. Hereafter abbreviated as "TT."

State of Utah v. Joseph Hillstrom, 46 Utah 341, 150 P. 935, appellant's brief, appeal from the Utah Third District Court, Utah Supreme Court, 1915.

U.S. Bureau of the Census, Thirteenth Census of the United States, 1910, and Fourteenth Census of the United States, 1920 (Washington, D.C.: National Archives and Records Administration).

Journal and Magazine Articles

Hesslink, George K., "Kimball Young: Seminal American Sociologist, Swedish Descendant, and Grandson of Mormon Leader Brigham Young," *Swedish Pioneer Historical Quarterly* 25, no. 2 (1974): 115–32.

Jensen, Vernon H., "The Legend of Joe Hill," *Industrial and Labor Relations Review* 4, no. 3 (April 1951): 356–66.

Morton, James, with David G. Wittels, "I Was King of the Thieves," *SEP*, Aug. 5, 1950 (part 1); Aug. 12, 1950 (part 2); Aug. 19, 1950 (part 3).

Powell, Allan Kent, "Elections in the State of Utah," *Utah History Encyclopedia* (online: http://www.media.utah.edu/UHE/e/ELECTIONS.html).

Schirer, David L., "Murray, Utah, Families in Transition, 1890–1920," *Utah Historical Quarterly* 61, no. 4 (Fall 1993): 339–54.

Unpublished Typescript

Curtis, Joseph A., *Right Man? The Tragic Saga of Joe Hill*, Joseph A. Curtis Papers, Accn 1229, Special Collections, Marriott Library, University of Utah, Salt Lake City.

Web Sites

Ancestry.com, http://www.ancestry.com (subscription required); Genline FamilyFinder, http://www.genline.se (subscription required).

Notes

70 **"I've been shot"**: *DEN*, Jan. 14, 1914. As for the time Hill arrived at McHugh's office, the Jan. 14 editions variously reported it as eleven P.M., eleven-thirty, and eleven-fifty.

70 **met at the home**: *SLH-R*, Jan. 14, 1914. **crossed paths**: Haan (a Hill researcher in the 1940s) to Thompson (editor of the *IW*), Jan. 18, 1948. Haan wrote that McHugh had told him he had "seen Hill in a meeting or two."

70 **onto a couch**: *DEN*, Jan. 14, 1914. **Blood continued to spurt**: Ibid. **a "fresh" wound**: *SLH-R*, Jan. 14, 1914. **missed his heart**: *SLT*, Jan. 14, 1914.

71 **quarreled over a woman**: *SLT*, Jan. 14, 1914. **"got into a stew"**: *SLH-R*, Jan. 14, 1914. **McHugh would testify**: *SLH-R*, June 23, 1914. **"perfectly safe"**: *SLH-R*, Jan. 14, 1914. **"lots of pain"**: Ibid. **"no serious hemorrhage"**: Ibid.

71 **friend of McHugh's**: *SLT*, Jan. 15, 1914. **decided to drop in**: *SLTele*, Jan. 14, 1914. **ten years older**: The 1910 U.S. Census lists Bird's age as thirty-five and his "estimated birth year" as 1875; the 1920 U.S. Census gives McHugh's age as thirty-six and his birth year as about 1884. Ancestry.com; Thirteenth Census of the United States; Fourteenth Census of the United States.

71 **newspapers variously placed**: *SLT*, Jan. 14, 1914; *SLH-R*, Jan. 15, 1914; *DEN*, Jan. 14, 1914; *SLTele*, Jan. 14, 1914. **"about through dressing"**: McHugh to Jensen, Nov. 26, 1947.

71 **"large automatic revolver"**: *DEN*, Jan. 14, 1914. **he could not**: *SLTele*, June 22, 1914. **a good look**: *SLH-R*, June 23, 1914.

72 **their Swedish farmstead**: Swedish Church Records, Närke och Värmland; Värmland Rudskoga AI:26 36500 p.o/183, Household Examination 1891–1895, 2.4.4. GID: 519.42.36500, Genline FamilyFinder. **"one's windows broken"**: Mulder, 47. **"wild beasts"**: Hesslink, 122, quoting from the 1883 unpublished autobiography "History of Helena Rosbery."

72 **later deported**: "Historical Sketch of J.E. Forsgren," *Box Elder News*, Aug. 1, 1916. **thirty thousand Scandinavians**: Hesslink, 122–23. **Carl Eselius**: Swedish Church Records, Närke och Värmland; Värmland Rudskoga AI:26 36500 p.o/183, Household Examination 1891–1895, 2.4.4. GID: 519.42.36500, Genline FamilyFinder.

72 **first to emigrate**: Swedish Emigration Records, 1783–1951, Ancestry.com. (The record lists her destination as Springfield, Minnesota, but that was most likely a clerical error. Betty Eselius and her family were bound for Springfield, *Missouri*, forty miles northeast of Verona.) **established Swedish community**: For a concise history of the "Swedish colonies" in Lawrence County, Missouri, see Miller et al., 358. **sometime before 1910**: The 1910 U.S. Census lists the family in Murray.

72 *The Escape: SLH-R*, Jan. 10, 1914. **nightcap and tamales**: *SLT*, Jan. 15, 1914.

72–73 **"son of a gun"**: Joseph A. Curtis interview with John Eselius, in Curtis, 302–3. **"sullen and morose"**: *DEN*, Jan. 22, 1914. **"He still refuses"**: Ibid.

73 **boarded in Salt Lake**: She lived at 229 East South Temple. R. L. Polk, *Polk's Salt Lake City Directory*, 1913, 336; Erickson to Haan, June 22, 1949. **middle of August**: Hill and Appelquist roomed together at the Eseliuses for two weeks in August, according to *SLT*, Jan. 15, 1914.

74 **future son-in-law**: In a letter to Governor William Spry, O. Lindegren of Garfield, Utah, wrote, "Hilda . . . kept company with Applequist [*sic*] and the mother on Xmas Eve (previous to the murder) introduced him to me as her intended son in law." Sept. 28, 1915, SP, reel 2, part 2. **"got very angry"**: Erickson to Haan, June 22, 1949. **Hilda overheard Hill**: Ibid.

74 **tinkering with a motorcycle**: *SLT*, Jan. 16, 1914.

75 **"Hilda and I"**: Police found the note, along with five dollars and sixty cents, in Hill's pocket when he was searched upon arrest. *SLT*, Jan. 14, 1914.

75 **"We found Joe"**: Erickson to Haan, June 30, 1949.

75 **a snoozing Appelquist**: *SLT*, Jan. 15, 1914. **Appelquist was resolute**: Ibid.

75 **"What's the matter?"**: Erickson to Haan, June 22, 1949.

76 **"out in the country"**: Jensen, 358. The article is riddled with errors small—numerous incorrect dates, for instance—and large: "no [IWW] strike was ever won in Utah in those days"; Morrison "had taken part" in an arrest of Frank Z. Wilson; McHugh's office was "about two and one-half miles from the scene of the homicide" (it was twice that distance). Jensen also reads Hill's mind: when the sheriff entered Hill's room to arrest him, Jensen writes, Hill "made a move for his pistol, which *he thought* was by his bedside." (Emphasis added.) **Bird also pleaded**: *SLH-R*, Jan. 15, 1914.

76 **incredible, claim**: McHugh to Jensen, Jan. 26, 1948. **"wanted some money"** (footnote): Jensen, 358.

76–77 **"confidential and privileged"**: McHugh to Jensen, Jan. 26, 1948.

77–78 **nominee for governor**: The winner, Simon Bamberger, a Jewish émigré from Germany, was the first Utah governor who was non-Mormon and a Democrat, as well as the second Jewish governor of any state. Powell (online), n.p.

77–78 **"Dear Governor Spry"**: Dec. 7, 1915, SP, reel 2, part 2.

78 **"make him drowsy"**: Curtis, 295, citing DA, 86. **"might be arrested"**: *SLTele*, June 22, 1914. **large-caliber gun**: Hill, McHugh warned Peters, "had a big automatic pistol and might try to use it." *SLTele*, Jan. 14, 1914.

78–79 **"leaped from his bed"**: *SLH-R*, Jan. 14, 1914; **reached under his pillow**: *SLH-R*, Jan. 15, 1914. **"I fired immediately"**: *SLH-R*, Jan. 15, 1914. **"semiconscious condition"**: *SLH-R*, Jan. 14, 1914. **"officer's inefficiency"**: Hill to Utah Board of Pardons.

79–80 **five A.M. scoop**: *SLH-R*, Jan. 14, 1914.

80 **"size and height"**: *SLT*, Jan. 15, 1914.

80 **press verdict**: Jan. 14, 1914, edition of *SLT* and *SLH-R*.

80–82 **two o'clock services**: *SLT*, Jan. 15, 1914.

82 **boldface bulletin**: *SLT*, Jan. 14, 1914.

82 **physical characteristics**: Comparison of "Joe Hillstrom Criminal Record" and "F. Z. Wilson Criminal Record."

82–83 **"Applequisting"**: *DEN*, Jan. 19, 1914.

83 **the agent's correspondence**: Groom to Donnelley. **most recent known robbery**: See "Box Car Robbers in Town Last Night," *EDFP*, Jan. 10, 1914.

83 **brazen job**: *Nevada v. Morton*. Olson, as "James Morton," pleaded guilty on Feb. 10, 1914. For news coverage of the crime, see *SLTele*, Feb. 5, 1914; *EI*, Feb. 6, 1914; and *EDFP*, Feb. 10, 1914. The latter story reports that "Morton" is said "to have been one of the leaders of a gang of box car thieves who have been operating between Reno and Ogden." **couple of overcoats**: *EDFP*, Jan. 27, 1914, and Jan. 29, 1914.

83–84 **"Officers Winding Evidence"**: *SLTele*, Jan. 14, 1914. **"Winding the Meshes"**: *DEN*, Jan. 31, 1914. **"Forging the Chain"**: *SLT*, Jan. 31, 1914.

84 **whatever residual interest**: *SLTele*, Feb. 5, 1914. **confessed to a crime**: *SLTele*, Feb. 5, 1914.

84 **"not been involved"**: Ibid. **rife with grafters**: See, for example, Detective George Cleveland's efforts to exact "tribute" from an opium dealer: *DEN*, July 20, 1911, and Aug. 11, 1911. See also *SLTele*, July 13, 1915, for testimony by a former police officer turned whistle-blower at a police-corruption trial. He said that Detective W. C. Zeese was "protecting" sixteen gambling houses in the city. Zeese, who was one of the primary detectives on Hill's case, was reputed to be so dishonest that the district attorney, E. O. Leatherwood, declared in July of 1915 that he would "never again accept the uncorroborated testimony" of Zeese. See *DEN*, July 13, 1915. (Unfortunately for Hill, Leatherwood's declaration came a year after the district attorney had accepted Zeese's damaging testimony in his murder trial.) **"bought my way"**: Morton, *SEP*, Aug. 12, 1950, 28.

84 **"waive the formality"**: *SLTele*, Feb. 5, 1914. **pleaded guilty**: *Nevada v. Morton*; *EDFP*, Feb. 10, 1914.

84–85 **"model prisoner"**: *EDFP*, Apr. 15, 1916. **influential "connection"**: Morton, *SEP*, Aug. 12, 1950, 28.

85 **"My dear Jim"**: Emmet Boyle to James Morton, Sept. 26, 1916. The correspondence is included in Nevada State Prison Inmate Case Files, Morton, James, no. 1650. **"Despite this record"**: Clerk of the Boards of Pardons and Parole Commissioners to E. E. Vanderhoef, June 21, 1916, ibid. **"a great favor"** (footnote): Ibid.

85 **"King of the Box Car"**: *EDFP*, Apr. 15, 1916.

85–86 **first-time offender**: Nevada State Prison Inmate Case Files, Waite, Thomas, no. 1651. **"Man with Nightmare"** (footnote): *Nevada State Journal* and *Reno Evening Gazette*, Mar. 22, 1915. The headline appeared in the *Gazette*.

86 **"I am confident"**: *SLH-R*, Jan. 21, 1914.

86–87 **"a bad pair"**: Smith's letter is printed in its entirety in *DEN*, Jan. 22, 1914. **accomplished family**: *SLTele*, Jan. 23, 1914.

87 **an "unkempt" Hill**: *DEN*, Jan. 22, 1914. **"constantly drooped"**: Ibid. **"only half buttoned"**: Ibid.

87 **"enter my pleading"**: *SLH-R*, Jan. 23, 1914.
87 **"familiar with court"**: Ibid. **"wished to have"**: *DEN*, Jan. 22, 1914.
87–88 **"writer of songs"**: *DEN*, Jan. 22, 1914.

5. "The Thought for the Day and the Dream of the Night"

Sources

Books

Barton, H. Arnold, *Letters from the Promised Land*; Carlsson, Ingvar, and Anne-Marie Lindgren, *What Is Social Democracy?*; Dowie, J. Iverne, and Ernest M. Espelie, eds., *The Swedish Immigrant Community in Transition*; Foner, Philip S., ed., *The Letters of Joe Hill*; Haywood, William D., *The Autobiography of Big Bill Haywood*; Ibsen, Henrik, *Peer Gynt*; Ljungmark, Lars, *For Sale—Minnesota*; London, Jack, *The People of the Abyss*; McFarlane, James Walter, ed., *The Oxford Ibsen*, vol. 3; Misgeld, Klaus, et al., eds., *Creating Social Democracy*; Moberg, Vilhelm, *The Emigrants*; Montgomery, M. W., *A Wind from the Holy Spirit in Sweden and Norway*; Nelson, Marie C., and John Rogers, eds., *Mother, Father, and Child*; Nerman, Ture, *Joe Hill*; Nilsson, Ulf Ivar, *Gävle på 1800-talet*; Ramazzini, Bernardini, *Diseases of Workers*; Robinson, Michael, ed., *Strindberg's Letters*, vol. 1; Runblom, Harald, and Hans Norman, *From Sweden to America*; Rusten, Sharon O., *The One Year Book of Christian History*; Söderström, Ingvar, *En sång kan inte arkebuseras*; Stephenson, George M., *The Religious Aspects of Swedish Immigration*; Weindling, Paul, ed., *The Social History of Occupational Health*.

Documents

"An Overpopulated Countryside," from "From Sweden to America," published on the Web site of the Swedish Emigrant Institute (English version), http://www.utvandrarnashus .se/eng.

Branting, Hjalmar, "Why the Workers' Movement Must Become Socialistic," speech, Gävle, Sweden, Oct. 24, 1886, http://marxists.org/archive/branting/1886/workers-movement .htm.

Gefle arbetarsångförening/Manskören (Gävle Workers' Federation/Men's Chorus) Forum B1:2, Medlemsmatrikel 1901–1940, Arkiv Gävleborg, Gävle, Sweden.

GS 75, Examens-Katalog för Folkskolan Gossar I Stad, 1882–1894, F 4A:3, Gävle Kommun, Stadsarkivet, Gävle, Sweden. (Hill's report card.)

Joe Hill to E. W. Vanderleith, Sept. 4, 1914 (typescript "From Joe Hill's Letters"), General Correspondence, box 2, Frank P. Walsh Papers, Special Collections, Manuscripts and Archives Division, New York Public Library, New York City.

Personnel records, Book T1, Gävle-Dala Railway Co. archives, Swedish Railway Museum, Gävle, Sweden.

Real estate records, Gävle Municipal Archives, Gävle, Sweden.

Salvation Army (Gävle branch) papers (Gävle Frälsningsarmén), 1930–1990 F1:1, Arkiv Gävleborg, Gävle, Sweden.

Serafimerlasarettet (Royal Serafimer Hospital), Journal of Admitted Patients, 1900, Riksarkivet (National Archives), Arninge, Stockholm.

Interviews

Rolf Hägglund, Stockholm, August 2008; Eric Hedlund (telephone), August 2009; Sandra Lidberg (telephone), August 2009; Robert Herpai, archivist, Swedish Railway Museum, Gävle, Sweden, August 2008; Ulf Ivar Nilsson, Gävle, Sweden, August 2008; Peter Wennman (telephone), May 2008.

Journal and Magazine Articles

Blake, Donald J., "Swedish Trade Unions and the Social Democratic Party: The Formative Years," *Scandinavian Economic History Review* 8, no. 1 (1961): 19–44.

Gustafson, David M., "J.G. Princell and the Waldenströmian View of the Atonement," *Trinity Journal* 20, no. 2 (Fall 1999): 191–214.

Hesslink, George K., "Kimball Young: Seminal American Sociologist, Swedish Descendant, and Grandson of Mormon Leader Brigham Young," *Swedish Pioneer Historical Quarterly* 25, no. 2 (1974): 115–32.

Hildeman, Nils-Gustav, "Swedish Strikes and Emigration," *Swedish Pioneer Historical Quarterly* 8 (1957): 87–93.

Safstrom, Mark, "'America Is No Paradise'—Paul Peter Waldenström and Social Justice," *Pietisten* 21, no. 1 (Summer 2006), n.p (online: http://www.pietisten.org/summer06/pwsocialjustice.html).

Sköld, Peter, "From Inoculation to Vaccination: Smallpox in Sweden in the Eighteenth and Nineteenth Centuries," *Population Studies* 50 (1996): 247–62.

Thörn, Olof, "Glimpses from the Activities of a Swedish Emigrant Agent," *Swedish Pioneer Historical Quarterly* 10, no. 1 (1959): 3–24.

Waldenström, Paul Peter, "John 3:16,17 and Waldenström's Commentary," trans. Tommy Carlson, *Pietisten* 21, no. 1 (Summer 2006), n.p. (online: http://www.pietisten.org/summer06/waldenstrom.html).

Unpublished Typescripts

Hawkinson, Bernard A., "Paul Peter Waldenström: His Life and Contribution to the Swedish Free Church Movement," master's thesis, Andover-Newton Theological School, 1937.

Takman, John, "A Conversation with Joe Hill's Sister," interview with Ester Hägglund Dahl, Nov. 17, 1955, Joseph A. Curtis Papers, Accn 1229, Special Collections, Marriott Library, University of Utah, Salt Lake City.

Web site

Ancestry.com, http://www.ancestry.com (subscription required).

Notes

91 **220,000 of them**: Runblom and Norman, 118.

91–92 **proportion of Swedes**: Misgeld et al., xvii. **two in ten Swedes**: Ibid., xviii.

92 **isolated tenant farm**: Biographical material for the Hägglund family is from interviews and e-mail correspondence with Rolf Hägglund, Hill's grandnephew. Hägglund, a dogged genealogist, has documented his ancestry primarily through Church of Sweden records, which he shared with the author. Additional information was supplied by Peter Wennman, a grandnephew of Joe Hill's mother.

92 **more than double**: Figures in Nilsson, 17.

93 **"soft and clear soprano"**: Takman, 2.

94 *Nedre Bergsgatan* **28**: Real estate records, Första Quarteret, Möstaren 6, Gefle Stads, Lotbook, 98.

94 **two thousand crowns**: Ibid. **he earned yearly**: Personnel records, 64. **family could afford**: Takman, 1–2.

94–95 **Catharina tied mittens**: Takman, 2. **installed water pipes**: Ibid.

95 **"People of the soil"**: Moberg, xxvii. **"no other capital"**: "An Overpopulated Countryside."

95 **smallpox vaccine** (footnote): For more on smallpox eradication in Sweden, see Sköld.

96 **"born popular orator"**: Hawkinson, 76. **"easily the greatest"**: Stephenson, 106. **heavily lidded eyes**: For a more detailed description and a photograph, see Montgomery, 15 and frontispiece, respectively.

96 **"curiously deficient"**: Karl A. Olsson, "Paul Peter Waldenström and Augustana," *Swedish Immigrant Community in Transition*, 116.

97 **"savior who God"**: Waldenström, 2. **"social inequalities"**: Safstrom, 4. **"release the oppressed"**: Luke 4:18–19.

98–99 **"bird-cherries"**: Rolf Hägglund interview. **Olof was hurt**: Personnel records, 64. **he blamed himself**: Nerman, 33. **"pray for Pappa"**: Ibid., 34.

99 **"Blessed are the dead"**: Ibid.

99 **Bible-cradling soapboxer**: Ibid., 36–37.

99 **railroad paid Catharina**: Personnel records, 64. **taking in ironing**: Söderström, 29. **"hard to describe"**: Takman, 3.

99–100 **"high gents"**: The phrase, from the Social Democrats' *Arbetarbladet*, is cited in Jan Gröhndahl, "Single Mothers and Poor Relief in a Swedish Industrial Town (Gävle) at the Beginning of the Twentieth Century," Nelson and Rogers, 43. **"lazy and immoral"**: Ibid. **"enough of humiliations"**: Takman, 3.

100 **small alms**: Ibid. **quit technical school**: Ibid. **Paul, the next**: Personnel records, 83. **each was allotted**: Takman, 3.

101 **children would take up**: Söderström, 31. **almost certainly Olof**: This is informed speculation; no choir records from that era are preserved in the Bethlehem Chapel archives. **blended to great**: For more on Sandell and Oscar Ahnfelt, who composed many of her tunes, see Stephenson, 41; Rusten, 554–55.

101 **"reach the keys"**: Takman, 2. **played by heart**: Ibid., 5. **shooed him outdoors**: Söderström, 34.

101–2 **His report card**: GS 75, Examens-Katalog för Folkskolan Gossar I Stad. **Christian knowledge**: Ibid., 30.

102 **"gangly," "solitary" teenager**: Takman, 4. **"little more serious"**: Nerman, 41. **"there is no poetry"**: Hill to Vanderleith. **attributed his introversion**: Takman, 4. **"never be lonesome"**: Joe Hill to Katie Phar, n.d., 1915, reprinted in Foner, 25. **"I would rather"**: Joe Hill to Katie Phar, Mar. 4, 1915, ibid., 29.

103 **"taunting songs"**: Nerman, 38–39. **"see or imagine"**: Takman, 5. **"Mamma was angry"**: Ibid.

103 **from the hymnbook**: Nerman, 39, quotes Dahl as saying that "[Joel] used their [the Salvation Army's] melodies for taunting songs which he created about us." **founded its Gävle branch**: Salvation Army (Gävle branch) papers.

sought its financial assistance: Ibid. **"follow the directions"**: London, 131–32.

104 **"I had to go"**: Joe Hill to Katie Phar, n.d., 1915, reprinted in Foner, 25. **"kept on complaining"**: Takman, 6.

104 **destroyed five hundred houses**: Nilsson interview. **Gävle's population**: Nilsson, 17. **110 factories operating**: Nilsson interview.

104 **"lowest possible level"**: Branting.

104–5 **Founded in 1866**: For a description and brief history of the federation, see "Gävle Arbetareförening," *Gefle Dägblad*, June 2, 2008.

105 **"lese-majesty"**: Carlsson and Lindgren, 7.

106 **"courts and bayonets"**: Branting. **management made examples**: Söderström, 18. **summoned military troops**: Hildeman, 87. **Kjellberg went undercover**: Robinson, 175. **"thought for the day"**: Kjellberg's writing is cited in Hildeman, 88.

106 **"like Siamese twins"**: Blake, 21. Blake points out that the Siamese twin analogy "was a favorite elsewhere in European socialism."

106–7 **Continental Congress**: Haywood, 181.

107–8 **worrisome splotches**: In Nerman, 41, Joel's friend P. E. Hedblom recalls that by the time he returned from a three-year stint as a seaman in 1896, Joel was undergoing X-ray therapy for his skin disease. **As early as 1700**: In *Diseases of Workers*, first published in 1700, Dr. Bernardini Ramazzini devotes a short chapter (257–61 in the bilingual 1940 reprint) to the occupational hazards of flax and hemp manufacturing. He writes, "For a foul and poisonous dust flies out from these materials, enters the mouth, then the throat and lungs, makes the workmen cough incessantly, and by degrees brings on asthmatic troubles." **"higher tuberculosis rates"**: The report of the researcher, Sir George Newman, is cited in Weindling, 109.

108 **unable to work**: Takman, 4. **attached the bow**: Dahl, quoted in Nerman, 39. **from job to job**: Nerman, 40, quoting Ruben L. Eriksson, says Joel worked at the box factory and the bathhouse; Dahl, in Takman, 5, says he also worked at the wood refinery. (The precise dates of employment could not be determined.)

108 **ticket to Stockholm**: Details of Joel's two-year stay in Stockholm are from Nerman, 41–42; Söderström, 34–36.

108 **"hunger and cold"**: Nerman, 41. **"love of life"**: Takman, 6.

108–9 **Serafimer Hospital**: Serafimerlasarettet. **What he witnessed**: Nerman, 42.

109–10 **"This will pass"**: Söderström, 36. **diagnosed with a fistula**: Ibid. **"Greatest Protector"**: Ibid., 37.

110 **"industry and handicraft"**: Material on the expo is courtesy of Anna Forsberg, archivist at Länsmuseet Gävleborg (the county museum), in Gävle. **"Faith in the Future"**: Nilsson interview.

111 **playing piano occasionally**: Nerman, 40. **Paul and Efraim sang**: The choral roster is in Gefle arbetarsångförening/Manskören. **according to Ruben Sjödin**: Nerman, 40. **One Ibsen scholar**: Ibsen, viii.

111 **"decent burial"**: McFarlane, 324.

111–12 **bereft over another**: Rolf Hägglund interview.

112–13 **"bed and the cupboard"**: Barton, 110. **"Swedes, snuff and whiskey"**: Ibid., 111. Barton and others cite this quote—or variations thereof—but none cite the original source. Even so, as Barton told me in an e-mail, "if Hill did not actually say that, he could very well have." **Copies of pamphlets**: Ljungmark, 30. **one wistful emigrant**: Barton, 17. For thorough discussions on the early use of agents and one state's propaganda techniques, see Ljungmark; Thörn.

113 **In 1902 alone**: Runblom and Norman, 118.

114 **October 18, 1902**: Cunard Line, List or Manifest of Alien Immigrants for the Commissioner of Immigration, Saxonia, Sailing from Liverpool Oct. 18, 1902, Arriving at Port of New York, Oct. 28, 1902, New York Passenger Lists, 1820–1957; Swedish Emigration Records, 1783–1951, Paul E. Hägglund, Joel E. Hägglund, both Ancestry .com.

114 **"a dog's life"**: Takman, 8. **married an American**: This newly discovered biographical material was pieced together primarily by a California writer and genealogist, Dianne Carlson Cook, and from interviews the author conducted with Eric Hedlund and Sandra Hedlund Lidberg, two of Paul's three U.S.-born grandchildren.

6. "Hallelujah, I'm a Bum!"

Sources

Audio Recording
Utah Phillips, "The 1910 Spokane Free Speech Fight," transcript and audio link posted online at Labor Notes, http://labornotes.org/node/1662.

Books
Anderson, Nels, *The Hobo*; Brissenden, Paul Frederick, *The I.W.W.: A Study of American Syndicalism*; Bruner, Robert F., and Sean D. Carr, *The Panic of 1907*; Chaplin, Ralph, *Wobbly*; Dubofsky, Melvyn, *We Shall Be All*; Flynn, Elizabeth Gurley, *The Rebel Girl*; Foner, Philip S., ed., *Fellow Workers and Friends*; Foner, Philip S., *History of the Labor Movement in the United States*, vol. 4; Foner, Philip S., ed., *The Letters of Joe Hill*; Glasscock, C. B., *The War of the Copper Kings*; Gordon, John Steele, *The Business of America*; Green, Archie, et al., eds., *The Big Red Songbook*; Howard, Joseph Kinsey, *Montana: High, Wide, and Handsome*; Kornbluh, Joyce L., ed., *Rebel Voices*; Lukas, J. Anthony, *Big Trouble*; Nerman, Ture, *Joe Hill*; Smith, Gibbs M., *Joe Hill*; Stavis, Barrie, *The Man Who Never Died*; Thompson, Fred, and Patrick Murfin, *The IWW: Its First Seventy Years*; Tyler, Robert L., *Rebels of the Woods*.

Documents
Charles L. Anderson to Fred Thompson, Nov. 18, 1947, box 102, folder 1, IWW Collection, ALUA.

Richard Brazier to Fred Thompson, Dec. 21, 1966, box 12, folder 25, Fred Thompson Collection, ALUA.

Paul and Joel Hägglund to "B(est) B(rother) Efraim," Oct. 27, 1902. Translated by Rolf Hägglund (Efraim's grandson) for the author, who has a photocopy.

Frances E. Horn to Philip P. Mason, Jan. 29, 1980, box 13, folder 14, Fred Thompson Collection, ALUA.

Fred Thompson to J. N. Beffel, Apr. 14, 1948, box 4, folder 3, Beffel Collection, ALUA.

Fred Thompson to Gibbs Smith, Jan. 2, 1967, box 14, folder 4, Fred Thompson Collection, ALUA.

Interview

Shirley Rudberg (Karl Rudberg's daughter-in-law; telephone), May 2008.

Journal and Magazine Articles

Ashleigh, Charles, "The Floater," *International Socialist Review* 15, no. 1 (1914): 34–38.

Baker, Ray Stannard, "The Revolutionary Strike," *American Magazine*, May 1912, 19–30c.

Brazier, Richard, "The Story of the I.W.W.'s 'Little Red Songbook,'" *Labor History* 9 (Winter 1968): 91–105.

Chaplin, Ralph, "Joe Hill, a Biography," *Industrial Pioneer* 1, no. 7 (1923): 23–26.

Holbrook, Stewart, "The Wild, Wild Wobblies," *True*, October 1949, 126–36 (author used online version: http://www.workerseducation.org/crutch/others/true.html).

Odell, Kerry A., and Marc D. Weidenmier, "Real Shock, Monetary Aftershock: The San Francisco Earthquake and the Panic of 1907," working paper 9176, National Bureau of Economic Research, Cambridge, MA, September 2002.

"Spokane—Inland Empire Gateway," *Timberman*, November 1909, 47.

Walsh, J. H., "Developments at Spokane," *IUB*, Apr. 4, 1908.

——, "IWW 'Red Special' Overall Brigade," *IUB*, Sept. 19, 1908.

Pamphlet

St. John, Vincent, *The IWW: Its History, Structure and Methods* (New Castle, PA: IWW Publishing Bureau, n.d.).

Unpublished Typescripts

Kensel, William Hudson, "The Economic History of Spokane, Washington, 1881–1910," PhD diss., Washington State University, 1962.

Nerman, Ture, "Labor Singer JOE HILL, Murderer or Martyr," n.d., box 101, IWW Collection, ALUA. This thirty-two-page English-language typescript is excerpted from Nerman, *Arbetarsångaren Joe Hill, mördare eller martyr?* (Note: my edition is a paperback reprint of a 1968 edition, which drops "Folksinger" from the title.)

Web site

Ancestry.com, http://www.ancestry.com (subscription required).

Notes

115 **"Coming to America"**: Hägglunds to "B(est) B(rother) Efraim.

116 **5 Water Street**: This is the return address on the note to Efraim.

116–17 **swept the floors**: This itinerary is derived from three principal sources: Chaplin, *Wobbly*, 184–85; Chaplin, "Joe Hill," 23–26; Nerman, "Labor Singer," 5–6. All draw from stories told by John (or, in Nerman's article, Jim) Holland, who claimed to be Hill's cousin. Hill's sister Ester Hägglund Dahl later said she believed that Holland was probably her and Hill's brother, Paul Hägglund (who went by Paul Hedlund in the United States). **"word by word"**: Chaplin, *Wobbly*, 184–85.

118 **Christmas card**: Photocopy of the card in the author's possession, courtesy of Barrie Stavis.

118–19 **"I woke up"**: Hill wrote the article on Apr. 24, 1906. It was published on May 16, 1906. It is reprinted in Swedish in Nerman, *Joe Hill*, 50–52, and in English in Smith, 49–50.

120 **"Come with me"**: Horn to Mason.

121 **dousing the pulley**: Ibid.; Shirley Rudberg interview. **"exceptional demand"**: St. John, 19. **four largest mills**: Foner, *History*, 89. **nine-hour day**: St. John, 19. **"procession was formed"**: Foner, *History*, 89.

121 **appeal for solidarity**: Ibid., 91. **his first article**: *IW*, Aug. 27, 1910.

121–22 **"forced indirectly"**: St. John, 19. **"west coast progress"**: Thompson and Murfin, 34. **"new and strange"**: Reprinted in *Industrial Union Bulletin*, Apr. 27, 1907, and cited in Brissenden, 206.

122 **200 locals**: Brissenden, 207. **entire Mining Department**: Ibid., 129–30. **"nearly wiped out"**: Ibid., 211.

122 **economic chain reaction**: Odell and Weidenmier, 6–8. **Fritz Augustus Heinze**: For more on Heinze's background, see Glasscock, 122–30. For his copper-market manipulations, see Gordon, 67–71; Howard, 69–84.

122–23 **"take the places"**: *SS-R*, Oct. 12, 1907. **"perpetual warfare"**: Ashleigh, 35.

123 **"penniless and homeless"**: Brazier, 93. **cash his paycheck**: *SS-R*, Nov. 14, 1907. **of eight hundred**: Tyler, 30. **"black with jobless"**: Brazier, 93.

123–24 **charge of conspiring**: For a monumental study of the case, see Lukas. **ideology and rhetoric**: For a thorough discussion of the philosophical differences alluded to in the footnote, see Brissenden, chap. 5. **ten thousand dues-paying**: Ibid., 131.

124 **became a biweekly**: Ibid., 131–32.

124 **city's population**: For an analysis of Spokane's rapid growth, see Kensel, 92.

124–25 **"more commodious hall"**: Brazier, 93. The words are Brazier's, not Walsh's.

125 **private employment agencies**: Tyler, 34. **"jungled up"**: Phillips, quoting Edwards. **"order for thirty"**: *IW*, Mar. 25, 1909. **"Not one in fifty"**: Ibid.

125–26 **"rake-off"**: *SS-R*, Nov. 12, 1907. In a criminal case filed against one employment agency, a former employee testified to the rake-off arrangement and said that the contractor in question received "one-third of the fees paid" to the employment agency by men sent to that contractor. **"not merely inadequate"**: Anderson, 110. Anderson was describing agents in Chicago, where he was a graduate student at the University of Chicago. **"perpetual motion"**: Phillips, quoting Edwards.

126 **had been "robbed"**: *IW*, Mar. 25, 1909. **"real or imaginary"**: Ibid. **"beneficial and necessary"**: *SS-R*, Mar. 8, 1908.

126–27 **"under its heel"**: *SS-R*, Apr. 13, 1908. The quotation may not be verbatim; appended to it is the reporter's disclaimer "or words to that effect."

127 **"I'm working now"**: Brazier, 94–95.

127 **"eagerly listening assemblage"**: *SS-R*, Apr. 13, 1908.

127 **recalled Walsh's declaration**: Brazier, 94.

127–28 **distinctive red cover**: Ibid., 93. **"songs of anger"**: Ibid., 97.

128 **"Good-bye dollars"**: Lyrics in Green et al., 55–56.

128–29 **"I remember you"**: Ibid., 65.

129 **"word up songs"**: Walsh, "Developments."

129 **"some of the boys"**: Thompson to Beffel. Thompson here is reconstructing a conversation he had three years earlier with Carmody.

129–30 **"clear-thinking" countryman**: Anderson to Thompson.

130 **"used them effectively"**: Thompson to Beffel.

130 **"pesky go-abouts"**: The quote and description are from Green et al., 52. **"sold like hotcakes"**: Walsh, "IWW." **Scholars disagree** (footnote): One reason it is difficult to ascribe authorship is the song's many verses and iterations. The folklorist John Greenway's 1953 book *American Folksongs of Protest* gives credence to the authorial claim to at least some of the verses of Harry "Haywire Mac" McClintock, a Wobbly musician who once went to court over his claim of copyright. But the IWW's Richard Brazier writes that George Speed, a Wobbly "old-timer," "used to laugh himself sick at the idea that any one man ever wrote that song." Speed was a veteran of Jacob Coxey's Army of the Unemployed. He said that the army sang "Hallelujah" during its protest march to Washington, D.C., in 1894, when McClintock was ten years old (Brazier to Thompson). And according to the historian Joyce L. Kornbluh, it was also sung by soldiers in the Spanish-American War of 1898 (Kornbluh, 71). Jack Walsh, writing in the *IUB*, says that the "genius" of the songwriters in the Spokane IWW hall was "expressed in . . . the composition and rendition at the street meetings as well as in the hall of ['Hallelujah']" (Walsh, "Developments"). Fred Thompson, the IWW historian, wrote to a friend in 1948 that "I am satisfied Joe Hill was in Spokane in 1908 and had a hand at least in writing 'Hallelujah'" (Thompson to Beffel). For more on the various claims, see Green et al., 52–54.

131–32 **"Don't Buy Jobs"**: Foner, *History*, 178. **all the stiffs**: Description drawn from Ashleigh, 36.

132 **sharks' shady practices**: Flynn, 106.

132 **"any effort made," "best known example," and *Solidarity* also distinguished** (footnote): Foner, *History*, 135.

132 **"learn to fight"**: Foner, ibid., citing Mary E. Marcy, *Shop Talks on Economics* (Chicago: Charles H. Kerr, n.d.), 54. (Foner cites an incorrect page number.) **"hit the employer"**: Kornbluh, 37, citing Walker C. Smith, *Sabotage, Its History, Philosophy, and Function* (Spokane: Industrial Workers of the World, n.d.), 8.

132 **Associated Agencies**: Foner, *History*, 178, citing *IW*, July 20, 1911. **"beginning to pinch"**: *IW*, June 3, 1909.

132–33 **"good propaganda"**: Brazier, 91–92.

133 **"Coffee An'"**: Lyrics in Green et al., 108–9. **"itinerants first met"** (footnote): ibid., 108.

133 **"Nearer My Job"**: Lyrics in ibid., 127.

135 **"Mr. Block"**: Lyrics in ibid., 116–17.

135 **"pacified the multitude"**: *SS-R*, Jan. 18, 1909. **"hired Pinkertons"**: Thompson and Murfin, 48, citing *IUB*, Feb. 7, 1909.

135 **city's discriminatory intent**: For the specifics of the ordinance, see *IW*, Nov. 3, 1909.

135–36 **"Men to Fill"**: Thompson and Murfin, 48, citing *IW*, Oct. 28, 1909.

136 **form a blueprint**: For background on the fights, see Kornbluh, 94–98; Foner, *Fellow Workers*, 4–22. **"Wild, Wild Wobblies"**: Holbrook, 7–8.

136 **jailed and "disciplined"**: Chaplin, *Wobbly*, 150. **"Where are the cops?"**: Thompson and Murfin, 49. **"never to be forgotten"**: *IW*, Mar. 18, 1909. **"teeth kicked out"**: Flynn, 107.

136–37 **"howling, singing"**: Holbrook, 7–8. **city conceded defeat**: Kornbluh, 95. **jails were cleared**: Tyler, 39. **acted to regulate**: Ibid.

137 **"fought" with Hill**: *SOL*, Jan. 9, 1915. **"All I can say"**: Brazier to Thompson.

137 **"odd jobs"**: 1910 U.S. Federal Census, Los Angeles Assembly District 70, Ancestry.com. Westergren was listed as "Oscar West."

137–38 **"On the Road"**: *IW*, Aug. 27, 1910.

138–39 **"cloak of humor"**: From Hill's letter to the editor of *SOL*, Nov. 29, 1914, reprinted in Foner, *Letters*, 16. **". . . in the jungles . . ."**: The original subtitle of *The Little Red Songbook*. **"the curious lift"**: Baker, 30a.

7. A Suburb of Hell

Sources

Books
Cannon, James P., *Notebook of an Agitator*; Drury, Wells, and Aubrey Drury, *California Tourist Guide and Handbook*; Dubofsky, Melvyn, *We Shall Be All*; Foner, Philip S., ed., *Fellow Workers and Friends*; Foner, Philip S., *History of the Labor Movement in the United States*, vol. 4; Gottlieb, Robert, and Irene Wolt, *Thinking Big*; Green, Archie, et al., eds., *The Big Red Songbook*; Halberstam, David, *The Powers That Be*; Mayo, Morrow, *Los Angeles*; McDougal, Dennis, *Privileged Son*; Rawls, James J., *California: An Interpretive History*; Street, Richard Steven, *Beasts of the Field*; Woeste, Victoria Saker, *The Farmer's Benevolent Trust*.

Documents
1880 U.S. Federal Census, Grant, Cass, Missouri, Ancestry.com (subscription required).

Jail records, Fresno County, California, August 1910–March 1911, Fresno County Historical Society.

U.S. Commission on Industrial Relations, *Final Report and Testimony*, vol. 5 (Washington, D.C.: Government Printing Office, 1916).

Journal and Magazine Articles and Reports
California: Resources and Possibilities, Twenty-first Annual Report of the California State Board of Trade, for the Year 1910 (San Francisco: California Development Board, 1911).

Genini, Ronald, "Industrial Workers of the World and Their Fresno Free Speech Fight, 1910–1911," *California Historical Quarterly* 53, no. 2 (Summer 1974): 101–14.

Mason, Philip, "Joe Hill—Cartoonist," *Labor History* 25, no. 4 (Fall 1984): 553–57.

Robertson, William, "Empire-Building Irrigation: How an Inland Empire Has Been Created in Fresno County, Central California," *Sunset*, March 1910, 351–54.

Vaught, David, "Factories in the Field Revisited," *Pacific Historical Review* 66, no. 2 (1997): 149–84.

Unpublished Typescripts

Lehmann, Ted, "The Constitution Guarantees Freedom of Speech—Rats! The Fresno
    Free Speech Fight," May 25, 1971, California History and Genealogy Room, Fresno
    County Public Library, Fresno, CA.
Roscoe, Will, "The Murder of Frank Little: An Injury to One Is an Injury to All," July
    1, 1973, http://www.willsworld.org/butte/franklittle.pdf (also available at the Mon-
    tana Historical Society, Helena, MT). A published book, *The Truth About the Lynch-
    ing of Frank Little* (Butte, MT: Old Butte Publishing, 2003), plagiarizes nearly the
    entire text of Roscoe's work, according to an Associated Press story, Sept. 9, 2006.
    The book's value lies in its fine collection of period photographs and illustrations.
Weintraub, Hyman, "The IWW in California, 1905–1931," master's thesis, UCLA, 1947.

Web site

Ancestry.com, http://www.ancestry.com (subscription required).

Notes

141 **"game-warden roaring"**: Mayo, 191. **"General" Otis**: For details on how Otis
    enhanced his military rank, see McDougal, 12, 32. (Note, however, that McDou-
    gal lists Otis's discharge rank as major.) **"loaded shotguns"**: Gottlieb and Wolt,
    23. For more on Otis, his background, and how he came to acquire the *Times* and
    his antiunion ideology (he was once a union printer himself), see ibid., pt. 1;
    Halberstam, 135–51. **actually been discharged** (footnote): National Park Ser-
    vice, US Civil War Soldiers, 1861–1865, Ancestry.com.

142 **"cradle of industrial liberty"**: *LAT*, July 10, 1910. **"closed shop"**: Rawls,
    240–41.

142 **degree of solidarity**: See ibid., chap. 20.

142 **"labor union wolves"**: Gottlieb and Wolt, 84. **"Unionist Bombs Wreck"**:
    LAT, Oct. 1, 1910. Note: This edition is not included in electronic databases.
    The *Times* reprinted the front page of Oct. 1, 1910 in a retrospective published
    on Oct. 15, 1929.

142–44 **four thousand copies**: Foner, *History*, 150. **display and classified**: *IW*, Oct. 15,
    1910. **terse and typical**: *IW*, May 21, 1910.

144 **would be eleven**: Weintraub, 23. **"IWW never had"**: *IW*, July 20, 1911.

145 **"[mints] its millionaires"**: Robertson, 351. **city was smack**: A monument on
    the west side of the city marked it as the geographic center of California. **state's
    leading producer**: For Fresno County production of table grapes, wine grapes,
    and raisins in 1910, see *California: Resources and Possibilities*, 28–29. **world's
    largest supplier**: Drury and Drury, 265.

145 **"all California falls"**: *IW*, Nov. 2, 1910.

145–46 **personal letter**: Chester H. Rowell to W. M. Giffen, Dec. 10, 1909, cited in
    Vaught, 149. **exemplified that indivisibility**: For more on Rowell's public and
    private interests, which were many and varied, see his entry in the *Fresno Bee*'s
    2007 list of the twenty most influential people in the county's 150-year history,
    http://dwb.fresnobee.com/special/150/story/12749670p-13444876c.html. **"If you
    undertake"**: Street, 604, citing *SOL*, Mar. 11, 1911.

146 **"creating a disturbance"**: *FMR*, Aug. 27, 1910. **"talking socialism"**: *LAT*, Aug. 26, 1910. **"half Indian"**: See, for instance, the poem "To Frank H. Little," by his contemporary Phillips Russell, reprinted in Green et al., 180–81. For more on Frank Little, see Roscoe; Cannon, 32–36. **"perjured jury"**: Weintraub, 24, citing *IW*, Sept. 10, 1910. **"jails and dungeons"** and **"dark cell"**: *FMR*, Sept. 3, 1910. **"If a noose"** (footnote): *FMR*, Feb. 15, 1911. **mob hanged him** (footnote): For a summary of the circumstances of Little's death, see Dubofsky, 391–92. For a longer treatment, see Roscoe. **"an abiding horror"** (footnote): Biographer William F. Nolan quotes Hellman and assesses the impact of Little's death on Hammett in his introduction to a collection of Hammett's stories, *Nightmare Town* (New York: Knopf, 1999), viii.

146–47 **"All Aboard"**: Genini, 105, citing *IW*, Sept. 10, 1910.

147 **"Joe Dock"**: Jail records, Nov. 19, 1910, 349. Incidentally, the arrest date was five years to the day before Hill was executed.

147 **thriving little railroad**: In 1891, the Southern Pacific established Coalinga as a coaling station for its steam locomotives. The site was known originally as Coaling A, hence the town's name. For more, see the Coalinga Area Chamber of Commerce online article "The Boom Town That Lived," http://www.coalingachamber.com/about.html. **took their complaints**: *IW*, Oct. 8 and Oct. 19, 1910. (Note: with the Oct. 19 issue, the *IW* began publishing on Wednesdays rather than on its previous Saturday schedule.)

147 **"some real action"**: *IW*, Oct. 15, 1910.

148 **"out of reach"**: *IW*, Jan. 12, 1911. Perhaps he was working on the big downtown construction project, a "modern one-story business block," that had recently broken ground, according to the *FMR*, Sept. 3, 1910.

148 **"Der Chief"**: *IW*, Feb. 2, 1911.

150 **caricature of Rudberg**: The card, dated Jan. 24, 1911, is reproduced in Mason, 554.

150 **one of their songs**: Foner, *Fellow Workers*, 15, citing *SOL*, July 25, 1914.

150–51 **"agitators" advancing**: *FMR*, Oct. 19, 1910. **"One may not"**: *FMR*, Nov. 29, 1910. **Local 66 was evicted**: *IW*, Oct. 15, 1910; Oct. 19, 1910. **sympathetic Socialist**: *LAT*, Dec. 11, 1910; Genini, 108. **jail's bull pen**: *IW*, Oct. 19, 1910. **"Everyone is a vag[rant]"**: *IW*, Jan. 5, 1911.

151 **"IWW Plans to"**: *FMR*, Aug. 27, 1910. **"Armed Guards"**: *FMR*, Oct. 28, 1910. **"fierce, wild yell"**: *IW*, Oct. 26, 1910.

151–52 **one cheerful jailbird**: This Wobbly may not have been in the Fresno fight. The quote is from the *Kansas City Star*, Oct. 24, 1911, and is cited in Foner, *Fellow Workers*, 15. **"cat-o'-nine-tails"**: Oct. 12, 1910, excerpted in *IW* (under the headline ADVOCATES WHIPPING POST TO SUPPRESS FREE SPEECH), Oct. 26, 1910.

152 **"undesirable characters"**: *FMR*, Oct. 18, 1910. **"drive these men"**: Ibid.

152 **police court judge**: Ibid. **each man's bail**: Ibid. **going wage rate** (footnote): "Testimony of Mr. I.R. Bentley," general manager, California Fruit Canners' Association, Aug. 27, 1914, U.S. Commission on Industrial Relations, 4918. For immigrant groups' wage rates, see "Testimony of Mr. E. Clemens Horst," Aug. 27, 1914, ibid., 4924–25. Horst owned a large hop-growing firm bearing his name. **"chief agitator"**: *IW*, Oct. 26, 1910. **verdict would bind**: *FMR*, Oct. 18, 1910; Lehmann, 19.

153   **eighty-five troublesome**: Genini, 108. **one Wobbly's diary**: Minderman, "The Fresno Free-Speech Fight," in Foner, *Fellow Workers*, 112–13. The diary was obtained and printed by the U.S. Commission on Industrial Relations and is reprinted in Foner, 105–22.

153   **"use the toilet"**: Ibid., 105. **"Seventeen beds"**: Ibid., 106. **documents meals**: Ibid., 113. **"beans and punk"**: Ibid., 106. Foner says that punk was likely rotten meat. **underwear rations**: Ibid., 113. **visit from Salvation**: Ibid., 106. **"'shocking' and 'unpatriotic'"**: *LAT*, Dec. 1, 1910. The headline was ANARCHISTS GET NO AID.

153–54 *no such ordinance*: FMR, Dec. 9, 1910; Genini, 108.

154   **"Drive Out Loafers"**: *LAT*, Dec. 11, 1910.

154   **"reports were rife"** and **"tarred and feathered"**: *FMR*, Dec. 10, 1910.

154–55 **out of earshot**: *FMR*, Dec. 11, 1910.

155   **"uncontrollable fury"**: *FMR*, Dec. 10, 1910.

155   **"suburb of hell"**: *IW*, Feb. 9, 1911.

155   **telegraphed this message**: *IW*, Dec. 15, 1910.

155   **"Police Let Rioters"**: *Centralia Daily Chronicle*, Dec. 10, 1910. **"Mob Rule in Fresno"**: Cedar Rapids *Daily Republican*, Dec. 10, 1910. The Syracuse *Post-Standard* headline: DESTROYS HEADQUARTERS OF INDUSTRIAL WORKERS.

156   **"ideal climate"**: *IW*, Jan. 5, 1911. **"Land of Sunshine"** (footnote): Woeste, 45.

156–57 **derailed the plans**: *LAT*, Feb. 18, 1911. **"wet, cold and hungry"** and **"suffering terribly"**: E. M. Clyde, "On the Wobbly Train to Fresno," in Foner, *Fellow Workers*, 88. The diary originally appeared in *Labor History* 14 (Spring 1973): 264–90. It is reprinted in Foner, 79–105. **"those strange situations"**: Weintraub, 29, quoting from the *San Francisco Call*, Mar. 2, 1911.

157–58 **newly elected sheriff**: For a biographical sketch, and a bit more on his reformist leanings, see "Former Sheriffs of Fresno County, Walter S. McSwain," http://fresnosheriff.org/history/profiles/mcswain.htm.

158   **"Jail is full"**: *LAT*, Feb. 22, 1911. **"Fight Is Over"**: *IW*, Mar. 9, 1911.

8. Chicken Thieves and Outlaws

Sources

Books

Albro, Ward S., *Always a Rebel*; Blaisdell, Lowell L., *The Desert Revolution*; Bufe, Chaz, and Mitchell Cowen Verter, *Dreams of Freedom*; Cockroft, James D., *Intellectual Precursors of the Mexican Revolution*; Cohn, Alfred, and Joe Chisholm, *"Take the Witness!"*; Foner, Philip S., ed., *The Letters of Joe Hill*; Godoy, Jose F., *Porfirio Díaz, President of Mexico*; Gottlieb, Robert, and Irene Wolt, *Thinking Big*; Green, Archie, et al., eds., *The Big Red Songbook*; Johnson, William Weber, *Heroic Mexico*; Lundberg, Ferdinand, *America's 60 Families*; Mayo, Morrow, *Los Angeles*; McDougal, Dennis, *Privileged Son*; Meyer, Michael C., William L. Sherman, and Susan M. Deeds, *The Course of Mexican History*; Newell, Peter E., *Zapata of Mexico*; Pletcher, David M., *Rails, Mines, and Progress*; Pringle, Henry F., *The Life and Times of William Howard Taft*, vol. 2; Raat, W. Dirk, *Revoltosos*; Reesman, Jeanne Campbell, *Jack London's Racial Lives*; Robinson, W. W., *Bombs and Bribery*; Schoultz, Lars, *Beneath the United States*;

Tout, Otis B., *History of Imperial Valley*; Turner, Ethel Duffy, *Revolution in Baja California*; Turner, John Kenneth, *Barbarous Mexico*.

Documents

Joe Hill to Sam Murray, Sept. 30, 1915. Copy of original in the author's possession, courtesy of Archives Collection, Länsmuseet Gävleborg, Gävle, Sweden.

Ricardo Flores Magón to Eugene V. Debs, Apr. 6, 1911, available online at Archivo Electrónico Ricardo Flores Magón, http://archivomagon.net/ObrasCompletas/Correspondencia/Cor311.html

—— to Emma Goldman, Mar. 13, 1911, http://archivomagon.net/ObrasCompletas/Correspondencia/Cor306.html

—— to Samuel Gompers, Mar. 11, 1911, http://archivomagon.net/ObrasCompletas/Correspondencia/Cor305.html

General Services Administration, National Archives and Records Service, *Records Concerning Joseph Hillstrom, Alias Joe Hill, Etc.*, reference service report, Sept. 5, 1957, box 4, folder 6, Joseph A. Curtis Papers, Accn 1229, Special Collections, Marriott Library, University of Utah, Salt Lake City.

Revolutions in Mexico: Hearing Before a Subcommittee of the Committee on Foreign Relations, United States Senate (Washington, D.C.: Government Printing Office, 1913).

U.S. Department of State, *Papers Relating to the Foreign Relations of the United States* (Washington, D.C.: Government Printing Office, 1918).

U.S. Marine Corps Muster Rolls, 1798–1940, Online at Ancestry.com.

Journal and Magazine Articles and Reports

Brayer, Herbert O, "The Cananea Incident," *New Mexico Historical Review* 13, no. 4 (1938): 387–415.

Chamberlin, Eugene Keith, "Mexican Colonization Versus American Interests in Lower California," *Pacific Historical Review* 20, no. 1 (1951): 43–55.

Creelman, James, "President Díaz, Hero of the Americas," *Pearson's Magazine*, 19, no. 3 (1908): 231–77.

Gerhard, Peter, "The Socialist Invasion of Baja California, 1911," *Pacific Historical Review* 15, no. 3 (1946): 295–304.

"The Last Letters of Joe Hill," *Industrial Pioneer* 1, no. 8 (1923): 53–56.

Lorey, David E., ed., *United States–Mexico Border Statistics Since 1900*, 1990 update (Los Angeles: UCLA Latin America Center Publications, UCLA Program on Mexico).

Mason, Philip, "Joe Hill—Cartoonist," *Labor History* 25, no. 4 (Fall 1984): 553–57.

Turner, John Kenneth, "The Revolution in Mexico," *International Socialist Review* 11, no. 7 (1911): 417–23.

Unpublished Typescripts

Bryan, Anthony Templeton, "Mexican Politics in Transition, 1900–1913: The Role of General Bernardo Reyes," PhD diss., University of Nebraska, 1970.

Curtis, Joseph A., *Right Man? The Tragic Saga of Joe Hill*, Joseph A. Curtis Papers, Accn 1229, Special Collections, Marriott Library, University of Utah, Salt Lake City.

Hendricks, William Oral, "Guillermo Andrade and Land Development on the Mexican

Colorado River Delta, 1874–1905," PhD diss., University of Southern California, 1967.

Kerig, Dorothy Pierson, "Yankee Enclave: The Colorado River Land Company and Mexican Agrarian Reform in Baja California, 1902–1944," PhD diss., University of California, Irvine, 1988.

Myers, Ellen Howell, "The Mexican Liberal Party, 1903–1910," PhD diss., University of Virginia, 1970.

Web site

Ancestry.com, http://www.ancestry.com (subscription required).

Notes

159–60 **cheerfully called**: *LAT*, Mar. 1, 1911. **skillfully drawn**: *FMR*, Mar. 7, 1911. **"handle the exodus"**: *LAT*, Mar. 4, 1911.

160 **little-known tale**: For the best introductory account, see Blaisdell.

160–61 **rubber-limbed gent**: Mason, 555.

161 **"some smart jink"**: *IW*, May 25, 1911.

161 **life expectancy**: Meyer, Sherman, and Deeds, 455–56. The authors say that life expectancy was about thirty years, and that infant mortality averaged 30 percent during the Porfiriato. **confiscating the natural**: Turner, *Barbarous*, 105–06. **forced into peonage**: Ibid., 95.

161–62 **"Kill them on"**: Meyer, Sherman, and Deeds, 420. **frighteningly fearless**: For biographical material on Flores Magón and the influences on his early political development, see Albro, especially chaps. 1 and 2; Bufe and Verter, "Biographical Sketch," especially 21–35. And for primary source material, including a complete run of *Regeneración*, other published writing, and selected correspondence, see the Web site Archivo Electrónico Ricardo Flores Magón, http://archivomagon.net. **exposed the atrocities**: See, for example, an article in the issue of Dec. 31, 1900, translated and reprinted in Bufe and Verter, 121–22. **"vampires of finances"**: *Regeneración*, Mar. 11, 1911. **"insulting the president"**: Meyer, Sherman, and Deeds, 468–69; Bufe and Verter, 342. **"ridiculing public officials"**: Bufe and Verter, 343–44. **lower-court decree**: Albro, 20–21. **execution and exile**: Bufe and Verter, 344.

162 **"volcano of popular"**: U.S. Department of State, xi. **more than a billion**: Quoted in Raat, 238. **"injured or destroyed"**: U.S. Department of State, xi.

162–63 **"categorical declaration"**: Ibid., 413–14.

163 **"practice maneuvers"**: *NYT* and *LAT*, Mar. 8, 1911. **"save American lives"**: Quoted in Raat, 238.

163 **Francisco I. Madero**: See Raat, 203–26, on the origins of Madero's political philosophy. **"practically unanimous"**: Turner, *Barbarous*, 165–66.

164 **"malady that afflicts"**: *Regeneración*, Oct. 8, 1910, quoted and translated in Cockroft, 175. **"abolition of misery"**: Bufe and Verter, 74.

164 **T-shape**: For the topography and geology of the delta, see Hendricks, 22–25; Kerig, 42. **size of Massachusetts**: That state measures 10,554 square miles, according to the 2000 U.S. Census. See U.S. Census Bureau Web site, http://www

.census.gov/prod/cen2000/phc3-us-pt1.pdf, 71, table 17. **"cents an acre"**: Excerpted in Blaisdell, 66–67.

164–65 **"dingy" two-story**: *LAT*, Mar. 7, 1911.

165 **west to east**: Population figures for 1910, in Lorey, 25.

165–66 **"sound and justifiable"**: Gottlieb and Wolt, 168–69.

166 **including Taft's brother**: The many-tentacled Henry W. Taft was also a law partner of George A. Wickersham, the U.S. attorney general, whom Díaz had also rewarded with shares of stock in the Mexican National Railway. For both men's ties to the Mexican National Railway, see Turner, *Barbarous*, 232. For a list of the railway's directors—a who's who of American railroad executives and financiers—see *NYT*, Apr. 8, 1903. **"constant worry"**: *NYT*, Mar. 10, 1911. **"general uprising"**: *Revolutions in Mexico*, 249.

166 **"den of thieves"**: Albro, 12; 154, n. 32. *Manifesto to the Nation*: *Regeneración*, Sept. 30, 1905. **underground cells**: Cockroft, 125.

167 **"inciting the Mexicans"**: Brayer, 392–94. **"their own graves"**: Turner, *Barbarous*, 185. **"The little party"**: Ambassador David E. Thompson (Henry Lane Wilson's immediate predecessor) quoted Díaz in a June 5, 1906, telegram to U.S. Secretary of State Elihu Root. Cited in Cockroft, 145.

167–68 **seized the Liberals' mail**: For a discussion of what the historian James D. Cockroft calls an "international system of persecution" against the Liberals, see Cockroft, 127–28. See also Raat, chap. 7, for a vivid dissection of that system. **"bloodhound of Díaz"**: Quoted in Myers, 233.

168 **"set on foot"**: Turner, *Barbarous*, 253. And Turner, 256, cites the relevant text of the "neutrality laws": "Every person who, within the territory or jurisdiction of the US, begins, or sets on foot, or provides or prepares the means for, any military expedition or enterprise, to be carried on from thence against the territory or dominions of any foreign prince or state . . . with whom the US [is] at peace, shall be deemed guilty of a high misdemeanor, and shall be fined not exceeding $3,168; and imprisoned not more than three years."

168 **sympathetic railroad employees**: Bufe and Verter, 37; Cockroft, 124.

168–69 **"willful misrepresentations"**: Flores Magón to Goldman. **"cause of the disinherited"**: Flores Magón to Debs. **"promptly and decisively"**: Flores Magón to Gompers. **"gigantic money interests"**: Flores Magón to Goldman. **her "powerful appeals"**: *Regeneración*, May 13, 1911.

169 *Manifesto to the Workers*: *Regeneración*, Apr. 8, 1911.

169–70 **"real dope"**: *Revolutions in Mexico*, 199. **surgical care**: Ibid., 192. **"blasting purposes"**: Ibid., 193. **"operate machine guns"**: Ibid., 191–92. **"ready and willing"**: Ibid., 198–99.

170 **army had mustered**: Turner, *Revolution*, 6. **"labor exertions"**: Ibid.

170–71 **"astonishing ease"**: Ibid., 7. **shot him dead**: *LAT*, Jan. 30, 1911. **"Bandits Sack Mexicali"**: Ibid.

171 **department deployed**: *Regeneración*, Feb. 25, 1911. **"fomenting the present"**: Blaisdell, 67.

171 **"socialist agitator"**: *LAT*, Jan. 31, 1911. **"in the heart"**: *NYT*, Jan. 30, 1911. **"blood red" buttons**: *LAT*, Jan. 31, 1911. **road from Ensenada**: *LAT*, Feb. 1, 1911. **"borrowed" horses**: *LAT*, Jan. 31, 1911.

171–72 **"midnight assassins"**: *LAT*, Oct. 3, 1910. **"dear, brave comrades"**: *Los Angeles Citizen*, Feb. 11, 1911, reprinted in Reesman, 271–72.

172 **"rebel recruiting station"**: *IW*, May 25, 1911.

173 **traveled by boat**: According to notes of an immigration hearing held on June 25, 1913, Hill testified that "he left San Pedro the latter part of April 1911, went by boat to San Diego and entered Mexico at or near Tia Juana to join the rebel army and to help them overthrow Díaz." General Services Administration, *Records Concerning Joseph Hillstrom*. **"laid the catastrophe"**: *IW*, May 11, 1911. **graphic illustration** (footnote): Cohn and Chisholm, 197–201; Robinson, 29–33; McDougal, 57–58. For discrepancies between the confession of J. B. McNamara and the facts of the case, see Mayo, 185–88.

173–74 **soldier of fortune**: Gerhard, 301. **"General" Stanley Williams**: Little can be verified about Williams, including his real name. Blaisdell, 74, offers two other possibilities for his name and says he might have been from Cleveland, Ohio, not Canada. Turner, *Revolution*, 23, says he spent thirty days in jail in Spokane on bread and water. Gerhard, 297, says Williams was a former army sergeant from Holtville, CA, but it seems more likely that his only connection to Holtville was through its active IWW local. **had been a private**: Mosby enlisted on July 11, 1910, and deserted on Feb. 16, 1911, from Marine barracks at Mare Island, Vallejo, CA. U.S. Marine Corps Muster Rolls. **"yellow-backed dime novels"**: *Revolutions in Mexico*, 248. **Simon Berthold died**: Ethel Duffy Turner, who once edited the English-language page of *Regeneración*, personally knew Berthold and once harbored him in her house during a time when he was on the lam. See her *Revolution*, 33–34. **other original commander**: Gerhard, 298.

174–75 **la Bandera Roja**: *Regeneración*, May 13, 1911; *IW*, May 25, 1911. **"Liberty will spread"**: *NYT*, May 27, 1911.

175 **"Don't believe"**: *IW*, June 8, 1911.

175 **certain of victory**: *Regeneración*, May 20, 1911.

175 **damage and losses**: Harry Chandler reported the figures in a June 1 wire to Otis. Blaisdell, 174. **president would consent**: Harry Chandler to Francisco Madero, May 29, 1911, cited in Turner, *Revolution*, 40.

175–76 **"President Taft advises"**: Ibid. **took Taft up**: *Papers Relating to the Foreign Relations*, June 6, 1911, 499. **"shipped as baggage"**: Ibid., 503. **"face to face"**: Turner, *Revolution*, 38.

176 **"Republic of Díaz"**: For more on the strange case of Richard Ferris, see ibid., 44–51; Blaisdell, 60–64, 142–62.

176–77 **bunked with fellow**: Murray interview, in Curtis, 22. **"plug the federals"**: *IW*, June 8, 1911. **"was a piano"**: Murray interview, in Curtis, 22. **"a quiet man"**: Ibid.

177 **"Should I Ever"**: For the complete lyrics, see *IW*, Apr. 3, 1913; Green et al., 111–12. He borrowed the last line of the chorus from the Liberals' war cry.

177–78 **heavily armed force**: For details of the battle and its aftermath, some of which are contradictory, see Blaisdell, 180–81; Turner, *Revolution*, 63–64; Gerhard, 303–04. **killed en route**: Blaisdell, 195.

178 **convicted of flouting**: Gerhard, 304.

178–80 **"without being questioned"**: General Services Administration, *Records Concerning Joseph Hillstrom*. **"advance Freedom's Banner"**: Joe Hill to Oscar W.

Larson, Sept. 30, 1915, in Foner, 59. **"share of the fun"**: Hill to Murray. **enclosed a caricature**: The drawing was published with "The Last Letters of Joe Hill," 53.

9. "More Beast than Man"

Sources

Books

Akrigg, G. P. V., and Helen B. Akrigg, *British Columbia Chronicle, 1847–1871*; Blaisdell, Lowell L., *The Desert Revolution*; Brissenden, Paul Frederick, *The I.W.W.: A Study of American Syndicalism*; Cohen, Norm, *Long Steel Rail*; Davis, Mike, Kelly Mayhew, and Jim Miller, *Under the Perfect Sun*; Drury, Wells, and Aubrey Drury, *California Tourist Guide and Handbook*; Dubofsky, Melvyn, *We Shall Be All*; Flynn, Elizabeth Gurley, *The Rebel Girl*; Foner, Philip S., ed., *Fellow Workers and Friends*; Foner, Philip S., *History of the Labor Movement in the United States*, vols. 3 and 4; Foner, Philip S., *The Case of Joe Hill*; Foner, Philip S., ed., *The Letters of Joe Hill*; Fudge, Judy, and Eric Tucker, *Labour Before the Law*; Green, Archie, et al., eds., *The Big Red Songbook*; Kornbluh, Joyce L., ed., *Rebel Voices*; Leier, Mark, *Where the Fraser River Flows*; McWilliams, Carey, *California: The Great Exception*; Perlman, Selig, and Philip Taft, *History of Labor in the United States*, vol. 4; Perry, Louis B., and Richard S. Perry, *A History of the Los Angeles Labor Movement*; Person, Carl E., *The Lizard's Trail*; Phillips, Paul A., *No Power Greater*; Phull, Hardeep, *Story Behind the Protest Song*; Schroeder, Theodore, *Free Speech for Radicals*; Sinclair, Upton, ed., *The Cry for Justice*; Smith, Gibbs M., *Joe Hill*; Stavis, Barrie, *The Man Who Never Died*; Stavis, Barrie, and Frank Harmon, *The Songs of Joe Hill*; Townsend, John Clendenin, *Running the Gauntlet*; Vorse, Mary Heaton, *A Footnote to Folly*; Watson, Bruce, *Bread & Roses*; Winters, Donald E. Jr., *The Soul of the Wobblies*.

Documents

A Report to His Excellency Hiram W. Johnson, Governor of California, of Harris Weinstock, Appointed as Commissioner on Apr. 15, 1912, to Investigate Charges of Cruelty and All Matters Pertaining to the Recent Disturbances in the City of San Diego and the County of San Diego (Sacramento: State Printing Office, 1912). Hereafter abbreviated as "Weinstock report."

Report on Strike of Textile Workers in Lawrence, Mass. in 1912, Prepared under the direction of Chas. P. Neill, Commissioner of Labor (Washington, D.C.: Government Printing Office, 1912).

General Services Administration, National Archives and Records Service, *Records Concerning Joseph Hillstrom, Alias Joe Hill, Etc.*, reference service report, Sept. 5, 1957, box 4, folder 6, Joseph A. Curtis Papers, Accn 1229, Special Collections, Marriott Library, University of Utah, Salt Lake City.

U.S. Bureau of the Census, Thirteenth Census of the United States, 1910, and Fourteenth Census of the United States, 1920 (Washington, D.C.: National Archives and Records Administration).

Joe Hill to Sam Murray, Feb. 13, 1915, box 2, folder 1, Llano del Rio Collection, Department of Manuscripts, Henry E. Huntington Library, San Marino, CA.

Joe Hill to E. W. Vanderleith, Sept. 4, 1914, and n.d., (typescript "From Joe Hill's

Letters"), General Correspondence, box 2, Frank P. Walsh Papers, Special Collections, Manuscripts and Archives Division, New York Public Library, New York City.

Alexander MacKay to Aubrey Haan, Jan. 26, 1950. In the author's possession.

Alexander MacKay to Fred Thompson ("Fellow Worker Editor"), Nov. 27, 1947, box 102, folder 1, IWW Collection, ALUA.

Harry McClintock to Fred Thompson, July 9, 1950, box 102, folder 23, IWW Collection, ALUA.

Louis Moreau to Fred Thompson, Mar. 8, 1967, box 12, folder 28, Fred Thompson Collection, ALUA.

Fred Thompson to Richard Brazier, Dec. 18, 1966, box 12, folder 25, Fred Thompson Collection, ALUA.

Fred Thompson to Barry [sic] Stavis, Nov. 29, 1965, box 12, folder 24, Fred Thompson Collection, ALUA.

Journal and Magazine Articles and Reports

Baker, Ray Stannard, "The Revolutionary Strike," *American Magazine*, May 1912, 18–30C.

Chaplin, Ralph, "Joe Hill, a Biography," *Industrial Pioneer* 1, no. 7 (1923): 23–26.

McCormack, A. Ross, "The Industrial Workers of the World in Western Canada, 1905–1914," *Historical Papers* 10, no. 1 (1975): 167–90.

Miller, Grace L., "The IWW Free Speech Fight: San Diego, 1912," *Southern California Quarterly* 54 (Fall 1972): 211–38.

Reed, John, and Art Young, "The Social Revolution in Court," *Liberator*, September 1918, 22 (online at Marxists Internet Archive: http://www.marxists.org/history/usa/culture/pubs/liberator/1918/09/09.pdf).

Secor, Margaret A., "San Diego Looks at the Maderista Revolution in Mexico 1910–1911," *Journal of San Diego History* 18, no. 3 (Summer 1972): 1–8 (online: http://www.sandiegohistory.org/journal/72summer/maderista.htm).

Shanks, Rosalie, "The IWW Free Speech Movement, San Diego, 1912," *Journal of San Diego History* 19, no. 1 (Winter 1973): 1–16 (online: http://www.sandiegohistory.org/journal/73winter/speech.htm).

Stavis, Barrie, "Joe Hill: Poet/Organizer," *Folk Music Magazine*, June 1964, 2–4, 38–50.

Unpublished Typescripts

MacKay, Alexander, "The Preacher and the Slave: A Critical Review," n.d. (circa 1950). Copy of the original in the author's possession.

Ryan, Frederick L., "The Labor Movement in San Diego: Problems and Development from 1887–1957," Bureau of Business and Economic Research, San Diego State College, 1959.

Weintraub, Hyman, "The IWW in California, 1905–1931," master's thesis, UCLA, 1947.

Web Sites

Ancestry.com, http://www.ancestry.com (subscription required); FamilySearch.org, https://familysearch.org; Genline FamilyFinder, http://www.genline.se (subscription required).

Notes

181 **Hill "sojourned"**: MacKay to Thompson. **"true-blue rebel"**: *SLH-R*, Nov. 19, 1915.

181–82 **"Price of song"**: *IW*, July 6, 1911. **"long-haired preachers"**: Lyrics in Green et al., 99–100.

183 **"signature song"**: See, for instance, ibid., 99. **Hill's "masterpiece"**: Kornbluh, 132. **included in anthologies**: Hardeep. See also Sinclair, 476; Sandburg, 222.

183 **huge nationwide walkout**: *LAT*, Sept. 30, 1911. For a scholarly study of the strike in Los Angeles and its environs, see Perry and Perry, 53–67. For a clear, brief account of the issues and outcome of the nationwide walkout, see Perlman and Taft, 370–73. And for a most useful, if vitriolic, book-length attack on the craft unions (the Casey Joneses of the strike who "kept their junk piles running") by a participant, see Person (who edited the federation of shop workers' *Strike Bulletin*). **IWW supported the walkout**: "The men see the folly of dealing with such huge corporations, with separate crafts, and are working hard for the ONE BIG UNION," the *Industrial Worker* reported on Aug. 24, 1911.

183–84 **largest landowner**: Carey McWilliams, the state's preeminent mid-twentieth-century journalist, writes (95) that "as late as 1919, the Southern Pacific was still the chief landowner in California." With all that land, he writes (179), came unsurpassed economic power. "If ever a state was at the mercy of one corporation, California was at the mercy of the 'octopus'—the Southern Pacific." **"aggregation of moral germs"**: Carl E. Person, cited in Smith, 22 (footnote); Thompson to Stavis, Nov. 29, 1965.

184 **popular vaudeville song**: For various iterations of the song and the definitive discussion of its origins, see Cohen, 132–57. **In Hill's song**: Lyrics in Green et al., 103–04.

185–86 **"classic American song"**: Foner, *Case of*, 12. **"an awful [big] hit"**: Hill to Murray.

186 **"turned them loose"**: Shanks, 4 (online version). **"hysterical frenzy"**: Cited in Dubofsky, 190.

186 **"jerk water towns"**: Hill to Vanderleith, n.d.

186–87 **"Most Equable Climate"**: Display advertisement for U.S. Grant Hotel, *LAT*, Jan. 31, 1911. **secret meeting**: Ryan, 21. Others place the meeting in October 1911 (Davis et al., 40) or December 1911 (Townsend, 17). **"hero's welcome"** and **published maps** (footnote): Davis et al., 40.

187 **"determined to rid"**: *LAT*, Dec. 6, 1911.

187–88 **IWW was unfamiliar**: Brissenden, 284.

188 **cut their wages**: *Report on Strike*, 9. **thirty-two cents**: Watson, 12. **"short pay!"**: Kornbluh, 159. **half of the town's**: *Report on Strike*, 9. **"Better to starve"**: Flynn, 128.

188 **dues-paying members**: *Report on Strike*, 11. **"outlaw organization"**: *Boston American*, Jan. 21, 1912, cited in Watson, 67. **"not a strike"**: "Hearings on Strike at Lawrence, Mass.," Committee on Rules, U.S. House Document No. 671, Washington, 1912, cited in Foner, *History*, vol. 4, 339. **"bitter class hatred"**: Cited in Watson, 67.

188 **"nothing to cooperate"**: *New York Call*, Feb. 15, 1912, cited in Foner, *History*, vol. 4, 338.

189 **fifty-one nations**: Watson, 8. **forty-four languages**: Stavis, "Joe Hill: Poet/ Organizer," 41. **police killed**: *Report on Strike*, 13–14. **spring orders unfilled**: Dubofsky, 253. **Their offer provided**: For details of the agreement, see *Report on Strike*, 13, 15. **"most signal victory"**: Dubofsky, 253.

189 **"weld men together"**: Baker, 30A. **"seemed dangerous"**: Vorse, 6.

189–90 **"The Internationale"**: For complete lyrics, see Kornbluh, 174. **"suspicious intimacy"**: Cited in Smith, 27. **"most devastating attacks"**: Winters, 92. **"John Golden"**: Lyrics reprinted in Green et al., 109–10.

191 **ports of call**: *SPDN*, July 21, 1911, July 25, 1911, and Oct. 9, 1911. **"worked with Joe"**: McClintock to Thompson. **no corroborating evidence**: None of Hill's surviving correspondence mentions Hawaii; the steamship company's personnel records are nonexistent (although some of its historical materials are collected at the Huntington Library, San Marino, CA); and his name (or a variation thereof) was not published in the *Directory of Hawaii Island* for either 1911 or 1912. **"cadging drinks"**: Thompson to Brazier.

191 **"come to write"**: Cited in Kornbluh, 131.

192 **"likely to obstruct"**: Schroeder, 121. Chapter 10 of Schroeder's *Free Speech for Radicals* is a compilation of articles republished from Sunday editions of the *New York Call* beginning Mar. 15, 1914. **"beggars and crooks"**: Ibid.

192–93 **to cram seventy-eight**: According to a letter from Alexander MacKay, cited in ibid., 123. **"worse than animals"**: Weintraub, 43.

193–94 **most influential citizen**: For a biographical sketch of Spreckels, see the San Diego Historical Society's online article, https://www.sandiegohistory.org/bio/spreckels/spreckels.htm. For a list of his holdings, see *IW*, May 23, 1912. For more on his influence, see Blaisdell, 26. **"left labor galoot"** (footnote): Secor, 2 (online version). **"compelled to endure"**: Mar. 5, 1912, cited in Weinstock report, 17. **"guns and bloodshed"** (footnote): *SDU*, Feb. 10, 1912, cited in Townsend, 24. **"Hanging is none"**: *San Diego Evening Tribune*, Mar. 4, 1912, cited in Townsend, 18.

194–95 **Committee of 1000**: Its call to arms, as published in the letters column of the *SDU*, Apr. 12, 1912, and cited in Miller, 223–24: "We the law abiding citizens of this commonwealth think that these anarchists have gone far enough . . . and hereafter they will not only be carried to the county line and dumped there, but we intend to leave our mark on them in the shape of tar well rubbed into their hair, so that a shave will be necessary to remove it, and this is what these agitators . . . may expect from now on, that the outside world may know that they have been to San Diego." **"carried out unconscious"**: Tucker's letter to St. John was later printed by the U.S. Commission on Industrial Relations and reprinted in Foner, *Fellow Workers*, 138–41. For further description of the ambush at San Onofre, see also Charles Hanson letter to St. John, reprinted in ibid., 135–38; Schroeder, 149–50. **"jails are full"**: *SOL*, Mar. 30, 1912.

195 **"on the cushions"**: Feb. 29, 1912.

195–96 **who took passage**: In Tucker's letter to St. John reprinted in Foner, *Fellow Workers*, 139, he discusses the party who arrived by boat from San Pedro on Mar. 20, 1912. **they chose "Casey"**: Ibid. **"singing revolutionary songs"**: *LAT*, Mar. 23, 1912. **"third degree"**: Tucker, in Foner, *Fellow Workers*, 139.

196 **"L. Jorgensan"** *LAT*, Mar. 23, 1912.

196 **"side-door Pullman"**: John Reed used the phrase in his reportage of the IWW conspiracy trial in Chicago in 1918. See Reed, 22.

196–97 **"pale and pinched"**: *IW*, Apr. 11, 1912.

197 **"practiced sabotage"**: Ibid.

197 **"Loafers Coming South"**: *LAT*, Apr. 2, 1912.

198 **gold rush boomtown**: D. W. Higgins, quoted in Akrigg and Akrigg, 132.

198 **week to ten days**: Moreau to Thompson. **unsanitary and dangerous**: For a vivid, firsthand account of conditions, see *BCF*, June 22, 1912. **myriad deductions**: Cited in Phillips, 52. **"horse would run"** (footnote): *BCF*, July 27, 1912.

198–99 **"overalls and snuff"**: *BCF*, June 22, 1912.

199 **only known stanza**: Moreau to Thompson. And see Moreau to editor of *IW*, Nov. 15, 1947 (date of handwritten letter), for Moreau's recollection of a fragment of a song Hill wrote while in the Yale camp about Skookum Ryan, a construction superintendent "of the roaring variety." The fragment: "Skookum Ryan the Walking Boss / Came tearing down the line / Says he, you dirty loafers take your coats off / Or go and get your time."

199 **"men were cheaper"**: *BCF*, June 22, 1912.

199–200 **"vilest sort"**: Reprinted in Stavis and Harmon, 12. **discharged the waste**: *BCF*, June 22, 1912. **"becomes more beast"**: Ibid.

200–201 **"miniature republic"**: Quoted in McCormack, 178. **their spare time**: *IW*, Apr. 18, 1912. **"only two nationalities"**: Quoted in McCormack, 177. **wrote his first**: Moreau to Thompson. **decidedly unsentimental**: The song was first published in *IW*, May 9, 1912.

201–2 **"contemptible reptiles"**: *BCF*, June 29, 1912. **"could carry all"**: Ibid. **"you red necktie"**: Ibid. **"groaning brigade"**: Moreau to editor of *IW*, Nov. 15, 1947. For the lyrics, see Moreau to Thompson.

202–3 **"tore his hair"**: Moreau to editor of *IW*, Nov. 15, 1947. **send in strikebreaking**: Leier, 51; McCormack, 178. **"stupendous scheme"**: McCormack, 178. **"scum of humanity"**: *Vancouver Sun*, Apr. 8, 1912, cited in ibid., 179.

203 **private detectives**: Fudge and Tucker, 68–69. **"inciting to murder"**: Leier, 51. **250 men**: McCormack, 179.

203 **unloaded more board**: Drury and Drury, 158. **straw boss**: MacKay to Haan.

203 **"impossible to assimilate"**: Foner, *History*, vol. 3, 258. **"trouble-makers"** and **"nothing but seeds"**: Ibid.

203–4 **Lefferts later remembered**: Stavis, "Joe Hill: Poet/Organizer," 49.

204 **stevedore companies scoffed**: *San Pedro Pilot*, July 24, 1912. Neither the *LAT* nor the *SPDN* printed the workers' demands. **they shut down**: The steamer *Klamath* was unable to depart as scheduled, according to a shipping schedule in *LAT*, July 18, 1912. **another to unload**: The *Governor* had to unload at Redondo Beach. *SPDN*, July 23, 1912. **"Boss This Wharf"**: *LAT*, July 20, 1912. **"Grafters are Doomed"**: *SPDN*, July 23, 1912.

204 **"will employ Americans"**: *SPDN*, July 22, 1912.

204–5 **acknowledged as much**: *SLTele*, Aug. 22, 1915. **"old friend Otis"**: *IW*, Aug. 15, 1912.

205 **"practically black-balled"**: MacKay to Haan.

205 **MacKay had met Hill**: Ibid. **"Every blinded member"**: Weinstock report, 20.

205–6 **five were acquitted**: Ryan, 23. **"tar-paper shack"**: MacKay to Haan. **"jungle up"**: Ibid.

206 **1912 edition**: For the complete list of songs, see Green et al., 479; for those in the 1913 edition, see ibid., 479–80.

206 **"copious amount"**: MacKay to Haan. **"tremendous struggles"**: Ibid. **"most reticent cuss"**: MacKay to Thompson. **"actually knocked out"**: The quote is a composite drawn from the two letters of MacKay's previously cited here as well as from his typescript "The Preacher and the Slave."

207 **"No Law but Love"**: *LAT*, July 8, 1928. **Canadian-born minister**: Makins was born in about 1864 and emigrated from Canada in 1888, according to the 1920 U.S. Census. **Makins "liked Joe"**: Chaplin, 24. Chaplin based his narrative primarily on a chance interview he conducted in a Cleveland bar with a Swedish sailor who said his name was John Holland and who claimed he was Joe Hill's cousin. Some have speculated that Holland was actually Joe's brother Paul, who had changed his surname to Hedlund. But the story was laced with so many errors of biographical fact—Joe's family name, the year of his birth, and when and where he joined the IWW, to name a few—that it seems unlikely that Paul was Chaplin's source.

207 **"used our piano"**: Smith, 56; 215, n. 78, citing *Annual Report of the Sailors' Rest Mission, San Pedro, California*, Feb. 1, 1919, 2. **Hill wrote "Casey"**: Chaplin, 24. **Sailors' Rest provided**: *SPDN*, June 7, 1911, and Jan. 22, 1913. Most weeks, usually on Wednesday or Thursday, *SPDN* reported the musical acts scheduled at the mission.

207–9 **Otto Appelquist**: Appelquist was born on Feb. 2, 1890, according to his birth record and the church enumeration in his home parish. Research of original Swedish church records was conducted for the author by Randy Nelson of Seattle, WA, citing Swedish Church Records, Malmöhus; Helsingborgs Stadsförsamling AI:90 33400 p.0/2375, Household Examination 1891–1895, 3.0. GID: 1250.117.33400, Genline FamilyFinder. Once in the United States, however, Appelquist began listing his birth date as Feb. 2, 1887. One explanation for his adding three years to his age is to avoid induction for service in World War I. On registering for the draft on Sept. 15, 1917, he stated on his application card that he was born on Feb. 2, 1887. That would have made him thirty years and seven months old—seven months past the maximum age for compulsory service. See Otto Wilhelm Appelquist, World War I Draft Registration Card, Orleans County, Louisiana, Roll: 1684817, Ancestry.com. **John and Ed**: Ed was born in Aug. 1880, John in Feb. 1883, both in Rudskoga, Värmland, Sweden. Biographical sources of information on the Eselius brothers: 1910 U.S. Census for Murray City, Utah; Swedish emigration records posted on Ancestry.com; FamilySearch.org; and obituary of John Eselius, *SLTele*, Aug. 28, 1948. **"common pacific coast"**: Hill to Vanderleith, Sept. 4, 1914.

209 **structural ironworker**: The only known photograph of Appelquist, a detail from a group shot with fellow construction workers in Ogden, appeared in *SLH-R*, Jan. 15, 1914.

209 **"sweat great gobs"**: MacKay to Haan.

209 **arrested on suspicion**: General Services Administration, *Records Concerning Joseph Hillstrom*. **robberies rippling across**: *LAT*, Apr. 28, 1913. **One such job**: For details, ibid.; *SPDN*, Apr. 2, 1913. **Five weeks later**: In a letter written Jan. 16, 1914—two days after Hill's arrest in Salt Lake City—Smith told the Salt Lake City police of his arrest of Hill the previous June. The Salt Lake newspapers published the letter Jan. 23, 1914.

209–10 **offense was vagrancy**: General Service Administration, *Records Concerning Joseph Hillstrom*. **"little too active"**: *SLTele*, Aug. 22, 1915.

210 **class of alien**: For the pertinent language from the act, see General Services Administration, *Records Concerning Joseph Hillstrom*. And for all quotations from the hearing, see ibid.

210–11 **July 8, 1913**: General Services Administration, *Records Concerning Joseph Hillstrom* **year to the day**: Salt Lake newspapers, July 9, 1914.

10. Bracing for War

Sources

Books

Cannon, Frank J., and Harvey J. O'Higgins, *Under the Prophet in Utah*; Foner, Philip S., *The Case of Joe Hill*; Foner, Philip S., ed., *The Letters of Joe Hill*; Hyndman, Henry Mayers, *Further Reminiscences*; Schmidt, Ronald J. Jr., *This Is the City*; Smith, Gibbs M., *Joe Hill*; Warrum, Noble, ed., *Utah Since Statehood*; White, Joseph, *Tom Mann*.

Documents

Hilda Erickson to Aubrey Haan, June 22, 1949. In the author's possession.

Aubrey Haan to Fred Thompson, Jan. 18, 1948, box 102, Correspondence, Jan. 1948, IWW Collection, ALUA.

Joe Hill to Utah Board of Pardons, "A Few Reasons Why I Demand a New Trial," Oct. 3, 1915, published in *DEN*, Oct. 4, 1915; Foner, *Letters*, 64–74.

State of Utah v. Joseph Hillstrom, appellant's brief, appeal from the Utah Third District Court, Utah Supreme Court, n.d.

State of Utah v. Joseph Hillstrom, no. 2764, 46 Utah 341; 150 P. 935, Utah Supreme Court, 1915.

Journal and Magazine Articles

Parker, Carleton H., "The California Casual and His Revolt," *Quarterly Journal of Economics* 30, no. 1 (1915): 110–26.

"Unemployed and Employed Workers Attention!," *Wooden Shoe* 1, no. 20, Jan. 22, 1914, Science, Industry and Business Library, New York Public Library, New York City.

Unpublished Typescripts

Curtis, Joseph A., *Right Man? The Tragic Saga of Joe Hill*, Joseph A. Curtis Papers, Accn 1229, Special Collections, Marriott Library, University of Utah, Salt Lake City.

Morris, James O., *The Joe Hill Case*, 1950, Labadie Collection, Special Collections Library, University of Michigan, Ann Arbor.

Notes

215–16 **"This is hard"**: *SOL*, Sept. 25, 1915. **"law or anarchy"**: *SLH-R*, Sept. 30, 1915. **"against the workers"**: *SOL*, Sept. 25, 1915.

  216 **"soaked with blood"**: *DEN*, Jan. 14, 1914.

216–17 **"meeting or two"**: Haan to Thompson. **"writer of songs"**: *DEN*, Jan. 22, 1914. Commander Smith confused the "bad pair": he cited Appelquist as the songwriter. **"Men Who Robbed"**: *SLTele*, Jan. 23, 1914.

  217 **"trail of crime"**: *DEN*, Jan. 22, 1914.

  217 **"was mixed up"**: *SLH-R*, Jan. 24, 1914. **mug shots**: *DEN*, Jan. 24, 1914.

217–18 **swelled from mere**: For a summary of the rumors and allegations, see *SLT* and *DEN*, Oct. 16, 1915; *SLH-R*, Oct. 17, 1915.

  219 **statutory standard**: *Compiled Laws of the State of Utah*, sec. 9279 (5015), 1907, cited in Morris, 41. **"complete and unbroken"**: For a discussion of the standard of proof and relevant case law, see *Utah v. Hillstrom*, appellant's brief, 22–24.

  219 **"Thrilling Scene"**: *SLTele*, June 19, 1914.

  220 **"our pants down"**: *IW*, July 7, 1945, cited in Foner, *Case of*, 17. **"Every construction camp"**: *SOL*, Sept. 26, 1914.

220–21 **"Garden of Paradise"**: *SOL*, Jan. 3, 1914.

  221 **"marked" him**: *SLTele*, Oct. 20, 1913. **"do not anticipate"**: Ibid. **"tirade against capitalism"**: *DEN*, Nov. 10, 1913.

221–22 **"definite and increasing"**: *SLT*, Jan. 9, 1914.

  222 **"We want work"**: *DEN*, Mar. 3, 1914.

222–23 **wire service report**: *DEN*, Mar. 5, 1914. See also *SLH-R*, Mar. 5, 1914; *SLT*, Mar. 7, 1914. **"terrorize the peaceful"**: *DEN*, Mar. 7, 1914. **"by warlike measures"**: *SLT*, Mar. 7, 1914. **"put into practice"** (footnote): *SLT*, Apr. 24, 1914.

  223 **staggering unemployment**: Parker, 122. **"want and misery"**: "Unemployed and Employed."

  223 **"Rained on and starved"**: Parker, 124. **"arrayed against them"**: *DEN*, Mar. 11, 1914. **"shiftless outsiders"**: Ibid.

223–24 **"starving amid plenty"**: "Unemployed and Employed." **"at its mercy"**: *SLTele*, Mar. 17, 1914; *NYT*, Mar. 18, 1914.

  224 **declined Rowan's offer**: Smith, 89. Smith's source is William Chance, a member who accompanied Rowan and whom Smith interviewed in 1967. **" 'go it' alone"**: Hill to Utah Board.

  225 **it was "immaterial"**: Hill to Utah Board.

  225 **"keenness and cunning"**: *DEN*, Jan. 29, 1914.

  225 **"in my presence"**: Hill to Utah Board. **"I *believe* that"**: *SLH-R*, Jan. 14, 1914.

  225 ***Herald-Republican*'s account**: *SLH-R*, Jan. 29, 1914.

  226 **Erickson had proved**: *SLT*, Jan. 15, 1914.

  226 **"This man's"**: *SLT*, Jan. 29, 1914.

  226 **"That is all"**: *SLH-R*, Jan. 29, 1914.

  227 **heard the commotion**: *SLT*, Jan. 29, 1914. **gazing out**: Ibid. **"resembling Hillstrom"**: *SLH-R*, Jan. 29, 1914. The words are the reporter's, not a direct quote.

227 **Supreme Court record**: *State v. Hillstrom*, 937. **"quarter to ten"**: Curtis, 193. *SLT*, June 19, 1914, reported that Merlin testified that the shootings had occurred "about 9:45."

227 **"more resembled Otto"**: *SLH-R*, Jan. 29, 1914.

227 **deflate the testimony**: Ibid.

227–28 **cowboy-style**: Ibid.

228 **"can't say that"**: Hill to Utah Board.

228 **"lack of knowledge"**: *DEN*, Jan. 29, 1914.

228 **"stranger in town"**: Ibid. **He ran unsuccessfully**: Warrum, 171.

229 **Rowan could report**: *SOL*, May 23, 1914.

229–30 **"The main thing"**: Ibid.

11. The Majesty of the Law

Sources

Books
Alexander, Thomas G., *Utah: The Right Place*; Foner, Philip S., ed., *The Letters of Joe Hill*; Warren, Louis S., *Buffalo Bill's America*.

Documents
"F. Z. Wilson Criminal Record," Aug. 10, 1911, Salt Lake City Police "mug book," 496, Police Museum, Salt Lake City. Courtesy of Police Lt. Steve Diamond (ret.), curator.

Joe Hill to Utah Board of Pardons, "A Few Reasons Why I Demand a New Trial," Oct. 3, 1915, published in *DEN*, Oct. 4, 1915; Foner, *Letters*, 64–74.

"Joe Hillstrom Criminal Record," Jan. 14, 1914, Salt Lake City Police "mug book," n.p., Police Museum, Salt Lake City. Courtesy of Police Lt. Steve Diamond (ret.), curator.

Salary Schedule for Police, 1911–1914. Courtesy of Police Lt. Steve Diamond (ret.), curator of the Salt Lake Police Museum.

Heber C. Kimball, certificate of death, State of Utah, Mar. 29, 1936, online, along with his obituary, *DEN*, Mar. 31, 1936, http://www.jared.pratt-family.org/orson_family _histories/joseph-kimball-death.html.

Memorial Addresses, Elmer O. Leatherwood, Late a Representative from Utah, 71st Cong., 2nd sess., House Document no. 505 (Washington, D.C.: Government Printing Office, 1930).

Nevada State Prison Inmate Case Files, Farmer, James, no. 1182, Nevada State Library and Archives, Carson City.

State of Utah v. Joseph Hillstrom, no. 3532, vol. 2, transcript of evidence introduced on behalf of the defendant (note: vol. 1 missing), Utah Third District Court, 1914. Hereafter abbreviated as "TT."

State of Utah v. Joseph Hillstrom, appellant's brief, appeal from the Utah Third District Court, Utah Supreme Court, n.d.

State of Utah v. Joseph Hillstrom, no. 2764, 46 Utah 341; 150 P. 935, Utah Supreme Court, 1915.

Film

The West, episode 7, "The Geography of Hope" (Public Broadcasting Service, 2001), with a biographical note on Cody online, http://www.pbs.org/weta/thewest/people/a_c/buffalobill.htm.

Journal and Magazine Articles

McCormick, John S., "Hornets in the Hive: Socialists in Early Twentieth-Century Utah," *Utah Historical Quarterly* 50, no. 3 (Summer 1982): 224–40.

Shor, Francis, "Biographical Moments in the Written and Cinematic Text: Deconstructing the Legends of Joe Hill and Buffalo Bill," *Film and History* 14, no. 3 (1984): 61–68.

Sillito, John R., "Women and the Socialist Party in Utah, 1900–1920," *Utah Historical Quarterly* 49, no. 3 (Summer 1981): 220–38.

Unpublished Typescripts

Curtis, Joseph A., *Right Man? The Tragic Saga of Joe Hill*, Joseph A. Curtis Papers, Accn 1229, Special Collections, Marriott Library, University of Utah, Salt Lake City.

Hilton, O. N., "Funeral Oration in Memoriam of Joe Hill," West Side Auditorium, Chicago, Nov. 25, 1915. In the author's possession.

Morris, James O., *The Joe Hill Case*, 1950, Labadie Collection, Special Collections Library, University of Michigan, Ann Arbor.

Owens, Stephen W., *Joe's Foe: Elmer O. Leatherwood*, paper written for Honors Class 374H-2, Ronald J. Yengich, adjunct professor, University of Utah, Salt Lake City, 1991. Copy in the author's possession.

Notes

231 "blood-sweating behemoth": *SLT*, June 7, 1914. "half history lesson": *The West*. "still looked wonderful": Quoted in Warren, 537.

231–32 "progress" and "civilization": Warren, 552, fn. 8, notes that the phrase "progress of civilization" was "a common refrain after the Civil War, evoking the triumph of modern, white America." "barbarism and savagery": Ibid.

232 small and insular: *SLTele*, Apr. 27, 1914, reported the U.S. Census figure of 109,530 (up from 92,777 just four years earlier). bestrode those circles: For Leatherwood's memberships, see *Memorial Addresses*, 36; for Ritchie's, see his obituaries, *SLTele* and *DEN*, Feb. 5, 1929.

234 "very much time": Curtis, 172. "under bounden obligation": Curtis, 173.

234 seemed "very surprised": Hill to Utah Board. "chosen between panels": *SLTele*, June 12, 1914. "hand-picked jury": Hilton, 8.

235 "very old man": Hill to Utah Board. Heber C. Kimball: Heber C. Kimball, certificate of death. forty-five wives: Alexander, 189. fellow board members: Ritchie obituaries, *SLTele* and *DEN*, Feb. 5, 1929. "unanimously endorse" (footnote): *SLT*, Dec. 28, 1915.

235–36 owed his political: *SLT*, Mar. 27, 1914, and Aug. 25, 1914. For biographical material, see *Memorial Addresses*; Owens. his opening statement: *SLH-R*, June 18, 1914. would narrowly lose (footnote): He lost to the Democrat/Progressive "fusion" candidate, James H. Mays, by 195 votes out of more than 50,000 cast.

236 **"just one thing"**: *SLH-R*, June 18, 1914.

236–37 **"only survivor"**: *SLT*, June 19, 1914. **told the *Tribune***: *SLT*, Jan. 15, 1914. **he ducked into**: *SLT*, June 19, 1914.

237 **Leatherwood's leading questions**: *SLH-R*, June 19, 1914.

237 **stop "squabbling"**: *SLTele*, June 18, 1914.

237–38 **"gently" reviewing** and **"torn to pieces"**: *SLTele*, Aug. 24, 1915. Scott wrote the bylined column HILLSTROM COULD HAVE SAVED SELF, SAYS HIS LAWYER in response to Hill's letter to the editor, which the *Telegram* had published two days earlier. The letter outlined his case for a new trial, including his charge of inadequate representation.

238 **"blandly informed me"**: *SLTele*, Aug. 22, 1915.

238 **"get rid of"**: Hill to Utah Board.

238 **neat blue suit**: *SLTele*, June 18, 1914. **"more hatchetlike"**: *SLTele*, June 19, 1914.

238 **"Everyone realized"**: Ibid.

239 **"three prosecuting attorneys"**: The account of Hill's attempt to dismiss his attorneys is drawn from *State v. Hillstrom*; *Utah v. Hillstrom*, appellant's brief; and all four Salt Lake dailies, June 19–20, 1914.

240 **"May Mr. Harms"**: Curtis, 216.

240–41 **"let them pass"**: Ibid., 218.

241 **"Did this man"**: The exchange is quoted in *State v. Hillstrom*, 939.

241–42 **"As *amicus curiae*"**: Curtis, 219.

242 **"great deal alike"**: *State v. Hillstrom*, 939. **"light bushy hair"**: Hill to Utah Board. **"Just the same"**: *Utah v. Hillstrom*, appellant's brief, 7.

243 **"suggestion and invitation"**: Ibid.

243 **"My counsel seem"**: Ibid., 48.

243 **"sensation after sensation"**: *SLT*, June 20, 1914. **"he had confidence"**: *Utah v. Hillstrom*, appellant's brief, 52.

243 **"no brainstorm either"**: *State v. Hillstrom*, 944.

243 **MacDougall stood up**: *SLTele*, June 19, 1914.

244 **to confer privately**: *SLH-R*, June 20, 1914. **"fair-haired"**: *SLT*, June 20, 1914. **"sweetheart of Hillstrom"**: *SLH-R*, June 20, 1914. **"greeted each other"**: Ibid. **"like a clam"**: *SLT*, June 20, 1914.

244 **"You want the court"**: Curtis, 235–36.

245 **"I said that"**: Ibid., 238.

245 **"some important points"**: *SLH-R*, June 20, 1914.

246 ***Tribune* pointed it**: *SLT*, June 21, 1914.

246 **Virginia Snow Stephen**: For biographical information, see Sillito, 231–34. **"prominent in educational"**: *SLT*, June 20, 1914. **Mormon Socialist** (footnote): For a table on the demographics and characteristics of party membership in Utah, see McCormick, 232. **"evils of capitalism"**: Ibid., 237–38, quoting Paul Avrich.

246–47 **"violent" opposition**: *SLH-R*, June 21, 1914. **much taken with**: *SLT*, June 21, 1914, published the lyrics of both songs.

247 **"simply could not"**: Ibid. **finished both songs**: Ibid.

247 **"cold-blooded right"**: *SLH-R*, June 21, 1914.

247 **Alfred Sorensen**: *SLT*, June 21, 1914. **nationally eminent**: See his obituaries in *Denver Post*, Dec. 16, 1932; *New York Times* and *Rocky Mountain News*, Dec. 17,

1932. **preparing to depart**: *SLH-R*, June 20, 1914. **union's chief counsel**: *Rocky Mountain News*, Dec. 17, 1932. **"Sit in Hillstrom"**: *SLH-R*, June 20, 1914.

247–48 **"perfectly reliable" source**: *SLH-R*, June 21, 1914. **"every available deputy"**: Ibid.

248 **to "pay tribute" (footnote)**: *DEN*, July 20, 1911, and Aug. 11, 1911. With the "tribute," Cleveland sought to supplement his annual salary of $1,260. (According to department historian and police museum curator Steve Diamond, uniformed policemen of the day had to provide their own uniform, and mounted police provided their own mount, tack, and feed.) **"within an hour"**: Curtis, 192.

248–49 **customarily loaded**: Ibid., 481–83.

249 **only lead bullets**: TT, 511. **"I have not"**: Ibid., 605–7.

249 **Arling did shoot**: *SLT*, June 26, 1914. **left shoulder blade**: TT, 530–31.

249 **directed verdict**: *SLH-R*, June 23, 1914.

249–50 **"uncalled for outbreak"**: *SLTele*, Aug. 24, 1915. **"suspicion with suspicion"**: TT, 449. **"answering the general"**: Ibid. **"terms of logic"**: Cited in *Utah v. Hillstrom*, appellant's brief, 25.

250 **"Holdups Kill Father"**: *SLT*, Jan. 11, 1914. **"wanted my life"**: *SLTele*, Jan. 12, 1914.

250 **"This fellow knows"**: *SLH-R*, Jan. 11, 1914.

251 **"incompetent, immaterial"**: TT, 485.

251 **"This is the theory"**: Ibid., 485–86.

251 **"take his life"**: Ibid., 485–87.

251 **"One sufficient reason"**: Ibid., 487.

252 **"burn it down"**: *EI*, Sept. 19, 1913.

252–53 **Southern Pacific agent**: Nevada State Prison Inmate Case Files.

253 **he was spotted**: *SLT*, Jan. 11 and 12, 1914; *SLTele*, Jan. 12, 1914.

253 **suspect was lying**: *SLT*, Jan. 14, 1914. **facts and figures**: "Joe Hillstrom Criminal Record" and "F. Z. Wilson Criminal Record."

253–54 **"either fell down"**: TT, 539–42.

254–55 **"acted suspiciously"**: Ibid., 553. **"smell any booze" and "rawboned"**: Ibid., 554. **interview with police**: *SLH-R*, Jan. 13, 1914; TT, 555–56. **"Does he resemble"**: TT, 556.

255 **"worse from wear"**: *SLH-R*, Jan. 13, 1914. **"use all speed"**: *SLH-R*, Jan. 11, 1914.

255 **"walking leisurely"**: Ibid.

255 **"he was shivering"**: *SLTele*, Jan. 12, 1914. **"taking a walk"**: *DEN*, Jan. 12, 1914. **police jailed him**: Carlson, TT, 602, affirmed that he had arrested a man who was "supposed to be lodging at the Salvation Army," but he could not recall his name. **bloody handkerchief**: *SLT*, Jan. 11, 1914; *SLH-R*, Jan. 11, 1914; *DEN*, Jan. 12, 1914.

256 **MacDougall asked him**: TT, 608. **"You had in custody"**: Ibid., 608–9.

256 **"Immaterial and irrelevant"**: Ibid., 609.

256 **Judge Ritchie agreed**: Ibid., 609–10.

256 **"indirect and circumstantial"**: Ibid., 610.

256–57 **"The question here"**: Ibid..

257 **"I take it"**: Ibid., 611.

257 **Lead typically flattened**: Ibid., 529–30.

258 **"a perpendicular position?"**: Ibid., 534.

258 "above his head": *SLH-R*, June 24, 1914.

259 supposedly advised him: *SLH-R*, June 25, 1914. unspecified damaging evidence (footnote): Curtis, 581–85.

259 He was "crestfallen": *SLH-R*, June 7, 1914. "Remember selling Luger": Hill to Utah Board.

259 "The defendant rests": TT, 614.

259–60 "some brute": *SLH-R*, June 25, 1914. "monstrous Cyclops": *SLT*, June 25, 1914.

260 "bullets and cartridges": *SLH-R*, June 25, 1914.

260 "hand of fate": *SLT*, June 25, 1914. "indelible mark": *SLH-R*, June 25, 1914. "Murder will out": *SLT*, June 25, 1914.

260–61 "veritable sledge hammer": Ibid.

261 "It just disappeared": Hill to Utah Board.

261–62 "without a motive": *SLH-R*, June 26, 1914. "then began shooting": *SLT*, June 26, 1914. "acquit this man": Ibid.

262 "a frame-up": *SLH-R*, June 27, 1914.

262 "It is true": *SLT*, June 27, 1914.

262 "presumption of innocence": *SLH-R*, June 27, 1914. "would rather kill": *SLTele*, June 26, 1914.

263 "do his bidding": *SLH-R*, June 27, 1914.

263 "I resent it": *DEN* and *SLH-R*, June 27, 1914.

264 "My blood boils": *SLT*, June 27, 1914.

264 "in God's name": *DEN* and *SLH-R*, June 27, 1914.

264 "parasites on society": *SLT*, June 27, 1914.

265 *Tribune* editorial (footnote): *SLT*, Apr. 7, 1914.

265–66 "sufficient to authorize": TT, 619; *SLH-R* and *SLT*, June 27, 1914.

266 "morally and logically": Morris, 46.

266 elected as foreman and jurors began deliberations: *SLT*, June 27, 1914. informally agreed and unanimous first ballot: *SLH-R*, June 28, 1914.

266 "Sheriff Is Watchful": *SLT*, June 27, 1914.

266 At exactly ten: *SLH-R*, June 29, 1914.

266 "have you agreed": TT, 629.

266–67 Hill swiveled halfway: *DEN*, June 27, 1914.

267 "We, the jurors": TT, 629.

267 have recommended "mercy": *SLT*, June 28, 1914.

267 "flutter of an eye": *DEN*, June 27, 1914.

267 "I'll take shooting": *SLT*, July 9, 1914.

12. "New Trial or Bust"

Sources

Books

Brissenden, Paul Frederick, *The I.W.W.: A Study of American Syndicalism*; Camp, Helen C., *Iron in Her Soul*; Chace, James, *1912*; Constantine, J. Robert, ed., *Letters of Eugene V. Debs*, vol. 2; Dubofsky, Melvyn, *We Shall Be All*; Flynn, Elizabeth Gurley, *The Rebel Girl*; Foner, Philip S., *The Case of Joe Hill*; Foner, Philip S., ed., *The Letters of Joe Hill*;

Green, Archie, et al., *The Big Red Songbook*; Holbrook, Stewart H., *Holy Old Mackinaw*; Kornbluh, Joyce L., ed., *Rebel Voices*; Link, Arthur S., ed., *The Papers of Woodrow Wilson*, vols. 35 and 49; Malmquist, O. N., *The First 100 Years*; Roper, William L., and Leonard J. Arrington, *William Spry*; Smith, Gibbs M., *Joe Hill*; Stavis, Barrie, *The Man Who Never Died*; Stavis, Barrie, and Frank Harmon, *The Songs of Joe Hill*.

Documents

Hilda Erickson to Aubrey Haan, June 22, 1949, June 30, 1949, and n.d., 1949. In the author's possession.

Constantine Filigno to Aubrey Haan, Feb. 4, 1950. In the author's possession.

Gov. William Spry Papers, series 2941, Joseph Hillstrom Correspondence, 1914–1916 (microfilm), Utah History Research Center, Salt Lake City (correspondence is filed alphabetically by sender's surname, and then by date). Hereafter abbreviated as "SP."

Aubrey Haan to Agnes Inglis, July 21, 1948, Labadie Collection, Special Collections Library, University of Michigan, Ann Arbor.

Joe Hill to Sam Murray, Sept. 15, 1914, Dec. 2, 1914, Mar. 22, 1915, Sept. 9, 1915, and Sept. 30, 1915. Copies of originals in the author's possession, courtesy of Archives Collection, Länsmuseet Gävleborg, Gävle, Sweden.

Joe Hill to Sam Murray, Feb. 13, 1915, June 6, 1915, and Aug. 12, 1915, box 21, folder 1, Llano del Rio Collection, Department of Manuscripts, Henry E. Huntington Library, San Marino, CA.

Joe Hill to Utah Board of Pardons, "A Few Reasons Why I Demand a New Trial," Oct. 3, 1915, published in *DEN*, Oct. 4, 1915; Foner, *Letters*, 64–74.

Joe Hill to E. W. Vanderleith, Sept. 4, 1914, and n.d. (typescript "From Joe Hill's Letters"), General Correspondence, box 2, Frank P. Walsh Papers, Special Collections, Manuscripts and Archives Division, New York Public Library, New York City.

"Hillstrom Documents," RG 59 General Records of the Department of State, 1910–1929, decimal file 311.582H55, Joseph A. Curtis Papers, Accn 1229, Special Collections, Marriott Library, University of Utah, Salt Lake City. Hereafter abbreviated as "HD."

O. N. Hilton to Joe Hill, July 19, 1915, and July 20, 1915, box 371, Elizabeth Gurley Flynn Joe Hill Case Papers, 1915, Tamiment Library & Robert F. Wagner Labor Archives, New York University, New York City.

State of Utah v. Joseph Hillstrom, no. 3532, vol. 2, transcript of evidence introduced on behalf of the defendant (note: vol. 1 missing), Utah Third District Court, 1914. Hereafter abbreviated as "TT."

State of Utah v. Joseph Hillstrom, appellant's brief, appeal from the Utah Third District Court, Utah Supreme Court, n.d.

State of Utah v. Joseph Hillstrom, no. 2764, 46 Utah 341; 150 P. 935, Utah Supreme Court, 1915.

Journal and Magazine Articles

Hill, Joe, "How to Make Work for the Unemployed," *International Socialist Review* 15, no. 6 (1914): 335–36.

"The Last Letters of Joe Hill," *Industrial Pioneer* 1, no. 8 (1923): 53–56.

"Religion: Again, Bishop Jones," *Time*, Nov. 11, 1929.

Unpublished Typescripts

Curtis, Joseph A., *Right Man? The Tragic Saga of Joe Hill*, Joseph A. Curtis Papers, Accn 1229, Special Collections, Marriott Library, University of Utah, Salt Lake City.

Hilton, O. N., "Funeral Oration in Memoriam of Joe Hill," West Side Auditorium, Chicago, Nov. 25, 1915. In the author's possession.

Web Site

Ancestry.com, http://www.ancestry.com (subscription required).

Notes

268 **"never be effaced"**: Unsigned letter to Spry, Aug. 5, 1914, SP, reel 2, part 1. The letter carried the return address of "Gladheim," an estate owned by Henry K. Dyer in Woods Hole, MA. **"in his Blodd"**: Anon. to Spry, n.d., SP, reel 2, part 2.

268 **"forty thousand letters"**: Spry to W. H. Price, Dec. 22, 1915, SP, reel 2, part 2.

268–69 **major American cities**: J. B. Knox to Spry, Aug. 23, 1914, SP, reel 2, part 2; *NYT*, Nov. 10, 1915; T. E. Latimer to Spry, Sept. 27, 1915, SP, reel 2, part 2; *SLH-R*, Nov. 10, 1915. **English docks**: *SOL*, Jan. 9, 1915, reports that during an "enthusiastic" meeting, the English IWW resolved to join with "fellow workers in America in demanding the unconditional release of Hill." **Australian goldfields**: For the resolution mailed to Governor Spry from Boulder City, West Australia, see *DEN*, Sept. 4, 1915.

269 **"Tin-Jesus"**: Hill to Vanderleith, n.d.

269 **state tennis champion** (footnote): *SLT*, July 5, 1914.

270 **"my last day"**: Hill to Vanderleith, Sept. 4, 1914. **heard oral arguments**: *SLH-R*, Sept. 2, 1914. **"any further ceremony"**: Ibid.

270 **immediately filed notice**: Ibid.

270 **"This is Sept. 4"**: Hill to Vanderleith, Sept. 4, 1914. **"man can prepare"** (footnote): *SLT*, Dec. 20, 1914. **"all joking aside"**: Hill to Vanderleith, Sept. 4, 1914.

271 **final three stanzas**: *SOL*, Sept. 12, 1914.

271 **"first class toadstool"**: Joe Hill to "Gus," Jan. 3, 1915, Foner, *Letters*, 19. **"fellow like myself"**: Joe Hill to E. G. Flynn, Mar. 10, 1915, ibid., 30. **"good correspondent"**: "Joe Hill to Gus," Jan. 3, 1915, ibid., 19.

272 **published the lyrics**: *SOL*, Sept. 19, 1914. **is derivative of**: Stavis and Harmon, 42.

273 **"unemployed and hungry"**: *SLTele*, Feb. 13, 1915. **membership had fallen**: Brissenden, 333, 335, for 1912 and 1914 figures, respectively. **attributed the declining**: Vincent St. John of the IWW mentioned the rampant joblessness among West Coast Wobblies in testimony before the U.S. Commission on Industrial Relations. Ibid., 337.

273–74 **"Wherever I go"**: Brissenden, 330. **legend had it** (footnote): Ibid., 279–80, 438–39.

274 **"Ta-Ra-Ra"**: Lyrics in Green et al., 165–66.

275 **"of IWW intent"** (footnote): Kornbluh, 143.

275 **"make the job last"**: Hill, "How to Make," 335–36.

276 **"dope something out"**: Hill to Murray, Dec. 2, 1914.

276 **printed Hill's "Soupline"**: In a parenthetical note within a published copy of

Hill's letter to Murray of Feb. 13, 1915, Murray writes, "We had secured nearly 50 dollars by selling it for 5 cents for the Joe Hill Defense. For the text of the letter with Murray's note, see "The Last Letters of Joe Hill," 54. And for the song lyrics, see Kornbluh, 145.

277 *Solidarity* maintained: *SOL*, Feb. 27, 1915. "parody on 'Tipperary'": *DEN*, Feb. 15, 1915. "like the smallpox": Hill to Murray, Mar. 22, 1915. "Sup Court will": Hill to Murray, Feb. 13, 1915. "for my benefit": Hill to Murray, Mar. 22, 1915.

277 "about a dozen": Ibid. company of soldiers: *SOL*, Feb. 20, 1915. encouraged a young: The girl was Katie Phar, of Spokane, the daughter of an IWW member. No date, probably January 1915, according to Foner, *Letters*, 25. "would rather play": Joe Hill to Katie Phar, Mar. 4, 1915, ibid., 29.

277–78 "What Socialism Will": Flynn, 53. leather-lunged: Her biographer, Camp, calls Flynn a "small, intense, Irish woman with . . . leather lungs." 18. "hellion that breathed": Holbrook, 211–12. "She-Dogs": Camp, 18. "quick brain": Ibid. "pot-hooks, curves, dots": Ibid., xxiii. "perpetual inebriate": Ibid.

278 wrote to Flynn: Foner, *Letters*, 21. "Saw your address in the 'Sol'"—*Solidarity*—he wrote by way of introduction. "I want to thank you for what you have done for me and for the interest you have taken in my welfare, but on the square I'll tell you that all the notoriety stuff is making me dizzy in the head and I am afraid I am getting more glory than I really am entitled to." "like Tommy Edison": Joe Hill to Elizabeth Gurley Flynn, Mar. 10, 1915, Foner, *Letters*, 30. "boil spuds": Joe Hill to Elizabeth Gurley Flynn, Sept. 7, 1915, ibid., 54.

278–79 "are more exploited": *SOL*, Dec. 19, 1914.

279 "help to line up": Hill to Murray, Feb. 13, 1915. "you was right": Joe Hill to Elizabeth Gurley Flynn, Nov. 18, 1915, Foner, *Letters*, 82. "The Rebel Girl": Lyrics in Green et al., 174–75.

280 "tall, good looking": *SOL*, May 22, 1915.

280 Am I leaving: She revealed her thoughts in her *SOL* article. "He's a Mormon": Flynn, 193.

280–81 "unusually large attendance": *SLT*, May 29, 1915. "intended clearly": *Utah v. Hillstrom*, appellant's brief, 49–50.

281–82 "I now ask": Curtis, 458. *SLT*, May 29, 1915, offers a similar but truncated account.

282 "no way prejudiced": *SLT*, May 29, 1915. Without access to the respondent's brief, I have had to rely on brief extracts in the Supreme Court opinion and on press reports. If Higgins presented more than a token case for the state, neither the court opinion nor the newspaper coverage reflected it.

282 granted "speedy relief": Hilton, "Funeral Oration," 15. the judges' "comments": Ibid., 16. "getting a reversal": Hill to Murray, June 6, 1915.

282 "fair and impartial": *State v. Hillstrom*, 947. "Supreme Court Says": *SLT*, July 4, 1915.

283 McHugh had testified: *Utah v. Hillstrom*, appellant's brief, 12. "I should judge": Ibid. "hazard an opinion": *SLT*, Jan. 29, 1914. matter of fact: *State v. Hillstrom*, 938.

283–84 Straup's opinion stated: Ibid. "ears chopped off": Ibid., 941. "The only explanation": Ibid., 941–42.

284 "He had a right": Ibid., 942. "not a witness": Ibid., 939.

284 **"Since the evidence"**: Ibid., 943.

285 **"drain the resources"**: Joe Hill to Elizabeth Gurley Flynn, July 24, 1915, Foner, *Letters*, 43. **"case is dropped"**: Joe Hill to Ed Rowan, July 22, 1915, ibid., 42.

285 **"starve themselves"**: Joe Hill to Orrin Hilton, July 14, 1915, ibid., 37–38.

285 *"good game people"*: Hilton to Hill, July 19, 1915.

285 **"Nothing except this"**: The exchange is quoted in *SLTele*, Aug. 2, 1915.

286 **"may be futile"**: Hilton to Hill, July 20, 1915. **"correctly informed"** (footnote): Copies are filed with the letters of writers to whom the governor's office replied. See any and all microfilm reels of Joseph Hillstrom Correspondence, SP. **"depraved and malignant"**: *State v. Hillstrom*, 943.

286–87 **"alive than dead"**: *SLTele*, Sept. 30, 1915.

287 **Hill's terse reply**: Ibid.

287 **"give me life"**: Joe Hill to Elizabeth Gurley Flynn, envelope dated Aug. 18, 1915, Foner, *Letters*, 53.

287 **"I never 'licked' "**: Ibid. **"drop in the bucket"**: Joe Hill to Ed Rowan, July 14, 1915, ibid., 36.

287 **"Arouse, Ye Slaves"**: *SOL*, Sept. 25, 1915. Upon her brother's lynching in 1917, Emma wired the editor of *SOL*, "Telegraph Frank's funeral arrangements. Save few of Joe Hill's ashes for me." *SOL*, Aug. 4, 1917.

288 **forty-eight states**: *NYT*, Mar. 18, 1916. **"measure for measure"**: John Walsh to Spry, Sept. 12, 1915, SP, reel 3. **"intensify the class"**: Hermon F. Titus to Spry, Sept. 11, 1915, SP, reel 3. **"like a tornado"**: H. R. Thomas to Spry, Sept. 10, 1915, SP, reel 3. **"will never kill"**: Ernest Fitch to Spry, Sept. 17, 1915, SP, reel 2, part 1.

288 **"I cannot believe"**: Ernest D. Condit to Spry, July 17, 1915, SP, reel 1. **"Thousands of intelligent"**: *BG*, Nov. 19, 1915. Keller also wired President Wilson to urge his intervention. Link, 206, 210. **large IWW banner**: *IW*, Oct. 3, 1912. The *IW* excerpted an interview in which Keller was asked if she "favored the Socialist cause." "I do," she replied, "for under Socialism only can everyone obtain the right work and be happy."

289 **"an instant reversal"**: Ernest D. Condit to Spry, July 17, 1915, SP, reel 1. **"despised and militant"**: A. M. Hodge, Sept. 29, 1915, SP, reel 2, part 1.

289 **"to have shaken"**: Stavis, 59. **"condemning the peace"** (footnote): *SLTele*, Oct. 11, 1917. **"promulgating unpatriotic doctrines"** (footnote): "Religion: Again." **"no objection to"** (footnote): *Myton Free Press*, Aug. 28, 1919. Jones went on to help found and work for the Fellowship of Reconciliation, the distinguished interdenominational peace organization. For a lucid account, see John R. Sillito and Timothy S. Hearn, "A Question of Conscience: The Resignation of Bishop Paul Jones," *Utah Historical Quarterly* 50, no. 3 (Summer 1982): 209–24. **"many possible doubts"**: Stavis, 59–60.

289–90 **he looked "immaculate"**: Sept. 19, 1915. **cited the infamous**: Ibid. For the absorbing and gruesome full chronicle of the Frank case, see Steve Oney, *And the Dead Shall Rise* (New York: Pantheon, 2003).

290 **"rather cut off"**: *SLT*, Sept. 19, 1915.

290 **"Say Hilton"**: Hilton, "Funeral Oration," 20.

291 **"just as soon"**: Ibid.

291 **"Now Mr. Hillstrom"**: *SLT*, Sept. 19, 1915.

291 **"little proposition"**: Ibid.

292 **Hilda among them**: Erickson to Haan, June 30, 1949. **Swedish emigration records**: On June 30, 1917, he left Norfolk, VA, on the ship *Baltic*, and on Apr. 17, 1918, he left New York on the ship *Magda*. On both ships, his job title was *Eldare*, or "fireman." Swedish Emigration Records, 1783–1951, Ancestry.com. **World War I**: Otto Wilhelm Appelquist, World War I Draft Registration Card, Orleans County, Louisiana, Roll: 1684817, Ancestry.com.

292–93 **six pallbearers**: Erickson to Haan, n.d. She wrote in reply to a letter from Haan dated June 13, 1949. **"fair-haired"**: *SLT*, June 20, 1914. **excerpts from both**: *SLT*, June 21, 1914, published the lyrics of both songs.

293–94 **"Considerable importance"**: *DEN*, June 19, 1914.

294 **won a fellowship**: Haan to Inglis. **possible subversive leanings**: E-mail to author from Haan's daughter Mary Haan, December 2010.

297 **"the power exerted"**: Filigno to Haan.

298 **one-sentence valedictory**: *SLTele*, Sept. 20, 1915.

298–99 **"Hillstrom Is Denied"**: *SLT*, Sept. 19, 1915.

299 **"your own head"**: *DEN*, Sept. 20, 1915. **"campaign of intimidation"**: *SLT*, Sept. 19, 1915. **"order of K.O.D."**: *SLT*, Sept. 22, 1915, reproduced the first sheet.

299 **"about my business"**: *SLH-R*, Sept. 26, 1915. **stringent security measures**: Ibid. **thirty Pinkerton operatives**: *DEN*, Sept. 27, 1915.

299 **"miscarriage of justice"**: Frank Polk to William Spry, telegram, September 25, 1915, HD. The wire includes the text of one sent that day by Wilhelm Ekengren to the State Department.

300 **"as a courtesy"**: *SLT*, Sept. 26, 1915. **lengthy manifesto**: Published in all four Salt Lake dailies. *SLTele* and *DEN*, Sept. 25, 1915; *SLT* and *SLH-R*, Sept. 26, 1915.

300 **"As I understand"**: *DEN*, Sept. 27, 1915.

300 **"nothing except arguments"**: Ibid.

300–301 **was a fixer**: Edith's husband, John Sergeant Cram, worked as counsel to Charles Murphy, the Tammany boss. See Cram's obituary, *NYT*, Jan. 19, 1936. **Later that day**: Flynn, 193–94. In her memoir, Flynn recalls that they met on Sept. 28; contemporary accounts suggest the meeting was the next evening. **promised to contact**: *NYT*, Sept. 30, 1915.

301 **"insufficient to warrant"**: Wilhelm Ekengren to Woodrow Wilson, telegram, Sept. 29, 1915, HD. **"Please wire me"**: *SLH-R*, Oct. 1, 1915.

301 **"Barring a miracle"**: *LAT*, Sept. 30, 1915.

13. Law v. Anarchy

Sources

Books

Albert, Peter J., and Grace Palladino, eds., *The Samuel Gompers Papers*, vol. 9; Blanchard, Leola Howard, *Conquest of Southwest Kansas*; Chace, James, *1912*; Dubofsky, Melvyn, *We Shall Be All*; Flynn, Elizabeth Gurley, *The Rebel Girl*; Foner, Philip S., *The Case of Joe Hill*; Foner, Philip S., *The Letters of Joe Hill*; Gentry, Curt, *Frame-Up*; Gompers,

Samuel, *Seventy Years of Life and Labor*, vol. 1; Link, Arthur S., ed., *The Papers of Woodrow Wilson*, vol. 35; Masterson, W. B. (Bat), *Famous Gunfighters of the Western Frontier*; Preston, William Jr., *Aliens and Dissenters*; Roper, William L., and Leonard J. Arrington, *William Spry*; Smith, Gibbs M., *Joe Hill*; Stavis, Barrie, *The Man Who Never Died*.

Documents

General Services Administration, National Archives and Records Service, *Records Concerning Joseph Hillstrom, Alias Joe Hill, Etc.*, reference service report, Sept. 5, 1957, box 4, folder 6, Joseph A. Curtis Papers, Accn 1229, Special Collections, Marriott Library, University of Utah, Salt Lake City.

Gov. William Spry Papers, series 2941, Joseph Hillstrom Correspondence, 1914–1916 (microfilm), Utah History Research Center, Salt Lake City (correspondence filed alphabetically by sender's surname, and then by date.) Hereafter abbreviated as "SP."

Joe Hill to O. N. Hilton, Oct. 20, 1915, and Oct. 27, 1915 (the latter is a typescript), box 371, Elizabeth Gurley Flynn Joe Hill Case Papers, Tamiment Library & Robert F. Wagner Labor Archives, New York University, New York City.

Joe Hill to Sam Murray, Sept. 30, 1915, box 21, folder 1, Llano del Rio Collection, Department of Manuscripts, Henry E. Huntington Library, San Marino, CA.

Joe Hill to E. W. Vanderleith, n.d. (typescript "From Joe Hill's Letters"), General Correspondence, box 2, Frank P. Walsh Papers, Special Collections, Manuscripts and Archives Division, New York Public Library, New York City.

"Hillstrom Documents," RG 59 General Records of the Department of State, 1910–1929, decimal file 311.582H55, Joseph A. Curtis Papers, Accn 1229, Special Collections, Marriott Library, University of Utah, Salt Lake City. Hereafter abbreviated as "HD."

O. N. Hilton to Elizabeth Gurley Flynn, Nov. 15, 1915, box 371, Elizabeth Gurley Flynn Joe Hill Case Papers, Tamiment Library & Robert F. Wagner Labor Archives, New York University, New York City.

Reed Smoot to Mr. EDC (most probably Ernest D. Condit, of New York), p. 2 of two-page letter (p. 1 missing), n.d., box 371, Elizabeth Gurley Flynn Joe Hill Case Papers, Tamiment Library & Robert F. Wagner Labor Archives, New York University, New York City.

University of Utah Board of Regents, minutes, Oct. 7, 1915, 453, University Archives, University of Utah, Salt Lake City.

Journal Article

Sillito, John R., "Women and the Socialist Party in Utah, 1900–1920," *Utah Historical Quarterly* 49, no. 3 (Summer 1981): 220–38.

Unpublished Typescripts

Curtis, Joseph A., *Right Man? The Tragic Saga of Joe Hill*, Joseph A. Curtis Papers, Accn 1229, Special Collections, Marriott Library, University of Utah, Salt Lake City.

Reed Smoot Diaries, box 2, vol. 7, book 20 (1915–1916), Reed Smoot Papers, Special Collections, Marriott Library, University of Utah, Salt Lake City.

Notes

302 **courtroom cuspidor:** *SLTele*, Sept. 30, 1915. **"my good clothes":** Ibid.

302 **"Respectfully ask":** Woodrow Wilson to William Spry, telegram, Sept. 30, 1915, HD.

302 **"That's nice":** *SLTele*, Sept. 30, 1915.

303 **"granted this respite":** *SLT*, Oct. 1, 1915. **"only case on record":** *SLH-R*, Oct. 1, 1915.

303–4 **"undisputed records":** William Spry to Woodrow Wilson, telegram, Sept. 30, 1915, HD; *SLH-R*, Oct. 1, 1915.

304 **"must be granted":** *SLH-R*, Oct. 1, 1915.

304–5 **"Law or Anarchy":** *SLH-R*, Sept. 30, 1915.

305 **"tacit approval":** *SLH-R*, Oct. 1, 1915.

305 **"experiencing abnormal disorder":** Governors Hiram Johnson, James Withycombe, Ernest Lister, and William Spry to Franklin Lane, telegram, Oct. 5, 1915, Department of Justice File 150139-48, cited in Preston, 60. **"chiefly of panhandlers"** (footnote): Simon J. Lubin to Thomas Gregory, Nov. 26, 1917, Department of Justice File 150139-46, cited in Preston, 60–61.

306 **"Friends and F.W.'s":** *SOL*, Oct. 9, 1915.

306 **"Well Gurley":** Foner, *Letters*, 62.

306–7 **"This dying business":** Hill to Murray.

307 **"unswerving courage":** *SOL*, Oct. 9, 1915.

307–8 **"old Shakespeare himself":** Foner, *Letters*, 75, 80. **"bull moose!"** (footnote): Chace, 117.

309 **in northern Mexico:** For documentation of Hill's whereabouts on that day, see General Services Administration, *Records Concerning Joseph Hillstrom.* **admitted his error:** *SLH-R*, Oct. 17, 1915.

310 **"will be pardoned":** *SLTele*, Oct. 16, 1915.

310 **"would not do":** *SLTele*, Oct. 17, 1915. **governor later denied:** *SLT*, Oct. 19, 1915. **"corroborated by responsible":** *SLTele*, Oct. 17, 1915.

310 **"board not satisfied":** *SLH-R*, Oct. 17, 1915. **"utterances in connection"** (footnote): *DEN*, Nov. 30, 1915. **board fired her** (footnote): University of Utah Board of Regents. See also Sillito, 233. **"attending an anarchistic"** (footnote): Sillito, 233.

310–11 **"nothing to say":** *SLH-R*, Oct. 17, 1915.

311 **"any further light":** Ibid. The article includes the text of the board's resolution.

311 **long black overcoat:** *SLH-R*, Oct. 19, 1915.

311 **"I am here":** *SLT*, Oct. 19, 1915.

311 **"Open Letter":** Full text in *DEN*, Oct. 20, 1915.

312 **"as much notoriety":** *SLT*, Oct. 21, 1915. **"deceive the public":** Ibid. **"shamefully unprofessional":** *SLH-R*, Oct. 21, 1915.

313 **Hill congratulated Hilton:** Hill to Hilton, Oct. 20, 1915. **"accepting your challenge":** Hill to Hilton, Oct. 27, 1915.

313 **sensational, unsigned letter:** Curtis, 640–41, quoting from enclosure in Hilton to Wilhelm Ekengren, Oct. 22, 1915. Curtis cites "Swedish Legation Hillstrom file 840," which the author has not seen.

313–14 **"This letter gives":** Text in Smith, 162–63.

314 **"trump card"**: *SLH-R*, Oct. 29, 1915.

314–15 **"dark days"**: *SLH-R*, Mar. 11, 1914. **"We have prestige"**: *DEN*, Oct. 25, 1915. **"quaint provision"**: *BG*, Nov. 7, 1915.

315 **"constitutional guarantees"**: Frank P. Sibley to Spry, Nov. 7, 1915, SP, reel 3. **buried its president**: For accounts of Horton's funeral, see *SLH-R*, *SLT*, and *SLTele*, Nov. 8, 1915. The press was scandalized that none of the half dozen eulogists mentioned God or offered a word of prayer. Instead they focused on the need to organize to prevent similar outrages. As Virginia Stephen told the assembled, "It is only by organization and making use of such tragedies as the Horton case [that] they [the "working class"] will ever get justice. The money spent on this funeral would be better spent in furthering the principles for which the workers of the country are fighting. This would be in harmony with the dead man's wishes."

315 **Dodge City, Kansas**: Masterson, 36. For more on Myton's gunfighting career, see the *Irrigator* newspaper (Garden City, KS), Oct. 24, 1885; Blanchard, 122. For his Utah background, see *SLTele*, Oct. 31, 1915, and Nov. 1, 1915.

315–16 **shot the unarmed**: For first-day coverage of the killing, see Salt Lake City papers for Oct. 31, 1915. **"Major Myton's friends"**: *SLTele*, Nov. 2, 1915. **involuntary manslaughter**: Smith, 128; *SLTele*, Nov. 20, 1915. **"Deeds of blood"**: *SLH-R*, Nov. 2, 1915.

316 **deliberated for less**: *SLTele*, Feb. 20, 1916.

316 **"searchlight of criticism"**: *BG*, Nov. 8, 1915.

316 **"six hired gunmen"**: *SLH-R*, Nov. 10, 1915.

316 **spoke only briefly**: *SOL*, Nov. 20, 1915. For Flynn's and Reed's remarks, see *SLH-R*, Nov. 10, 1915.

316 **"spare your tears"**: *SOL*, Nov. 20, 1915.

316–17 **"biggest protest ever"**: *SOL*, Oct. 23, 1915. **a provocateur intent**: His name was Herbert F. Gerry, and he ran a small agency, Intermountain Protective Service (INFORMATION OBTAINED ON ANY SUBJECT, ANY TIME, ANYWHERE). According to Sheriff John Corless, Gerry not only tracked down information about the IWW and offered protection, for a daily retainer, from its supposed depravities, but also *authored* many, if not most, of the ominous and pseudonymous threats that created the fear that fueled the demand for his protective services. See, for instance, "Sheriff Probes Activities of New Concern," *DEN*, Oct. 22, 1915; "Believe Letters May Be Local Threats," *SLTele*, Oct. 22, 1915; "Sheriff Believes Gerry Is Crazy," *SLTele*, Nov. 30, 1915.

317 **"perfectly useless"**: Wilhelm Ekengren to Henry C. Grey, telegram, Oct. 8, 1915, cited in Curtis, 583. **"anything you can"**: *SLT*, Oct. 10, 1915. **"offered an insult"**: Smoot Diaries, 20–21. **"taken no interest"** (footnote): Smoot to Mr. EDC.

317–18 **"quite resigned"**: Orrin Hilton to Wilhelm Ekengren, telegram, Oct. 13, 1915, cited in Curtis, 589. **"appeals of humanity"**: Joe Ettor to Woodrow Wilson, telegram, Nov. 17, 1915, HD.

318 **"greeted us cordially"**: Flynn, 194.

318 **"Well, that's true"**: Ibid.

318 **"deluge" of correspondence**: Robert Lansing to Woodrow Wilson, Dec. 3, 1915, in Link, 283. **United Hebrew Trades**: Resolution of Nov. 15, 1915, HD. **"writ of error"**: Central Labor Council of Alameda County to Woodrow Wilson, Oct. 20,

1915, HD. **Cloak and Suit**: Cloak and Suit Tailors Union, No. 9, to Woodrow Wilson, telegram, Nov. 17, 1915, HD.

318 **"great social wisdom"**: Robert Valentine to Woodrow Wilson, Nov. 15, 1915, HD. **"nation's helpless sons"** and **"very much touched"**: Link, 206; *BG*, Nov. 17, 1915.

318–19 **needed one another**: Gompers later recalled that he came to hold Wilson in the highest regard: "My respect for him grew into a feeling of well-nigh reverential admiration." Gompers, 545.

319 **"in the bigness"**: *SLTele*, Nov. 3, 1915. **given the hostilities**: See, for instance, Hill's "Mr. Block" and "John Golden and the Lawrence Strike." **"radical fungus"**: Gompers, 425.

319 **met just once**: Gentry, 63. **Mooney himself** (footnote): For further reading on Mooney and his case, see Gentry.

319–20 **"new and fair"**: For the text of the resolution, see *SLH-R*, Nov. 17, 1915. **resolution passed unanimously**: Albert and Palladino, 343–44. **"With unaffected hesitation"**: Link, 210.

320 **three drafts**: The two unsent drafts are in Nov. 18, 1915, SP. For the unabridged final version, see *SLH-R*, Nov. 19, 1915, or Link, 213–15.

321 **"champions of lawlessness"**: *SLH-R*, Nov. 18, 1915. **"stooped from the dignity"**: Ibid., **"hysterical effort"**: *DEN*, Nov. 18, 1915.

321 **"unwarranted and indefensible"**: *SLH-R*, Nov. 19, 1915.

322 **"Joe Hill Special"**: *SOL*, Nov. 13, 1915.

322 **singing soapboxer warmed**: *SLH-R*, Nov. 19, 1915. **"powers that be"**: *BG*, Nov. 18, 1915. **"Do you hear"**: *LAT*, Nov. 19, 1915.

14. To Be Found Dead in Utah

Sources

Books

Buhle, Paul, and Nicole Schulman, eds., *Wobblies!*; Chaplin, Ralph, *Wobbly*; Dubofsky, Melvyn, *We Shall Be All*; Dylan, Bob, *Chronicles*, vol. 1; Flynn, Elizabeth Gurley, *The Rebel Girl*; Foner, Philip S., *History of the Labor Movement in the United States*, vol. 7; Foner, Philip S., *The Letters of Joe Hill*; Green, Archie, et al., eds., *The Big Red Songbook*; Link, Arthur S., ed., *The Papers of Woodrow Wilson*, vol. 49; May, Lowell, and Richard Myers, eds., *Slaughter in Serene*; Murphy, Mary, *Mining Cultures*; Preston, William Jr., *Aliens and Dissenters*; Schmidt, Regin, *Red Scare*; Sinclair, Upton, ed., *The Cry for Justice*; Smith, Gibbs M., *Joe Hill*; Stavis, Barrie, *The Man Who Never Died*.

Documents

Hilda Erickson to Aubrey Haan, June 30, 1949. Letter in the author's possession.

Joe Hill to O. N. Hilton, Oct. 27, 1915 (typescript), box 371, Elizabeth Gurley Flynn Joe Hill Case Papers, Tamiment Library & Robert F. Wagner Labor Archives, New York University, New York City.

"Hillstrom Documents," RG 59 General Records of the Department of State, 1910–1929, decimal file 311.582H55, Joseph A. Curtis Papers, Accn 1229, Special Collections, Marriott Library, University of Utah, Salt Lake City. Hereafter abbreviated as "HD."

Fred Lee to Utah Phillips (a retrospective account of Lee's efforts to reclaim Hill's ashes for the IWW), Mar. 12, 1990, in the author's possession, courtesy of Fred Lee.

Ed Rowan to Elizabeth Gurley Flynn, telegram, Nov. 19, 1915, box 371, Elizabeth Gurley Flynn Joe Hill Case Papers, Tamiment Library & Robert F. Wagner Labor Archives, New York University, New York City.

S. P. Wise to Ralph Chaplin, Feb. 12, 1948, MS 71, box 2/11, Ralph Chaplin Papers, Washington State Historical Society, Tacoma, WA.

U.S. Department of Labor, Bureau of Labor Statistics, Economic News Release, Jan. 21, 2011, available online, http://www.bls.gov/news.release/union2.nro.htm.

Journal and Magazine Articles

Bruere, Robert W., "Copper Camp Patriotism," *Nation*, Feb. 21, 1918, 202–3.

Fogel, Chuck, "Joe Hill's Ashes," UAW *Solidarity*, May 1988, n.p.

Hill, Joe, "How to Make Work for the Unemployed," *International Socialist Review* 15, no. 6 (1914): 335–36.

Kerson, Roger, "What Ever Happened to Joe Hill?," *Chicago Reader*, Nov. 24, 1988.

Mayer, Gerald, "Union Membership Trends in the United States," CRS Report for Congress, Aug. 31, 2004, available online, http://digitalcommons.ilr.cornell.edu/cgi/viewcontent.cgi?article=1176&context=key_workplace.

"Menace of the IWW," *New York Times Magazine*, Sept. 2, 1917, 57–58.

Modesto, Zapata, "The Death of Joe Hill," *Mainstream* 15, no. 9 (1962): 3–16.

Preston, William,, "Shall This Be All? U.S. Historians Versus William D. Haywood et al.," *Labor History* 12, no. 3 (Summer 1971): 434–53.

Unpublished Typescripts

Curtis, Joseph A., *Right Man? The Tragic Saga of Joe Hill*, Joseph A. Curtis Papers, Accn 1229, Special Collections, Marriott Library, University of Utah, Salt Lake City.

MacKay, Alexander, "The Preacher and the Slave: A Critical Review," n.d. (circa 1950). In the author's possession.

Reed Smoot Diaries, box 2, vol. 7, book 20 (1915–1916), Reed Smoot Papers, Special Collections, Marriott Library, University of Utah, Salt Lake City.

Takman, John, "A Conversation with Joe Hill's Sister," interview with Ester Hägglund Dahl, Nov. 17, 1955, Joseph A. Curtis Papers, Accn 1229, Special Collections, Marriott Library, University of Utah, Salt Lake City.

Video Documentary

The Return of Joe Hill, directed by Eric Scholl (New York: Cinema Guild, 1990).

Web Site

"The Bisbee Deportation of 1917," University of Arizona exhibit, http://www.library.arizona.edu/exhibits/bisbee/history/overview.html.

Notes

323   "my busy day": *SLTele*, Nov. 18, 1915. "seeing a minister": *SLT*, Nov. 19, 1915.

323–24 wore a coarse: *SLH-R*, Nov. 19, 1915. "all bones": Ibid. "a mentally clear":
        Ibid.

324   "Why should I": Ibid. "only public curiosity": *SLTele*, Nov. 18, 1915.

324   "am not vindictive": *SLH-R*, Nov. 19, 1915. "on my knees": *SLTele*, Nov. 18,
        1915. "properly and advantageously": *SLH-R*, Nov. 19, 1915.

324   "IWW any harm": Ibid.

324   "commit willful murder": Curtis, 731.

324   letter of reference: *DEN*, Nov. 19, 1915.

325   "In case someone": Hill to Hilton.

325   "march right on" and "true-blue rebel": *SLH-R*, Nov. 19, 1915.

325–26 "shoved it across": Chaplin, 188–89. "here to Wyoming": *SLH-R*, Nov. 19, 1915.

326   "Goodbye, Joe": Chaplin, 189.

326   "He was overjoyed": Stavis, 95.

326   "refused to be": Smith, 56; 215, n. 78, citing *Annual Report of the Sailors' Rest
        Mission, San Pedro, California*, Feb. 1, 1919, 2. Makins's telegram: *LAT*, Nov.
        20, 1915.

326   "days of yore": *SLH-R*, Nov. 19, 1915.

326   sent best wishes: *SLH-R*, Nov. 19, 1915. "We the members": *SLTele*, Nov. 19, 1915.

326–27 "Composed new song": *SLH-R*, Nov. 19, 1915. Hill's final song (footnote):
        For complete lyrics, see Green et al., 172–73. "Dear Friend Gurley": Original
        reproduced on back cover of Flynn. Also in Foner, *Letters*, 82.

327   "As for trinkets": Quote from *SLH-R* reprinted in *SOL*, Nov. 27, 1915.

327–28 "do solemnly swear": Text of affidavit in *Seattle Star* and *DEN*, Nov. 19, 1915;
        LAT, Nov. 20, 1915.

328   *"Do you hear"*: *LAT*, Nov. 19, 1915. "Good Old Wooden": Hill used the phrase
        as the last line of his poem "The Rebel's Toast," *SOL*, June 27, 1914. "make the
        job": Hill, 335.

328   wired the text: *Seattle Star*, Nov. 19, 1915. "information and consideration":
        Robert Lansing to William Spry, telegram, Nov. 19, 1915, HD. Hilton at once:
        LAT, Nov. 20, 1915.

328–29 repair a motorcycle: *SLT*, Jan. 16, 1914. "found Joe": Erickson to Haan.

329   "She demanded": Smoot Diaries, 41.

329   "shut her off": Ibid.

329–30 barricaded himself: The account is drawn from *SLH-R* and *NYT*, Nov. 20,
        1915.

330   "loot and kill": *SLTele*, Oct. 16, 1915.

330   "strong stimulants": *DEN*, Nov. 19, 1915. "pretty stiff ordeal": Modesto, 11.
        The story is unsourced.

331   at seven-twenty: *SLTele*, Nov. 19, 1915. had furtively entered: *SLH-R*, Nov.
        20, 1915. improvised shooting gallery: *DEN*, Nov. 19, 1915.

331   prison gates opened: Ibid.

331   "guy that pinched": Ed Rowan to Elizabeth Gurley Flynn, Dec. 27, 1915, ex-
        cerpted in Stavis, 98. changed his mind: *SLTele*, Nov. 19, 1915.

331–32   **Sheriff Corless lead**: Ibid. **"stepped with uncertainty"**: *SLH-R*, Nov. 20, 1915. **having just inspected**: Ibid. **"ordinary arm chair"**: *DEN*, Nov. 19, 1915. **chair was placed**: *SLH-R*, Nov. 20, 1915, reported the distance as twenty-five feet; *DEN*, Nov. 19, 1915, and *SLT*, Nov. 20, 1915, said thirty-five feet.

332   **signaled the firing**: *SLTele*, Nov. 19, 1915.

332   **"easily and naturally"**: *SLT*, Nov. 20, 1915.

332   **"clear conscience"**: Ibid.

332   **four-inch-wide square**: *SLH-R*, Nov. 20, 1915. **"Aim so death"**: *BG*, Nov. 18, 1915.

332   **"Ouch!"**: *SLT*, Nov. 20, 1915.

333   **stand-back order**: *SLH-R*, Nov. 20, 1915.

333   **"I am going"**: Ibid.

333   **"Well, goodbye, boys"**: *SLT*, Nov. 20, 1915.

333   **cold, clear morning**: *DEN*, Nov. 19, 1915, reported a temperature of thirty-seven degrees at 6 A.M.

333   **"Yes, aim"**: *SLTele*, Nov. 19, 1915.

333   **threw back his head**: *SLH-R*, Nov. 20, 1915.

333   **"shots rang out"**: Ed Rowan to Elizabeth Gurley Flynn, letter excerpted in Stavis, 98.

333   **"send for Joe"**: Ibid.

333   **"shot at sunrise"**: Rowan to Flynn. **similarly to** *Solidarity*: *SOL*, Nov. 27, 1915.

333–34   **"morbidly curious"**: *SLTele*, Nov. 21, 1915. **"slumber room"**: Ibid. **locked the doors**: Ibid. **"of all stations"**: *SLH-R*, Nov. 21, 1915. **"well-known people"**: *SLTele*, Nov. 21, 1915.

334–35   **thousands upon thousands**: Ibid. **placed two roses**: *SLT*, Nov. 21, 1915. **IWW button**: Wise to Chaplin. He wrote, "The IWW button on Fellow Worker Joe's coat was put on by me and another Fellow Worker."

335   **"best rebel funeral"**: *SLH-R*, Nov. 22, 1915. **"could be secured"**: Ibid.; *SLTele*, Nov. 22, 1915.

335   **"name of God"**: *SLTele*, Nov. 22, 1915. **"we are indignant"**: *SLH-R*, Nov. 22, 1915.

335   **"Poor Joe understood"**: Ibid.

336   **they held aloft**: Ibid.

336   **"intelligent prostitute"**: Ibid. And see Sinclair, 476.

336   **"backbone nor guts"**: *SLH-R*, Nov. 22, 1915. **"I am glad"**: Ibid.; *DEN*, Nov. 22, 1915.

336–37   **"higher tribunal"**: *SLH-R*, Nov. 22, 1915. **call his "valedictory"**: *SOL*, Nov. 27, 1915. **"My Last Will"**: Ibid.; *SLTele*, Nov. 19, 1915. Original in Elizabeth Gurley Flynn Joe Hill Case Papers.

338   **Dusk was settling**: Description of the cortege drawn from *SLH-R*, Nov. 22, 1915.

339   **"tear-stained faces"**: *SLT*, Nov. 22, 1915. **inspired afterthought**: Ibid. **"do no more"**: *SLH-R*, Nov. 22, 1915.

339   **accompanied the body**: *SLT*, Nov. 24, 1915. **fog and rain**: *SOL*, Dec. 4, 1915. **"weather-beaten men"**: Ibid.

339   **mercury soared**: *CDT*, Nov. 26, 1915. **five thousand persons**: *SLTele*, Nov. 26, 1915. **"brutal murder"**: *SLT*, Nov. 26, 1915.

339   **"solidly for three"**: *CDT*, Nov. 26, 1915. **mile-long procession**: Ibid.

340   **"short but stirring"**: *SOL*, Dec. 4, 1915. **"stricken with undisguised"**: Ibid.

340 **six hundred packets**: *CDT*, Nov. 20, 1916; Chaplin, 193.

340–41 **"fight has just begun"**: Spry's press conference, from which this is drawn, was covered in all four local papers: *DEN* and *SLTele*, Nov. 19, 1915; *SLT* and *SLH-R*, Nov. 20, 1915.

341 **"criminal syndicalism" legislation**: For the language of one state's law (Idaho's), see Foner, *History*, 297. **"Capitalists of America"**: *IW*, Feb. 10, 1917, cited in Preston, *Aliens*, 89. **IWW was surging**: Dubofsky, 349–50.

341 **Bisbee, Arizona**: In Bisbee, authorities broke a copper miners' strike by rounding up nearly twelve hundred men, packing them like cattle into manure-coated boxcars in the extreme heat of mid-July, and "deporting" them to a remote patch of New Mexico desert without shelter, food, or water. For an excellent online presentation about the incident, see the University of Arizona Web exhibit "The Bisbee Deportation of 1917." And for a near contemporaneous account, See Bruere, 202–03. **Butte, Montana**: On August 1, 1917, as described earlier, vigilantes in Butte, Montana, kidnapped, tortured, and lynched Frank Little, the oft-beaten and -jailed organizer who had gone there to support striking copper miners following an underground fire in the Speculator mine that had killed 167—the worst metal-mining disaster in American history. On the fire, see sources listed in Murphy, 39, n. 50.

341 **"this diabolical association"**: "Menace of the IWW," 57.

342 **"stamp them out"**: Cited in Foner, *History*, 297. **"Don't scotch 'em"**: Ibid., 294.

342 **"seditious or disloyal"**: Preston, *Aliens*, 105.

342–43 **"ring leaders"**: Ibid., 124–25. **"certainly are worthy"**: Woodrow Wilson to Thomas Gregory, quoted in Schmidt, 71, n. 194. **"menace to organized"**: Preston, *Aliens*, 128. **"necessary in time"**: Link, 438–39.

343 **"broadest search warrants"**: Dubofsky, 406. For a seriocomic description of the raids at headquarters and his home, see Chaplin, 220–24.

343 **"essentially a criminal"**: Preston, *Aliens*, 120. **"out of business"**: Dubofsky, 407. **infiltrated its ranks** (footnote): Preston, *Aliens*, 129.

343 **four separate counts**: For a cogent summary of the charges, see ibid., 119–21. **"love my flag"** (footnote): Ibid., 89.

344 **return the verdict**: Dubofsky, 436. **"using poor English"**: Ben Fletcher, who incidentally was the lone African American defendant, quoted in Buhle and Schulman, 173.

344 **"a dog's life"**: Takman, 8.

345–46 **"folk heroes seriously"** and **"an anesthetic"** and **"enormous condescension"**: Preston, "Shall This Be All?," 436.

346 **"working clothes on"**: Quoted in *DEN*, May 4, 1915.

347 **Union power peaked**: Mayer, 3. **11.9 percent**: U.S. Department of Labor, Economic News Release. **over seventy years**: *NYT*, Jan. 21, 2011. **"in the gutter"**: Preston, *Aliens*, 41.

347 **"out of the guts"**: MacKay, 3–4. **"needed to know"**: Dylan, 52.

347 **"accidentally mutilated"**: Fogel, n.p.

347–48 **"treason, insurrection"**: Ibid. **"intensely 'IWW' "**: Preston, *Aliens*, 147. **"Christian Singing Society"** (footnote): Ibid., 148.

348 **newly discovered arcana**: Kerson, n.p.

348 **should human remains**: Lee to Phillips.

348–49 **dedicate a memorial**: For the complete telling of the Columbine strike, see May and Myers. **"It's high time"**: Scholl.

SELECTED BIBLIOGRAPHY

Akrigg, G. P. V., and Helen B. Akrigg. *British Columbia Chronicle, 1847–1871: Gold & Colonists*. Vancouver: Discovery Press, 1977.

Albert, Peter J., and Grace Palladino, eds. *The Samuel Gompers Papers*, vol. 9, *The American Federation of Labor at the Height of Progressivism, 1913–1917*. Urbana: University of Illinois Press, 2003.

Albro, Ward S. *Always a Rebel: Ricardo Flores Magón and the Mexican Revolution*. Fort Worth, TX: Texas Christian University Press, 1992.

Alexander, Thomas G. *Grace & Grandeur: A History of Salt Lake City*. Carlsbad, CA: Heritage Media, 2001.

———. *Mormonism in Transition: A History of the Latter-day Saints, 1890–1930*. Urbana and Chicago: University of Illinois Press, 1986.

———. *Utah: The Right Place, the Official Centennial History*. Salt Lake City: Gibbs Smith, 1995.

Alexander, Thomas G., and James B. Allen. *Mormons & Gentiles: A History of Salt Lake City*. Boulder, CO: Pruett Publishing, 1984.

Anderson, Nels. *The Hobo: The Sociology of the Homeless Man*. Chicago: University of Chicago Press, 1923.

Andrews, Thomas G. *Killing for Coal: America's Deadliest Labor War*. Cambridge, MA: Harvard University Press, 2008.

Arrington, Leonard J. *Brigham Young: American Moses*. Urbana: University of Illinois Press, 1986.

Asch, Moses, ed. *American Folksong; Woody Guthrie*. New York: Oak Publications, 1961 (reprint).

Avrich, Paul. *Anarchist Voices: An Oral History of Anarchism in America*. Princeton, NJ: Princeton University Press, 1995.

Barton, H. Arnold. *A Folk Divided: Homeland Swedes and Swedish Americans, 1840–1940*. Carbondale: Southern Illinois University Press, 1994.

———. *Letters from the Promised Land: Swedes in America, 1840–1914*. Minneapolis: University of Minnesota Press, 1975.

Bird, Stewart, Dan Georgakas, and Deborah Shaffer. *Solidarity Forever: An Oral History of the IWW*. Chicago: Lake View Press, 1985.

Blaisdell, Lowell L. *The Desert Revolution: Baja California, 1911*. Madison: University of Wisconsin Press, 1962.

Blanchard, Leola Howard. *Conquest of Southwest Kansas*. Wichita, KS: Wichita Eagle Press, 1931.

Brawley, Edward Allan. *Speaking Out for the Poor: A Millionaire Socialist in the Progressive Era*. Amherst, NY: Humanity Books, 2007

Brissenden, Paul Frederick. *The I.W.W.: A Study of American Syndicalism*. New York: Columbia University, 1919.

Brody, David. *Workers in Industrial America: Essays on the Twentieth Century Struggle*. New York: Oxford University Press, 1980.

Bruner, Robert F., and Sean D. Carr. *The Panic of 1907: Lessons Learned from the Market's Perfect Storm*. Hoboken, NJ: John Wiley and Sons, 2007.

Bruns, Roger A. *The Damndest Radical: The Life and World of Ben Reitman*. Urbana: University of Illinois Press, 1987.

Bufe, Chaz, and Mitchell Cowen Verter. *Dreams of Freedom: A Ricardo Flores Magón Reader*. Oakland, CA: AK Press, 2005.

Buhle, Mari Jo, Paul Buhle, and Dan Georgakas, eds. *Encyclopedia of the American Left*. New York: Garland Publishing, 1990.

Buhle, Paul, and Nicole Schulman, eds. *Wobblies! A Graphic History of the Industrial Workers of the World*. New York: Verso, 2005.

Camp, Helen C. *Iron in Her Soul: Elizabeth Gurley Flynn and the American Left*. Pullman: Washington State University Press, 1995.

Cannon, Frank J., and Harvey J. O'Higgins. *Under the Prophet in Utah*. Boston: C. M. Clark Publishing, 1911.

Cannon, James P. *Notebook of an Agitator*. New York: Pathfinder Press, 1973 (1st ed., 1958).

Carlson, Peter. *Roughneck: The Life and Times of Big Bill Haywood*. New York: Norton, 1983.

Carlsson, Ingvar, and Anne-Marie Lindgren. *What Is Social Democracy?* Stockholm: Arbetarrörelsens Tankesmedja, 2007. (Available online in English at Socialdemokraterna, http://www.socialdemokraterna.se/upload/Internationellt/Other%20Languages/WhatisSocialDemocracy.pdf.)

Chace, James. *1912: Wilson, Roosevelt, Taft & Debs—the Election That Changed the Country*. New York: Simon & Schuster, 2004.

Chaplin, Ralph. *Wobbly: The Rough-and-Tumble Story of an American Radical*. Chicago: University of Chicago Press, 1948.

Cockroft, James D. *Intellectual Precursors of the Mexican Revolution, 1900–1913*. Austin: University of Texas Press, 1968.

Cohen, Norm. *Long Steel Rail: The Railroad in American Folksong*. Urbana: University of Illinois Press, 1981.

Cohn, Alfred, and Joe Chisholm. *"Take the Witness!"* New York: Frederick A. Stokes, 1934.

Constantine, J. Robert, ed. *Letters of Eugene V. Debs*, vol. 2, *1913–1919*. Urbana: University of Illinois Press, 1990.

Cory, H. T. *The Imperial Valley and the Salton Sink*. San Francisco: John J. Newbegin, 1915.

Curtis, Joseph A. *Right Man? The Tragic Saga of Joe Hill*. Unpublished monograph. Special Collections, Marriott Library, University of Utah, Salt Lake City.

Davis, Mike, Kelly Mayhew, and Jim Miller. *Under the Perfect Sun: The San Diego Tourists Never See*. New York: New Press, 2003.

Dowie, J. Iverne, and Ernest M. Espelie, eds. *The Swedish Immigrant Community in Transition*. Rock Island, IL: Augustana Historical Society, 1963.

Drury, Wells, and Aubrey Drury. *California Tourist Guide and Handbook*. Berkeley, CA: Western Guidebook, 1913.

Dubofsky, Melvyn. *We Shall Be All: A History of the IWW.* New York: Quadrangle Books, 1969.

Dylan, Bob. *Chronicles, Volume One.* New York: Simon & Schuster, 2004.

Faulkner, Harold Underwood. *The Quest for Social Justice, 1898–1914.* New York: MacMillan, 1931.

Flynn, Elizabeth Gurley. *The Rebel Girl.* New York: International Publishers, 1955.

Foner, Philip S. *The Case of Joe Hill.* New York: International Publishers, 1965.

——, ed. *Fellow Workers and Friends: IWW Free Speech Fights as Told by Participants.* Westport, CT: Greenwood Press, 1981.

——. *History of the Labor Movement in the United States,* vol. 3, *The Policies and Practices of the American Federation of Labor, 1900–1909.* New York: International Publishers, 1964.

——. *History of the Labor Movement in the United States,* vol. 4, *The Industrial Workers of the World, 1905–1917.* New York: International Publishers, 1965.

——. *History of the Labor Movement in the United States,* vol. 7, *Labor and World War 1, 1914–1918.* New York: International Publishers, 1987.

——, ed. *The Letters of Joe Hill.* New York: Oak Publications, 1965.

Fudge, Judy, and Eric Tucker. *Labour Before the Law: The Regulation of Workers' Collective Action in Canada, 1900–1948.* Toronto: Oxford University Press, 2000.

Gentry, Curt. *Frame-Up: The Incredible Case of Tom Mooney and Warren Billings.* New York: Norton, 1967.

Glasscock, C. B. *The War of the Copper Kings.* Helena, MT: Riverbend Publishing, 2002 (1st ed., 1935).

Godoy, Jose F. *Porfirio Díaz, President of Mexico, The Master Builder of a Great Commonwealth.* New York: G. P. Putnam's Sons, 1910.

Goldman, Emma. *Living My Life,* vol. 1. New York: Dover Publications, 1970 (1st ed., 1931).

Gompers, Samuel. *Seventy Years of Life and Labor,* vol. 1. New York: E. P. Dutton, 1925.

Gordon, John Steele. *The Business of America.* New York: Walker, 2001.

——. *The Great Game.* New York: Scribner, 1999.

Gottlieb, Robert, and Irene Wolt. *Thinking Big: The Story of the Los Angeles Times.* New York: G. P. Putnam's Sons, 1977.

Graham, John, ed. *"Yours for the Revolution."* Lincoln: University of Nebraska Press, 1990.

Green, Archie, et al., eds. *The Big Red Songbook.* Chicago: Charles H. Kerr, 2007.

Halberstam, David. *The Powers That Be.* New York: Dell, 1980 (1st ed., 1979).

Hampton, Wayne. *Guerrilla Minstrels.* Knoxville: University of Tennessee Press, 1986.

Haywood, William D. *The Autobiography of Big Bill Haywood.* New York: International Publishers, 1977 (1st ed., 1929).

Holbrook, Stewart H. *Holy Old Mackinaw: A Natural History of the American Lumberjack.* New York: Macmillan, 1957.

Howard, Joseph Kinsey. *Montana: High, Wide, and Handsome.* New Haven: Yale University Press, 1959.

Hunter, Robert. *Poverty.* New York: Garrett Press, 1970 (1st ed., 1904).

Hyndman, Henry Mayers. *Further Reminiscences.* London: Macmillan, 1912.

Ibsen, Henrik. *Peer Gynt.* Trans. Horace M. Finney. New York: Philosophical Library, 1955.

Jensen, Vernon H. *Heritage of Conflict.* Ithaca, NY: Cornell University Press, 1950.

Johnson, William Weber. *Heroic Mexico: The Violent Emergence of a Modern Nation*. New York: Doubleday, 1968.

Kazin, Michael. *The Populist Persuasion*. New York: Basic Books, 1995.

Kornbluh, Joyce L., ed. *Rebel Voices: An IWW Anthology*. Ann Arbor: University of Michigan Press, 1964.

Leier, Mark. *Where the Fraser River Flows: The Industrial Workers of the World in British Columbia*. Vancouver: New Star Books, 1990.

Limerick, Patricia Nelson. *The Legacy of Conquest: The Unbroken Past of the American West*. New York: Norton, 1987.

Link, Arthur S., ed. *The Papers of Woodrow Wilson*, vols. 35 and 49. Princeton, NJ: Princeton University Press, 1980.

Ljungmark, Lars. *For Sale—Minnesota: Organized Promotion of Scandinavian Immigration, 1866–1873*. Stockholm: Scandinavian University Books, 1971.

London, Jack. *The People of the Abyss*. New York: Lawrence Hill Books, 1995 (1st ed., 1903).

Lukas, J. Anthony. *Big Trouble*. New York: Simon & Schuster, 1997.

Lundberg, Ferdinand. *America's 60 Families*. New York: Vanguard Press, 1937.

Malmquist, O. N. *The First 100 Years: A History of the Salt Lake Tribune, 1871–1971*. Salt Lake City: Utah State Historical Society, 1971.

Masterson, W. B. (Bat). *Famous Gunfighters of the Western Frontier*. Houston: Frontier Press of Texas, 1957 (1st ed., 1907).

May, Lowell, and Richard Myers, eds. *Slaughter in Serene: The Columbine Coal Strike Reader*. Denver: Bread and Roses Workers' Cultural Center and the IWW, 2005.

Mayo, Morrow. *Los Angeles*. New York: Knopf, 1932.

McCormick, John S. *The Gathering Place: An Illustrated History of Salt Lake City*. Salt Lake City: Signature Books, 2000.

McCormick, John S., and John R. Sillito, eds. *A World We Thought We Knew: Readings in Utah History*. Salt Lake City: University of Utah Press, 1995.

McDougal, Dennis. *Privileged Son: Otis Chandler and the Rise and Fall of the L.A. Times Dynasty*. Cambridge, MA: Perseus Publishing, 2001.

McFarlane, James Walter, ed. *The Oxford Ibsen*, vol. 3. London: Oxford University Press, 1972.

McWilliams, Carey. *California: The Great Exception*. Berkeley: University of California Press, 1949.

Meyer, Michael C., William L. Sherman, and Susan M. Deeds. *The Course of Mexican History*. New York: Oxford University Press, 1999 (6th ed.).

Miller, Jessie C., et al., eds. *Lawrence County Missouri History*. Mt. Vernon, MO: Lawrence County Historical Society, 1974.

Milner, Clyde II, Carol A. O'Connor, and Martha A. Sandweiss, eds. *The Oxford History of the American West*. New York: Oxford University Press, 1994.

Misgeld, Klaus, et al., eds. *Creating Social Democracy: A Century of the Social Democratic Labor Party in Sweden*. State College, PA: Penn State Press, 1992.

Moberg, Vilhelm. *The Emigrants*. St. Paul: Minnesota Historical Society Press, 1995 (1st ed., in Swedish, 1949; 1st English-language ed., 1951).

Montgomery, M. W. *A Wind from the Holy Spirit in Sweden and Norway*. New York: American Home Missionary Society, 1884.

Mulder, William. *Homeward to Zion: The Mormon Migration from Scandinavia*. Minneapolis: University of Minnesota Press, 1957.

Murphy, Mary. *Mining Cultures: Men, Women, and Leisure in Butte, 1914–41*. Urbana: University of Illinois Press, 1997.

Nelson, Marie C., and John Rogers, eds. *Mother, Father, and Child: Swedish Social Policy in the Early Twentieth Century*. Uppsala, Sweden: Family History Group, Department of History, Uppsala University, 1990.

Nerman, Ture. *Joe Hill, Mördare eller martyr*. Stockholm: Tryckeri AB Federativ, 1989 (1st ed., 1951, published as *Arbetarsångaren Joe Hill, mördare eller martyr?* [Folksinger Joe Hill, murderer or martyr?]).

Newell, Peter E. *Zapata of Mexico*. Montreal: Black Rose Books, 1997.

Nichols, Jeffrey. *Prostitution, Polygamy, and Power: Salt Lake City, 1847–1918*. Urbana and Chicago: University of Illinois Press, 2002.

Nilsson, Ulf Ivar. *Gävle på 1800-talet* (Gävle in the 1800s; in Swedish). Gävle, Sweden: Kultur & Fritid Gävle, 2006.

Parker, Carleton A. *The Casual Laborer, and Other Essays*. New York: Harcourt, Brace and Howe, 1920.

Perlman, Selig, and Philip Taft. *History of Labor in the United States, 1896–1932*, vol. 4. New York: Augustus M. Kelley, 1966.

Perry, Louis B., and Richard S. Perry. *A History of the Los Angeles Labor Movement, 1911–1941*. Berkeley: University of California Press, 1963.

Person, Carl E. *The Lizard's Trail: A Story from the Illinois Central and Harriman Lines Strike of 1911 to 1915 Inclusive*. Chicago: Lake Publishing, 1918.

Phillips, Paul A. *No Power Greater: A Century of Labour in British Columbia*. Vancouver: B.C. Federation of Labour, 1967.

Phull, Hardeep. *Story Behind the Protest Song: A Reference Guide to the 50 Songs That Changed the 20th Century*. Westport, CT: Greenwood Press, 2008.

Pletcher, David M. *Rails, Mines, and Progress: Seven American Promoters in Mexico, 1867–1911*. Ithaca, NY: Cornell University Press, 1958.

Pourade, Richard F. *Gold in the Sun*. San Diego: Copley Press, 1965.

Preston, William Jr. *Aliens and Dissenters: Federal Suppression of Radicals, 1903–1933*. 2nd ed. Urbana and Chicago: University of Illinois Press, 1994 (1st ed., 1963).

Pringle, Henry F. *The Life and Times of William Howard Taft*, vol. 2. New York: Farrar & Rinehart, 1939.

Raat, W. Dirk. *Revoltosos: Mexico's Rebels in the United States, 1903–1923*. College Station: Texas A&M University Press, 1981.

Ramazzini, Bernardini. *Diseases of Workers*. Latin text of 1713, with trans. and notes by Wilmer Cave Wright. Chicago: University of Chicago Press, 1940.

Rawls, James J. *California: An Interpretive History*. New York: McGraw-Hill, 1998 (7th ed.).

Reesman, Jeanne Campbell. *Jack London's Racial Lives: A Critical Biography*. Athens: University of Georgia Press, 2009.

Reisner, Marc. *Cadillac Desert: The American West and Its Disappearing Water*. New York: Penguin Books, 1993 (Rev. ed.).

Robinson, Earl. *Ballad of an American: The Autobiography of Earl Robinson*. Lanham, MD: Scarecrow Press, 1998.

Robinson, Michael, ed. *Strindberg's Letters*, vol. 1, *1862–1892*. Chicago: University of Chicago Press, 1992.

Robinson, W. W. *Bombs and Bribery*. Los Angeles: Dawson's Book Shop, 1969.

Roper, William L., and Leonard J. Arrington. *William Spry: Man of Firmness, Governor of Utah*. Salt Lake City: Utah State Historical Society, 1971.

Rudolph, Alan, and Robert Altman. *Buffalo Bill and the Indians; or Sitting Bull's History Lesson*. Screenplay. New York: Bantam Books, 1976.

Runblom, Harald, and Hans Norman. *From Sweden to America: A History of the Migration*. Minneapolis: University of Minnesota Press, 1976.

Rusten, Sharon O. *The One Year Book of Christian History*. Carol Stream, IL: Tyndale House Publishers, 2003.

Sandburg, Carl, ed. *The American Songbag*. New York: Harcourt, Brace, 1927.

Schmidt, Regin. *Red Scare: FBI and the Origins of Anticommunism in the United States*. Copenhagen: Museum Tusculanum Press, 2000.

Schmidt, Ronald J. Jr. *This Is the City: Making Model Citizens in Los Angeles*. Minneapolis: University of Minnesota Press, 2005.

Schoultz, Lars. *Beneath the United States: A History of US Policy Toward Latin America*. Cambridge, MA: Harvard University Press, 1998.

Schroeder, Theodore. *Free Speech for Radicals*. Riverside, CT: Hillacre Bookhouse, 1916.

Sinclair, Upton, ed. *The Cry for Justice: An Anthology of the Literature of Social Protest*. New York: Barricade Books, 1996 (1st ed., 1915).

Smith, Gibbs M. *Joe Hill*. Salt Lake City: University of Utah Press, 1969.

Söderström, Ingvar. *En sång kan inte arkebuseras: Berättelsen om Joe Hill* (A song cannot be executed by a firing squad: The story of Joe Hill). Stockholm: Bäckströms Förlag, 2002.

Stavis, Barrie. *The Man Who Never Died: A Play About Joe Hill, with Notes on Joe Hill and His Times*. New York: Haven Press, 1951.

Stavis, Barrie, and Frank Harmon. *The Songs of Joe Hill*. New York: Oak Publications, 1955.

Stegner, Wallace. *Joe Hill: A Biographical Novel*. New York: Penguin Books, 1990 (1st ed., 1950, published as *The Preacher and the Slave*).

———. *Mormon Country*. Lincoln: University of Nebraska Press, 1981 (1st ed., 1942).

Stenhouse, Thomas B. H. *The Rocky Mountain Saints: A Full and Complete History of the Mormons*. New York: D. Appleton, 1873.

Stephenson, George M. *The Religious Aspects of Swedish Immigration*. New York: Arno Press, 1969.

Stevens, Joseph E. *Hoover Dam: An American Adventure*. Norman: University of Oklahoma Press, 1990.

Street, Richard Steven. *Beasts of the Field: A Narrative History of California Farmworkers, 1769–1919*. Stanford, CA: Stanford University Press, 2004.

Stringham, Nathaniel G., and Bryant S. Hinckley. *Briant Stringham and His People*. North Salt Lake, Utah: Stringham Family Association, 1994.

Swanberg, W. A. *Citizen Hearst*. New York: Scribner's, 1961.

Terkel, Studs. *Talking to Myself: A Memoir of My Times*. New York: Pantheon Books, 1973.

Thompson, Fred, and Patrick Murfin. *The IWW: Its First Seventy Years, 1905–1975.* Chicago: Industrial Workers of the World, 1976.

Tout, Otis B. *History of Imperial Valley, Southern California, USA.* San Diego: Otis B. Tout, 1931.

Townsend, John Clendenin. *Running the Gauntlet: Cultural Sources of Violence Against the IWW.* New York: Garland Publishing, 1986.

Turner, Ethel Duffy. *Revolution in Baja California: Ricardo Flores Magón's High Noon.* Detroit: Blaine Ethridge Books, 1981.

Turner, John Kenneth. *Barbarous Mexico.* Austin: University of Texas Press, 1969 (1st ed., 1910).

Tyler, Robert L. *Rebels of the Woods: The I.W.W. in the Pacific Northwest.* Eugene: University of Oregon Press, 1967.

Vorse, Mary Heaton. *A Footnote to Folly.* New York: Arno Press, 1980 (1st ed., 1935).

Warren, Louis S. *Buffalo Bill's America: William Cody and the Wild West Show.* New York: Knopf, 2005.

Warrum, Noble, ed. *Utah Since Statehood*, vol. 1. Chicago and Salt Lake City: S. J. Clarke Publishing, 1919.

Watson, Bruce. *Bread & Roses: Mills, Migrants, and the Struggle for the American Dream.* New York: Viking, 2005.

Weindling, Paul, ed. *The Social History of Occupational Health.* London: Croom Helm, 1985.

White, Joseph. *Tom Mann.* Manchester, UK: Manchester University Press, 1991.

Winters, Donald E. Jr. *The Soul of the Wobblies: The IWW, Religion, and American Culture in the Progressive Era, 1905–1917.* Westport, CT: Greenwood Press, 1985.

Woeste, Victoria Saker. *The Farmer's Benevolent Trust: Law and Agricultural Cooperation in Industrial America, 1865–1945.* Chapel Hill: University of North Carolina Press, 1998.

Worster, Donald. *Rivers of Empire: Water, Aridity, and the Growth of the American West.* New York: Oxford University Press, 1985.

Young, John P. *Journalism in California: Pacific Coast and Exposition Biographies.* San Francisco: Chronicle Publishing, 1915.

INDEX

Page numbers in *italics* denote illustrations or captions.

A NOTE ON THE AUTHOR

William M. Adler is the author of *Land of Opportunity*, about the rise and fall of a crack cocaine empire, and *Mollie's Job*, which follows the flight of one woman's factory job from the U.S. to Mexico. He has contributed to numerous publications, including *Esquire*, *Rolling Stone*, *Mother Jones*, and *Texas Monthly*. Adler lives with his wife and son in Denver, Colorado.